Supplementary
Education

Supplementary Education

The Hidden Curriculum of High Academic Achievement

Edmund W. Gordon,
Beatrice L. Bridglall, and
Aundra Saa Meroe

ROWMAN & LITTLEFIELD PUBLISHERS, INC.
Lanham • Boulder • New York • Toronto • Oxford

To the next generation, Andrew, Armand, Devin, Ishan, Isobel, Jade, Kai, Kenan, Scott, Stephen, Susan Rosa, and Wyatt, grand children all.

ROWMAN & LITTLEFIELD PUBLISHERS, INC.

Published in the United States of America
by Rowman & Littlefield Publishers, Inc.
A wholly owned subsidary of The Rowman & Littlefield Publishing Group, Inc.
4501 Forbes Boulevard, Suite 200, Lanham, Maryland 20706
www.rowmanlittlefield.com

PO Box 317
Oxford
OX2 9RU, UK

British Library Cataloguing in Publication Information Available

Library of Congress Cataloging-in-Publication Data

Gordon, Edmund W.
  Supplementary education: The Hidden Curriculum of High Academic Achievement /
Edmund W. Gordon, Beatrice L. Bridglall, and Aundra Saa Meroe.
    p. cm.
  Includes bibliographical references and index.
  ISBN 0-7425-4260-2 (cloth: alk. paper) — ISBN 0-7425-4261-0 (pbk.: alk. paper)
1. Compensatory education—United States. 2. Children with social disabilities—
Education—United States. 3. Academic achievement—United States. I. Bridglall,
Beatrice L., 1968- II. Meroe, Aundra S., 1967- III. Title.
  LC213.2.G67 2005
  370.111

                                                                          2004009250

∞™ The paper used in this publication meets the minimum requirements of American
National Standard for Information Sciences—Permanence of Paper for Printed Library
Materials, ANSI/NISO Z39.48-1992.

Contents

Foreword

Child guidance and counseling, Head Start, compensatory education, Title I of the Elementary and Secondary Education Act, equal educational opportunity, career education, human diversity and pedagogy, dynamic assessment and pedagogy, and now supplementary education are aspects of education that have claimed the attention of the senior editor of this book. In fact, some of these terms had their origins in his work and that of his colleagues. After almost sixty years devoted to the field of education, many of those years devoted to effort at improving the quality of schooling for less advantaged children, Edmund W. Gordon, with the assistance of his young colleagues Beatrice Lallmanie Bridglall and Aundra Saa Meroe, has turned his attention to the examination of several nonschool factors that they claim may enable schooling to be effective. They do so in this collection of essays and papers, some of which were initially presented in the 1999 Invitational Conference on Supplementary Education that was sponsored by The College Board and the Laboratory for Student Success at Temple University.

Gordon and his colleagues argue that affluent and educationally sophisticated parents have long recognized that not only what happens in school is important for high academic achievement but also factors in the daily lives of children that happen out side of school and are in support of academic development are important. Gordon, Bridglall, and Meroe borrow a notion that I have advanced (*Waiting for a Miracle: Why schools can not solve our problems and how we can*). Directing their attention to a variety of experiences of persons from low-income families and people of color who have gone on to high levels of achievement, the editors develop the rationale for the importance of what they call "intellective competence"—critical literacy and numeracy, problem solving, analogical reasoning, knowledge and skill transfer, self-regulation abilities—the metaproducts of high levels of academic achievement. With a high degree of consistency, Gordon and his colleagues claim that these persons have been the beneficiaries of experiences in a wide variety of developmental and enrichment activities that tend to be ubiquitous in the lives of children who grow up in privileged environments and tend to be absent in the lives of children who do not. It is this wide variety of activities that are complementary to school but are non–school based, that they call supplementary education.

Supplementary education activities include things like preschool education and child care, summer camp, dance and music lessons, travel, adequate health and nutrition, positive and caring adult models, reading to and with self and others, dinner table talk, peer and parental expectations, tutoring, and specialized professional help when needed. These are the things that those of us who know try to make available, as a matter of course, for our own children. Thus supplementary education is not at issue because it is new; rather it is problematic because such experiences are not available to many of the children for whom schooling is of limited effectiveness. The authors of the papers collected here do not advocate that these non–school based activities should replace or supplant the things that schools do. By implication they argue that the impact of schooling should be strengthened. They rather explicitly argue for making these supplements more broadly available.

Supplementary Education addresses a challenge that has been in plain view, but is generally either missed, ignored, or underestimated. I was recently reminded of the power of the mainstream child rearing experience when my daughter, son-in-law, and granddaughter Nicole, who live on the West Coast, visited me for a few days on the East Coast. I was struck with the matter-of-fact and yet systematic way Nicole's parents were providing her with what it will take to be successful. It caused me to reflect on the fact that I received a similar kind of experience growing up—even in a low-income, but well-functioning, high aspiration family. We provided my daughter with the same. In our competitive society, this mainstream child rearing and exposure style gives an advantage. But we will all be better off, and we will have a chance to create a better world, when all children are reared and exposed in a way that gives them a reasonable chance to be successful. *Supplementary Education* explores the issues and points the way.

James P. Comer, M.D.,
Maurice Faulk Professor of Psychiatry and
Associate Dean of the College of Medicine,
Yale University
April 2004

Preface

Our concept of supplementary education rests on Pierre Bourdeiu's notion that academic achievement is related to access to and participation in various forms of education-related capital such as health and nutrition, the material resources that money provides, cultural capital, human capital, polity capital, and social capital. We posit that access to such capital may be necessary if schools are to succeed at enabling academic achievement for students in general, and students of color in particular. We contend that it is the unequal distribution of access to these forms of capitals that severely limits the effectiveness of schools. The redistribution of access to such capitals may be beyond our immediate reach, but all may not be lost because concerned communities and families can and should influence the effectiveness of schooling.

In *Supplementary Education*, we argue that, while access to schools that enable and expect academic achievement is a necessary ingredient for the education of students, good schools alone may not be sufficient to ensure universally high levels of academic development. Supplemental educational experiences may also be needed. The idea of supplementary education is based on the assumption that high academic achievement is closely associated with exposure to family- and community-based activities and learning experiences that occur both in and out of school in support of academic learning. For low income and some ethnic minority student groups, opportunities to participate in such activities are generally under-resourced and underutilized in comparison to the access to and participation in such activities by many European Americans and Asian Americans from mid to high socioeconomic backgrounds.

This book is organized into three sections. The first makes the case for supplementary education. Specifically, it focuses on the need for universal access to high levels of academic achievement and the challenge of reducing the "achievement gap" that exists between Asian American and European American students and their African American, Hispanic American, and Native American counterparts. Having posed the problem, the second section of the book is directed toward defining the construct and provides in-depth descriptions of some of the more colloquial expressions of supplementation in after school care, youth development, and other forms of supplemental education. The book closes with a discussion of the emerging institutionalization and need for more thoughtful and rigorous research on the supplementary education movement and a reflection by the senior editor, Edmund Gordon, on the idea of supplementary education. In this reflection, Gordon perceives supplementary education as an instrument in the negotiation of sociocultural marginality and places supplementary education within the context of family and community as forces that (1) influence the quality of academic achievement and (2) shape the political economic integrity of the societies that spawn them. Supplementary education, indeed, may be the hidden curriculum of high academic achievement.

ACKNOWLEDGEMENTS

We, as editors of this collection of papers that began with a small conference in 1999, gratefully acknowledge our indebtedness to the late Professor Margaret Wang, who provided the initial support for that conference. Since that time, other contributors have been added. We are grateful for the strength these papers have added to the collection. We especially appreciate the support of Dean Birkenkamp, former editor, and our current editor at Rowman & Littlefield, Alan McClare. We also want to acknowledge the invaluable bibliographic assistance and support of Ms. Ines Sucre, reference librarian and information specialist at the Institute for Urban and Minority Education at Teachers College. Thanks goes to The College Board, which in the past two years, has provided support for the scholarly work of the senior editor.

Edmund W. Gordon
Beatrice L. Bridglall
Aundra Saa Meroe
February 2004

1

CONCEPTUAL FOUNDATIONS FOR
SUPPLEMENTARY EDUCATION

Universal Access to Academic Excellence

Donald M. Stewart

Supplementary education diverges, some would say, from the rather single-minded focus on school and curricular variables that have dominated school improvement efforts and our public dialogue on improving academic achievement. In fact, a Committee for Economic Development report a few years ago typified the call for greater focus on the school's quite specific academic achievement goals; dilution of purpose only dilutes results, we were urged. And indeed, such an approach may be most valuable when implemented in concert with the kinds of supplementary educational initiatives being discussed in this book. Questions regarding the effective interplay and balance among in-school and out-of-school variables go, I believe, to the heart of this book's underlying theme.

But supplementary education diverges a bit from dominant discourse, dear reader. Today in our national discourse, when definitions of key terms and even of key phrases have received considerable attention at the highest levels, perhaps we might consider how we define the work of education in our republic, and specifically the role we assign to particular institutions like schools within the broader configuration of external educating agencies. What is it we ask of schools? Where does their responsibility begin and end, and where do we recognize the domain of other, supplementary educating agencies such as the family, health and social services, churches, athletic teams, and so forth?

According to recent opinion polls conducted by the Public Agenda Foundation, values rate high among the top concerns of parents, students, and teachers, just after learning the basics in a safe environment. In particular, parents seek personal attention for their children, want them to be pushed academically, and want them to learn values of honesty, hard work, respect, and tolerance for others. This, of course, should not surprise us, unless we read too many policy reports, since the moral upbringing of the young has long been central to education, and our public schools have long been a key component of our civic religion, even if unfulfilled in practice. Certainly, we are also witnessing a strange indulgence at the national level in moral posturing, with self-impressed wags pointing fingers at the private moral lapses of various public leaders. How self-righteous it all sounds, how clarion and resonant the call to fundamental values of truth, justice, and personal piety! And yet most of the public appears to demur, wondering why we cannot move past sex scandals and a tabloid-littered public square. This is not for the public's lack of concern with values but, I suspect, recognition that we embarrass ourselves in our narrowed sense of values, our obsession with private indiscretions, our kinky interest in lusty details. Our discussion of values does not seem to diverge into more public questions, issues less personal but far more pressing—inequities such as those in education, both school-bound and supplementary, where indeed we should lament, to turn Bill Bennett's phrase, the death of outrage.

For where is our outrage at the educational inequities we allow to persist and at our anorexic sense of public ends in education? These inequities and this inattention to public ends are not, I would maintain, unrelated; we face persistent—and, in some cases, increasing—educational gaps at the same time that our schools' accountability systems barely refer to their competency in advancing the republic, this democratic experiment, or its many public ends. It is not coincidence that we seem unable, at the very same time, to marshal effective dialogue surrounding the privatization of the forms of schooling, not even to suggest how private institutions might share responsibility for the constant social reconstruction of the republic. Have we, in fact, accepted the privatization of the ends of education? Have we accepted that schools are to be measured solely on their ability to move private individuals along in their private ambitions, with scorekeeping kept solely by measures of individual achievement? If we aggregate these private accomplishments, does that equal the public outcomes we should seek for public education? Do we have no public educational goals beyond the sum of our individual academic competencies?

Should not public education be about democratic community building? How have we kept score on that objective? How do we measure that? How many efforts are underway today to gauge our success as a nation? Any international comparisons underway? The broader supports for "academic socialization" and "intellective development"—the building of social, community mechanisms that support a constant, critical spirit of inquiry—is that not part of what John Dewey meant when he saw democracy as a profoundly educational enterprise? Do we not understand that we—in schools and in supplementary education—are constructing a citizenry, a vision, and a competency in real kids' minds about what this nation should be about? Are these not values we share today? Do we not value outcomes for public education to which individual success alone is supplementary? Are these not values whose violation should yield public outrage, whose death too many herald? Has not our lack of attention to these public ends of education, to the role of schools as central entities in the creation of local democratic life, forced us to speak of community life, of social conditions, of the health and well-being of our youth as supplemental to education itself? As ancillary to the central purposes of public institutions touted for their homage to traditions of local community control? Yet, if the community, the broader social lives we live, is considered supplemental to public education's purposes, if democracy building has been supplanted by career building or test taking alone, then we have privatized the ends of our most public of institutions. The forms of governance will, one day perhaps all too soon, simply catch up to a total abdication of principle.

But I would ask you: Can we still hear, above the din of social policy jargon and the comforting bromides of technological salvation, the voices of public mindedness from our American educational tradition? Can we hear Doxey Wilkerson, renowned African American social scientist—with whom, by the way, our own Ed Gordon coauthored a College Board book on compensatory education some thirty-eight years ago—can we hear him lamenting back in the 1930s the effects of school segregation for weakening "both the Negro race and the country as a whole"? Do we evaluate today our educational institutions by whether or not from them "emanate that able and wholesome leadership so sorely needed"? Can we hear the voice of Teachers College sociologist George Counts earlier this century, chiding Americans for their "sublime faith in education . . . convinced that education is the one unfailing remedy for every ill to which man is subject, whether it be vice, crime, war, poverty, riches, injustice, racketeering, political corruption, race hatred, class conflict, or just plain original sin"?

If education is to be so beneficent and powerful, argued Counts nearly seventy years ago, educators must "abandon easy optimism, subject the concept of education to the most rigorous scrutiny, and be prepared to deal much more fundamentally, realistically, and positively with the American social situation than has been their habit in the past."

Should, then, part of our development of supplementary education involve the means by which to hold education accountable for its public responsibilities? Does public education build a public, fulfill the needs for leadership, sustain the principles and practices of this experiment in democracy? Or have we too long ago lost the language of public ends? What are we willing to demand of perhaps our most central and public institution? The late historian Lawrence Cremin, in explaining how so many in education have failed, through their training and by their performance, to link their work to the aims of the republic, would relate the story told to him by a political scientist friend. When his friend was asked why so many people did not seem to care terribly much about defending the principle of freedom of speech, the political scientist would answer, "It is because they do not have that much to say." Do we, yet, have much to say about what role schools should play in the democratic development of our communities? Do we have the vocabulary and the will to argue that not only must we provide supplementary support to the academic development occurring in schools, but that we must also supplement the individualistic, private ends of schools with their role in supporting the community's development?

Now, even if we seem unable to recapture a proud tradition of public mindedness in education, we might still be heard on grounds of fundamental fairness in regards to educational inequities. In discussing those factors surrounding formal education, we must, with targeted research and application, develop greater access to what Ed Gordon calls "intellective development and academic socialization opportunities." It seems to me that such efforts can address underachievement for students of color, a key component in establishing a more just republic. I applaud and support such initiatives; indeed, as you know, the National Task Force on Minority High Achievement is one key way in which the College Board is engaged in this effort.

But let us also remind ourselves of what we know about formal educational inequities, the world the College Board tends to inhabit, and how they affect achievement, if at least to refine further our understanding of supplementary education's critical role. Let me suggest just two areas in which the College Board is working, and invite your assistance and your guidance regarding how supplementary education can buttress these key components of academic achievement. These are likely areas with which you are already quite familiar. What role can supplementary education play, and in what form, regarding (1) differences in teacher preparation and effectiveness, and (2) access to challenging academic work?

With respect to differences in teacher preparation and effectiveness, we have long known the critical role of teachers in student achievement, and although the work is still developing, recent research in Tennessee, Texas, and elsewhere has begun to quantify that role more systematically. In Tennessee elementary schools, for example, Professor William Sanders and colleagues estimate that roughly 40 percent of the variance in student achievement relates to teacher effectiveness, making it "the single most dominant factor affecting student academic gain. . . . Groups of students with comparable abilities and initial achievement levels may have vastly different academic outcomes as a result of the sequence of teachers to which they are assigned." Further, it appears that the effects are both "additive and cumulative, with little evidence of compensatory effects of more effective teachers in later grades." These effects, over a three-year period of elementary school, can result in a range of mean student percentiles of over fifty points.

We now know a great deal more about the differences in teacher preparation in high-poverty and minority-dominant schools. A recent federal study indicated that

of all teachers who taught at least one high school mathematics class, for example, almost one-third did not have a college major or minor in mathematics or mathematics education. . . . Public high schools with 50 percent or more students receiving free or reduced-price lunches (high-poverty schools) had higher levels of out-of-field teaching in mathematics, science, and English than did public high schools with fewer than 20 percent of these students (low-poverty schools). In mathematics, for example, 40 percent of public high school teachers in high-poverty schools taught out of field, compared to nearly 28 percent of mathematics teachers in low-poverty schools.

These statistics are all too familiar, and their effects on student academic achievement are becoming increasingly obvious. My challenge to readers, however, is rather straightforward: How can supplementary education efforts—parental supports, advocacy, research—help address the inequitable differences in teacher preparation and effectiveness?

Second, with respect to access to challenging academic work, the College Board's EQUITY 2000 school district reform initiative has been at the heart of our work. We know too much about too many impediments, even for those students prepared to succeed in demanding coursework. For example, the educational pipeline, starting far back in elementary school, appears to narrow so early and so harshly for so many disadvantaged students that their academic "merits," however defined, rarely get a chance to see the light of a senior high school classroom, let alone a college admissions office. In California, for every one hundred white students in public elementary school, thirty-one end up eligible for admission to the University of California, having taken the "A-F requirements." For their African American and Hispanic American classmates, fewer than fifteen end up as eligible. Nationally among urban high schools, the data suggest that fewer than half of ninth graders graduate within four years. This is a brutal selection process in which the opportunity funnel narrows early in one's schooling, from elementary school forward—a harsh sorting not done on the basis of academic merit, and one that demands our most concentrated collective attention. A study a few years ago of some northern California schools showed Hispanic and African American students twice as likely to be misassigned into lower academic tracks, half as likely to be in college prep math courses, and most likely to have teachers ignorant of college entrance requirements. In one southern California district, according to data from the Achievement Council, of the top quartile of scorers on the California Test of Basic Skills, roughly 90 percent of the whites and Asians were put into algebra; fewer than half of their high-scoring African American and Hispanic classmates ended up in algebra. My friends, we do not need very sophisticated research to tell us what needs to happen in such a district!

The College Board's experience in this matter, beyond that of the task force, has moved in two rather distinct directions within schools. First, EQUITY 2000 has built upon a district-level policy requiring all students to take the same algebra and geometry, along with the commitment to build the necessary safety nets to enable all students to succeed. While our evaluation efforts are still ongoing, it is clear that such a policy change can be an effective lever for advancing student achievement, helping more students to succeed in math than ever before. Second, we have been working in curriculum enhancement with teachers from middle school through senior year. The goals include (1) to put in more challenging and responsive curriculum, such as Pacesetter and advanced placement (AP), and (2) to support teachers in preparing students well before they enter their junior and senior years. Our work in vertical teams, for example, brings together English and math teachers from across the middle school and high school years in order to coordinate their work in developing critical thinking in their students, thereby increasing student access to rigorous courses.

Our recent research has reinforced our confidence in getting more students to achieve at challenging academic work, and this research suggests a way in which a larger pool of students can be offered rigorous academic experiences. High schools that offer AP courses, for example, are confronted with the need to identify students who may be successful in these courses. As college-level courses, AP courses are intended for students who have already completed relevant secondary school work in the subject and have the skills and motivation to complete college-level course work during their high school studies. Teacher recommendations, self-nomination, previous courses completed, grades in relevant previous high school courses, discussions with students, and scores on achievement tests are successfully used to varying degrees by schools in identifying students for placement in AP courses. However, such procedures may not identify all students who can potentially benefit from AP courses and be successful in them.

Recent analyses have shown that student performance on the PSAT can be useful in identifying additional students who may be successful in AP courses. PSAT scores can identify students who may not have been initially considered for an AP course through teacher or self-nomination or other local procedures. For many AP courses, students with moderate scores on the PSAT have a high probability of success on the examinations. For example, a majority of students with PSAT verbal scores of 46–50 (PSAT scores range from 20 to 80) received grades of 3 or above on nearly all of the twenty-nine AP examinations studied, while over one-third of students with scores of 41–45 achieved grades of 3 or above on five AP examinations. (AP grades of 3 or above are usually accepted for credit or placement by colleges.) What this all means, of course, is that we must be diligent in our use of student assessment data—with all the necessary qualifications—in order to identify talent, to promote academic achievement, and not to inappropriately limit educational access or opportunity. We must, as Ed Gordon suggests, be about affirmative development, at a time when affirmative action seems ever more constrained. Proper use of solid data can further that human development agenda.

Another challenge is this: how can supplementary education efforts help address the inequitable access to challenging academic work and develop the tools to promote practices of affirmative development in our educational systems? This brings me back to the theme of my title: universal access to academic excellence. Our aim, if divergent from the dominant conversation about student achievement, does not diverge but rather returns front and center to what our educational systems should be about in this republic. First, we must not give up the public ends of education as supplementary in any way; they are why we have a system of publicly supported education in the first place. Second, we must recognize supplementary education as central to advancing, in reality and not just in rhetoric, higher academic achievement for more of our disadvantaged students. Our efforts must be carefully targeted and must build upon the careful, data-driven work being done in many schools. We at the College Board welcome the assistance and collaboration of those who are mindful that our values, our shared small-r republican values, demand a collective resurrection of outrage at our educational inequities.

2

The Challenge, Context, and Preconditions of Academic Development at High Levels

Edmund W. Gordon and Beatrice L. Bridglall

THE CHALLENGES AND MAGNITUDE OF MINORITY HIGH ACADEMIC ACHIEVEMENT

It was about a century ago that W. E. B. Du Bois first called attention to the critical importance of giving consideration to the intellective development of the "talented tenth" among people of color. Du Bois argued that no society could afford to neglect the nurturance of that segment of its population. Like Plato and others, he saw that pool of talented people as the source of cultural, economic, political, and social leadership. At the time that he was advancing this somewhat elitist notion, he was greatly influenced by the prevailing conception of what it meant to be an educated person. Du Bois was better educated than most people in his generation. He was among the very few African American persons to have the privilege of a liberal arts education at that time. Early in his life he had become convinced of the popularly held view that the German universities provided the best education in the world. He was so convinced that he went to the University of Heidelberg to pursue his PhD. Some think that early signs of the racism that was to consume that nation led to the refusal of the faculty to let him complete the degree. Du Bois had to settle for a PhD degree from Harvard, where his dissertation became the inaugural volume of the prestigious Harvard University History Series.

But it is not Du Bois's biography that is of concern now; our concern is with the Du Boisian notion of the talented tenth and their education. The education that Du Bois advocated was the classical study of the liberal arts and sciences. He was later to call them the "liberating arts, humanities, and sciences" (Du Bois, personal communication with Gordon, 1958) because he was convinced that once the human intellect had been developed through

10

such studies, people could never again be enslaved. Having so much respect for classical education, Du Bois was wedded to the encyclopedic mastery of knowledge and an understanding of the relatedness of the several knowledge domains; his own competence reflected this bias. He seemed to know everything about almost every subject and held his audiences spellbound with his erudition. However, in one of the last lectures he delivered in this country before resigning his U.S. citizenship to become a citizen of Ghana and to live there, he indicated that the exquisite knowledge that he once advocated for the talented tenth would some day become the universal expectation for all educated people. He predicted that modern societies would increasingly depend on the products of human intellect and that meaningful participation in such societies would require that we educate, not just train, all people.

It is by no means clear that Du Bois was so advanced in his thinking that he anticipated more recent developments in our understanding of what it means to be an educated person. But his conception of the educated person as one who has encyclopedic knowledge or even deep mastery of one or more disciplines is being displaced by more fluid conceptions of what Gordon calls intellective competence (2001). By intellective competence, we refer to the metacognitive command of affective, cognitive, and situative processes to access, know, understand, interpret, and utilize knowledge and technique. Intellective competence is apparent in such capacities as

- Critical literacy
- Critical numeracy
- Mastery of some knowledge domains and their related tacit understandings
- Analogical reasoning
- Problem identification and the formulation of researchable questions
- Accession and taxonomic ordering of information (bringing order to chaos in the service of problem solving)
- The capacity to conduct analysis, to achieve synthesis, and to create synergy; and
- Movement from knowing to understanding.

We like to think of the capacity to engage in and manipulate these processes as "sense-making." This concern for the achievement of intellective competence brings us to the core of our problem: educating so as to enable the development of these intellective capacities. The goal of education so conceived requires a pedagogy that goes beyond the simple transfer of knowledge and skill to the mediation of understandings and appreciations and the adjudication of values in the service of prosocial human ends. We recognize that the demand for such educational achievement is increasingly universal.

The problem is not that the know-how for the conduct of such pedagogy is scarce but that will to provide it is seemingly nonexistent. At the same time, we are painfully aware that there exist serious gaps between the achievement of these educational goals and social divisions such as class, ethnicity, gender, and language proficiency. It is in the context of this complex problem that the National Task Force on Minority High Achievement, which investigated the extent, nature, and causes of this problem, was created. The task force's report, *Reaching the Top: A Report of the National Task Force on Minority High Achievement* (College Board 1999), presents some findings and recommendations for action. While little is new in this report, it is a codification of what is currently known about this problem. Specifically, *Reaching the Top* addressed:

1. The significance of academic underachievement in minority students;
2. The magnitude of the minority academic underachievement problem;
3. Sources of achievement disparities; and
4. Existing strategies for improving minority achievement.

The Significance of Academic Underachievement in Minority Students

The continuing shortage of African American, Hispanic American, and Native American students who achieve at very high levels academically is the national problem that guided the work of the National Task Force on Minority High Achievement (College Board 1999), a group of thirty-one prominent leaders from education and other sectors organized by the College Board in 1997. Its resulting report, *Reaching the Top*, (1) predicted that it will be "virtually impossible" to thoroughly "integrate the professional and leadership ranks of our society . . . until many more students from these underrepresented groups become high achievers"; (2) documented the variables associated with this shortage; and (3) recommended complementary strategies for redressing the imbalance underscored by the large number of European American and Asian American students who earn high grades in school, score highly on standardized tests, and earn bachelor's and advanced degrees.

Specifically, African American, Hispanic American, and Native American students are underrepresented among the students who perform in the top 25th percentile of students in elementary, secondary, and postsecondary education in the United States. To address this problem, the task force focused on four categories of work: (1) the identification and creation of strategies in school reform that show promise for reversing this condition; (2) the identification and replication of those programs and strategies in higher education that are directed at enhancing the academic achievement of students of color;

(3) the exploration of current developments in, and the effects of, supplementary education as factors influencing the academic achievement of students of color; and (4) the development of a comprehensive program of research concerning the correlates of high achievement in a variety of ethnic groups.

Equally significant is the report's finding that the pervasiveness of ethnic minority underachievement exists not just among low-income students but among students of color at all socioeconomic levels, including those students of color who are often unable to maintain the same high level of academic achievement in college despite having done very well in high school. Most problematic is the finding that the differentials in academic achievement increase as socioeconomic status (SES) increases. In other words, higher class status is not associated with smaller differences in achievement.

Magnitude of the Minority Academic Underachievement Problem

Given these important achievement differences between ethnic and SES groups. Some data sets such as the Scholastic Achievement Test (SAT) suggest that these differences are often substantial and may be larger among high-SES students than among low-SES students. For example, in 1993 the gap in average difference in the combined SAT math and verbal scores between white and black test takers, with at least one parent with a graduate degree, was 183 points (1024 for whites and 841 for blacks), while it was 137 points (796 and 659) between whites and blacks with no parent with a high school diploma. We are especially concerned that students of color are not only grossly underrepresented in the high end of the academic achievement distribution but that the quality of the contribution of this achieving group to the pool of relatively high academic achievers is lower than might otherwise be expected. It appears that the gap between majority and some ethnic minority students in their academic achievement cannot be narrowed unless we can reduce this gap in scores at the high end of the distribution.

It is sobering that African American, Hispanic American, and Native American students made up only 8 percent of the students nationally in 1995 with a combined math and verbal SAT score of 1400 or higher. These ethnic minority groups accounted for just 5 percent of the total number of students who scored 1200 or higher on the SAT, yet total 30 percent of all U.S. nationals under age eighteen. By contrast, Asian Americans account for 4 percent of the under-eighteen population, yet comprise 18 percent of those scoring 1400 or higher (Miller 1995).

These within-socioeconomic-group gaps are particularly costly from a high academic achievement standpoint. All racial/ethnic groups in the United

States draw a disproportionate number of their highest achieving students from their high-SES segments. Indeed, worldwide, high achievers are heavily drawn from high-SES students. However, if middle-class ethnic minority students are not doing nearly as well in relative terms as high-SES European and Asian American groups, it makes it very difficult to reduce the high achievement gaps that exist. For example, if all Puerto Rican SAT test takers with no parent with a high school diploma had scored as well in 1993 as those with at least one parent with a graduate degree, their average combined SAT math and verbal score would have increased from 686 to 861. Yet, 861 was still 163 points lower than the 1024 average for this segment of high-SES European American students.

At the elementary and middle school levels, the pervasive shortage of these groups among high-achieving students surfaces quickly in the early years of school and changes little thereafter (College Board 1999). For example, minority and majority test-score gaps on the federal government's National Assessment of Educational Progress (NAEP) reading, math, and science tests in the fourth grade parallel those found on NAEP tests in the twelfth grade. Among high school seniors in 1998, blacks, Hispanics, and Native Americans comprised only about one-tenth of the students who scored at the highest level on NAEP tests and are represented by only one in twenty of the students who had very high scores on the SAT I, scores typical of individuals admitted to first-tier colleges and universities (College Board 1999).

What is also distressing is that top black and Hispanic students enrolled at selective institutions do less well than their European American and Asian American peers. Indeed, the data clearly indicate that African Americans, Hispanic Americans, and Native Americans are considerably underrepresented among higher education degree recipients (College Board 1999). For instance, while comprising about 30 percent of the under-eighteen population in 1995, these minority groups received only 13 percent of the bachelor's degrees, 11 percent of the professional degrees, and 6 percent of the doctoral degrees presented by U.S. colleges and universities. Clearly, it is important for these students to sustain their gains not just on the elementary and secondary levels but also on the graduate and undergraduate levels.

Sources of Achievement Disparities

The research continues to reinforce the idea that attempts at reducing achievement disparities among ethnic minority groups, especially as they relate to the near absence of high-achieving students of color, must seriously take into account the range of challenges that disadvantaged children, their families, and the schools that serve them constantly encounter. Family and school instability, for example, ranks high among the research-based findings of poverty-related barriers. Indeed, disadvantaged families are (1) more likely to move often, especially in urban areas, and (2) may not be aware that these school changes may interfere with their children's education. For students who are more settled, however, learning is disrupted by frequent student turnover, and effective teaching is compromised by the presence and high turnover rate of inexperienced and unqualified teachers. Given that Hispanic Americans (who now make up the largest minority group) and blacks make up a growing number of disadvantaged students, this issue becomes even more problematic because the effects of poverty on racial and ethnic achievement gaps will continue to be considerable (College Board 1999).

Another factor affecting the racial and ethnic achievement gap revolves around variation in the education levels of minority parents. Unlike parents with a high school education or less, most parents with college degrees understand and emphasize academic achievement by supplementing their children's education with tutors and facilitating access to college preparatory classes. The research indicates that substantial numbers of European American and Asian American parents have college degrees, while large numbers of black, Hispanic American, and Native American parents are still without high school diplomas. Given the negative consequences of parental illiteracy, activities aimed at increasing the level of developed academic ability in parents need to be woven into multilevel efforts to increase the number of students of color among top academic achievers.

Racial and ethnic prejudice and discrimination continue to affect minority high achievement in a number of ways. First, African American, Hispanic American, and Native American students frequently encounter lower academic expectations. Second, the damaging effect ingrained stereotypes (which inaccurately posit that minority students are less intelligent than European American or Asian American students for genetic or cultural reasons) have on minority students' confidence and performance in challenging academic situations (College Board 1999). Third, it is not inconceivable that some minority students deliberately minimize their academic efforts out of a perception that success in school is only for white or Asian students (College Board 1999) or that their performance may serve to confirm existing stereotypes.

In addition to the above sources of achievement disparities, some research findings have suggested that both school-related and family/community-related cultural differences contribute to the achievement gaps among minority and majority groups. School-related differences might involve a curriculum that does not effectively draw on students' cultural experiences (College Board 1999). Similarly, family and community differences speak to the distressing lack of economic and academic resources that families and communities need in order to facilitate their children's academic development. Unlike most disadvantaged parents and communities, academically successful parents and communities draw on their personal resources to provide a broad range of activities and supports designed to supplement their children's education. Taken together, these sources of academic disparities continue to impact, on a number of levels, the ubiquitous underrepresentation of students of color among high students.

Existing Strategies for Improving Minority Achievement

Several extant strategies focus on students at risk of failing to achieve acceptable academic success. These include initiating and reinforcing preschool and parent education programs; raising elementary and secondary school academic standards; and improving curriculum, instruction, teacher professional development, and home–school interaction. In the interest of raising academic standards and ultimately achievement, school districts in many states are now expected to disaggregate data by race and ethnicity. This monitoring effort by states, however, does not include an emphasis on interventions designed to increase minority representation among high-achieving students. The same can be said of current efforts at evaluations of preschool and parent education programs, curriculum, instruction, and teacher professional development, which largely gauge the number of low-performing students brought to acceptable achievement levels, and rarely on their capacity to increase the number of high-achieving students. This emphasis on the use of test data to drive accountability is understandable, but it does little to inform or enable more appropriate opportunities to learn.

Despite inherent weaknesses in the evaluation/accountability focus of these approaches, the following research-based approaches can support efforts to increase the number of students of color who perform at high achievement levels (College Board 1999). These strategies include:

- Academically rich and rigorous curricula;
- Instruction that provides the assessment and mediation opportunities that students need to grasp key knowledge, techniques, and understanding;
- The development of strong home–school relationships;
- Supporting the continual and differentiated professional development of teachers; and
- The enabling of adult support for the academic and personal development of students.

As detailed earlier, most academically promising black and Hispanic students are not performing as well as their European American and Asian American counterparts at the college/university level. Despite this reality, some higher education officials are not recognizing the need for diverse efforts geared at generating a critical mass of high-achieving minority students. These efforts should include personal support and advising, opportunities for knowledge and skill development, opportunities to develop strong academically oriented peer networks, and sufficient financial aid to reduce pervasive concerns about finances (College Board 1999).

Most initiatives, however, have followed the lead provided by efforts at general school reform, which tend to focus on raising student achievement across the board. These efforts have had little specific impact, however, on reducing the gap between low- and high-achieving students of color and more privileged students (Treisman and Surles 2001).

THE CONTEXT AND PRECONDITIONS
FOR MINORITY HIGH ACHIEVEMENT

How is it possible to identify signs of improvement in academic achievement without sufficiently objective evidence that these initiatives have resulted in significant progress in reducing the academic achievement gap between high- and low-achieving groups? We argue that the in-school initiatives—school reforms—have not been sufficient to the general need and, in particular, have not been directed at the high-achieving end of the distribution. We argue further that the problem of the academic achievement gap is not a problem of schooling alone. Some of us are beginning to believe that without the capital to invest in human resource development, it is impossible to achieve meaningful participation in an advanced technological society. What is the nature of that capital? Several of us have included the following categories (Bourdieu 1986; Coleman 1987, 1990; Gordon and Meroe 1999; Miller 1995):

- Cultural capital
- Financial capital
- Health capital
- Human capital
- Personal capital
- Polity capital
- Social capital

Obviously, when we speak of capital, we are speaking of more than money and material resources. Capital is the accumulated accessibility and control of resources and power. Schools and other social institutions seem to work when persons served bring to these institutions the varieties of capital that enable and support human development.

The relationship between family income and academic achievement had become obvious by the middle of the twentieth century. Sexton's *Education and Income: Inequalities of Opportunity in Our Public Schools* (1961), the prodigious work of Cloward and Piven (1974), and the race-based studies of Kenneth Clarke have highlighted the tendency of academic achievement to rise with increases in family income. So noticeable were these associations that at least one investigator claimed that income is the best single predictor of academic achievement in the United States. However, mid-century United States was more concerned with the relationship between race and educational opportunity than with the impact of income. As a result, the great body of research from that period gave more attention to the impact of racial isolation and integration than to factors concerning income. However, if we are correct in assuming that the effectiveness of schools and other human resource development institutions is in part a function of the availability of wealth-derived capital for investment in human development, we may have in this relationship a catalyst for political and social intervention.

In the 1966 report *Equality of Educational Opportunity*, James Coleman and colleagues created some controversy when they asserted that variations in the quality of schooling did not adequately explain the variance in academic achievement. In fact, they argued that differences associated with families and family status accounted for the largest portion of the variance in school achievement. In a subsequent reanalysis of disaggregated data, Pettigrew (1967) reported that this relationship was not as strong for black and some other low-income children. For these less-advantaged children, quality of schooling appears to be more important. This may be the case because school is more likely to be the only place where they experience systematic supports for academic learning. The Coleman finding of family background as a primary correlate of academic achievement appeared to take the onus away from racial isolation and racial integration and the implicit differences in the quality of schooling available to blacks and whites in the schools of the nation. The finding also exacerbated the understandably negative reaction of minority groups and some liberal friends to the idea that something was wrong with black families that explained the relatively low level of academic achievement in that population. Some of us may recall that this report appeared at about the same time as the Moynihan report on black families (1965) and Lewis's work on Hispanic American families (1966).

The deflection of attention away from problems with the schools to problems with the victims of the school's failure and their families was met with a defense of the cultures and cultural identities of the victims. Neglected in this skirmish were factors related to the resources available to these families and the manner in which academic achievement was supported or not supported by the lifestyles that they experienced. It was almost as if the field was blind to any comprehensive sensitivity to or understanding of the broader context in which academic learning functions. For example, in the same period, a rather prominent historian of education was advancing the notion that our conception of education needed to be broadened to include the variety of institutions that provide education services or contribute to the effectiveness of education. Lawrence Cremin's (1976) list of educational institutions included families, faith-based institutions, museums, libraries, community centers, youth development organizations, recreation services, and so forth—the resources we are now calling *supplementary education*. Cremin saw schools as just one of the many institutions of learning, and thought that it was a mistake for professional educators to neglect these extra-school experiences and resources. Despite the prominence of the author and the logical consistency of the idea, Cremin's concern did not shake the centrality of the colloquial focus on schools as primary sources of education.

This overidentification of education with schooling is perhaps a function of our cultural history in which the school has played the central role educationally for most members of the society. As both the common socializing and nation-building influence and the primary source of exposure to formal didactic experience with the disciplines, most of us perhaps think first of school when we think of academic learning. Despite this colloquially accepted notion, increasingly we are convinced that universal academic development and high achievement require more than schools can deliver. In fact, after reviewing the evidence, it is difficult to avoid the conclusion that the achievement of the optimal benefits of schooling, as reflected in high levels of developed academic ability, depends on factors outside of the control and influence of schools. In other words, while schools may be necessary to the achievement of intellective competence in the general population, they may not be sufficiently enabling of this goal. Thus, schools alone cannot solve the ubiquitous underproductivity of schooling and some of the populations served (Comer 1997; Steinberg 1996; Berliner and Biddle 1995).

THE PRECONDITIONS FOR MINORITY HIGH ACHIEVEMENT

There is wide agreement of the characteristics of well-resourced schools and effective teaching and learning situations. These include:

* Effective leadership,
* Well-prepared staff,
* Clear sense of purpose and goals,
* Adequate human and material resources, and
* Sense of trust and security.

While these well-resourced schools may be necessary, the effectiveness of the teaching and learning situations may be a function of the requisite preconditions that provide the foundation and scaffolding for high levels of academic achievement. These foundations and scaffolds—supports for academic and personal development—provide the preconditions that enable good schooling to be effective. Perhaps best conceptualized by Schultz (1961), Bourdieu (1986), Coleman (1987, 1990), and more recently by Miller (1995), the preconditions of high levels of academic achievement are seen as the availability of education-relevant resources (Miller 1995, 88), which these authors refer to as "capital." They argue that the access some families have to various capital enables them to invest in their children's education. It is this hidden curriculum (Strodtbeck 1964) that accounts for the differential effectiveness of schools for children from well-resourced families.

According to Coleman, "The resources devoted by the family to the child's education interact with the resources provided by the school—and there is greater variation in the former resources than in the latter" (1987, 35). Given this conceptualization, Miller (1995) suggests that:

1. To ensure academic success, the family or the school must provide children with a substantial quantity of resources.
2. In contemporary America, there are significant differences among families and schools in the amounts and forms of these resources that are available for the education of children. The differences among families are greater than the differences among schools.
3. Even the best-resourced school under existing arrangements is usually not able to compensate fully for a substantial shortfall on the family side.
4. Even when there is no resource-quantity problem on either side, there may be incompatibility of resource forms between the family and the school (for example, language or other cultural differences) that can adversely affect the educational experience of the child.

These nonschool-based, education-relevant resources (varieties of capital) that are necessary for schooling to be effective in the development of high levels of academic ability are identified and elaborated here for emphasis.

Cultural Capital

Cultural capital is the accumulated beliefs, knowledge, techniques, technologies, ways of doing, being, and the identities and rituals of a people. The experience with the artifacts of one's culture and the foci of one's cultural identity not only influence the development of one's attitudes and behaviors but also important developmental resources. Hirsch (1988) has argued eloquently (some may say too narrowly) for the importance of cultural capital. There is no question, however, about the validity of his claim that cultural knowledge is an important resource. In a multicultural society, familiarity with the central elements of the hegemonic culture may be difficult for some members of diverse cultural groups, but it is nonetheless an essential resource. Since schools are not typically organized to privilege these diverse cultures in routine teaching and learning transactions, students who do not have a command of the central elements of the hegemonic culture are placed at a disadvantage. But familiarity is not always sufficient. Culture is a ubiquitous phenomenon; simply knowing the custom or how to do it may not be sufficient. It is sometimes necessary that one identify with the culture in order to function in it with automaticity. Thus, culture is an essential capital with which to invest in the pursuit of one's education (Gordon 1997a).

Financial Capital

Financial capital is so obvious a human need that it appears superfluous to isolate it. It refers to income, wealth, and the material resources necessary for survival and developmental investment in a society where commodification is privileged. This concern with financial capital must be approached at multiple levels. The society must have money to invest in education. The school must have the finances necessary to be adequately resourced. The family must have the money to access the material resources necessary for its existence and advancement. There are considerable research findings that document the relationship between family access to financial capital and school achievement (Bowles and Gintis 1976; Sexton 1961; Coleman 1990). The National Research Council's report on school finance provides a definitive review of the relationships between societal and/or school-level finances and the quality of schooling (Ladd, Chalk, and Hansen 1999). However, the usual focus on available income is not sufficient to enable the understanding of the complex relations between financial resources and school achievement. Jaynes and Williams (1989) have documented the same phenomenon, as well as differentials in the impact of wealth on black and white families when income or wealth is controlled as an independent variable. Even in the presence of income that is adequate to the comfortable existence of a family, the absence of wealth (accumulated assets) can leave the family that has achieved middle-class status one paycheck away from poverty. Almost half a century ago, E. Franklin Frazier (1966) described the ersatz character of the attempt to re-create the hegemonic culture in some middle-class black families. This strategy, however, seems to simply exacerbate the impact of differences in access to financial capital (income and wealth) as an education-relevant resource.

When Title I was established in 1965, it reflected a recognition among educators and government policymakers that poverty is strongly related to low academic achievement. Since that time, we have learned a great deal about poverty's multiple impacts on student achievement. Importantly, researchers have learned that children experiencing chronic long-term poverty are among the most at risk educationally. These youngsters frequently have health problems that undermine learning. As suggested earlier, their families also tend to move frequently, resulting in serious discontinuities in the children's education as they travel from one school to the next. Researchers have also found that a high concentration of poor youngsters in schools is associated with lower achievement for poor and well-off students alike. But poverty concentration need not be extreme to have a negative impact. Some research findings indicate that in schools with a 25 percent student poverty rate, both poor and well-off youngsters do less well academically than their counterparts in schools with very low student poverty rates (Miller 1995).

Health Capital

Clearly one of the prerequisites for high academic achievement, health capital is one of the categories of education investment capital that Bourdieu (1986) introduced. This conceptual framework highlights the critical relationships between health and academics that Birch and Gussow (1970) systematically describe in their book, *Disadvantaged Children: Health, Nutrition and School Failure*. Their central message concerns the importance of good health and adequate nutrition as resources for effective schooling. For children to succeed academically in school, they generally need to be in good health and adequately fed. The literature from the mid-twentieth century to the present clearly documents the fact that when children cannot bring good health into the classroom, attendance, attention, some aspects of learning, sustained learning, and task engagement suffer. In a modern industrialized nation, with a large middle class and a supposedly small number of poverty-stricken members, it may seem unnecessary to single out health as a major resource needed to ensure school success, because in such a society most children are thought to be in good health. But in less-developed countries in which the middle class is small and a large proportion of the population is poor, improving children's health may be an essential component of effective strategies for increasing the academic success of students.

Although the United States is an affluent nation, it has a relatively large number of children who are poor and who have health problems severe enough to undermine prospects for their academic success. A recent report (Proctor and Dalaker 2003) indicates that the United States has the largest number of children living in poverty of any of the industrialized nations. These children are also disproportionately members of racial/ethnic minority groups in the United States. They are consequently placed at risk of failure to thrive by the quality and nature of their economic, ethnic/cultural, polity, and health capital. Consequently, health capital is included among the resources required when examining variations in family and school resources as they relate to academic achievement.

This is especially important since national health statistics continue to show significant disparities in the number of low-income people of color with poor health outcomes and limited access to health care compared to the general population in the United States (despite some progress in public policies regarding racial discrimination over the last century). For example, African Americans and Hispanic Americans comprise 56 percent of the more than 700,000 cases of AIDS reported to the U.S. Centers for Disease Control and Prevention (CDC) since the beginning of the epidemic in 1981 (CDC 2000). AIDS remains the leading killer of African Americans age twenty-five to forty-four (CDC 2001). In addition, approximately four million new cases of sexually transmitted diseases (STDs) each year occur in adolescents, with African Americans and Hispanics having higher rates of STDs than whites (U.S. Department of Health and Human Services 2000), while the prevalence of diabetes in African Americans is nearly 70 percent higher than in whites and the prevalence in Hispanics is almost double that of whites (U.S. Department of Health and Human Services, n.d.).

Birch and Gussow (1970) postulated that children who are better nourished perform better in school. Although there was a dearth of scientific evidence at the time, recent empirical evidence about the role of nutrition in cognitive development and intellectual performance confirms the accuracy of their assumption. The CDC's *Guidelines for School Health Programs* (1996), for example, asserts that not having breakfast can affect children's intellectual performance. That is, hungry children are more likely to have behavioral, emotional, and academic problems at school (CDC 1996). Corroborating evidence of recent studies in developing countries have shown that improvement in nutrition among children results in periodic gains in mental tests and on motor development (Martorell 1998; Sigman and Whaley 1998).

The exposure to and impact of environmental pollutants on children's cognitive abilities also need to be recognized. In the last thirty years, environmental chemicals and their potential effects on human health and children's cognitive abilities have received considerable attention. Lead-based paint, for example, continues to be the main source of exposure for children who develop lead poisoning, and it is entirely preventable (Wasserman and Factor-Litvak 2001). According to the Centers for Disease Control, 890,000 children in the United States ages one to five had noticeable lead levels in their blood in 1991; by 1999–2000, the estimated number of children with elevated blood lead levels was 434,000 (CDC 2003a). Over one-fifth of African American children living in housing built before 1946 have elevated lead levels. Other common exposures include lead carried home on shoes or clothing, lead in water, consumption of imported foods, and folk medicines and practices. Over the years, research has increasingly recognized that lead affects nearly every system in the body. It is particularly harmful to the developing brain and the central nervous system and when ingested can cause learning disabilities and behavioral problems. If ingested at very high levels, it can result in seizures, coma, and even death (CDC 2003b).

Human Capital

Human capital refers to the developed abilities/expertise of those in one's environment. Throughout history, novices have benefited from the guidance, examples, modeling, and shared experiences of more sophisticated learners. When one's surroundings are rich in such persons, and novice learners have access and can participate in meaningful experiences, it can be said that one is rich in human capital. Human capital is represented in the intelligence, information, substantive knowledge, technical skills, tacit knowledge, social competence, and other education-derived abilities of the people in one's social network. Thus the children of college-educated parents have more human capital than those of high school dropouts. For example, Aunt Evangeline, the college professor, is a part of the human capital available to her nephew John. One of the senior author's students at Yale wrote her senior essay on the families of high-achieving Korean students. In the essay, she concluded that one of the factors influencing the achievements of these students was the presence of well-educated parents in the home, one of whom stayed at home to raise the children. She reasoned that the constant exposure of these children to adults with well-developed academic abilities gave them a human capital advantage that she associated with their academic competence. But it is not simply formal education and substantive knowledge that is important. Others who have lived the experience and have tacit knowledge of the problem or of the experiential phenomenon are examples of human capital. The "green-thumbed" farmer is a part of the human capital of the novice gardener. This definition so far gives emphasis to the characteristics of the valued person, but access to such persons is equally important and is related to another category of human resource development capital that we call social capital.

Personal Capital

Personal capital refers to resources that are intrinsic to the person—to characteristics of the learning person or the assets or resources that the person carries with the self. Here we refer to agency, attitudes, aspirations, developed abilities, dispositions, efficacy, and one's sense of power. This domain of human behavior, sometimes associated with resilience, combines tangible developed abilities and skills with aspects of the affective domain that have to do with feelings about oneself and the targeted human activity. It involves intentionality and purpose. It is reflected in deliberately deployed effort and the willingness to exert it. Gordon (2001) has introduced the construct *intellective competence* while Greeno (2001) prefers *intellective character* to refer to the combination of developed ability and these existential affective characteristics of the person that form the context for human action. It is the capital intrinsic to the person that one brings to and continues to develop in learning situations.

Polity Capital

Polity capital references the reciprocal concern and respect, communal commitment, welcomed participation, and group affinity and inclusiveness that are associated with societal membership. The slogan for a major financial service corporation is "membership has its privileges." Polity refers to sense of membership. If I sense that I belong to the group, I tend to identify with the goals and values of the group. If I sense that I do not belong, then the values, standards, and expectations of the group are less important and more easily ignored. If society recognizes me as a member, it is more likely to be concerned about my welfare and more willing to support the needs of other members who are like me. For example, if the people who use the public schools are "like me," it seems easier to raise tax-levied funds to support those schools. If the schools serve "those unlike me," public school budgets are likely to suffer. Societies and other human groups tend to emerge to meet the needs of those who are thought to belong or share polity. Of all the human resource development capitals, polity capital may be the most important, since having it signals collective responsibility for my welfare.

Social Capital

Social capital refers to the access that one has to resources by virtue of social networks that exists within human groups. Being able to call a friend for a job or school application reference is a common example. A more pejorative example is "'the old boys' club." Some teenage boys rely on loose networks of gang members to "protect their backs." Some of the craft unions are said to require family, friendship, or ethnic connections for admission to membership. When schooling was being made needlessly difficult for one of his children, the senior author was able to call a highly placed school official to resolve the problem. Social capital refers to such networks and the capacity and freedom to tap into them. Social capital also refers to the tacit knowledge (1) that such networks exist; (2) of how one goes about accessing them; and (3) of the social norms, cultural styles, and the privileged values by which others recognize that one is eligible to participate. There is a third kind of social capital that is reflected in the traditional conceptions of polity. For most of the senior author's life, he has functioned in social and professional settings where blacks were not expected. He has functioned remarkably well even without the social capital associated with being a white male. When women enter male-dominated fields, when English-language learners enter English-dominant groups, when lower-class and black students enter highly selective colleges or jobs, they do so without the social capital of the more privileged.

INTRODUCING SUPPLEMENTARY EDUCATION TO THOSE IN NEED

At this point, the question in our readers' minds may be concerned with what those of us who are serious about raising high academic achievement for students of color. We can start by systematically introducing supplementary education activities for African American, Hispanic American, and Native American ethnic minority group students. These activities and strategies include:

Empowering Support

The empowerment of parents of color and other adults to support more adequately the academic and personal development of their children. This strategy is supported by Gordon and Wilkerson's (1966) finding that parents can enable the academic aspirations for their children with access to the know-how to turn these aspirations into academic success. Parents need to receive instruction, guidance, hands-on technical assistance, and supported experience in the exercise of those behaviors and the creation of those conditions that are known to be supportive of academic achievement. In addition to more sustained parent involvement in the affairs of the school, parents need to be taught and encouraged to intervene at school on behalf of their children. Parents who are unfamiliar with the time demands for sustained engagement in serious study need to be oriented to the demands of modern academic pursuits. Parents need to be introduced to and guided in their interactions with the many networks by which higher educational and supplementary educational experiences are available.

Providing Comparable Supplementary Education

The provision of supplementary education activities comparable to those that many affluent and academically sophisticated parents make available to their children. There may be limits to what we can expect to achieve for students of color through the current efforts at school reform, which are primarily focused on accountability and high standards of educational achievement. It may be necessary that students, families, and communities be strengthened in their capacity to extract what they need from the schools as they exist. As evidenced in our earlier discussion of human resource capital, education appears to be more effective when it is built upon an adequate base of human resource capital—that is, health, material resources, social networks, tacit knowledge about how schooling works, polity as reflected in a sense of membership, cultural versatility, and political socialization. These resources are not equally distributed among members of the society. Supplementary education activities seek to provide some of this human resource capital that is naturally available to children from better-advantaged homes. Included are services related to health and nutrition, guidance, tutorials, mentoring, summer educational enrichment, travel, exposure to institutions of "high" culture, and the social networks through which opportunities for upward mobility are mediated.

Cooperative Learning Opportunities

The utilization of cooperative learning communities, peer group supports, and social climates. These types of opportunities privilege academic achievement behaviors, political socialization, and athletic-style academic coaching (Gordon 1986). One of the models examined in this volume (see chapter 10) is the recruitment of small groups of students who attend school together, study together, support each other, collectively understand that mastery of the tasks of schooling is a political as well as an academic endeavor, and are responsible to each other and for each other's success (Gordon 1997b). Our own experiences and extant research indicate that students who sense cultural and political relevance in their learning experiences tend to sustain engagement and invest more time on tasks in the learning experiences so perceived (Gordon and Song 1994). Through purposive attention to political socialization, emphasis should be placed on making explicit the link between the integrity of one's cultural identity, the exercise of political power (acting collectively to pursue common goals), and success in education. The models for cooperative learning (Fullilove and Treisman 1990; Lockhead and Clement 1979) need to be adapted to take advantage of collective approaches to academic study. This is in contrast to the colloquial notion that isolated study and individual approaches to learning are the secret to academic success.

Direct Instruction

Direct instruction to ensure the enhancement of cognitive and metacognitive competencies, effective teaching and learning experiences, diagnostic-targeted remediation, and academic socialization. The development and implementation of this strategy relates to Gordon's (1986) ideas on learning about thinking and thinking about learning, in which students are enabled to better understand the operation of their own mental processes and to use this understanding to manage their intellectual pursuits. The theory holds that those who understand how they think and learn are better positioned to appropriately target their mental processes and self-correct. Similarly, the use of diagnostic strategies to identify specific aspects of academic dysfunction should inform remediation that is targeted to specific problems (Gordon 1986). The implementation effort needs to include state-of-the-art mediation of intensive teaching and learning transactions, such as AP courses, Pacesetter, and extended SAT-preparation types of tutorials. Through academic socialization, students need to be taught study skills, oriented to the conditions necessary for effective study, and influenced in the shaping of dispositions and behaviors that traditionally have proved to be effective in high-quality academic pursuits. The assumption is that many persons learn these competencies, dispositions, and strategies in the natural course of their lives with academically sophisticated adults and peers. For some students of color, this has not been the case. Consequently, the acquisition of these attitudes, skills, and competencies cannot be taken for granted, but must be taught directly or through specially orchestrated opportunities.

Access to Technology

The development and provision of ready access to advanced computer technology and telecommunications. The availability of such programs (1) provides access to a wide range of information sources and (2) enables students, teachers, parents, and sponsors to communicate with each other. We need to utilize such systems as the Internet or World Wide Web as vehicles to achieve the goals of this initiative. A "home page" (also known as a "website") is a related mechanism through which online information and services can be widely distributed to targeted audiences. Through this system, these audiences can be provided with the following services:

- Online guidance and tutorial assistance
- Group or individual communication and consultation
- Access to data banks, directories, and library services
- Online discussion and conference participation
- Computer-mediated educational assessment and tutorial or self-evaluation via telecommunication
- Access to information concerning college admissions and institutions of higher or continuing education

The telecommunications system needs to function as an electronic hotline as well as a medium of general support for learning. The system needs to provide a web server, which would enable planners to design and maintain a tree of information pages, process instructional materials, and develop training programs for users of the system. Users would need access to a computer, modem, and telephone line. The development and implementation of this strategy also has to consider the problems of equipment and service cost to users with limited incomes. We suggest that organizations like churches, community centers, schools, libraries, and local sponsors can serve as viable sources through which interventions based in the domain of supplementary education can be promoted.

CULTURAL HEGEMONY, IDENTITY, AND DISSONANCE

In a society that, all too often has been ready to look for the causes of failure to thrive in the intrinsic and even genetic characteristics of learners, it is interesting that so little attention has been given to what learners actually do and feel about the academic learning experience. This may be due in part to the reluctance to place the blame for school failure at the doorstep of populations that are known to be underserved. Blaming the quality of their genetic material may be more acceptable because it means that neither they nor the society can do anything about it. Nonetheless, a discussion of the context and conditions that enable high academic achievement must include attention to such learner phenomena as one's personal sense of agency or power, one's sense of efficacy, and ultimately the quantity and quality of effort deployed in the service of the achievement of academic goals. The research literature is replete with relevant evidence. In Coleman's report (1966), he and his associates conclude that a five-item probe of students' sense of power (ability to do something about one's life) enabled them to account for a proportion of the variance in academic achievement second only to the impact of family background. In other words, to the extent that students felt that they had the power to influence or control their environments and lives, differences between higher- and lower-status blacks and whites declined. Howard (1995) designed a curriculum intervention around findings that show effort and productivity increasing as sense of efficacy increases. Sullivan (1990) places human agency—the intentional orchestration and deployment of one's energy and other resources on purposeful behavior directed at self-specified ends—at the center of his science of human behavior.

Behavioral scientists have been able to identify social psychological circumstances that influence agency, efficacy, sense of power, and effort. Katz (1967) and Steele (1997) respectively established associations between test takers' perceptions of the ethnicity of test administrators or the ethnicity of the persons with whom they were to be compared, and the performance on the tests. More recently, Steele and his colleagues have determined that if test takers' perceptions of what is being measured can be mapped onto contemporary stereotypes concerning one's primary reference group, test scores go down (Steele and Aronson 2000). Steele calls this phenomenon *fear of stereotype confirmation*. Fordham and Ogbu (1986) have identified the phenomenon they call *fear of acting white* as a deterrent to serious academic pursuit on the part of some African American students. Gordon (1999) reports of African American students who have had to hide their books and other academic pursuits from peers to avoid being laughed at or "dissed" by their black youth peers. These affective and existential phenomena are a part of the context in which academic development must occur for many of the children with whom we are concerned.

These structural, functional, and existential factors, in addition to other sets of contextual factors, are associated with the dissonance created by the coexistence of hegemonic and subordinated cultural groups in a modern, technologically advanced society like the United States.

CONCLUSION

Clearly, the referenced varieties of capital form the essential context and foundation for high levels of academic learning. As resources for human development, however, they are often taken for granted. Not surprisingly, too little attention is given to their importance for academic learning, and almost no attention is paid to the fact that these capitals are unevenly distributed among the majority and minority school population. It may well be that some of the variance that Coleman assigns to family background is accounted for by the strong association between family SES and access to the variety of education-related capital we regard as enabling of success in school. In the presence of these capitals, well-resourced and effective schools, coupled with appropriate family and community supports for academic development, are among the essential conditions for the development of academic excellence.

Given this broader context, the unequal distribution of these capitals severely limits the effectiveness of schools. The redistribution of access to such capitals may be beyond our immediate reach, but all may not be lost because concerned communities and families can find alternatives to the school-related benefits otherwise derived from access to such capital.

REFERENCES

Berliner, D. C., and B. J. Biddle. 1995. *The manufactured crisis: Myths, fraud, and the attack on America's public schools*. Redding, MA: Addison-Wesley Publishing.

Birch, H. G., and J. D. Gussow. 1970. *Disadvantaged children: Health, nutrition and school failure*. New York: Harcourt Brace and World.

Bourdieu, P. 1986. The forms of capital. In *Handbook of theory and research for the sociology of education*, edited by J. Richardson, 241–58. Westport, CT: Greenwood.

Bowles S., and H. Gintis. 1976. *Schooling in capitalist America*. New York: Basic Books.

Centers for Disease Control and Prevention. 1996. *Guidelines for school health programs to promote lifelong healthy eating*. Morbidity and Mortality Weekly Reports and Recommendations no. 45. Washington, DC: U.S. Government Printing Office.

————. 2000. *HIV/AIDS Surveillance Report*. Vol. 12(1). Washington, DC: U.S. Department of Health and Human Services. Available online at www.cdc.gov/hiv/stats/hasr1201.htm.

————. 2001. *HIV/AIDS among African Americans: Key facts*. Washington, DC: U.S. Department of Health and Human Services. Available online at www.cdc.gov/hiv/pubs/Facts/afam.pdf.

————. 2003a. *Children's blood lead levels in the United States*. Washington, DC: U.S. Department of Health and Human Services. Available online at www.cdc.gov/nceh/lead/research/kidsBLL.htm.

————. 2003b. *Surveillance for elevated blood lead levels among children: United States, 1997–2001*. U.S. Department of Health and Human Services. Available online at www.cdc.gov/mmwr/preview/mmwrhtml/ss5210a1.htm.

Cloward, R. A., and F. F. Piven. 1974. *The politics of turmoil: Essays on poverty, race, and the urban crisis*. New York: Pantheon Books

Coleman, J. S. 1987. Families and schools. *Educational Researcher* 16:32–38.

————. 1990. *Equality and achievement in education*. Boulder, CO: Westview Press.

Coleman, J. S., E. Q. Campbell, C. J. Hobson, J. McPartland, A. M. Mood, F. D. Weinfeld, and L. R. York. 1965@ p. 18. *Equality of educational opportunity*. Washington, DC: U.S. Government Printing Office.

College Board. 1999. *Reaching the top: A report of the National Task Force on Minority High Achievement*. New York: College Entrance Examination Board.

Comer, J. 1997. *Waiting for a miracle: Why schools can't solve our problems—and how we can*. New York: Dutton.

Cremin, L. A. 1976. *Public education*. New York: Basic Books.

Fordham, S., and J. U. Ogbu. 1986. Black students' school success: Coping with the "burden of acting white." *Urban Review* 18(3): 176–206.

Frazier, E. F. 1966. *The Negro family in the United States*. Rev. and abridged ed. Chicago: University of Chicago Press.

Fullilove, R. E., and P. U. Treisman. 1990. Mathematics achievement among African American undergraduates at the University of California, Berkeley: An evaluation of the Mathematics Workshop Program. *Journal of Negro Education* 59(3): 463–78.

Gordon, E. W. 1986. Designing, implementing, and evaluating programs to facilitate cognitive development. *Special Services in the Schools* 3(1, fall) and (2, winter).

————. 1997a. Cultural identity and behavioral change. *Case Western Reserve Law Review* 47(2): 389–98.

————. 1997b. *An evaluation of the POSSE Foundation Program*. Pomona, NY: Gordon and Gordon.

————. 1999. *Education and justice: A view from the back of the bus*. New York: Teachers College Press.

————. 2001. *The affirmative development of academic ability*. Pedagogical Inquiry and Praxis, no. 2. New York: Teachers College, Columbia University.

Gordon, E. W., and A. S. Meroe. 1999. Common destinies—Continuing dilemmas. In *Education and justice: A view from back of the bus*, edited by E. W. Gordon. New York: Teachers College Press.

Gordon, E. W., and L. D. Song. 1994. Variations in the experience of resilience. In *Educational resilience in inner-city America: Challenges and prospects*, edited by M. C. Wang and E. W. Gordon. Hillsdale, NJ: Lawrence Erlbaum.

Gordon, E. W., and D. Wilkerson. 1966. *Compensatory education for the disadvantaged: Programs and practices, preschool through college.* New York: College Entrance Examination Board.

Greeno, J. 2001. Students with competencies, authority and accountability: Affording intellective identity in classrooms. Unpublished paper, College Board, Division of Academic Affairs, New York

Hirsch, E. D. 1988. *Cultural literacy: What every American needs to know.* New York: Vintage Books.

Howard, J. 1995. You can't get there from here: The need for a new logic in education reform. *Daedalus: Journal of the American Academy of Arts and Sciences* 124(4).

Jaynes, G. D., and R. J. Williams Jr., eds. 1989. *A common destiny: Blacks and American society.* A report from the Committee on the Status of Black Americans, National Research Council. Washington DC: National Academy Press.

Katz, I. (1967). Motivation and equal education opportunity. Paper presented at the APA Division 15 Symposium, University of Michigan, September 3.

Ladd, H. F., R. Chalk, and J. S. Hansen, eds. 1999. *Equity and adequacy in education finance: Issues and perspectives.* Washington, DC: National Academy of Sciences Press.

Lewis, O. 1966. *La vida: A Puerto Rican family in the culture of poverty—San Juan and New York.* New York: Random House.

Lockhead, J., and J. Clement, eds. 1979. *Cognitive process instruction: Research on teaching thinking skills.* Philadelphia, PA: Franklin Institute Press.

Martorell, R. 1998. Nutrition and the worldwide rise in IQ scores. In *The rising curve: Long-term gains in IQ and related measures*, edited by U. Neisser, 183–206. Chicago: American Psychological Association.

Miller, S. 1995. *An American imperative: Accelerating minority educational advancement.* New Haven, CT: Yale University.

Moynihan, D. P. 1965. *The Negro family: The case for national action.* Washington, DC: U.S. Department of Labor.

Pettigrew, T. F. 1967. The consequences of racial isolation in the public schools—Another look. Paper presented at the National Conference on Equal Educational Opportunity in America's Cities, November, Washington, DC.

Proctor, B. D., and J. Dalaker. 2003. *Poverty in the United States: 2002.* Current Population Reports, P60-222. Washington, DC: U.S. Census Bureau.

Schultz, T. W. 1961. Investment in human capital. *American Economic Review* 51(1): 1–17.

Sexton, P. 1961. *Education and income: Inequalities of opportunity in our public schools.* New York: Viking Press.

Sigman, M., and S. E. Whaley. 1998. The role of nutrition in the development of intelligence. In *The rising curve: Long-term gains in IQ and related measures*, edited by U. Neisser. Chicago: American Psychological Association.

Slavin, R. E., and N. A. Madden. 1989. Effective classroom programs for students at risk. In *Effective programs for students at risk*, edited by R. E. Slavin, N. L. Karweit, and N. A. Madden. Boston, MA: Allyn and Bacon.

Steele, C. M. 1997. A threat in the air: How stereotypes shape intellectual identity and performance. *American Psychologist* 52(6): 613–29.

Steele, C. M., and J. Aronson. 2000. Stereotype threat and the intellectual test performance of African Americans. In *Stereotypes and prejudice: Essential readings*, edited by C. Stangor, 369–89. Philadelphia, PA: Psychology Press.

Steinberg, L. 1996. *Beyond the classroom: Why school reform has failed and what parents need to do*. New York: Simon and Schuster.

Strodtbeck, F. L. 1964. The hidden curriculum of the middle class home. In *Urban education and cultural deprivation*, edited by C. W. Hunnicutt. Syracuse, NY: Syracuse University Press.

Sullivan, E. 1990. *Critical psychology and pedagogy: Interpretation of the personal world*. Westport, CT: Greenwood Press.

Treisman, P. U., and S. A. Surles. 2001. Systemic reform and minority student high achievement. In *The right thing to do, the smart thing to do: Enhancing diversity in the health professions*, edited by B. D. Smedley, A. Y. Stith, L. Colburn, and C. H. Evans. Summary of the Symposium on Diversity in Health Professions in honor of Herbert W. Nickens, M.D. Washington, DC: National Academy Press.

U.S. Department of Health and Human Services. n.d. Eliminating racial and ethnic disparities in health. Available online at: http://raceandhealth.hhs.gov/3rdpgBlue/Diabetes/3pgGoalsDiabetes.htm.

———. 2000. *Healthy people 2010*. 2nd ed. Washington, DC: U.S. Government Printing Office. Available online at www.healthypeople.gov/Publications.

Wasserman, G. A., and P. Factor-Litvak. 2001. Methodology, inference and causation: Environmental lead exposure and childhood intelligence. *Archives of Clinical Neuropsychology* 16(4): 343–52.

3

After-School Programs, Youth Development, and Other Forms of Supplementary Education

Beatrice L. Bridglall

$\mathbf{A}$ wide variety of custodial, developmental, directed learning, and recreational experiences are provided for children outside of the schools' jurisdiction. These activities and services are more colloquially recognized as components of after-school programs and youth development or youth service programs. In addition to these more formally organized services, there is a host of activities that parents and other adults arrange for children outside of schooling that serve protective and recreational functions. Many of these activities also serve educational functions or are specifically designed to support the academic development of children. Gordon (1999) asserts that these activities may, in fact, enable schooling to be effective. We refer to these activities, services, and practices as supplemental to schooling or *supplementary education*. Discussions of these three categories of activity (after-school care, youth development services, and other forms of supplementary education) constitute the first part of this chapter. In addition to providing an inventory and analysis of the variety of current practices in supplementary education, we include in the second part of this chapter a definition, conceptual frame, and rationale for the construct of supplementary education. We conclude with a discussion of the relevant issues, provide a critique, and offer suggestions on the significant roles parents and families, young adolescents, community organizations, schools, health organizations, higher education institutions, research and evaluation organizations, funders (including businesses and corporate philanthropies, media), and our government can play and the diverse contributions they can make in the lives of youth.

FORMS OF SUPPLEMENTARY EDUCATION

After-School Care

For over a century, schooling has served both educative and child-care purposes. The extension of the school day to include various forms of after-school care emerged as a response to (1) the increased demand for child-care services at the end of the school day as the number of family members who worked outside the home increased, and (2) greater sensitivity to the need for children to be protected from patterns of youth crime and youth victimization that occur between the hours of 2 p.m. and 8 p.m. (Newman, Fox, Flynn, and Christeson 2000). Some would add the possibility that support for after-school care came from a source that also supported public schooling—those who were primarily interested in keeping children out of the labor force. Although the need for child care and child protection outside the home has continued, the use of after-school care to extend and support academic development crept into the after-school movement before the middle of the twentieth century. This was reflected in the introduction of tutorials and makeup time for academics into after-school programs. By the end of the twentieth century, concern for the ubiquitous academic achievement gap between majority and some ethnic minority groups had begun to recast the way parents, educators, and policymakers think about the various ways in which the academic, personal, and protective needs of children can be served through after-school programs. We regard this range of after-school and other out-of-school services for children as forms of supplementary education. Conceptions of after-school care, however, continue to be the most widely used single category of these services.

The concept of after-school care within the broader domain of supplementary education is not new. A review of the literature indicates that it is a century-old issue (Seppanen, deVries, and Seligson 1993). Indeed, day nurseries and private charities began providing care for school-age children as early as 1894 (Seligson, Genser, Gannet, and Gray 1983). The mission of these early services was twofold: (1) to provide care for children from poor, troubled homes, and (2) to help immigrant children to assimilate.

The use of arts and crafts, dramatic play, and recreational activities (referred to as "progressive" educational constructs) began to affect private-school practices in the early 1920s. These developments soon spread to less-privileged children through the introduction of "play schools" that were organized in housing projects, community centers, settlement houses, and public schools in major urban areas across the nation. By the late 1920s and 1930s, the practice of play school began to meet the needs of families who were faced with the loss of traditional forms of child care precipitated by the increasing numbers of mothers in the out-of-home labor force and the population shift from rural to urban areas.

The start of World War II and the related need for female workers to maintain the war effort propelled the demand for school-age child care into a public policy issue, which resulted in the allocation of federal funds to meet the increased need for child care for youngsters. Seligson and his colleagues documented that almost 3,000 extended-day school programs served over 100,000 school-age children during the war years. Additionally, several hundred combined school-age/nursery child-care programs and 835 child-care centers served another 30,000 (Seligson et al. 1983, 21). During this time, the federal Office of Education (OE) sponsored about 95 percent of all day-care centers, most of which were located in schools built in the 1930s by the Works Project Administration (WPA). In addition to this effort, the OE endorsed the increase of child-care services by disseminating information on how to start after-school programs, suggested that local community leaders form child-care committees, and advocated the idea that schools were the -most practical places for these programs.

Federal funding of child-care programs ended, however, when the war ended and women were no longer needed to replace male workers. A few state and local governments, California and New York, for example, continued to fund these programs because affordable school-age child-care services remained in demand as women's participation in the workforce grew. "As a national policy, however, child-care and the role of the public schools in providing school age care did not reemerge until the 1970s" (Seppanen, deVries, and Seligson 1993).

According to the U.S. Bureau of Labor Statistics (as cited in Willer et al. 1991), between 1970 and 1990, the proportion of American children under age eighteen with mothers in the labor force rose from 39 percent to 62 percent. The 1990 employment rate for mothers whose youngest child was ten to twelve years of age was 70 percent, with 49 percent working full time and 21 percent part time. And according to the 1990 National Child Care Survey (NCCS), care arrangements for five- to twelve-year-old children in families with employed mothers were as follows: care by relatives, the most frequently reported arrangement, accounted for 25 percent of the children; centers served 14 percent; family day care, 7 percent; in-home care, 3 percent; and other, 7 percent. Alarmingly, no arrangements were made for 44 percent of the children. The NCCS study also projected that school-age children accounted for some 2.5 million (or nearly one-third) of the 7.6 million children under the age of thirteen registered in center-based child care in 1990. The study suggests that one of the appeals of school-based programs may be the expectation that students will have exposure to staff who are not only adequately trained and compensated but are also dependable and can enable students to develop personally and academically. This finding is significant given the increase in the number of public school programs from 13,500 in 1991 (Seligson, Gannet, and Coltin 1992) to more than 18,000 in 1993–1994 (National Child Care Information Center 1997). Dryfoos (1999) suggests that this number is also expected to increase given the focus of new after-school funding initiatives for schools.

According to the 1991 National Study of Before- and After-School Programs, nonprofit organizations, including public schools, community organizations, social service agencies, and religious groups, operated most of the after-school programs (66 percent) (Seppanen, deVries, and Seligson 1993). For-profit day-care centers operated 29 percent of the after-school programs, and for-profit private schools and other entities operated about 5 percent of programs. Approximately 35 percent of these after-school programs were located in child-care centers, 28 percent were located in public schools, 19 percent were located in religious institutions or schools, and 18 percent were found in other locations (Seppanen, deVries, and Seligson 1993).

Recently, the number of programs housed in schools has increased considerably, with the largest increase occurring in elementary schools. The programs located in schools are operated under the guidance of the school's principal or through the community education department in the local district, for example. These programs are also managed by other youth service organizations and agencies (which include community centers, youth service organizations, parent organizations, churches, and national organizations with local affiliates (such as Girls, Inc., Boys and Girls Clubs, 4-H, the National Urban League, YMCA, and YWCA) within the community and may be located at the school under a collaboration or a leasing agreement (Miller 1995). Similarly, parent groups and other members in the community may also organize and manage after-school programs (Miller 1995).

Youth Development Services

According to various sources, about seventeen thousand youth development organizations were active in the United States in 1990 (*New Nonprofit Almanac and Desk Reference* 2002; Carnegie Council on Adolescent Development 1992). Given the range and diversity of school activities, programs, and organizations (mostly private and voluntary) that comprise youth development, it is not surprising that a standard definition of a youth development program does not exist. Specifically, some programs are associated with national youth-serving organizations while others are supported by public institutions or agencies, including parks and recreation departments, libraries, schools, and police athletic leagues. Still others are operated by private organizations with humanitarian missions such as religious groups, museums, civic organizations, and independent "grassroots" community-based organizations.

Accordingly, program content (sports, academic enrichment, vocational guidance, or community service) and goals not only differ for each category (national organizations, independent [grassroots] organizations, private, public, and religious organizations) but they also differ on a structural level. Some programs provide facilities where youths can gather; others connect youths to a mentor or troop that can meet anywhere. Some programs concentrate on a particular activity—sports or the arts, for example—while others provide a broad range of choices to youth participants. Many groups that once considered themselves as providing recreation are reconceptualizing their services as "informal education" or youth development and are more deliberate about teaching and encouraging young people to apply new knowledge, skills, and abilities.

Youth development programs can be distinguished from the broad range of development services by their focus on supporting the normal socialization and healthy development of young people. "If the entire spectrum of youth services can be thought of as a continuum, youth development services would be at one end and social control and incarceration would be at the other. In between these ends of the continuum would fall primary prevention (of problems such as substance abuse, adolescent pregnancy, juvenile crime, and the like); short-term intervention; and long-term treatment" (Quinn 1999). While some youth services organizations may provide prevention and intervention programs, their emphasis is on supporting normal development, offering relationships and environments that challenge and support young people, shaping their intellectual and social competencies, and regarding them as assets.

Other Forms of Supplementary Education

One of the concerns parents share with educators and others is the creation of safe out-of-school opportunities for the personal and academic development of children. By guiding their children toward productive learning activities and experiences outside the school, parents enable them to access new areas of knowledge (while reinforcing various concepts from the school curriculum) and knowledgeable adults, such as coaches, employers, youth workers, parents, and other peers. These experiences and activities not only enable adolescents to appreciate and assess new ideas, examine social issues, and develop different approaches for resolving their own problems but also exposes them to a range of role models who can influence and help the adolescents to form their own identities. Research has demonstrated that high-achieving students tend to spend at least twenty hours a week outside of school engaged in productive formal and informal learning (Carnegie Council on Adolescent Development 1992). Parents play a critical role in organizing these opportunities and guiding their children's participation (Gordon and Bridglall 2002).

Informed parents, scholars, and educators have known for some time now that schools *alone* cannot enable or ensure high academic achievement (Coleman et al. 1966; Wilkerson 1985; Gordon 2001). James Comer asserts this position more forcefully in *Waiting for a Miracle: Why Our Schools Cannot Solve Our Problems—and How We Can* (1997). Colloquial knowledge among many parents "in the know" reflects awareness that there are a number of experiences and activities that occur outside of school that appear to enable schooling to work. Examples can be found in the many education-related opportunities that affluent and sophisticated parents make available to their children—for example, travel, dance lessons, scouting, tutoring, summer camp, and so forth. In 1966, James Coleman concluded that differences in the family backgrounds of students, as opposed to school characteristics, accounted for the greatest amount of variance in their academic achievement. This finding was later found to be less so for low-income and ethnic minority children than for the general population (Gordon 1999), but typically, family background and income stand as strong predictors of achievement in school (Sexton 1961; Gordon and Meroe 1999; Jaynes and Williams 1989). In related works, Mercer (1973) and Wolf (1966, 1995) posit that it is the presence of family environmental supports for academic development that may explain this association between family status and student achievement. They made the now-obvious point that books, positive models, help with homework, and a place to study in the home are associated with school achievement.

In *Pedagogical Inquiry and Praxis*, Gordon (2001) referenced Bourdieu's (1986) notion that varieties of human development capital are among the resources necessary for effective schooling.[1] While access to these varieties of capital is unequally distributed, it is this access that enables a wide variety of supplementary education experiences. It is the inferred association between access to human development capital and supplementary education, and between supplementary education and the effectiveness of education, that led to the inclusion of supplementary education as a component of Gordon's (2001) advocacy for the affirmative development of academic ability. (See chapter 2 for a more complete description of the varieties of capital.)

THE IDEA OF SUPPLEMENTARY EDUCATION

The idea of supplementary education (Gordon 1999) is based on the premise that beyond proficiency with the school's formal academic curriculum, high academic achievement is closely associated with exposure to family and community-based activities and learning experiences that occur outside of school. For most students of color, these opportunities are generally underdeveloped. In the home environment, for example, high-achieving students benefit from literate adults, home computers, collections of books, magazines, journals, and the academic assistance and encouragement of older siblings and parents. In terms of community resources, the combination of local library privileges, the organization of mentoring and tutoring programs, peer-based study groups, Saturday and/or after-school academies, participation in various folk and "high" cultural events, and faith-based activities influence the development of proactive and engaged dispositions toward academic learning.

In general, high degrees of congruency between values promulgated at school, at home, and in one's immediate community are associated with high academic achievement. What may be equally critical are students' perceptions that what happens at school matters and is consistent with what parents and other family members consider important (Wilkerson 1985). This is conveyed through expectations, physical provisions for academic pursuits, attitudes toward intellectual activity, and the models that are available for children to emulate. Participation in these supplementary activities contributes to the development of a sense of membership in high-performance learning communities and shared values for the importance of academic achievement for personal fulfillment, community development, and social and political upward mobility (Gordon 1999).

We define supplementary education as the formal and informal learning and developmental enrichment opportunities that are provided for students outside of school and beyond the regular school day or year. Some of these activities may occur inside the school building but are over and above those included in the formal curriculum of the school. After-school care is perhaps the most widely used of these activities. Supplementary education includes the special efforts parents exert in support of the intellective and personal development of their children (Gordon 1999). These efforts may range from provisions for good health and nutrition to extensive travel, socialization to life in the academy, and mediated exposure to selected aspects of both indigenous and hegemonic cultures. Many activities, considered routine in the settings in which they occur, are nonetheless thought to be implicitly and deliberately engaged in to ensure adequate intellective and social development of young people. These routines include reading to and with one's children; dinner-table talk and inclusion in other family discussions of important issues; exposure to adult models of behaviors supportive of academic learning; active use of the library, museums, community, and religious centers as sources of information; seeking help from appropriate sources; and investing in reference and other education materials (Gordon 1999).

In a related but different domain are efforts directed at influencing the choice of friends and peers; guiding and controlling the use of spare time; guided and limited time spent watching TV; and participation in high-performance learning communities. Thus, we find a wide range of deliberate and incidental activities that serve to supplement the more formal and systematically structured learning experiences provided through schooling. These naturally occurring child development practices are no doubt dually responsive to the folk knowledge of academically sophisticated families and the empirically derived knowledge of experts in child development and education (Gordon 1999).

Rationale for Supplementary Education

It seems that parents have come to realize that schools are limited in their ability to address all of the needs of individual children. Those of us who are parents can recall situations in which our own children have experienced difficulty with school subjects and we have felt the need to hire tutors or seek the help of counselors. Many of us have had experience with children who were in trouble or were disturbed in some way (beyond our capacity to help or endure), and we have sought guidance for them and/or ourselves. Most of us who are able and well informed will, almost automatically, seek out the additional help that our children need. In less-critical situations, many of the things we do quite naturally for recreation, for cultural pleasure, or out of anxious concern for the optimal development of our children are implicitly supplemental to schooling. The problem is that not all children have parents who know how or are well positioned to engage their children in these activities and experiences. In advocating for increased access to supplementary education, we are arguing for making available and accessible, to all children, those supplements that many of us automatically provide to ensure the effectiveness of education for our own children.

We have found no evidence that specific individuals or groups have formally agreed on the need for the components of what we call supplementary education. Our review of high-quality programs suggests that they are comprised of three key components: positive relationships with peers and adults, enriching experiences and activities, and a safe place. Often, the most effective after-school and youth development programs have both academic and recreational content. Academically, effective programs are often connected to the school-day curriculum, staffed by qualified personnel, and provide one-to-one tutoring (Fashola 1998). High-quality programs also enable young people to examine various topics, skills, or projects that interest them deeply but may not be clearly linked to the school curriculum. (Examination of this sort may also increase young people's capacity for creative thinking and problem solving). A program's recreational components can help students acquire important skills that are not always or explicitly taught in the classroom, such as good sportsmanship. Enabling social competence (Gordon 2001) is usually one of the key goals of after-school and youth development programs that are also enabling of positive peer relations, social skills, and a sense of belonging.

The Need for Supplementary Education

In studies of high-achieving students, many of whom have been exposed to a wide range of supplementary education efforts, we find that these students seemed actively engaged in school events and extracurricular activities (see Everson and Millsap's chapter 7); identified with high achievement values; acquired good study skills and other learner behaviors; demonstrated personal skills such as independence, interpersonal facility, and flexibility; and maintained positive ties with adults (parents and mentors) and peers who continually advocated high expectations for academic achievement. These students tend to come from adequately resourced families and experience less housing mobility and greater social stability than their lower-achieving counterparts. Support for their intellectual and personal development appears to flow from parents, peers, and school environments that encourage and expect high academic achievement (see Gordon and Meroe's chapter 4).

Obviously, some of these circumstances and conditions are school dependent. Mastery of the academic content of schooling may be disproportionately a function of exposure to and participation in effective schooling. With the exception of a relatively small number of students who are effectively educated at home, we see strong and adequate schooling as an essential feature of modern societies. However, much of what it means to be an educated and intellectively competent person involves attitudes, appreciations, dispositions, tacit knowledge, and metacognitive abilities that depend on good schooling and good out-of-school activities and experiences. Thus we argue that those cultural and social factors associated with academic learning are as important as the substance of what is to be learned and the processes by which it is to be learned. Consequently, those of us concerned with replicating the circumstances and conditions associated with high academic achievement need to focus on creating positive social and psychological conditions for academic learning. This includes developing and implementing cooperative and supportive learning experiences, explicating and mediating the critical demands of learning situations, organizing tutorial and study groups, using mentoring and athletic coaching models, and creating ubiquitously high expectations. We must also be aware of the need to reduce the dissonance between hegemonic and ethnic minority cultural identities as is reflected in the phenomenon described as "fear of acting white" (Fordham and Ogbu 1986) and "fear of stereotype confirmation" (Steele 1997; see Gordon and Bridglall's chapter 2 for a more detailed description of this phenomenon).

Additionally, given that high-achieving students are greatly influenced by the social contexts in which they develop, their academic achievements and competencies may be dependent upon the extent to which their social contexts, both natural and contrived, support their desired ends. Some of these essential contextual supports have been described as various forms of human and social capital that enable and facilitate academic learning and personal development. The necessary human capital includes adults and peers who themselves are sources of know-how and are models of the behaviors and achievements that students can emulate. The social capital is represented in the networks of support, the connections to sources of information and resources, and the expectations of the group within which one travels. For students who are not naturally exposed to academically demanding environments, parents as well as educators need to create high-performance learning communities (whether they are in the form of families, peer groups, classrooms, social groups, or institutions) where serious academic work is respected, standards are explicit, and high achievement is rewarded (Gordon 1999). Some parents may need help in developing the capacity to advocate for and access varieties of human development resource capital and to place them at the disposal of their children's academic and personal development. We advocate the following targeted strategies:

1. The facilitation of cooperative learning cadres among student peers in social environments that encourage and nurture academic achievement as instrumental to personal and political agency;
2. The implementation of specific interventions designed to enhance students' skills and understanding, including
   • socialization to the demands of serious academic engagement,
   • metacognitive competence and metacomponential strategies—an understanding of how one thinks and learns, and strategies of how to use this understanding in the self-regulation of one's learning behavior, and
   • diagnostically targeted instruction and remediation;
3. Developing the facility to use electronic and digital technology for accessing various types of information, resources, and extended learning experiences; and
4. The academic and political socialization to the requirements and rewards of high levels of achievement as instruments of personal agency and social responsibility.

The concern for political socialization suggests that for low-SES students and/or students of color, negative school experiences such as low-level tracking, persistent failure, and manifestations of racism can result in failure to develop positive self-concepts and the outright rejection of aspirations for academic achievement (see chapter 5 by E. T. Gordon). These reactions may be ameliorated through school-, community-, peer-, and family-mediated supplementary education interventions that allow students to grasp the relevance of education not only for potential individual gains in future careers but also as a means for developing an informed understanding of issues of social justice and for recognizing that developed academic abilities can be vehicles for political advocacy and action. Moreover, familiarity with the knowledge and skills used in struggles for emancipation and justice can add an element of political sensitivity in pedagogy. In the process, students can be socialized to cultivate an agentic perspective (Bandura 2001) to understand the potential relationships between academic mastery and their own political agendas. According to E. T. Gordon, raised political consciousness can be seen as a particular form of supplementary education and an organizing principle for the creation of high-performance learning communities among subaltern populations.

The Variety of Supplementary Education Experiences

Related types of supplementary education interventions include those that are implicit (parenting, nutrition, family talk, parental employment, decision making, reading along with children, socialization and acculturation, social networks, travel, and environmental supports [Mercer 1973; Wolf 1966]) and those that are explicit (academic development, tutorials, advocacy, remediation, SAT preparation, one-on-one tutoring, Saturday academies, specialized services, sociocultural opportunities, and child-centered social groups). In the youth development area, the organizations sponsoring sports, academic enrichment, vocational guidance, or community service are broadly categorized as national youth-serving organizations, independent (grassroots) organizations, religious organizations, and public and private organizations. These categories of interventions are further impacted by the ethos of students' homes and communities, cultural and socioeconomic demographics, the economic and cultural infrastructure students and families may or may not have access to, incidental and informal experiences, formal and explicit exposure to high-performance learning communities, aspirations, expectations, and access to available resources. These interventions can be directed at students who are achieving academically at different levels and achievement ranges: to those students who are at risk of underachievement and to those who are high achievers.

An example of an implicit intervention includes reading to and with one's children. Parents who deliberately read with and to their children and subsequently engage in conversations with their children appreciate the role and purpose of these activities in enabling children's language skills to grow. For example, reading "predictable" books to preschool children helps them to grasp how stories progress. A child can easily learn familiar phrases and repeat them, thus pretending to read. "Pretend reading" gives a child a sense of power and courage to keep trying. Parents' storytellers' voices help their child to hear the sounds of words and how they are put together to form meaning. Parents also know that when they collect and read books as part of their family life, they send their children messages that books are important, enjoyable, and full of new things to learn. This is especially important because as children learn reading skills in school, they often come to associate reading with work, not pleasure, and as a result, they may lose their desire to read. And it is that desire—the curiosity and interest—that is the cornerstone to using reading and related skills successfully.

An example of explicit intervention includes academic tutoring, which is an established, effective approach used to enhance learning. Although cost restraints may prevent it from being used as often as needed, tutoring is highly recommended as an in- or out-of-school effort at reducing school failure (Slavin, Karweit, and Wasik 1991). Usually conducted on a one-to-one or small-group basis, supplementary programs engage peers, volunteers, paraprofessionals, and professional teachers as tutors. This approach is in wide use because it is thought to produce better results than large-group instruction (Gaustad 1992; Gyanani and Pahuja 1995). Specifically, one-on-one tutoring relationships can increase learning outcomes by interpreting necessary learning cues and fostering appropriate student participation necessary to make the learning process effective. Another advantage is that the direct contact between tutee and tutor decreases the likelihood of miscommunication due to cultural, cognitive, emotional, or overall learning differences that are common to group instruction (Gaustad 1992). Tutoring is often the first method employed by parents and teachers in order to address specific academic needs. It can also be effective with all students, be they at risk or high achieving. In general, tutoring is an effective approach for strengthening specific skills, correcting problems in any subject, and reinforcing socialization and study habits.

ISSUES, CRITIQUE, AND EMERGING PRINCIPLES

It is reasonable to assume that the most academically successful populations (primarily European Americans and Asian Americans from mid- to high-SES backgrounds) tend to have combinations of strong home and school resources to support their academic development. The least successful groups (African American, Hispanic American, Native American, and the poor) have, on average, a much weaker combination of home and school resources (Birch and Gussow 1970; Gordon and Meroe 1999; College Board 1999). Some of the interrelated issues that directly impact academic and personal development include low participation levels for some ethnic minority populations, lack of access for youths in low-income communities, inadequate financial resources, lack of evaluations concerning program effectiveness, lack of coordination with other youth-supporting services (including schools), and the incongruence between actual activities and perceived needs of adolescents.

The Issue of Participation

Clearly, socioeconomic status, race, and geographic location determine who can participate in after-school, youth development, and other forms of supplementary education services and programs. It is interesting that these variables and levels of academic achievement also seem to influence who actually participates in civic and volunteer activities as young adults. According to the National Center for Education Statistics report *Coming of Age in the 1990s: The Eighth-Grade Class of 1988 Twelve Years Later* (Ingels, Curtin, Kaufman, Alt, and Chen 2002), "young adults who show high mathematics achievement as eighth-graders were more likely than their peers who showed low mathematics achievement at that time to have volunteered in a youth organization and to have participated in a political campaign in the last 12 months" (66). Additionally,

> students' method of completing high school and family socioeconomic status also showed a relationship with young adults' volunteer efforts. About 21 percent of students who earned high school diplomas had volunteered for a youth organization, compared to 8 percent of high school dropouts. Cohort members who came from the highest SES quartile were twice as likely as those from the lowest SES quartile to have volunteered for a civic/community organization (28 percent vs. 13 percent. (66)

Given this finding, it is distressing that low-income neighborhoods in urban and rural areas are the least likely to provide a wide range of developmental opportunities and related support to young teens (Ianni 1990). Littell and Wynn's (1989) comparison of the existing community resources for youth ages eleven to fourteen in a low-income, African American neighborhood in Chicago with an affluent, predominantly white suburb indicated that the suburban community provided three times as many services as the inner-city

community. Specifically, it offered a wide range of opportunities that underscored educational development, while the inner-city programs emphasized
personal support and academic remediation. Additionally, public agencies in
the suburban community not only provided more resources but were themselves considered resources compared to those in the inner-city site. The public middle schools in the suburban community also provided nearly seven
times as many extracurricular activities per week, and the public park districts
offered eight times the number of activities during an average week. In the
inner-city neighborhood, however, churches performed a larger role. Clearly,
the prevalence of unequal access to programs and supportive institutions is one
of the key factors influencing disparate participation rates between low-
income and affluent young people.

Differing participation rates can also be partially explained by the fact that
existing programs may not meet the developmental needs or interests of
young teens. (This issue of incongruence between youth needs and actual activities is addressed later in this chapter.) Additionally, these adolescents may
have more independence about how to use their free time than younger children. As a result, after-school and youth organizations have to be conscientious about developing and implementing different strategies for appealing to
and retaining young adolescents in their programs. Young people often refer
to "fun and friends" and "voice and choice" (Quinn 1999) when asked to describe what appeals to them best about participating in supplementary education programs.

The Issue of Access

The previous discussion on lack of participation by low-income youths is
clearly linked to access. Some of the key barriers to participation that directly
impact adolescents living in low-income areas include location of services,
safety considerations, transportation, and whether or not there are fees for services for basic items like uniforms. Although we have indicated that some
adolescents, typically those in affluent communities, have a wide range of developmental activities to participate in during the nonschool hours, gaining
access to productive, positive activities during the "witching hours" of 2 to 8
p.m. is a very real problem for many youths, not only the poorest, although
they have the greatest need. In the first section of this chapter, we discussed
how changing employment demographics have partially resulted in more parents with young children (in all socioeconomic groups) who are often not at
home during after-school hours to organize and guide activities or to provide
transportation. Another consequence that is of concern to policymakers, educators, and parents is the finding that, on average, 40 percent of adolescents'

discretionary time is spent socializing, 20 percent watching television (Carnegie Council on Adolescent Development 1992), and very little on reading, arts involvement, sports, or hobbies (Zill, Nord, and Loomis 1995). Gordon's (1999) concept of the affirmative development of academic ability, based on the assumption that academic abilities are not simply inherited but are developed through pedagogical and social interventions (Gordon and Bridglall, in press) is an attempt to counteract Zill et al.'s conclusion that "American adolescents are spending little time on activities that strengthen their ties to society or provide them with the necessary skills to succeed in school or in the labor force" (1995, 24–25).

Among the more subtle issues of access for young minority teens is the sponsoring organization or program's ability to genuinely welcome their participation. Additionally, we cannot overlook how the impact of race, class, geographic location, and physical ability and/or disability issues affect adolescent perspectives of access and related decisions about participation. Clearly, many minority youth live in economically poor families and neighborhoods. Subtle discrimination and overt manifestations of racism are facts of life for these young people and their families. Supplementary education planners and implementers should recognize that many of these young people face substantial risks associated with low-income status, social stratification, and limited resources. Given this reality, program planners must therefore avoid replicating these structural inequalities, however inadvertent, and develop concrete strategies to assist young people in overcoming negative effects. The Carnegie Council on Adolescent Development (1992) suggests that supplementary education programs focus on these challenges by deliberately planning targeted outreach programs. One of the ways supplementary education organizations can extend their reach to underserved youths is to take their services to the neighborhoods where low-income youths live or attend school. These organizations should also recruit, train, and support diverse staff and volunteers to work with low-income populations; ensure safety in program settings; implement targeted job-skills programs; and provide paid employment for youth. But providing access and enabling participation and outreach for low-income youths has financial implications, and funding is perceived as one of the pivotal issues with which different supplementary organizations grapple.

The Issue of Funding

The existing research about after-school and youth service organizations is not systematic enough to extrapolate their funding patterns; it does, however, suggest that although financial support for after-school and youth development programs have increased in recent years, issues of diversity, instability, inadequacy, and inequity continue to have far-reaching impacts. The Carnegie Council on Adolescent Development suggests that funders should focus on the four major problems that preoccupy those organizations providing supplementary education: "instability of core support, inadequacy of total financial resources, a crisis orientation toward fixing problems rather than deliberately promoting healthy development, and a single-issue approach to youth problems rather than a comprehensive one" (1992). Specifically, funders should reinforce and secure the funding base by moving from categorical funding to core support of after-school and youth organizations, combine public with private funds, and facilitate associations among schools and fragmented supplementary education organizations. Similarly, funders should concentrate new resources on low-income neighborhoods and craft, as funding priorities, professional development of staff, assessment of programs, replication of programs that work, and effective advocacy for and on behalf of youth. Among the critical challenges are bringing coherence and stability to funding sources, ensuring that the total investment is adequate to the task, and developing mechanisms to channel more financial resources to the places they are needed most—low-income communities. This strategy should assist in eliminating the amount of time supplementary education organizations spend establishing adequate financial support to do their work.

The Issue of Program Effectiveness

As discussed in chapter 15, there has been little systematic examination of the effectiveness of supplementary education programs despite the broad reach and the capacity they have for supporting academic and social development for youth. Until recently, these organizations have counted on inconclusive evidence of their effectiveness, including self-reports and testimonials from young people and their parents (Quinn 1999). Given the current emphasis on accountability and results, these organizations' leaders should recognize that such anecdotal evidence is of limited value and move toward determining formative and summative evidence about program effectiveness. A review of current programs suggests that outcome evaluations center on two categories of programs: those that seek to prevent or reduce problem behaviors such as substance abuse and adolescent pregnancy (Quinn 1999) and those that promote normal socialization and positive development (Gordon 1999). Programs that seek to prevent or reduce particular behaviors are identified as "categorical" programs (and, as discussed in the above discussion on funding, are supported through categorical funding). Quinn (1999) suggests, however, that in many youth organizations, initiatives designed to promote normal socialization and positive development are thought of as the "core" program and sometimes both categorical and core programs are combined in a discrete organization.

The Issue of Coordination with Other Youth Services

Given the increasing recognition of the interdependence between schools and communities, both professional and volunteer staff of after-school and youth development programs are reconceptualizing how they partner and work with other community institutions, especially schools. Specifically, these organizations are shifting away from a perception that schools are responsible for academic achievement while they (after-school and youth organizations) are responsible for providing recreation and custodial care. As a result of this shift, schools, communities, and youth organizations across the country are exploring partnerships with each other and changing, in the process, the traditional ways of planning, funding, and implementing the services that include increasing access to safe places, supplementary education, and dependable relationships for children and youth. As suggested, these collaborations take many forms, from the federally supported 21st Century Community Learning Centers, in which the public school is the lead agency and grantee, to the Children's Aid Society's Community Schools, in which the public school and youth agency collaborate equally in all phases, from the conceptualization of services to actual implementation.

Thus far, we have suggested that children's needs are best addressed when there is coordination between the formal school-day curriculum and the after-school and youth organizations. On a practical level, however, these goals are difficult to achieve. Currently, some after-school programs are implemented separately from the school-day curriculum, resulting in neglected opportunities to strengthen children's academic and personal development. Similarly, after-school and youth programs miss potential opportunities to engage children in supplemental learning through experiences that are different from what happens during the school day. This phenomenon may be a function of the fact that the programmatic default is remediation (especially tutoring) and help with homework in many after-school programs. While we can agree that some of these services may be necessary, the focus for after-school and youth programs should be academic and social development and the provision of learning opportunities that supplement and complement what happens during the regular school day.

Supplementary education programs can improve children's and young people's ability to stay focused without repeating exactly what happens during the school day. Innovative program designers are aware that reading, math, and science can also be learned through performing and visual arts, individual and team sports, woodworking and cooking classes, and in the planning and implementing of programs for the community. Additionally, activities such as technology classes and chess clubs provide ideal opportunities to practice logic, persistence, concentration, and critical thinking skills. These alternative approaches for engaging children and youth are clearly important, given the finding that students whose out-of-school time includes twenty to thirty-five hours of productive learning experiences and activities per week perform at academically high levels. It bears reiterating that these productive learning experiences and activities include discussions with knowledgeable adults or peers, composing letters, writing diaries or journals, homework, reading for pleasure, hobbies, chores, and problem-solving games (Clark 1988).

Currently, the national attention on increasing children's learning time, represented by federal commitment through the 21st Century Community Learning Centers, presents valuable opportunities for applying available knowledge and restructuring community resources for children and young adolescents. The challenge is ensuring that schools and community organizations are equal partners in this work, and that young people's interests, needs, and opinions are respected in the process of program development.

The Issue of Incongruence

There is a substantial discontinuity between actual activities and perceived needs of adolescents for many of our students. One of the more subtle but no less critical issues concerns the incongruent relationship between actual program activities and what youths perceive they need. This issue was addressed in some detail in the Carnegie report (Carnegie Council on Adolescent Development 1992), which elaborated the disparity between the developmental needs of youth and existing practices. The following illustrate the developmental needs of youth (critical habits of mind, information, dependable relationships, life skills, reliable bases for decision making, usefulness, belonging, and autonomy) and provides a brief summary of actual practices:

- Programs that concentrate on only one aspect of development (recreation, for example) do not avail participants of the potential opportunities to acquire *critical habits of mind*—for example, metacognition and the discipline—that enable academic achievement.
- Although youths have identified their need for straightforward *information*, some youth organizations evade contentious issues, often the very issues that teens consider important. An obvious example of such an issue is human sexuality. Many American youth organizations sidestep or

dilute discussions of human sexuality in their programs and materials, despite young people's often articulated need for guidance in understanding and examining this topic.

- High staff turnover occurs in some supplementary education programs because of inattention to staff development and low salaries. Similarly, inadequate funding within the youth sector results in organizational instability, which contributes to lack of *dependability in staff and volunteer relationships* with youth.

- Given that *life skills* are developed through experience, not lecture, some supplementary education programs need to reassess their didactic methodology. Likewise, some programs need to rethink the frequency and duration of their programs and related activities since skills also develop through practice.

- The youth development literature illustrates that young adolescents *are engaged in important decision making* about substance abuse, sexual activity, gang involvement, and a number of other significant behaviors. However, some supplementary education organizations concede to political pressure that they not address contentious issues or that they not acknowledge young people's independence in making behavioral choices. The "Just Say No" programs that seek to prevent substance use and adolescent sexual activity, for example, typically do not provide practice in active decision making.

- Although many supplementary education organizations do offer young people community service opportunities, these opportunities are not available to enough youth, especially those in low-socioeconomic groups. On another level, young people have few opportunities to feel *useful* and are often not consulted in organizational decision making, concerning the goals and methods of programs, for example.

- In a review of some supplementary education organizations, it appears that the stress is on symbols of membership that are good for the organization (such as uniforms, which provide revenue and visibility) and not enough importance is attached to relevant symbols associated with real ownership of the ideals of these programs. Young people indicate that they want to belong to a valued group of peers and want to decide for themselves what, if any, symbols of membership are fitting in that context. One of the appeals of youth gangs is its emphasis on this sense of *belonging*.

- The above illustrations of belonging and usefulness also apply to the concept of autonomy. Clearly, the programs provided to young people are constrained to those that adults consider. Similarly, adults also decide the agendas of many after-school and youth organizations, often on a national level. However, given the voluntary nature of youth agencies, this implies that young people should have some degree of autonomy in deciding on activities in which they will participate.

Coordination of Efforts

Given the importance of working in tandem to create, implement, and promote supplementary education programs, we provide suggestions on how parents and families, young adolescents, community organizations, schools, health organizations, higher education institutions, research and evaluation organizations, funders (including businesses and corporate philanthropies), the media, and our government can not only play significant roles but also can contribute to producing young people who privilege academic and social competence while simultaneously taking responsibility for themselves.

Parents and Families

Parents and families can help young adolescents make wise choices about constructive use of nonschool time by seeking information about community programs; volunteering as leaders, board members, or fund-raisers; offering feedback about the quality of current community services for youth; advocating for their own children (and others) in community forums; and participating in parent-family events, including parent education workshops and recognition events.

Young Adolescents

With appropriate adult supervision, young people can participate in their community by tutoring their peers and younger children, volunteering in area hospitals and social service agencies; and registering voters, for example.

Community Organizations

Initially, these organizations may need to consider whether to realign and/or reconfigure existing resources. As a result of this consideration, they may need to produce specific resources to meet identified needs. Community-wide planning and implementation efforts may also need to consider issues of staff development; draw on one another's demonstrated strengths and abilities in expanding available training efforts; provide access to services for all adolescents; explore relevant factors such as location, transportation, and fees; and actively encourage young people in the planning process.

Schools

Schools need to work with community agencies in constructing a coherent system of supplementary education interventions that acknowledges the common goals of schools and community agencies while respecting their inherent differences and strengths. These common goals could foster joint planning and decision making; the shoring-up of existing institutional and organizational resources; and the sharing of costs in assessing needs, defining service gaps, improving access to and coordination of current resources, and providing new services as needed. A collaboration with these characteristics may enable schools to convey high expectations for students' use of out-of-school time in addition to enabling schools to guide students in making positive choices.

Health Organizations

Both public and private health and mental health agencies need to collaborate with supplementary education organizations in deliberate efforts to increase adolescents' access to health information and services. One of the ways health and mental health organizations can collaborate is by working with these organizations to expand their current health and fitness programs. By working in tandem, these organizations can sponsor joint programs, develop and implement mutual referral systems, team up as advocates for youth, and cooperate on staff development activities. Additionally, health organizations—including health clinics and community mental health agencies—can themselves offer community-based programs for youth, including mental health counseling and parent education workshops.

Higher Education Institutions

It is now necessary for higher education institutions, including community colleges, four-year colleges, and universities, to become substantively involved with community programs to develop the knowledge base from which supplementary education programs function; increase these organizations' accountability (particularly through systematic and rigorous evaluation); improve pre- and in-service training efforts for supplementary education practitioners and volunteers; and organize joint programs that directly serve young people.

From a research perspective, it is also critical that faculty at higher education institutions conduct scientifically rigorous yet socially relevant research that can be applied to supplementary education programs; assist planners in designing theory-based interventions; convene forums for researchers and practitioners to collaborate in developing data-based agendas for service delivery improvement; and inform particularly the education, research, and policy communities about the actual and potential contributions of supportive services for young people. Faculty can also improve practice by designing and conducting program evaluations of supplementary education organizations. In the most effective models, university-based researchers perceive themselves as colleagues in this process and take the time to familiarize themselves with the strengths, needs, weaknesses, and constraints of an organization's setting before suggesting any particular evaluation approach.

Faculty in higher education can contribute new information and strategies to train, recruit, and retain practitioners. One of the ways they can disseminate their research is by collaborating with supplementary education organizations at both the national and local levels to provide training workshops that enable program developers and practitioners to stay abreast of current research and theories about adolescent development. At the same time, faculty will be able to learn more about the experiences of young people from those who work with them on a regular basis. Another role research faculty can play is preparing practitioners for careers in providing supplementary education services. Additionally, schools of social work, academic departments of human development, and schools of theology and public health can actively incorporate academic content emphasizing adolescent development and group facilitation skills. Schools of education can also prepare teachers and school administrators to work collaboratively with supplementary education organizations to provide academic enrichment programs, offer young people opportunities to explore college campuses, meet slightly older peers, and learn about admissions processes and financial aid.

Research and Evaluation Organizations

Research organizations that specialize in social science research can play key roles in assisting supplementary education organizations to strengthen their conceptions of youth development and provide training and technical assistance for these efforts.

Funders (Including Businesses and Corporate Philanthropies)

It's worth emphasizing that funders can play a crucial role in strengthening and stabilizing the funding base for supplementary education programs and services. They can begin to shift from categorical (problem-specific) funding to core support for youth development; to focus resources to low-income neighborhoods; and to institute funding priorities that emphasize professional development, outcome evaluations, replication of proven programs, and advocacy on behalf of youth with local United Ways and other community foundations, national foundations, corporations, and other businesses, for example.

Media

The media—television, radio, magazines, newspapers, and films—can play a pivotal role in disseminating information about supplementary education services. Given that public opinion is often influenced by what gets filtered through the media, it can also shape the willingness of elected officials and community leaders to make youth a priority. The media can advocate supplementary education programs in four ways: through expanded coverage of youth activities and legislative and programmatic efforts designed to support adolescents; through increased publication or broadcasts of editorial opinions, news stories, and videos written or produced by young people; through programs that feature young adults in new anchor roles, such as the show *Radio Rookies*, which is produced by WNYC-TV, New York City's public television station; and by increasing the use of the media to publicize these services directly to young audiences and their families.

Government

Ideally, the government needs to be integrated at local, state, and federal levels through public policies that emphasize expanding support for basic supplementary education services; by directing services to areas of greatest need; by giving priority to locally generated solutions; and by actively supporting and nurturing community involvement. The elements of such a system would be built on existing best practices and on principles from youth development (see chapter 14 for further description) and community problem solving. Local governments should collaborate with community organizations to convene a community-wide planning task force, for example, whose charge would be to improve direct service delivery for children and youth and generate or allocate needed financial resources to support these supplementary education services. Strong staff leadership and facilitation of services for all of the community's young people are the hallmark of effective local governments.

State governments could contribute to local efforts by coordinating education, health, and social services; allocating or generating new resources to support supplementary education services; and focusing new and reallocated resources to low-income areas. While improving school-based services is one important effort that states can initiate, it is also important for them to recognize local strategies. States can enable local efforts by offering technical and financial assistance for planning and coordination efforts, in addition to direct services.

Policies on the federal level, including employment, poverty, housing, health, education, civil rights, and specific youth development policies, contribute to the climate of improvement or deterioration of adolescent well-being. The federal government currently shows some commitment to the promotion of supplementary education initiatives from a legislative and funding perspective. They should also allocate public resources to supplement the already considerable but clearly inadequate private support for youth development services nationwide, with a focus on expansion of services in impoverished areas. Further, federal policy should encourage and empower communities to take a more integrated approach to the provision of health and social services for youth by modifying eligibility requirements within existing federal programs to enable the use of categorical funds for comprehensive services.

Another issue the federal government can mitigate is to continue to expand the Youth Development Information Center. Clearly, expansion of that effort could address an important, documented national need for a permanent information source that is available to all. These solutions, if fully funded and conscientiously implemented, could enable more solid long-term change that would ultimately recognize young people as having the wherewithal to enrich the entire country with each succeeding generation.

National Youth Organizations

Given their extensive resources and reach, national youth organizations are in a unique position to increase their work with young people (especially those living in poor neighborhoods). However, it is crucial that these groups approach this strategy in ways that will resonate with the young people who most need their services. These approaches may include accurate data collection and use with respect to the target population; an emphasis on increasing the skills of paid and volunteer staff in working with diverse populations; and deliberate local and national advocacy efforts.

Taken together, these various institutions and organizations (including parents, families, and youth themselves) have a responsibility to improve life in neighborhoods with substandard schools, little or no medical care, and few supportive and healthy activities during the nonschool hours. The creation, implementation, funding, and evaluation of supplementary education interventions has enormous potential to enable young people to not only cope with the demands of the contemporary American workplace but also to develop the academic, social, and intellectual competence to fulfill the demands of citizenship, family, and parenthood.

CONCLUSION

Despite efforts to improve schools on a wide-scale basis for students from the least successful groups have produced many positive results, formidable obstacles to eliminating the differentials in academic achievement between students from high-status and low-status families persist. In our program of affirmative development of academic ability (Gordon 2001), we have identified several in-school initiatives that we believe will contribute to the closing of this gap, but we are pessimistic with respect to the possibility that schooling alone will solve the problem. We therefore propose concentrated efforts at introducing a wide variety of supplementary education opportunities for low-income families and communities of color. It may be simplest to start with an initiative that has already taken root. After-school programs are among the most widespread forms of supplementary education, and are being reconceptualized as opportunities to influence the narrowing of this pervasive academic achievement gap between majority and some ethnic minority student groups. The After School Corporation, for example, cited some of the educational impacts of this form of supplementary education (1999). They include improved academic performance and school behavior, improved attendance and graduation rates, improved family relationships, and decreased pregnancy and drug use rates.

Our literature review indicates that although the after-school movement addresses a range of student needs, it is giving increased attention to the academic development of students. This direction of the after-school movement should be encouraged and conjoined with similar trends in youth development services and the wide range of less-structured activities that we call supplementary education.

School districts and communities that serve low-income populations and families of color might well take a page from Koreatown, Los Angeles, where some three hundred or more agencies provide supplementary education services, most of which require that parents pay for them (see a description of this phenomenon in chapter 13). Not only do our communities need to have such facilities readily available but consideration must also be given to ways of involving families in the financial support of these services within their ability to pay. While we are sensitive to the problem of placing additional financial burdens on already hard-pressed families, Gordon has raised the possibility that a parent's decision to invest in supplementary education may be an important part of the process (see chapter 16). When parents extend themselves or even make sacrifices to make an extra education service available, the message to the children is that parents consider this to be important. Furthermore, organizations like ASPIRA, NAACP, Urban League, Jack and Jill, the Links, faith-based institutions, and so forth can and should become local community sponsors of these activities, with the cost subsidized by philanthropic or public sources. The core idea here is that if supplements to schooling are important (and we consider them to be essential), we must find ways to ensure the availability of such services independent of family status.

Much of our rationale for the availability of supplementary education opportunities has been grounded in the urgent need to increase the academic productivity of many students of color and the schools that serve them. However, the outcomes from the deliberate implementation of supplementary education interventions may be broader than academic. Gordon (2001) and Greeno (2001) have respectively introduced complementary notions of "intellective competence" and "intellective character." Both of these scholars suggest that the metaexpression of academic achievement may be reflective at the level of competence and/or the character of the person. Much of what we see in these extensive supplements to the education of some of our most privileged members of the population is directed not only at improved academic content mastery but the development of attitudes, appreciations, dispositions, and habits of mind. Good supplementary education is not simply further academic instruction, but is enabling of broader aspects of affective, cognitive, and personal development.

REFERENCES

After School Corporation. 1999. *After school programs: An analysis of need, current research and public opinion.* Prepared for TASC by the National Center for Schools and Communities. New York: Fordham University.

Benson, P. 1995. *Developmental assets among Minneapolis youth: The urgency for promoting healthy community.* Minneapolis, MN: Search Institute.

Birch, H., and J. D. Gussow. 1970. *Disadvantaged children: Health, nutrition and school failure.* New York: Harcourt Brace and World.

Bourdieu, P. 1986. The forms of capital. In *Handbook of theory and research for the sociology of education,* edited by J. Richardson, 241–58. Westport, CT: Greenwood.

Carnegie Council on Adolescent Development. 1992. *A matter of time: Risk and opportunity in the nonschool hours. Report of the Task Force on Youth Development and Community Programs.* New York: Carnegie Corporation of New York.

———. 1995. *Great transitions: Preparing adolescents for a new century.* New York: Carnegie Corporation of New York.

Clark, R. M. 1988. *Critical factors in why disadvantaged children succeed or fail in school*. New York: Academy for Educational Development.

Coleman, J. S., E. Q. Campbell, C. J. Hobson, J. McPartland, A. M. Mood, F. D. Weinfeld, and L. R. York. 1966. *Equality of Educational Opportunity*. Washington, D.C.: U.S. Government Printing Office.

College Board. 1999. *Reaching the top: A report of the National Task Force on Minority High Achievement*. New York: College Entrance Examination Board.

Comer, J. 1997. *Waiting for a Miracle: Why Our Schools Can't Solve Our Problems—and How We Can*. New York: Dutton.

Dryfoos, J. 1999. The role of the school in children's out-of-school time. *Future of Children* 9(2): 117–34.

Fashola, O. S. 1998. *Review of extended day and after-school programs and their effectiveness*. Baltimore, MD: Johns Hopkins University, Center for Research on the Education of Students Placed at Risk.

Fordham, S., and J. Ogbu. 1986. Black students' school success: Coping with the burden of "acting white." *Urban Review* 18:176–206.

Gaustad, J. 1992. Tutoring for at-risk students. *OSSC Bulletin* 36(3). Eugene: Oregon School Study Council, University of Oregon.

Gordon, E. W., ed. 1999. *Education and justice: A view from the back of the bus*. New York: Teachers College Press.

———. 2001. "The affirmative development of academic ability." *Pedagogical Inquiry and Praxis*, no. 2. New York: Teachers College, Columbia University.

Gordon, E. W., and B. L. Bridglall. 2002. "The idea of supplementary education." *Pedagogical Inquiry and Praxis*, no. 3. New York: Teachers College, Columbia University.

———. In press. *The affirmative development of academic ability*. Boulder, CO: Rowman and Littlefield.

Gordon, E. W., and A. S. Meroe. 1999. Common destinies—Continuing dilemmas. In *Education and justice: A view from the back of the bus*, edited by E. W. Gordon. New York: Teachers College Press.

Greeno, J. 2001. Students with competencies, authority and accountability: Affording intellective identity in classrooms. Unpublished paper prepared for the Division of Academic Affairs, College Board.

Gyanani, T. C., and P. Pahuja. 1995. Effects of peer tutoring on abilities and achievement. *Contemporary Educational Psychology* 20:469–75.

Hofferth, S. L., A. Brayfield, S. Deich, and P. Holcomb. 1991. *National child care survey, 1990*. Washington, DC: Urban Institute Press.

Ianni, F. A. J. 1990. *The search for structure*. New York: Free Press.

Ingels, S. J., T. R. Curtin, P. Kaufman, M. N. Alt, and X. Chen. 2002. *Coming of age in the 1990s: The eighth-grade class of 1988 twelve years later*. Washington, DC: U.S. Department of Education, National Center for Education Statistics. NCES 2002-321.

Jaynes, G. D., and R. J. Williams Jr., eds. 1989. *A common destiny: Blacks and American society. A report form the Committee on the Status of Black Americans, National Research Council*. Washington DC: National Academy Press.

Littell, J., and J. Wynn. 1989. *The availability and use of community resources for young adolescents in an inner-city and suburban community*. Chicago: University of Chicago, Chaplin Hall Center for Children.

Mercer, J. 1973. *Labeling the mentally retarded: Clinical and social system perspectives on mental retardation*. Berkeley: University of California Press.

Miller, B. M. 1995. *Out-of-school time: The effects on learning in the primary grades*. Wellesley, MA: Wellesley College, School-Age Child Care Project, Center for Research on Women.

National Child Care Information Center. 1997. *Child Care Bulletin* 17 (September/October). Available online at www.nccic.org/ccb/ccb-so97/ccb-so97.html.

New nonprofit almanac and desk reference. 2002. Washington, DC: Urban Institute and the Independent Sector.

Newman, S. A., J. A. Fox, E. A. Flynn, and W. Christeson. 2000. *America's after-school choice: The prime time for juvenile crime, or youth enrichment and achievement*. Washington, DC: Fight Crime: Invest in Kids

Quinn, J. 1999. Where need meets opportunity: Youth development programs for early teens. *Future of Children* 9(2): 96–116.

Seligson, M., E. Gannet, and L. Coltin. 1992. Before and after-school child care for elementary school children. In *Issues in Child Care: Yearbook in Early Childhood Education*. Vol. 3, edited by B. Spodek and O. N. Saracho, 125–42. New York: Teachers College Press.

Seligson, M., A. Genser, E. Gannet, and W. Gray. 1983. *School-age child care: A policy report*. Wellesley, MA: School-Age Child Care Project, Wellesley College, Center for Research on Women.

Seppanen, P., D. deVries, and M. Seligson. 1993. *National study of before- and after-school programs*. Washington DC: U.S. Department of Education, Office of Policy and Planning.

Sexton, P. 1961. *Education and income: Inequalities of opportunity in our public schools*. New York: Viking Press.

Slavin, R. E., N. L. Karweit, and B. A. Wasik. 1991. *Preventing early school failure: What works?* Baltimore, MD: Johns Hopkins University, Center for Research on Effective Schooling for Disadvantaged Students.

Steele, C. 1997. A threat in the air: How stereotypes shape intellectual identity and performance. *American Psychologist* 52:613–29.

Wilkerson, D. A. 1985. *Educating all our children*. Westport, CT: Mediax.

Willer, B., S. L. Hofferth, E. Kisker, P. Divine-Hawkins, E. Farquhar, and F. Glantz. 1991. *The demand and supply of child care in 1990*. Washington, DC: National Association for the Education of Young Children.

Wolf, R. M. 1966. The measurement of environments. In *Testing problems in perspective*, edited by A. Anastasi. Washington, DC: American Council on Education.

———. 1995. The measurement of environments: A follow-up study. *Journal of Negro Education* 64(3): 354–59.

Zill, N., C. Nord, and L. Loomis. 1995. *Adolescent time use, risky behavior, and outcomes: An analysis of national data*. Rockville, MD: Westat.

NOTE

1. Bourdieu asserts that health, social networks, educated humans, money, membership, and culture are forms of capital that are invested in the development of successfully educated persons.

4

Supplementation and Supplantation as Alternative Education Strategies

Edmund W. Gordon and Aundra Saa Meroe

In this chapter, we present a brief overview of such school reforms as curriculum intensification, the implementation of performance indicators (i.e., standardized testing on national and state levels), and the professional development of teaching staff. We then discuss the core features of promising programs directed toward students of color. Next, we consider the possible strengths and weaknesses of the recent movement for the privatization of schools and the devolution of institutional management from the federal and state levels to individual schools. Finally, we turn to the issue of the need for involving family and community members more vigorously in the support and supervision of academic achievement through various forms of supplementary education as an alternative to the supplantation of public schools with privatization.

VARIETIES OF SCHOOL REFORM

Over the past three presidential administrations, there have been a number of proposals for school reforms that bear the stamp of various constituencies' visions for an adequate education. The unanimous assumption underlying these reforms is that public schools are not performing as well as they ought. The distinguishing characteristics among these reforms have to do with a sense of esteem held for the idea of public education and various conceptualizations of the weaknesses and ultimate purposes of public education.

For example, proposals for "intensification" assume that public schools are not offering rigorous and sufficient saturation in core items of traditional curricula (e.g., English literacy, mathematics, and the natural sciences). Not only should students be exposed to more course material, but they also should be exposed for longer periods by the extension of the school day and the school year and the assignment of more work to be completed at home.

Reforms that go by the names of "accountability" and "performance indicators" advocate the further implementation of standardized testing and other achievement assessments in light of heightened academic standards (supposedly reflected in intensification reforms). Additionally, these new standards can entail stricter codes for student conduct (e.g., behavior and dress, etc.). Systems designed to encourage student compliance with these new regulations include, on one hand, awards and honors for high achievement and, on the other hand, grade retention or reduced academic opportunities and extracurricular privileges if students fail to meet GPA minimums, as well as more punitive sanctions for misconduct. Furthermore, school administrations and staff members would also be subject to continuous assessments, rankings, and competitions for financial rewards.

In the course of the narrowing of traditional core curriculums, some reforms have suggested the dismantling of transitional bilingual education (TBE) and the reinstitution of full English immersion programs. This runs counter to research findings that language minority students in multiyear TBE programs not only develop bilingual literacy but also outperform immersion cohorts in math and science achievement. Nevertheless, the rationale for the abolition of TBE is that educational institutions should be promoting a homogeneous curriculum (for the production of homogeneous populations) (Berliner and Biddle 1995; Brisk 1998; Lucas, Henze, and Donato 1990; Miller 1995; Rivera and LaCelle-Peterson 1993; Trueba 1989; Zentella 1997).

In a similar vein, some reforms demonstrate a growing dismissal of the special needs of some students in favor of gifted and talented programs. While this move resonates with the general call for higher standards and core curriculum intensification, countless researchers have called attention to the de facto segregation between high-SES, Asian American, and European American students and low-SES African American, Hispanic American, and Native American students when it comes to the populations most likely to be served by gifted versus special education curriculums (e.g., Darling-Hammond 1998; Oakes 1985).

These types of school reform proposals have troubling implications for the academic welfare of low-SES ethnic minority students who are currently having problems in our educational institutions. As many commentators note, if certain groups of students are presently struggling from underachievement, what likelihood is there that the universal elevation of academic standards will attend to their needs? This is not to say that these students would not benefit from enriched curriculums; however, without sufficient interventions for their present challenges, more rigorous standards have a strong potential for amplifying cycles of failure and the displacement of these students from the mainstream endowments of schooling.

PARTICULAR REFORMS FOR STUDENTS OF COLOR

There are smaller-scale programs and interventions that have demonstrated promise in reversing the patterns of underachievement among ethnic minority students. A review by Borman, Stringfield, and Rachuba (1998) identifies interventions that target student and school characteristics relevant to enhancing academic performance. Student characteristics include engagement with school events and practices, identification with high achievement values, and personal skills for resiliency such as independence, interpersonal facility, flexibility, and the maintenance of positive ties with adults (typically parents) and peers with high and stable expectations for achievement. High-achieving ethnic minority students also tend to come from higher-SES backgrounds and experience less housing mobility than lower-achieving counterparts.

Features of the school environment that encourage academic success are teachers' positive attitudes and high expectations for students regardless of ethnic or SES group membership and lower percentages of poverty among the student population. Additionally, such schools employ pedagogical strategies that are student centered, emphasize comprehension and personal relevance (as opposed to rote memorization), and demonstrate instructional flexibility and respect for cultural diversity. Also, students of color who are exposed to gifted and talented curricula tend to develop higher levels of proficiency. It is, of course, unclear whether this is a function of the superior education treatment, a result of selection bias, or a combination of the two.

Reviewing the reforms of the Calvert School, the Comer School Development Model, Core Knowledge, Paideia, and Success for All, Borman et al. find that programs such as the Comer Model and Success for All take a holistic approach to the well-being of students by focusing on academic, psychological, and social needs. Success for All and Paideia both use cooperative learning strategies between school peers while the latter program uses exploratory and meaning-focused group discussion (of a Socratic style). The Calvert School emphasizes the development of expertise through revisions of student work.

Overall, these are programs that offer challenging curricula, student-centered and cooperative pedagogical methods (between students and with teachers), diverse and integrated student bodies (in terms of ethnicity and SES), and shared values for high achievement among peers, family, and community members.

Fashola and Slavin (1997) find that, among the variety of national educational reforms implemented in elementary and middle schools, the most effective programs have the following characteristics: they are developed in the context of university-based, national, or regional initiatives in contrast to more commercial packages; they focus on a well-defined cluster of goals that are pursued with clear guidelines, coherent curricula, and instructional methods; there are clear standards and procedures for professional development among the faculty that involve intensive training, staff cooperation, and technical support; and educational outcomes are repeatedly assessed throughout the course of implementation.

Analyses of the common characteristics of effective school settings (for all grades) suggests that smaller class sizes and school populations facilitate stronger interpersonal ties between students and teachers and may promote more interaction between students of different ethnicities; diversified curriculums and learning experiences outside the classroom are more engaging and challenging for students and teachers; cooperative learning strategies and school curriculum and governance procedures that centrally involve student input promote a greater sense of students' academic agency, identification, responsibility, and community with peers; and extended periods of school-related contacts that support interpersonal continuities allow for more comprehensive monitoring of student progress throughout the years (e.g., longer school years, consistent relationships over the years between a group of students and a homeroom teacher, etc.) (Darling-Hammond 1998; Jones 1998; McQuillan 1997; Wang, Oates, and Weishew 1995).

The school reforms discussed above point to at least two main issues for reversing student underachievement. First, such students greatly benefit from exposure to enriched educational environments and practices directed at intellective development. High academic expectation and values, challenging course materials, engaging teaching methods, and sufficient material resources—conditions typically available to our most privileged and academically able young citizens—are equally critical to the achievement of students of color (if not more so). Secondly, effective school reforms for minority and low-income students tend to employ holistic approaches for addressing the needs particular to the individual student and the communities from which these students hail. Inventiveness and good intentions alone will not be sufficient for the further propagation of these programs; the effective implementation of these interventions demands adequate financial resources in the way of curriculum, teaching, assessment, and professional development (Borman, Stringfield, and Rachuba 1998; Darling-Hammond 1998; Fashola and Slavin 1997).

FULL FUNDING OF EDUCATION

Compared to other Western countries, the United States has a legacy of un-equal—and inequitable—funding of education. In contrast to other industrialized nations that establish federal statutes for educational expenditures, most school funding in the United States is generated from local and state tax bases. This translates into significant discrepancies between states and between school districts with healthier tax bases and those in poorer rural and central-city locales. As a result, schools districts serving middle- to high-SES populations can allocate 1.5 to even 5 times more tax dollars per student than poorer districts (Berliner and Biddle 1995; Darling-Hammond 1998; Kozol 1991; Miller 1995).

In turn, the school district's resources also determine the quality of school resources and teaching staff. Consequently, there can be great differences in the quality of educational resources varying across districts and states and, almost universally, these disparities impact the poor and people of color. Given that these populations typically arrive at school with greater needs than more socioeconomically privileged students, it is not enough for schools to be funded equally. Schools need to be funded equitably, that is, in proportion to the existing demands of the clientele served (Gordon 1985, 1999; Miller 1995). As many have noted, future endeavors in educational research, school reforms, and budgetary considerations should incorporate the notion that high achievement should *not* be dependent upon students' middle- or upper-class status or the presence of two highly sophisticated parents (with one working solely in the home) (Berliner and Biddle 1995).

Gordon (1999) and Miller (1995) propose even more comprehensive approaches to educational funding. Namely, expenditures to promote high academic achievement should also address the larger issue of the distribution of wealth in the United States. It may not be sufficient to solely ameliorate the poverty-induced disabilities that children bring to their schools. Interventions must enhance these students' chances of growing up in less-oppressive communities and familial circumstances and justify their academic efforts with the likelihood of improved life chances.

PROFESSIONAL DEVELOPMENT OF ADMINISTRATIVE, TEACHING, AND COUNSELING STAFF

The development of high-achieving ethnic minority students is certainly related to the professional standards and expertise required of their teachers. We already know that lower-SES students are more likely to be taught by less experienced and less capable teachers than student populations from higher-SES groups. Compared to other Western countries and other domestic professions, teaching staff in the United States endure middling levels of professionalization, expertise, autonomy/authority, and financial reward. Gordon (1999) suggests that the future professional development of teachers address the following three domains: (a) the content of preservice and in-service education for teachers; (b) the diversification and flexibility of the methods by which continuing education is made available to teaching staff; and (c) the organizational and logistical characteristics of professionalization programs.

Programs for teacher education have typically focused on the sufficient mastery of particular subjects and the use of newly initiated pedagogical strategies. In addition to these central foci, Gordon encourages the explicit development of teachers' recognition and demonstration of requisite features of intellective competence. In other words, it is conducive to both higher levels of teacher confidence and student comprehension if teachers possess expertise in the subject matter as well as the cognitive competence and disciplinary repertoires that undergird that mastery.

In Darling-Hammond's (1999) terminology, teachers must have expertise in "pedagogical content knowledge" as well as in "pedagogical learner knowledge." That is, teachers must develop facility not only with the "art" of teaching but also an understanding of the scientific knowledge and practices underlying pedagogical innovations (e.g., cognitive and developmental psychology). Teachers should be comfortable with employing flexible methods for the ongoing analysis, assessment, and documentation of student comprehension and progress as well as the relative efficacy of various teaching approaches according to subject matter, student needs, classroom characteristics, and available resources. As far as encouraging student engagement, it is critical that teachers have a wide repertoire for relating to the variety of individual and cultural differences that students bring to the classroom and understanding how these differences might demand diverse strategies for motivating each student (also see Oakes and Lipton 1998).

Griffin (1999a) and Darling-Hammond (1999) are strong advocates of the refashioning of traditional models of teacher education. In their view, the preparation of teachers should be elaborated beyond what is typically available in undergraduate programs of education. For example, Darling-Hammond (1996, 1999) supports the trend for graduate-level teacher preparation, as is the case in many European nations. In addition to years of undergraduate training within the university, prospective teachers would be required to undergo two to three years of graduate training in accord with the standards of other professions.

Furthermore, the professionalization process must involve placing prospective teachers within actual school settings. For example, within an "apprenticeship" mode, student teachers are more likely to effectively integrate pedagogical theory with practice and to be prepared for the constant challenges of teaching once they enter the profession. As is the case with the instruction of students, teacher education itself should diversify its techniques beyond traditional didactic and passive learning methods. Teacher education should involve in situ and collaborative problem solving with other teachers and expert supervision. The introduction of novel technical supports, instructional materials, and resources should be integrated within performative and hands-on training experiences (Darling-Hammond 1999; Goodlad 1990; Griffin 1999a; Whitford and Metcalf-Turner 1999).

In the case of the logistical features of programs for teacher development, measures should be taken to ensure that administration staff and pedagogical experts do not issue educational reforms without the input of teaching and counseling staff (McClure 1999). Neglect to encourage cooperative efforts with teaching staff and to ensure the provision of additional temporal and financial resources can result in teachers' disenchantment with and resistance to promising innovations. Additionally, pressures on school staff to produce heightened student performances on standardized assessments undermine the possibility of teachers experimenting with and tailoring their expertise according to new pedagogical methods (i.e., the likelihood of "teaching to the test"). The need for closer analysis and supervision of individual student progress (i.e., adaptive education) entails a negotiable teacher-student ratio. Teacher development programs that attend to the range of these demands promise greater intellective gains for student achievement, competence, and confidence; nonetheless, without high standards for teachers' proficiency, ongoing training, professional status, and agency, any such practices are likely to be less effective (Darling-Hammond 1999; Griffin 1999a).

SCHOOL CHOICE AND PRIVATIZATION

Issues concerning parental choice in the education of children have emerged among minority populations in response to the perceived crisis in education. African American parents in particular understandably harbor considerable doubts about the extent to which their children are adequately served by public schools. African American pundits for school choice are likely to cite the importance of educational options, increased personal control of the distribution of education-directed revenue, freedom from the political fetters of teachers' unions, more institutional accountability, and the potential for greater parental advocacy (Chubb 1997; Chubb and Moe 1990; Fulani 1999; Vanourek, Manno, Finn, and Bierle 1997). Among other segments of the population, choice appears to be increasing in popular acceptance as much out of concern for social insulation (from lower-SES and ethnic minority groups) as for the pursuit of high-quality education.

Approaches to school choice range from state and federal level proposals for vouchers, tax credits, and rebates for parochial and private school tuition expenses to opportunities for parental choice among districtwide public, magnet, charter, and alternative/community schools. Most central to the national debate have been the potential gains and hazards of implementing wide-scale voucher and charter school programs. Although the campaign to introduce voucher programs began more than thirty years ago, the actual distribution of vouchers and the development of charter schools are less than a decade old. As such, assessments of these relatively new interventions are usually inconclusive (Anyon 1997; Henig 1994; Sarason 1998; Whitty 1997).

In general, proponents of voucher programs claim that parents should have the right to send their children to a public school of their choice or to parochial or private facilities if they are dissatisfied with the performance of assigned schools. With Adam Smith–like faith in the tendencies of the free market toward social equilibrium, voucher advocates (starting with Friedman's [1962] proposals in *Capitalism and Freedom*) look to deregulated parental choice as a means of addressing educational resource disparities and encouraging competition between private and public schools. By this logic, access to a sufficient education is less of a universal right than it is a private good for purchase. Intertwined with the appeals for an educational marketplace are the larger trends toward the privatization of social welfare services in general and the dismantling of federal, state, and labor union jurisdiction (Henig 1997; Whitty 1997).

Voucher-type options do present a reasonable means for protecting students' interests against those of large, and perhaps inflexible, school-related bureaucracies. However, vouchers, scholarships, and/or tax credits do not necessarily remedy the great disparities between the levels of resources that lower- versus higher-SES families are able to allocate for educational expenses beyond tuition (e.g., transportation, study aids, etc.). Furthermore, the financial allowances that are provided by vouchers to lower-income families typically are insufficient for covering the tuition costs of high-quality private institutions. Rather, for lower-SES families, these benefits are usually only applicable to parochial school attendance. Research does indicate that students of color demonstrate higher levels of achievement in private institutions, a great majority (approximately 90 percent) of which are church affiliated. Bryk, Lee, and Holland (1993) find that African American students who attend Catholic schools are more likely to graduate from high school and attend four-year colleges. Available research does not enable definitive causal statements. It is unclear as to whether these schools are better or if the families who choose to use them are more academically motivated and are more active in the support of the academic development of their children. Nevertheless, there are a number of problems with the use of public funds for the support of parochial schools. First, voucher programs present a violation of the constitutional separation of church and state. The redirection of public funds to such private institutions not only results in the funding of religious organizations but also in the loss of the taxpayer's voice with regard to the particular practices instituted in these schools. Additionally, the transference of funds from public school budgets to those of parochial and private institutions risks weakening the resources available to the least-advantaged students who do not enroll in voucher programs (Berliner and Biddle 1995; Darling-Hammond 1998; Doerr, Menendez, and Swomley 1996; Whitty 1997).

In comparison to voucher-type programs, there appears to be even greater public support for charter schools (Berliner and Biddle 1995; Henig 1994). Charter schools are autonomously operated institutions that are funded with public revenue. There are two basic types of charter schools: (1) those that have been converted from formerly public facilities, and (2) those that are newly formed by teachers, parents, community residents, school administrators, institutions for higher education (e.g., colleges and universities), not-for-profit institutions (e.g., museums, institutes, etc.), or for-profit business firms. Existing private institutions are usually not eligible for conversion to charter status.

Most charter schools are purportedly based upon the following objectives: (a) to improve academic achievement, especially among "at-risk" populations; (b) to increase educational options for families and encourage greater parental involvement; (c) to create wider professional opportunities for administrative and teaching staff; and (d) to shift the accountability systems from those based upon rules to those more attentive to performance. A more tacit assumption about charter schools refers to colloquial notions about the benefits of market competition. The idea is that charter schools, if successful, will drive traditional public schools to improve their own services in order to remain viable.

Supporters of charter schools claim that low-income students of color tend to make greater gains in achievement after enrolling in charter schools (Chubb and Moe 1990; Vanourek, Manno, Finn, and Bierle 1997). Charter schools also hold specific attractions for underserved ethnic minority populations, given charter schools' liberty to focus on particular educational concerns. For example, some charter schools explicitly target at-risk students of color; promote the development of advanced proficiency in the sciences, mathematics, arts, or business; proactively generate stronger coalitions between school staff, parents, and community-based institutions; feature smaller class sizes and overall student bodies; and/or create school environments and curricula that focus on specific ethnocultural worldviews and subject matter (Nathan 1996; Sarason 1998).

Critics of the school choice movement voice concern about two central issues: the dismantling of the public school system and the potential for educational resegregation (Berliner and Biddle 1995; Henig 1996; Orfield 1996; Orfield and Eaton 1996; Whitty 1997). In terms of the distribution of school-allocated funds, the district's per-student allowances follow the student. Therefore, the transfer of students to charter schools also means the loss of funds for the public schools that once served these students. If a school is perceived as ineffective, it is more likely to be divested of funds that might otherwise be redirected into its future school-based reforms. If the districtwide demand for charter schools exceeds the supply, students remaining in traditional public schools will be likely to suffer from the depletion of much-needed resources.

Admission to charter schools is usually determined by lottery or first-come–first-served policies. At the same time, there are selection mechanisms that undermine universal access to these facilities. Many charter schools actively recruit students according to the particular emphasis of the school and subsequently select the most "appropriate" students—often, this can mean academically or artistically gifted students. As Whitty (1997) observes in his review of the "quasi-privatization" of education in New Zealand, the United Kingdom, and the United States, in a marketplace atmosphere, the likelihood for charter schools to resort to "cream-skimming"—choosing the best-prepared students—is high. In demonstrating that their services are among the best available, focus will be given to the quality of the "products"—that is, the students themselves. Less attention will be given to the effectiveness of the school in enhancing levels of student performance. Instead, consumers will look to present levels of student achievement (which often reflect the extant strengths that students bring to the school) instead of to the gains that students have made since enrolling in the school.

Furthermore, parent consumers tend to approach the educational marketplace with traditional and entrenched conceptions of "a good school." A number of charter school applicants are generated by word of mouth among parents. Parents are also more likely to choose institutions that are conveniently located and pose fewer concerns about social integration. These tendencies present the likelihood that if charter schools open in relatively segregated communities (in terms of ethnicity and SES), the student body will most likely reflect these same characteristics if not closely regulated by the licensing agencies (Henig 1996; Orfield 1996; Orfield and Eaton 1996).

Sarason (1998), drawing upon observations of charter schools in Arizona, Connecticut, Illinois, and Massachusetts, warns that in order for charter schools to meet their goals there must be some understanding of the "contributing factors you seek to prevent." In short, the attitudes and practices of school agents (e.g., administration and teaching staff) in the past have contributed to part of the problem; therefore, those who develop and implement charter initiatives must confront the adverse consequences of their "overlearned" and counterproductive repertoires. Sarason anticipates a number of specific problems that charter schools might encounter:

In terms of institutional and programmatic planning, there is an underlying presumption that subsequent reforms or improvements will not be necessary for charter institutions. As such, there is no alternative plan required if the charter school encounters difficulties, such as changes in leadership or the need for additional resources. Financially, the state aid formulas for per-pupil costs are not realistic for the creation of a new school and the expectations of superior outcomes. Without subsidies from external sources (e.g., for-profit corporations such as Boston's Edison Project), insufficient start-up funds and monies for continuing expenses are among the most central challenges for founders of charter schools (also see Henig 1994; Nathan 1996). In short, the redistribution of funds for education via charter programs is not the same as the investment of greater amounts of financial resources in U.S. education.

As for the governance of charter schools, a well-defined structure of decision making is not required in the application of a charter and, therefore, a wide disparity exists in this area. The reality of a shared power model of governance—offering students, parents, teachers, and administrators equal voices—tends to be much more laborious and time-intensive than initially expected. Schools that envision an environment in which students are also policymakers (and feel a sense of ownership) can lack a clear vision, resulting in difficulty with setting appropriate limits and establishing discipline policies. When parents are among the founders of charter schools, there is the additional dilemma of accommodating parents' private interests in their own children along with the welfare of the student body as a whole. Often schools spend so much time addressing pressing organizational issues that educational issues are not given their needed focus. Teachers (who are typically European American, middle-class, young, and relatively inexperienced) and principals put in longer hours, increasing the possibility of early burnout. Also, ethnic diversity among the student population is often compromised for smaller classes and autonomy.

It is not uncommon for charter schools to operate within a hostile community environment that feels charter schools are taking money away from public schools. Given that most public schools probably will not welcome the presence of new charter schools, this institutional and professional isolation may frustrate many opportunities for collaborative efforts. As such, Sarason suggests that charter schools attempt to create networks among themselves for the sharing of important resources such as technical assistance and support.

Once reliable data has been collected on the various charter school programs developing around the country, Sarason predicts that we are likely to see an encouraging subset of successful charter programs among a majority of inadequate or failing experiments. Other scholars note that, despite the laudable intentions of charter school founders, a national laissez-faire policy with regard to educational reform can potentially create new subsets of troubles in addition to those we are already seeking to ameliorate (Berliner and Biddle 1995; Henig 1996; Orfield 1996; Orfield and Eaton 1996; Whitty 1997).

THE LIMITATIONS OF EXISTING SCHOOL REFORMS

Even the best programs are not radically altering minority achievement on a mass scale given the uneven levels of quality and quantity in the delivery of these interventions. Success for All is, perhaps, the most carefully and rigorously engineered and implemented of these reform initiatives. As is true of other interventions, this initiative has been associated with improvements in the achievement of targeted students. However, Success for All and the best of the remaining reform programs still leave 30 to 40 percent of the targeted population seriously behind in terms of academic development. Several years ago, Benjamin Bloom introduced "Mastery Learning," a program based upon rigorous teaching and repeated exposure to unlearned material. Bloom boasted about the capacity of mastery learning to bring 65 percent of the targeted population up to grade level. Most of these reform programs do make a difference and are to be encouraged, but they have not solved the problems of academic underproductivity in African American, Hispanic American, and Native American children.

If one is to take seriously the importance of human resource development capital and the extensive use of supplementary educational experiences by more affluent and successful students, it becomes obvious that many of the factors contributing to high levels of academic achievement come from outside the school. Schooling may work because it builds upon a variety of capital resources that children bring with them to school. As such, schooling must build upon or compensate for the absence of these varieties of human resource development capital. Students' exposure to high-quality educational programs will be enhanced by economic and social stability in the family as well as familial, peer, and community involvement with and in support of academic development. These challenges require more comprehensive public policies that go beyond educational institutions to additionally target raising the quality of living standards for all citizens in the form of employment opportunities, political participation, health care, housing, and the continued implementation of civil/human rights.

Similarly, many affluent and sophisticated parents do not depend exclusively on what happens in school for the education of their children. These families use a wide range of supplements to schooling to ensure that adequate academic and personal development is achieved. This strategy involves using the public schools for whatever they can provide and to supplement those educational services with the additional services that are thought necessary to the adequate education of each child. Discussed later in this chapter, these supplements include guidance and tutoring, travel, expectation and demand, modeling, exposure to high culture, supports for academic development in the home, and other factors.

What is clear from our survey of school reform movements is that there are limits to what we can expect. Even if schooling were perfected and distributed equitably, it is possible that low-status minorities would still be left behind, in part because it does not appear that schools can be made to function as efficiently as may be needed, and because schooling, at its best, is insufficient to meet the academic and personal development needs of most children. Schooling, public and private, appears to require supplementation by a host of additional educative experiences. We see the need for continued efforts to improve and reform schools and increase access to society's broader range of educative facilities and functions. At the same time, we hold that there are limits to what can be immediately expected from school reform and that there are numerous problems with the supplantation of public schools with private institutions.

THE DEVELOPMENT OF HIGH-PERFORMANCE LEARNING COMMUNITIES

At least since the first major investigation and assessment of the equality of educational opportunities (Coleman et al. 1966), we have been aware that schools alone cannot ensure high academic achievement. On the other hand, we also know that high academic attainment is related to well-endowed capital resources that are not easily garnered by the populations with which we are most concerned.

In general, high degrees of congruency between values promulgated at school, at home, and in one's immediate community are associated with high academic achievement. What may be important are students' perceptions that what happens at school matters and is consistent with what parents and other family members consider important. This is conveyed through expectations, physical provisions for academic pursuits, attitudes toward intellectual activity, and the models that are available for children to emulate. These supplementary practices contribute to the development of high-performance learning communities and shared values for the importance of academic achievement for personal fulfillment, community development, and social and political mobility.

The notion of "high-performance learning communities" refers to the establishment of proacademic community-based initiatives and cultures that support academic achievement within family/home, peer, community, and school environments. With respect to community as a context for human learning, we proceed from the assumption that community can be thought of as an institution or a locale — people and places where common kinship, purpose, mores, and values are shared. Community can also be more symbolic, that is, not identifiable as a concrete place but strongly expressed through association at the level of shared belief and in communal spirit. Community, in this latter sense, functions more like a culture (Gordon and Armour-Thomas 1991). In this proposed initiative, high-performance learning communities are not formal institutions (e.g., schools) but close-knit associations between people (families and peer groups) in which relationships are nurtured, where commitment to high academic achievement is a shared purpose, where academic socialization occurs naturally, where proacademic and prosocial mores and values are promoted, where students learn how to support the academic development of each other, and where members are expected to achieve and are rewarded for academic and personal excellence — individually and collectively. The idea is to convert the actual families and peer groups to which selected participants belong into high-performance learning communities where the application of one's intellective competence to high-level academic endeavors is culturally and socially legitimized (Fordham and Ogbu 1986; Steele 1992). We believe that supplementary education and high-performance learning communities are necessarily interdependent practices; that is, an effective component of supplementary education would involve the formation of high-performance learning communities, and a high-performance learning community would most likely rely upon a variety of supplementary education practices grounded in the following conceptions of human learning:

Social and Cooperative

At the core of the initiative is the view of human learning as a social and cooperative endeavor (Vygotsky 1978; Slavin et al. 1996; Sarason 1998; Cole,

Gay, Glick, and Sharp 1971; Gordon and Armour-Thomas 1991). We consider that situative—the cultural and social—factors that are associated with academic learning are as important as the substance of what is to be learned and the process by which it is learned. Consequently, attention should be given to the creation of positive social conditions for academic learning, such as cooperative learning experiences, organized tutorial and study groups, the use of athletic-style academic coaching, and the creation of ubiquitous high expectations. In addition, attention should be given to reducing the dissonance between hegemonic and ethnic minority identities as is reflected in the phenomenon described as "fear of acting white" (Fordham and Ogbu 1986). The principal vehicles for addressing the social cooperative nature of learning can occur through the creation of high-performance learning teams of fifteen students and a coach and teams of parents and teachers who work together in support of the academic and personal development of these teams of students.

Social Contexts

Human learners are viewed as greatly influenced by the social contexts in which they develop and their achievements are viewed as dependent upon the extent to which social contexts support the aspired ends. Some of these essential contextual supports have been described as various forms of human development resource capital, which enable and facilitate academic learning and personal development.

For example, the Parents for Rockland Youth Supplemental Education (RYSE) (see chapter 12) is a supplementary education initiative developed by the senior author and Patti Smith. Briefly, Parents RYSE was created in two suburban communities north of New York City to serve communities of color that were experiencing problems in the academic achievement of their children. The program goals included providing families with some of the human resource and social capital that is naturally available to families from more-advantaged homes and making explicit the link between education, cultural integrity, and political power through purposeful attention to political socialization and cultural celebration in the context of a multicultural society. These goals were achieved by providing parent education that focused on:

1. better understandings of the school's curriculum and educational services;
2. familiarity with the respective responsibilities of teachers, counselors, and parents and the importance of developing parent-teacher alliances;
3. facility with implementing educational practices for their children outside of school; and

4. the development of highly effective parenting and student advocacy skills.

Supplementary education services in the form of Saturday schools and individual tutoring were also provided for the children of these families. These direct services to students were to elaborate upon the students' schoolwork and to model effective out-of-school academic experiences that were necessary for high academic achievement. Family members involved with the RYSE program participated in trips to colleges, universities, and cultural events. Parents organized smaller cottage meetings in their homes for mutual support, collective strategizing, and information sharing. Occasionally, more sophisticated (e.g., academically, professionally, etc.) members of ethnic minority communities were invited to share their experiences and act as mentors for RYSE parents and students. Ultimately, this package of parent and student services increased parents' understanding of the scope and breadth of experiences necessary for their children to succeed and excel in a competitive academic environment.

Underlying Assumptions and Targets

We assume that the students selected to participate in this intervention are already in functioning schools that are at least adequate in fostering reasonable levels of achievement among some students. We assume that these students do not need a different pedagogical approach to their education. What these students need is the additional support that many children from affluent and more academically sophisticated families receive. As such, components of this initiative should target:

- The practical know-how of parents to advocate for and support their children's academic interests and personal development;
- The development and provision of high-quality supplementary educational activities comparable to those available to more affluent and/or academically savvy populations;
- The facilitation of cooperative learning cadres among student peers and social environments that encourage and nurture academic achievement;
- Specific interventions designed to enhance students' skills in academic socialization, a personal understanding of how one thinks and learns, strategies to boost these capacities, and diagnostically targeted remediation;
- The development of computer literacy for accessing various types of academically related information and resources;

- The ongoing use of research and evaluation processes to track the overall progress (e.g., strengths and shortcomings) of this initiative and to develop and distribute accessible and culturally tailored guidelines for the implementation of similar programs.

Academic and Political Socialization to Academic Achievement

For low-SES students and/or students of color, negative school experiences such as low-level tracking, persistent failure, and racism can result in disidentification and the outright rejection of aspirations for academic achievement. Furthermore, a familiarity with the history of the use of knowledge and skill in the struggle for emancipation and justice can add an element of politicization as an instrument of pedagogy. In the process, students are socialized to their responsibility for self-empowerment and the empowerment of others as well as an understanding of the potential relationships between academic mastery and one's political objectives. Politicized consciousness can be seen as a particular form of supplementary education and a guiding principle for high-performance learning communities (see chapter 5).

SUPPLANTATION VERSUS SUPPLEMENTATION IN PUBLIC EDUCATION

Causing some controversy, Coleman et al.'s (1966) study, *Equality of Educational Opportunity*, concluded that differences in the family backgrounds of students, as opposed to school characteristics, accounted for the greatest amount of the variance in their academic achievement. In later works, Wolf (1966, 1995) posited that it is the presence of family environmental supports for academic development that may explain this association between family status and student achievement. The literature on the relationship between academic achievement and quality of schooling is less definitive for all students, but it is clear that features of schooling account for a considerable portion of the variance in the academic achievement of low-income and ethnic minority students. It is reasonable to assume that the most academically successful populations (which in the United States are mainly European American, Asian American, and the middle, professional classes) tend to have a combination of strong home and school resources to support their academic development. The least successful groups (mainly African American, Hispanic American, Native American, and the poor) have, on average, a much weaker combination of home and school resources.

Efforts to improve schools on a widespread basis for students from the least successful groups have produced some good results, but there are formidable obstacles to providing high-quality schooling to minority populations on a consistent basis. Available evidence also suggests that racial/ethnic group differences in achievement remain, even in schools that are regarded as well resourced and serve mostly advantaged (middle-class) students. These differences also exist within classrooms (as is the case with demanding college preparatory courses and advanced placement courses).

Reform of School Governance

Most of the action on the school reform front has been directed at changes in the organizational structure and governance of schools. In a number of school systems across the nation, efforts are underway to increase teacher participation in decisions concerning what happens in schools. This notion rests on the logical conclusion that people are likely to work more effectively when they are pursuing goals and actions of their own choosing—when they feel some sense of ownership of the programs and projects in which they are involved. The basic idea is consistent with related developments in the industrial sector and is thought to partially explain the reported differences between the productivity of Japanese and U.S. workers.

Site-based management seems to have become the current panacea for much that is considered to be wrong with schooling, despite findings that such efforts to date have done more for teacher morale than for student achievement (Ogawa and White 1994; Whitty 1997; Wohlstetter 1995). Most advocates for this approach to school reform argue that real change cannot occur without support from staff, and that site-based management is the supposed route to such involvement and support. But active participation in the decision making and management of schools requires more than authorization to participate. It requires know-how, resources, and societal commitment—none of which is in adequate supply. With respect to know-how, until we strengthen the pedagogical and substantive competence of our teaching force, their involvement in decision making and school improvement is likely to be limited. In addition, if the primary goal of many of our efforts at school reform is to reduce the incidence of school failure among students who present very diverse characteristics to the school and who are served poorly by our schools, the current reforms in school governance hardly seem to be the treatment of choice.

Efforts at Accountability and Higher Standards

Many of the states, and certainly the federal government, have staked their hopes for school reform and the improvement of education for students at risk of failure on the imposition of higher standards of academic achievement and some attempts at establishing systems whereby schools can be held accountable for their productivity. There is no question but that the standards by which we judge academic achievement and to which we consistently fail to hold schools accountable are too low. They compare poorly to the standards achieved in other technologically advanced countries. However, it can be argued that our standards and achievement are low not simply because our sights are set too low, but because our practices of and provisions for education are inappropriate to the requirements of educational excellence.

Among the most prominent efforts at goal and standard setting were the National Education Goals, set by the president and fifty governors in 1990 and signed into law in 1994 (*Goals 2000: Educate America Act*) and the nongovernmental New Standards Project (National Center on Education and the Economy 1998). While for some the National Goals were measured by a new educational achievement test, New Standards proposed a new system of education assessment. The latter was headed in the right direction with respect to assessment but both gave woefully little attention to the importance of educational inputs. One cannot argue with the substance of the National Education Goals, however, which clearly still apply in today's social and political climate.

1. By the year 2000, all children in America will start school ready to learn.
2. By the year 2000, the high school graduation rate will increase to at least 90 percent.
3. By the year 2000, American students will leave grades four, eight, and twelve having demonstrated competency in challenging subject matter (e.g., mathematics, science, English, history, and geography), and every school will ensure that all students learn to use their minds well in preparation for responsible citizenship, further learning, and productive employment in our modern economy.
4. By the year 2000, U.S. students will be first in the world in science and mathematics achievement.
5. By the year 2000, every adult will be literate and will possess the knowledge and skills necessary to compete in a global economy and to exercise the rights and responsibilities of citizenship.

In each instance, we see iterated a rational expectation of what will be required of our students if they are to have meaningful, satisfying, and responsible participation in the social order. The values reflected in such goals, especially the third goal listed above, send a powerful message to school systems concerning what the nation expects from its educational institutions. However, an extremely negative message is sent by the promulgation of such goals in the absence of the resources, know-how, and a national commitment to ensure that schools and students are enabled to meet these goals. Nothing in the national efforts speaks to the desperate need for staff development and the improvement of the quality of the labor force in schools. Nowhere in that effort is attention given to the states' responsibility for ensuring that schools have the capacities to deliver the educational services necessary to the realization of such goals. Nowhere is there any recognition of the circumstances beyond the school that are conducive to these objectives. Without attention to these extra-school forces, it is folly to expect that the national effort will address questions of responsibility for ensuring that these enabling conditions will prevail.

In the report of the New York City Chancellor's Commission on Minimum Standards (Gordon 1986), the case was made for the importance of symmetry in the pursuit of school accountability. After identifying achievement-level targets as standards, the report proposed that standards also be set for professional practice and institutional capacity. New York City, other school districts, the federal government, and New Standards have yet to seriously engage standards for practice and capacity. Yet if we are to expect that children at risk of failure (and other children as well) will experience great improvements in their academic performance, it is more likely to come from the imposition of higher standards upon those of us who manage their education and guide their learning. The problem is that it is relatively easy to arrive at agreement on what students should know and know how to do, while it is very difficult to agree on what the educational inputs should be to achieve these aims without becoming overly prescriptive or without facing—what is more problematic politically—questions concerning entitlement and the fixing of responsibility for costs. If the field can ever agree on a set of standards for professional practice and school capability, do we then have a basis for asking the courts to hold schools or states responsible for making them available, especially to children at risk of school failure?

The Problem with Supplantation

The most aggressively pursued models for the implementation of choice in elementary/secondary education are efforts directed at the privatization of the delivery of educational services. These efforts would result in the supplantation of public education with a vast array of commercially and privately sponsored deliverers. (To supplant is *to take the place* of or *substitute* for.) Discouragement with the effectiveness of public schools is an understandable response to the failure of these institutions to adequately serve low-status populations, but the crisis in public education in this country may indeed be as "manufactured" as Berliner and Biddle (1995) claim. Public schools can and do work: for some people and under conditions of appropriate support. Privatization is not the answer.

1. We object to any retreat from public responsibility for the education of all members of our society.
2. We object to the allocation of public funds to support private endeavors. (This can be seen in the nation's dependence on the privatized delivery of health care which has resulted in one of the world's most advanced collection of medical technology and one of the weakest systems of health care delivery).
3. The problem is not one of parental choice of schools but parental and community support of schooling.
4. Supplanting public with private schools will not address two of the most neglected problems in education: (1) the inequitable distribution of human resource development capital necessary for investment in the academic and personal development of children (see chapter 2); and (2) the underpreparation of the teaching force required for the delivery of adequate and sufficient opportunities to learn.

The Potential of Supplementation

James Comer's book *Waiting for a Miracle: Why Our Schools Can't Solve Our Problems—and How We Can* (1997) persuasively details the limitations of school reform. An even more cogent argument is made for the importance of families and communities taking responsibility for improving and supplementing what happens in school to ensure that the education of our children is effective. Comer suggests that the maximization of the academic/intellective development of minority groups and the poor will require substantial investments in making available to them supplementary supports comparable to those that are available to better-advantaged students. Supplementary education may be needed for both low- and high-SES segments of the population. Across ethnocultural groups, high support for academic achievement is not a universal condition. Supplements to formal schooling may fulfill two roles for populations of color in particular:

1. helping to compensate for the weaknesses of the schools attended by these students, and

2. providing students access to opportunities for intellective development, academic socialization, and high-achievement value orientations in the heart of their social networks—regardless of whether students attend weakly or strongly resourced schools.

REFERENCES

Anastasi, A., ed. 1966. *Testing problems in perspective*. Washington, DC: American Council in Education.

Anyon, J. 1997. *Ghetto schooling: A political economy of urban educational reform*. New York: Teachers College Press.

Berliner, D., and B. Biddle. 1995. *The manufactured crisis: Myths, fraud, and the attack on America's public schools*. New York: Addison-Wesley.

Borman, G., S. Stringfield, and L. Rachuba. 1998. *Advancing minority high achievement: National trends and promising programs and practices*. Baltimore, MD: Johns Hopkins University, Center for Social Organization of Schools.

Brisk, M. 1998. *Bilingual education: From compensatory to quality schooling*. Mahwah, NJ: Lawrence Erlbaum.

Bryk, A., V. Lee, and P. Holland. 1993. *Catholic schools and the common good*. Cambridge, MA: Harvard University.

Chubb, J. E. 1997. Lessons in school reform from the Edison Project. In *New schools for a new century: The redesign of urban schools*, edited by D. Ravitch and J. P. Viteritti, 86–122. New Haven, CT: Yale University Press.

Chubb, J., and T. Moe. 1990. *Politics, markets and America's schools*. Washington, DC: Brookings Institute.

Cole, M., J. Gay, J. Glick, and D. Sharp. 1971. *The cultural context of learning and thinking*. New York: Basic Books.

Coleman, J. S., E. Q. Campbell, C. J. Hobson, J. McPartland, A. M. Mood, F. D. Weinfeld, and L. R. York. 1966. *Equality of educational opportunity*. Washington DC: Government Printing Office.

Coleman, J., and T. Hoffer. 1987. *Public and private high schools: The impact of communities*. New York: Basic.

Comer, J. 1997. *Waiting for a miracle: Why our schools can't solve our problems—and how we can*. New York: Dutton.

Darity, W. 1997. Programmed retardation and the theory of noncompeting groups. Unpublished monograph.

Darling-Hammond, L. 1995. Cracks in the bell curve: How education matters. *Journal of Negro Education* 64(3): 340–53.

———. 1996. *The right to learn: A blueprint for creating schools that work*. San Francisco: Jossey-Bass.

———. 1998. Unequal opportunity: Race and education. *Brookings Review* 16(2): 28–32.

———. 1999. Educating teachers for the next century: Rethinking practice and policy. In *The education of teachers*, edited by G. Griffin, 221–56. Chicago: University of Chicago Press.

Doerr, E., A. Menendez, and J. Swomley. 1996. *The case against school vouchers*. Amherst, NY: Prometheus Books.

Fashola, O., and R. Slavin. 1997. Promising programs for elementary and middle schools: Evidence of effectiveness and replicability. *Journal of Education for Students Placed at Risk* 2(3): 251–307.

Fordham, S., and J. Ogbu. 1986. Black students' school success: Coping with the burden of acting white. *Urban Review* 18:176–206.

Friedman, M. 1962. *Capitalism and freedom*. Chicago: University of Chicago Press.

Fulani, L. 1999. *Reform Party reflects views of Black America on education options*. New York: Committee for a United Independent Party.

Fuller, B., R. F. Elmore, and G. Orfield, eds. 1996. *Who chooses? Who loses? Culture, institutions and the unequal effects of school choice*. New York: Teachers College Press.

Goodlad, J. 1990. *Teachers for our nation's schools*. San Francisco: Jossey-Bass.

Gordon, E. W. 1985. Social science knowledge production and the Afro-American experience. *Journal of Negro Education* 54:117–33.

———. 1986. *Foundations for academic excellence*. Brooklyn, NY: NYC Chancellor's Commission on Minimum Standards, New York City Board of Education.

———. 1987. *The truly disadvantaged: The inner city, the underclass and public policy*. Chicago: University of Chicago Press.

———. 1999. *Education and justice: A view from the back of the bus*. New York: Teachers College Press.

Gordon, E. W., and E. Armour-Thomas. 1991. Culture and cognitive development. In *Directors of development: Influences on the development of children's thinking*, edited by L. Okagaki and R. Sternberg, 83–100. Hillsdale, NJ: Erlbaum.

Griffin, G. 1999a. Changes in teacher education: Looking to the future. In *The education of teachers*, edited by G. Griffin, 1–17. Chicago: University of Chicago Press.

Griffin, G., ed. 1999b. *The education of teachers*. Chicago: University of Chicago Press.

Henig, J. 1994. *Rethinking school choice: Limits of the market metaphor*. Princeton, NJ: Princeton University Press.

———. 1996. The local dynamics of choice: Ethnic preferences and institutional responses. In *Who chooses? Who loses? Culture, institutions and the unequal effects of school choice*, edited by B. Fuller, R. F. Elmore, and G. Orfield. New York: Teachers College Press.

———. 1997. Patterns of school-level racial change in D.C. in the wake of Brown: Perceptual legacies of desegregation. *PS: Political Science and Politics* 30(3): 448–53.

Jones, V. 1998. Improving black student performance on a large scale: The lessons of Equity 2000 program. In *The state of black America*, 173–94. New York: National Urban League.

Kozol, J. 1991. *Savage inequalities*. New York: HarperCollins.

Lagemann, E., and L. Miller, eds. 1996. *Brown v. Board of Education: The challenge for today's schools*. New York: Teachers College Press.

Lucas, T., R. Henze, and R. Donato. 1990. Promoting the success of Latino language–minority students: An exploratory study of six high schools. *Harvard Educational Review* 60(3): 315–40.

McClure, R. 1999. Unions, teacher development, and professionalism. In *The education of teachers*, edited by G. Griffin, 18–62. Chicago: University of Chicago Press.

McQuillan, P. J. 1997. Humanizing the comprehensive high school: A proposal for reform. *Educational Administration Quarterly* 33 (supplement): 644–82.

Miller, L. S. 1995. *An American imperative: Accelerating minority educational advancement*. New Haven, CT: Yale University Press.

Nakanishi, D., and T. Nishida, eds. 1995. *The Asian American educational experience*. New York: Routledge.

Nathan, J. 1996. *Charter schools: Creating hope and opportunity for American education*. San Francisco: Jossey-Bass.

National Center on Education and the Economy with the University of Pittsburgh. 1998. *New Standards performance standards*. Vols. 1–3. Washington, DC: Author.

Oakes, J. 1985. *Keeping track: How schools structure inequality*. New Haven, CT: Yale University Press.

Oakes, J., and M. Lipton. 1998. *Teaching to change the world*. Boston: McGraw-Hill.

Ogawa, R., and P. White. 1994. School-based management: An overview. In *School-based management: Organizing for high performance*, edited by S. A. Mohrman, P. Wohlstetter and associates, 53–80. San Francisco: Jossey-Bass.

Orfield, G. 1996. Public opinion and school desegregation. In *Brown v. Board of Education: The challenge for today's schools*, edited by E. Lagemann and L. Miller. New York: Teachers College Press.

Orfield, G., and S. Eaton, eds. 1996. *Dismantling desegregation: The quiet reversal of Brown v. Board of Education*. New York: New Press.

Rivera, C., and M. LaCelle-Peterson. 1993. *Will the national education goals improve the progress of English language learners?* Washington, DC: George Washington University, Evaluation Assistance Center.

Sarason, S. 1998. *Charter schools: Another flawed educational reform?* New York: Teachers College Press.

Slavin, R., N. Madden, L. Dolan, B. Wasik, S. Ross, L. Smith, and M. Dianda. 1996. Success for all: A summary of research. *Journal of Education for Students Placed at Risk* 1:41–76.

Steele, C. 1992. Race and the schooling of black Americans. *Atlantic Monthly* 269(4): 68–78.

———. 1997. A threat in the air: How stereotypes shape intellectual identity and performance. *American Psychologist* 52:613–29.

Sternberg, R., ed. 1994. *The encyclopedia of human intelligence*. New York: Macmillan.

Trueba, H. 1989. *Raising silent voices: Educating the linguistic minorities for the 21st century*. New York: HarperCollins.

Vanourek, G., B. Manno, C. Finn, and L. Bierle. 1997. *Charter schools as seen by those who know them best: Students, teachers, and parents*. Charter Schools in Action Project, Final Report, Executive summary. Indianapolis, IN: Hudson Institute.

Villanueva, I. 1996. Change in the educational life of Chicano families across three generations. *Education and Urban Society* 29(1): 13–34.

Vygotsky, L. 1978. *Mind in society*. Cambridge, MA: Harvard University Press.

Wang, M., J. Oates, and N. Weishew. 1995. Effective school responses to student diversity in inner-city schools: A coordinated approach. *Education and Urban Society* 27(4): 484–503.

Whitford, B., and P. Metcalf-Turner. 1999. Of promises and unresolved puzzles: Reforming teacher education with professional development schools. In *The education of teachers*, edited by G. Griffin, 257–78. Chicago: University of Chicago Press.

Whitty, G. 1997. Creating quasi-markets in education: A review of recent research on parental choice and school autonomy in three countries. *Review of Research in Education* 22:3–47.

Wohlstetter, P. 1995. Getting school-based management right: What works and what doesn't. *Phi Delta Kappan* 77(1): 22–26.

Wolf, R. M. 1966. The measurement of environments. In *Testing problems in perspective*, edited by A. Anastasi, 491–503. Washington, DC: American Council in Education.

———. 1995. The measurement of environments: A follow-up study. *Journal of Negro Education* 64(3): 354–59.

Zentella, A. 1997. Latino youth at home, in their communities and in school: The language link. *Education and Urban Society* 30(1): 122–30.

5

Academic Politicalization: Supplementary Education from Black Resistance

Edmund T. Gordon

In thinking about supplementary education as a means of enhancing the academic achievement levels of the poor and students of color, careful consideration must be given to why it is that many of these young people are not achieving at levels commensurate with their capabilities. E. W. Gordon (1986) has suggested disidentification and limited engagement with traditional schooling as contributing causes. Understanding the mechanisms of this underachievement and marginalization could be instructive to the design of programs of supplemental education. Supplementary education programs must not reproduce the impediments to achievement often found in the more traditional educational institutions. These programs must also be attractive to students and must provide skills that are not only academically effective but also have relevance to their everyday lives out of school as well as in these institutions. In this chapter, I agree that cultural politics and resistance to the disciplinary technologies of traditional schools and other educational institutions play important roles in lowering the engagement and consequent academic achievement levels of many low-achieving students of color. It is suggested that education programs that take account of and build upon these students' cultural politics may have a better chance of success. Further, I argue that those opportunities to learn that occur outside of the jurisdiction of the school provide greater freedom for educators to address these cultural-political perspectives.

THE CULTURE PROBLEM IN EDUCATION

Culture is conventionally conceptualized as an essential historical tradition that is passively inherited. Culture from this perspective is seen as a uniform set of symbols, meanings, and practices received from previous generations and reproduced unconsciously by living members of a cultural community.

Based on this conception of culture, there are two ways in which scholars and educators have conceptualized cultural differences as a "problem" in the educational institutions of pluralistic societies. On the one hand, this problem is understood to be preeminently the problem of mismatched symbolic systems between the two cultures. Here it is generally held that in order to be effectively educated, students of subaltern cultures[1] must either learn the symbol systems of the dominant culture or the schools must employ the symbol systems of the subaltern students' cultures. This model is most often, though not exclusively, applied to groups of students who are not English speakers or for whom English is a second language.

On the other hand, the problem is conceptualized as the generalized pathology of the "ghetto" culture of the underclass. Students from a ghetto background are seen as caught in an unbroken cycle of poverty and social disorganization characterized by irresponsible unemployed and unattached males, promiscuous teenage females, dysfunctional matriarchal families, and inadequately socialized children. As a result of their backgrounds, these children are characterized as too unprepared and undermotivated to take advantage of the educational opportunities offered them.

This model is most often applied to African Americans. Accordingly, poorly socialized black children of both genders, unable to function effectively in educational settings, grow up with warped value systems and poor employment prospects. The joint result is their consignment to lives of poverty and social deviance and to the reproduction of their own dysfunctional families (Kempton 1991; Lemann 1986; Moyers 1986; Moynihan 1965, 1986, 1989). This perpetual cycle, conceptualized as a self-reproducing set of learned practices, is represented as a culture (albeit a dysfunctional one) that is often assumed to be coterminous with African American culture (e.g., D'Souza 1995).

Increasingly, a contrasting view of subaltern culture is emerging. From this perspective, culture is seen as invented, emergent, highly variable though circumscribed, and infused by past meaning and practice. Most importantly for this analysis, it is formed within the context of critically informed struggle against subordination/oppression; in other words, subaltern culture is a political philosophy (see, for example, Blassingame 1979; Gilroy 1987). This conceptualization of subaltern culture has critical implications for the education of student members of subaltern groups and especially African Americans.

RESISTANCE, ACCOMMODATION, AND THE CULTURAL CONTINUUM

An interesting and critically important aspect of the cultural repertoires of subaltern racial/cultural groups like African Americans is what I refer to as a "cultural range."[2] No culture is confined to a single set of symbols, meanings, or practices. A range always exists. This phenomenon is significantly enhanced in the case of subaltern racial/cultural groups living in pluralistic societies. These ranges often become quite large, stretching between "deeper," group-specific, often explicitly oppositional nodes and "standard," shared, often explicitly assimilationist nodes that are shifted in the direction of the culture of a dominant or other competing cultural group. As a result, within a given subaltern racial/cultural community, there appears a repertoire of practices and meanings that, when seen in relation to the dominant culture, extend from resistant to accommodative.

I characterize cultural practices as *resistant* or *accommodative* rather than simply different or similar with reference to the dominant culture because dominant cultures are understood as always (at least potentially) hegemonic and infused with hegemonic ideology (R. Williams 1977). As participants in pluralistic societies permeated by a hegemonic culture, there is constant pressure on subaltern racial/cultural individuals and groups to conform to "civilized," "normal," "national" hegemonic cultural practice—to assimilate and thereby symbolically to validate the superiority of the dominant group (B. F. Williams 1991). The production and reproduction of different cultural practice in these terms is therefore resistant and that of similar practice accommodative.[3]

The different cultural practices of subaltern racial/cultural groups are resistant in a number of ways. They are often parodic and/or filled with motifs of resistance. Sometimes they are directly and concretely confrontational, contesting and flaunting authority (Willis 1977), or even political in an organized and/or institutional manner. However, the practices of subaltern groups are also obliquely resistant. As signifier, they are forms of "refusal" to the power-laden meanings and practices of hegemonic culture, their difference a "symbolic violation of the social order" (Hebdige 1989, 2, 19). They also serve as the material and symbolic basis for the production and reproduction of positive alternative identity for subaltern groups, which "entails non-conformity to and dissent from 'claims about the condition and direction of society' (Geertz) made by those who control it" (Stutzman 1981, 76).

These concepts are particularly powerful when used in the analysis of African American culture. By way of demonstration, consider the culture of gender identity in our communities. For reasons of space, my analysisis confined to African American males.

BLACK MALE CULTURE: RESPECTABILITY–REPUTATION

The culture of male identity in our communities can be described as a continuum with the archetypal nodes referred to by P. Wilson (1969) as "reputation" and "respectability" at opposite ends. The tradition of black male respectability has its roots in Africa and slave cultures but was greatly strengthened during the period after slavery in rural areas of the U.S. South. During this period, the black community developed strong institutions that, as a result of segregation, were semi-independent of those of white society (Butler and Wilson 1990). Despite the injustice and hardships of apartheid, black males were able to play pivotal roles in such institutions as patriarchal extended families, black religious and educational institutions, the black media, and black owned and operated small businesses and farms. In this context, values that complemented positions of responsibility within these institutions and community survival—such as hard work, economic frugality and independence, community commitment and activism, mutual help and uplift, personal responsibility, religious faith, and conservative styles of self-presentation—were basic to the achievement of male status. Respectability remains today an important form of black male cultural practice, though increasingly associated with the middle class.

It is readily evident how respectability can be associated with accommodation. Many, though not all, of the core values and practices of respectability are shared with Anglo middle-class male culture. This is in part a result of the emulation of Anglo cultural practice by African American males and therefore an indication of cultural assimilation. It is also informed by black male concern with white perceptions of African American individuals and community. Respectability is understood by whites to be similar to their own valued practice and therefore nonthreatening.[4] This adds to respectability's accommodationist feel.

However, African American male respectability has a logic internal to the black community as well. In the past, it has primarily been a function of values and practices critically associated with the reproduction of established

African American social institutions. Moreover, although many of the values and practices are similar, historically there have been important differences between blacks and whites in the styles in which these practices are undertaken. For example, while respectable black males are expected to be involved in the church, the religious rituals, music, and even administrative styles are very different from those of the white church.

Increasingly, though, respectability must be understood as accommodationist. As black institutions have disintegrated with the urbanization of the black population and the end of segregation, respectable public-sphere practice has taken place increasingly within the context of Anglo institutions. In this situation, respectability is accommodationist in the sense that it serves to perpetuate racist institutions. It is doubly so because the styles employed by blacks within these institutions perforce conform to those of Anglos. Thus the assimilationist tendencies of respectability are accentuated.

"Reputation" is also a traditional component of African male culture with roots in Africa and slavery.[5] Contemporary reputational practice emerged after the 1940s with the increasing urbanization of U.S. blacks. It is most often identified with black entertainers, athletes, and outlaws (epitomized in the 1960s and 1970s by hustlers and in the 1980s by drug dealers) but perhaps best exemplified by black musicians who are preoccupied with individual improvisations in style and who are preeminently "cool." "Cool," following Nelson George (1992, 62), is a "fluid no-sweat attitude . . . a certain sartorial elegance, smooth charm, and self possession that . . . suggested a dude that controlled not only himself but his environment." An important aspect of the attitude is its thinly veiled hostility to establishment society and its marking of the individual affecting this behavior as someone who doesn't have to answer to anyone (George 1992, 62).

Contemporarily, reputation (P. Wilson 1969) or "cool pose" (Majors 1986) has developed into the most widely recognized (and pilloried) black male cultural practice. In the 1980s, as African Americans in general and males in particular were made increasingly expendable by the transformations of the U.S. postindustrial economy (and postsegregation society) (Marable 1983; W. J. Wilson 1980), "reputation" became more prevalent. Although there are many indications that all black males recognize and most aspire to respectability as an ideal type male behavior,[6] it is difficult for many black males to realize the standards of patriarchal male achievement and thereby realize social status through respectable practice (Cazenave 1981). African American males in such circumstances turn to reputation as an alternative and resistant cultural practice. In its radical (often parodic) difference from standard Anglo middle-class male practice, it signs opposition to the latter and thereby refusal to be judged on the basis of Anglo norms by the dominant society. Reputation is also an alternative criterion of male status achievement. It prescribes a standard of male cultural practice that these black males can reasonably hope to achieve. The status of individual black males involved in reputation practice does not depend on the judgment of Anglo society but upon that of the black community and most particularly upon the critical evaluation of black male peers.

Various cultural practices characterize reputation. Being "successful" with women—that is, able to establish relationships of dominance and exploitation of women ("getting over on," "doing it to") and to establish one's reproductive prowess in the production of offspring, proving one's virility and manhood—are essential to the creation of reputation. Reputation is also established through competition with and dominance over one's male peers. This is accomplished in one-on-one activity through fighting and other forms of physical violence, athletic contests, verbal bouts, drinking bouts, or music and dance contests. It is also an important aspect of intergroup competition such as that associated with gangs. Conspicuous material consumption and display are also important. Expensive cars, clothes, and jewelry, as well as generosity in peer group and other extradomestic spending, are important components of establishing reputation. Resistance to authority, often played out in illegal activities and in abrasive and confrontational relations with authority figures and whites in general, is another important characteristic of reputation.

Stylistic virtuosity and improvisation are fundamental aspects of reputation, which infuse all its other aspects. Firmly embedded in the African American aesthetic, body language, dress, music, dance, and verbal and athletic performance are all infused with "cool." Expressive styles and culture are at the heart of African American male culture of resistance. As much or more attention is paid to the style of practice than to its content.

Reputation is deeply resistant and oppositional. It rejects the hegemonic model of male culture as practiced by the white middle class and posits a cultural practice that emanates from the black community, providing a space for its practitioners to exercise their creative abilities and within which they can achieve status, identity, and dignity.[7]

Respectability and reputation occupy opposing ends of a cultural continuum. In any African American community, at any given time, there are individual males involved in practices that are characteristic of one or the other of the archetypal nodes. The everyday practice of the vast majority, however, is to be found somewhere in between the two ideal types, with each individual utilizing a unique combination of the range of behaviors characteristic of black males as a group. Similarly, on a day-to-day basis, each individual utilizes different combinations of elements along the continuum, shifting toward one node or the other depending upon the social contexts he find himself in.

Over longer periods of time, black males often shift up the continuum toward respectability as they get older and/or their class status changes. Each African American community as an aggregate of the practice of its constituent individuals can be identified with a particular position on the continuum of male cultural practice. This position also changes with time as the overall conditions in the community change and individual male cultural behavior is modified accordingly. All black males are acquainted with the full range of practices associated with the African American male cultural continuum from reputation to respectability. Most are able to and do engage in practices that extend over large sections of the continuum.

I have used the example of black male culture to explicate the invented aspect of culture and the related concepts of the cultural continuum and accommodative/resistant culture, many aspects of all subaltern cultures can be conceptualized utilizing these tools. Subaltern language is another good example. Consider the Puerto Rican community here in the United States. Many Puerto Ricans, especially those born in this country, speak both Puerto Rican Spanish and English as well as a number of linguistic varieties that mix various aspects of Spanish, English, and black English together in seeming infinite variety, depending upon the social context in which they find themselves. If one then considers the political (attitudes toward and relations of power) implications of the use of a particular variation in a particular social context, the validity and the value of these concepts should be clear.[8]

SUBALTERN CULTURE, RESISTANCE, AND EDUCATION

The educational system is an important component of dominant civil society in all Western nations. It is the archetypal ideological state apparatus (Althusser 1971) and a socializing agent of the first order. While schools do play the essential role of imparting knowledge, techniques, and intellectual skills, they are fundamentally involved in the forging of good citizens (obedient, conformist, patriotic) and good workers (disciplined, productive, skilled) (Bowles and Gintis 1976). As such, schools are purveyors of a disciplining institutional version of hegemonic Anglo culture and ideology (which includes racism). Along with the police and perhaps the welfare office, the school system is the most important state institution in African American and other subaltern U.S. communities. For good and bad, it is an important arm and symbol of the state and state power.

It follows that school for subaltern students is a particularly important site for the production and reproduction of resistant culture. Students placed in an institution that they find alien, threatening, representative of a dominating society, and in which they feel powerless engage in "micro-technologies of power" (Foucault 1979). They empower themselves by resisting in everyday ways (Scott 1986). Part of this resistance is expressed in random oppositional behavior. However, important aspects of so-called bad or deviant behaviors found in school settings are not arbitrary but learned patterned cultural practices (Solomon 1992; Willis 1977). There is a culture of "deviant" behavior (what I prefer to style resistant or alternative practice) in our schools that, in the case of young African American males, is intimately related to African American culture and reputation. Oppositional cultural practice associated with schools deflects negative judgments and outcomes imposed by the educational system; it makes them irrelevant. It provides an alternative basis for peer group and community judgment of individual stature and thus affords the possibility for personal dignity, status, and space (existential and material). However, it also tends to preclude standard forms of academic success.

There are two general types of subaltern students who succeed according to traditional academic standards. There are those who generally conform to school rules and procedures in an attempt to excel on the school's terms. In the case of black males, these are students who embrace the respectability side of the black male cultural continuum. At one extreme they may be students who become "raceless" and with whom there is the tendency to move beyond respectability within African American culture and to embrace white middle-class practices and identity (Fordham 1988). These students identify with Anglo-dominated educational institutions and are generally successful academically. More commonly, they are students who because of home environments and socialization usually associated with the black middle class are versed in respectable practice. They may react negatively to aspects of Anglo-dominated schools but have learned to conform enough to school disciplinary and respectable practices to be academically successful (Fordham 1988). They may also be students who, because they are especially sharp or for a variety of other reasons, have initial academic success and therefore feel confident of being able to win the academic game on its own terms.

The second type of successful subaltern student consists of those who recognize the continuum of behaviors available to them and who learn to master the contextual use of the continuum. These abilities can come from home socialization or from skilled teachers who teach the validity of subaltern culture as well as the utility of Anglo disciplinary school practice. These are usually extremely self-confident and assertive individuals. They are able to draw strength and a positive sense of identity and mission from their oppositional cultural practice that sustains them in their mastery of and participation in

Anglo-dominated educational institutions. Mastery of the continuum can be an extremely powerful tool.

The level of oppositional cultural practices in our schools on the part of subaltern students has increased over the last four decades. In the pre–*Brown vs. the Board of Education* era, U.S. schools were segregated at all levels. The level of student rebellion in schools during this period was comparably low for a number of reasons. In the case of African Americans, one of the most important was that schoolteachers and administrators were from the local community and were viewed as leaders and role models. Desegregation of U.S. schools, while only partial as regards student populations, has been much more complete at the faculty and administrative levels. The result is that while most subaltern children attend schools that are racially segregated at the student level, these schools are taught and directed by members of the dominant culture from outside the local community. These teachers and administrators as potent symbols of Anglo authority are rejected consciously and unconsciously by many black students. As the divisiveness of U.S. racial politics intensified during the late 1980s and through the early 1990s, and the socioeconomic circumstance of the bulk of black people has stagnated or in many areas deteriorated, resistant cultural practice has gained currency throughout the black community (rap music is but one example) and particularly in our schools. The continuing high level of black student underachievement in U.S. schools is at least partially attributable to this political phenomenon.

IMPLICATIONS FOR SUPPLEMENTAL PEDAGOGY

From this perspective, the culture "problem" in the education of subaltern youth is not so much a problem of "pathological" culture as it is of cultural resistance and the active production of oppositional cultural practices. There is a problem of mismatched symbol systems and the absence of shared practices and meanings between the cultures of many subaltern students and those of the dominant cultures as represented in the classroom. However, this is not necessarily in the same sense that many "Afrocentric" educators insist. Communication between teacher and student across the abyss of dominant and resistant cultures is difficult. In addition to the difficulty minority students have in grasping concepts and learning skills presented in alien cultural codes, there is the problem of their resistance to learning the dominant codes and their allegiance to oppositional concepts and skills that are not directly translatable to academic success.

Similarly, the position I have outlined above places the commonly held perception that low motivation, low self-esteem, and limited aspirations are among the preeminent problems faced by subaltern students in a new light. Subaltern cultures have created an alternative cultural standard for their members. What looks like low motivation and self-esteem from the perspective of the dominant culture in many cases is, in fact, an artifact of an individual engaging in practice oriented by a completely different set of goals and standards of valued behavior. These are oppositional and often disruptive (Solomon 1992; Willis 1977). As is the case with black males focused on achieving status through reputational practices, the student's self-esteem is based on an alternative system of status acquisition and aspiration toward success in that alternative system.

This leads us finally to the central question of this chapter: Can supplementary education positively address this situation? Two general sets of solutions have been proposed for the problem of cultural mismatches in education. Many have emphasized the need to teach subaltern children how to operate under the terms of the dominant culture (melt into the melting pot). As we know, these efforts have not worked well for many subaltern students. Others have proposed curricular change that emphasizes teaching styles, language, and content more in line with those of subaltern cultures. Again, Afrocentric teaching has had mixed results.

Recognizing that this mismatch is political as much as it is cultural, we find that an alternative is required with emphasis on the politics of education. On the one hand, to survive in a society in which they are a subordinate minority, it is necessary that subaltern students emerge from their educational experiences conversant in the meanings and practices of the dominant culture. Teaching these skills will be enhanced if the similarity between dominant cultural practice and that of the subaltern group is constantly emphasized so that it is clear that dominant practice or something similar is not just the practice of the dominant group. It is also important to emphasize to students that these skills are not necessarily accommodationist, that they do have utility in their communities' own institutions. Moreover, we need to make clear that these skills and concepts have defensive and resistance potential. They can be used positively as tools in the ongoing struggles of subaltern communities with dominant ones.

More importantly, command of a cultural continuum as an educational goal seems essential. In other words, students should be taught not only to be conversant in dominant *and* subaltern cultures but they should be taught the validity and utility of the continuum—the intrinsic interrelationship between its elements, their basic similarities, and the interrelatedness of its values, meanings, and modes of expression. Emphasis should be placed on learning how to contextually invoke different sets of meanings and practices from along the continuum depending upon the social context where the student finds her/himself.

However, subaltern cultures present another set of pedagogical problems that have been largely overlooked. These cultures are oppositional and resistant. They are therefore dynamic in the extreme when faced with incorporation (R. Williams 1977). Communities and individuals reproduce cultural difference in the face of oppression and marginalization. This process is accelerated when cultural elements are appropriated by the dominant society (West 1988). Unless subaltern students and communities are empowered in educational institutions, the attempt to utilize subaltern culture in academic settings may set off a continual process of cultural transformation away from the standard. This process will frustrate attempts to create translatability and enhanced contextual usage along a cultural continuum within the classrooms of our educational institutions.

Unfortunately, in the short term, it is unlikely that subaltern communities will be empowered in this manner. Supplementary education, therefore, may be our only immediate recourse if we are to privilege such values in the education of marginalized and subordinated populations. Accordingly, members of subaltern communities need to establish educational programs within their homes and communities, outside the schools, that are explicitly supportive of political and cultural resistance. These programs must provide learning experiences for our youth that teach the liberational potential of the full range of our cultural and social repertoire.

Specifically, we should establish in black communities in this country supplementary educational programs that focus on three types of political goals: cultural, scholarly, and policy. In the first, forms of popular African American expressive culture—music (for example, rap), dance (for example, hip-hop), graphic arts (for example, graffiti), and so forth—should be taken as the focal point for the formation of learning groups/classes. Their primary focus should be the formal teaching and achievement of virtuosity in these communicative forms. Literacy in indigenous genres should be stressed (for example, the ability to read music, choreograph body movements, play word games, improvise cadence in sounds). The history and sociology of these art forms as expressions of the black collective and aesthetic should also be critically studied. Special emphasis should be placed on the cultural politics of these forms, including the struggle over their validity in the face of denigration by the dominant society. Regular presentations of acquired virtuosity in these art forms accompanied by demonstration of scholarly politicized arguments for their validity should be presented in the sheltered environments of community and family-based learning that is supplemental to the regular school, as well as in settings dominated by the hegemonic culture.

Second, groups/classes should also be formed around the study and production of scholarly knowledge about the history and current circumstances of African American communities. Here, the primary focus should be on the acquisition of the skills in critical thinking, literacy, and research about their communities. This can be done with all age groups. Emphasis should be placed on the historic exclusion and misrepresentation of our communities from and in scholarly canons. Here, the politics of scholarship, including the role of dominant representation and privileged knowledge in the reproduction of this society's racial hierarchy and the ameliorating role of vindicationist scholarship and learning, should be stressed. Since there are few school settings where such emphases can be pursued, supplemental learning opportunities can be used for this purpose. We see examples of such activity in some of the tribal institutions controlled by Native American peoples where cultural traditions are celebrated and subjected to scholarly analysis. There should be regular opportunities for students to produce such knowledge and discuss implications for its use in struggles for change. In addition, the sponsors of such supplements to regular schooling will also need to create opportunities for these students to present the knowledge produced in these activities as scholarly political interventions in Anglo-dominated contexts.

Third, we should develop groups/classes that focus on the practical politics of the communities in which students are a part. This could be the racial politics of high schools or universities, grassroots neighborhood politics, local electoral politics, and so on, or any combination thereof. Emphasis should be placed on acquiring the knowledge production and critical thinking skills necessary to assess the problems to be addressed, developing political strategies to effect social change, and engaging in political activities suggested by this process. Key aspects of this should be the presentation of demands and arguments on their behalf in Anglo-dominated public spheres. Special attention should be paid to placing the students' contemporary political struggles within the historical context of African American struggle.

Supplementary educational efforts along these lines may enable the resolution of a number of the referenced impediments to meaningful engagement in academic pursuits and the resulting low academic achievement for students of color. The supplemental educator can utilize the impulse to resistance that is a stumbling block to academic achievement within schools to motivate students to take part in and learn from these programs of instruction. In this way, the supplemental educator creates groups of student peers in resistance that can develop oppositional alternatives that are academically adaptive to standards of success for participants. Through these programs, students will develop, in the service of resistance, critical thinking, literacy, and other skills and knowledge that can also be utilized to achieve academic success. Programs such as these will demonstrate to students that many of the skills taught in schools do have potential for use on the behalf of their communities and themselves. Similarly, they will demonstrate the value and techniques of virtuosity across the breadth of the African American cultural continuum as they come to realize through their groups' political activities that effective resistance requires effective communication with Anglos and successful negotiation of their institutions. Through supplementary programs like these, the politics of cultural resistance can become the politics of successful academic achievement.

REFERENCES

Althusser, L. 1971. *Lenin and philosophy, and other essays*. New York: Monthly Review Press.

Bickerton, D. 1975. *Dynamics of a Creole system*. London: Cambridge University Press.

Blassingame, J. W. 1979. *The slave community: Plantation life in the antebellum South*. New York: Oxford University Press.

Bowles, S., and H. Gintis. 1976. *Schooling in capitalist America*. New York: Basic Books.

Butler, J. S., and K. L. Wilson. 1990. *Entrepreneurial enclaves in the African American experience*. Washington, DC: Neighborhood Policy Institute.

Cazenave, N. A. 1981. Black men in America: The quest for manhood. In *Black families*, edited by H. P. McAdoo. Beverly Hills, CA: Sage Publications.

DeCamp, D. 1971 Toward a generative analysis of a post-Creole speech continuum. In *Pidginization and Creolization of languages*, edited by D. Hymes. Proceedings of a conference held at the University of the West Indies, Mona, Jamaica. London: Cambridge University Press.

Drummond, L. 1980. The cultural continuum: A theory of intersystems. *Man, New Series* 15(2): 352–74.

D'Souza, D. 1995. *The end of racism: Principles for a multiracial society*. New York: Free Press.

Fordham, S. 1988. Racelessness as a factor in black students' school success: Pragmatic strategy or Pyrrhic victory? *Harvard Educational Review* 58(1): 54–84.

Foucault, M. 1979. *Discipline and punish: The birth of the prison*. New York: Pantheon Books.

George, N. 1992. *Elevating the game: Black men and basketball*. New York: HarperCollins.

Gibson, M., and J. U. Ogbu, eds. 1991. *Minority status and schooling: A comparative study of immigrant and involuntary minorities*. New York: Garland.

Gilroy, P. 1987. *There ain't no black in the Union Jack*. London: Hutchison.

Gordon, E. W. 1986. *Foundations for academic excellence*. Brooklyn: New York City Board of Education, Chancellor's Commission on Minimum Standards.

Gordon, E. W., and D. Green. 1974. An affluent society's excuses for inequality: Developmental, economic, and educational. *American Journal of Orthopsychiatry* 44(1): 4–18.

Guha, R. 1988. Preface. In *Selected subaltern studies*, edited by R. Guha and G. C. Spivak. New York: Oxford University Press.

Hebdige, D. 1989. *Subculture: The meaning of style*. London: Routledge.

Hymes, D., ed. 1971. *Pidginization and Creolization of languages.* Proceedings of a conference held at the University of the West Indies, Mona, Jamaica. London: Cambridge University Press.

Kempton, A. 1991. Native sons. *New York Review of Books*, April 11.

Lemann, N. 1986. The origins of the underclass, part 1. *Atlantic Monthly* 257(6): 31–55; part 2, 258(1): 54–68.

Le Page, R. B., and A. Tabouret-Keller. 1985. *Acts of identity: Creole-based approaches to language and ethnicity.* Cambridge: Cambridge University Press.

Lewis, O. 1966. *La vida: A Puerto Rican family in the culture of poverty—San Juan and New York.* New York: Random House.

Majors, R. 1986. Cool pose: The proud symbol of black survival. *Changing Men: Issues in Gender, Sex, and Politics* 17:83–87.

Marable, M. 1983. *How capitalism underdeveloped black America: Problems in race, political economy and society.* Boston: South End Press.

McAdoo, H. P., ed. 1981. *Black families.* Beverly Hills, CA: Sage Publications.

Moyers, B. 1986. *The vanishing family: Crisis in black America.* Special Report (January). New York: Columbia Broadcasting System.

Moynihan, D. P. 1965. *The Negro family: The case for national action.* Washington, DC: U.S. Department of Labor.

———. 1986. *Family and nation.* San Diego: Harcourt, Brace, Jovanovich.

———. 1989. Toward a post-industrial social policy. *Public Interest* 96:16–27.

Naison, M. 1992. Outlaw culture and black neighborhoods. *Reconstruction* 1(4): 128–31.

Ogbu, J. U. 1991. Immigrants and minorities in comparative perspective. In *Minority status and schooling: A comparative study of immigrant and involuntary minorities*, edited by M. Gibson and J. U. Ogbu. New York: Garland.

Rodman, H. 1963. Lower class value stretch. *Social Forces* 42(2): 205–15.

Said, E. 1988. Foreword. In *Selected subaltern studies*, edited by R. Guha and G. C. Spivak. New York: Oxford University Press.

Scott, J. 1986. Everyday forms of peasant resistance in South-East Asia. *Journal of Peasant Studies* 13(2): 5–35.

Solomon, R. P. 1992. *Black resistance in high school: Forging a separatist culture.* Albany: State University of New York Press.

Stutzman, R. 1981. *El mestizaje*: An all-inclusive ideology of exclusion. In *Cultural transformations and ethnicity in modern Ecuador*, edited by N. E. Whitten. Urbana: University of Illinois Press.

Thompson, R. F. 1966. An aesthetic of the cool: West African dance. *African Forum* 2(2): 85–102.

West, C. 1988. *Prophetic fragments.* Grand Rapids, MI: Eerdmans, Africa World Press.

Whitten, N. E., ed. 1981. *Cultural transformations and ethnicity in modern Ecuador.* Urbana: University of Illinois Press.

Williams, B. F. 1991. *Stains on my name, war in my veins: Guyana and the politics of cultural struggle.* Durham, NC: Duke University Press.

Williams, R. 1977. *Marxism and literature.* Oxford: Oxford University Press.

Willis, P. 1977. *Learning to labor: How working-class kids get working-class jobs.* New York: Teachers College Press.

Wilson, P. 1969. Reputation and respectability: A suggestion for Caribbean ethnology. *Man, New Series* 4(1): 71–84.

Wilson, W. J. 1980. The *declining significance of race: Blacks and changing American institutions*. Chicago: University of Chicago Press.

NOTES

1. The term *subaltern* is generally used in reference to classes that are subordinate to a dominant class or classes (Said 1988, v–vi). Its use has been expanded by some to refer to "the general attribute of subordination whether this is expressed in terms of class, caste, age, gender and office or in any other way" (Guha 1988, 5). Following, with modifications, Ogbu's (1991) characterization of "involuntary minorities," subaltern racial/cultural groups are here understood to be segments of pluralistic societies that were brought into these societies involuntarily through colonial conquest or slavery, that are oppressed based on their perceived racial and cultural difference, that occupy subordinate positions within that society, whose members are conscious of this position as "institutionalized and enduring," that have developed cultures within the context of domination that share important commonalties with that of the dominant group while simultaneously being distinct and oppositional, that have developed shared collective oppositional identity and politics based on consciousness of group oppression and aspects of shared oppositional culture, and that have historic identification with territory controlled by the dominant group.

2. The idea of a "cultural range" correlated with the resistance/accommodation dialectic has a number of antecedents. Rodman's (1963) Lower Class Value Stretch contains important elements of the concept I am trying to develop. However, I have derived the basic idea from the "Post Creole Continuum" and related arguments about linguistic performance and identity put forth by a number of sociolinguists interested in the dynamics of Creole languages (Bickerton 1975; DeCamp 1971; Le Page and Tabouret-Keller 1985). Drummond's (1980) use of this concept to understand Guyanese cultural variations has also influenced my thinking.

3. It should be remembered that while we emphasize the resistant and accommodative aspects of the cultures of subaltern racial/cultural groups at this point in our analysis, this is only part of the logic of cultural production and reproduction. These cultures have their own internal dynamic as well. They are not just, or even predominantly, reactive and are therefore the basis of alternative as well as oppositional identity.

4. Respectability does not always ensure accommodative behavior. Martin Luther King Jr. and Malcolm X are two black males who were eminently respectable but engaged in very effective resistance against white oppression.

5. See Thompson (1966) for African forms of cool and traditional trickster figures.

6. Indications of the veracity of this assertion are the significant number of reputational figures—that is, professional athletes and even long-time drug dealers who take on the aura of respectability when they have accumulated the requisite material resources. Age also often effects a gradual transition from reputation to respectability in black males.

7. There are, of course, exceedingly problematic and destructive consequences of taking reputational practice to its farthest and, some would argue, logical extreme. The excesses of what Naison (1992) calls "outlaw culture" are well documented. They include predatory sexuality, rampant drug abuse, and ubiquitous violence. Naison gets to the core of the matter in his observation that this culture "has emerged among Black youth that has

rejected African American communal norms in favor of the predatory individualism of the capitalist marketplace." Reputation has a contradictory outcome from another perspective as well. By participation in this alternative male practice, black males many times effectively destroy any possibility for mobility through the dominant society's approved structure of male status, thereby reproducing their marginalized and exploited social positions within it (Willis 1977).

8. The idea that there are subaltern cultures that differ from the dominant culture, and whose divergence widens from that dominant culture at least in part as a function of class, needs to be distinguished from the concept of a "culture of poverty" as advocated by Lewis (1966) and more importantly Moynihan (1965, 1986, 1989) and his ilk. What is being proposed here departs from the culture of poverty formulation in at least two fundamental ways. Firstly, divergent subaltern cultural forms are not conceptualized pejoratively. They are seen instead as historically based with a logic internal to their particular subaltern community at the same time that they are resistant and therefore empowering. This is in marked contrast to cultures of poverty, which are characterized as pathological or deviant and disorganized responses to poverty. More importantly, the culture of poverty concept is an essentialized one. It is seen as diachronically and synchronically invariant. The concept of subaltern cultures being put forth here is much more dynamic. It involves the concept of a cultural continuum in which individuals and communities, instead of being condemned to the habitual reproduction of some standardized set of cultural meanings and practices, are seen as masters of a range of variant cultural behaviors that they invoke contextually and in an array of combinations.

6

Family Environments in Support of Academic Achievement

Richard M. Wolf

Consider the following chronology. In 1869, Sir Francis Galton published *Hereditary Genius,* a book in which he tried to apply Darwinian thinking to make the case that genius was an inherited characteristic. The basis for his conclusion was that many prominent men in England were the offspring of prominent men. It was a rather clumsy work but was the opening salvo in the heredity–environment controversy. In 1894, there was a spate of new articles on the issue while, at the same time, Binet (1909) was carrying out developmental work on the first mental test of intelligence. Around 1919, there was a fairly large outpouring of articles on the heredity–environment issue by people who were ardent hereditarians. Much of this writing was quite irresponsible and is critiqued by Gould in his book, *The Mismeasure of Man* (1981). In 1944 another round of articles was published on the topic, stemming from the National Society for the Study of Education's two-volume series on nature and nurture. In 1969 Jensen published his article on the issue in the *Harvard Educational Review*, and in 1994 Herrnstein and Murray published *The Bell Curve: Intelligence and Class Structure in American Life.*

What is notable about this chronology is that major outbreaks in the heredity–environment controversy have occurred every twenty-five years with astonishing regularity. It is as dependable as Halley's comet! By this reckoning, we can expect another eruption in 2019. Since we have some time before then, we can examine some of the evidence bearing on the issue.

Virtually all of the solid evidence on the heredity–environment issue comes from studies of identical twins reared together and reared apart. The basic evidence is quite clear-cut. There is clear evidence for the existence of genetic factors in intelligence and other human characteristics. There is also clear evidence in support of environmental factors in intelligence as well as other human characteristics. The question we cannot answer is how much of an individual's ability is due to what they were born with and how much is due to what they have lived through. The reason we cannot answer the question is because it is unanswerable! As D. O. Hebb once noted, it is like trying to answer the question, "What contributes more to the area of a field: its length or its width?" There is simply no answer to the question. Anastasi recognized this forty years ago when she published her article, "Heredity, Environment and the Question 'How?'" (1958). In that article, she stressed the need to understand how genetic and environmental factors influenced the development of human characteristics rather than trying to estimate how much each contributed to human development. A number of us, then young and fledgling researchers, followed Anastasi's recommendations and began to study the matter of how environmental variables influenced the development of human characteristics, especially intelligence and academic achievement. We were greatly assisted in our endeavors by Benjamin Bloom's book, *Stability and Change in Human Characteristics* (1964). In that seminal work, Bloom proposed a conceptualization of the environment in which a single physical environment was made up of a number of subenvironments, each influencing the development of a specific characteristic. Our research (Wolf 1966) and the research of others have only served to confirm Bloom's theory. I have summarized much of this research in an article in the *Journal of Negro Education* (Wolf 1995). What I want to do in this chapter is describe the home environment variables that make a difference in educational achievement and present the evidence supporting the efficacy of these variables. At the conclusion of the chapter, I issue a few caveats regarding these variables and how they can and cannot be used.

The home environment for academic achievement is composed of six variables, and each is further divided into several environmental process characteristics that give meaning to the environmental variables (Dave 1963). These are as follows:

1. Press for Academic Achievement
   a. Parental aspirations for the education of the child
   b. Parents' own aspirations
   c. Parental interest in academic achievement
   d. Social press for academic achievement
   e. Standards for reward for academic achievement
   f. Knowledge of the educational progress of the child
   g. Preparation and planning for the attainment of educational goals
2. Language Models in the Home
   a. Quality of the language use of the parents

    b. Opportunities for the enlargement and use of vocabulary and sentence patterns

    c. Keenness of the parents for correct and effective language usage

3. Academic Guidance Provided in the Home

    a. Availability of guidance on matters relating to schoolwork

    b. Quality of guidance on matters relating to schoolwork

    c. Availability and use of materials and facilities related to school learning

4. Activeness of the Family

    a. The extent and content of the indoor activities of the family

    b. The extent and content of the outdoor activities during weekends and vacations

    c. Use of television and other media

    d. Use of books and periodicals, and libraries and such other facilities

5. Intellectuality in the Home

    a. Nature and quality of toys, games, and hobbies made available to the child

    b. Opportunities for thinking and imagination in daily activities

6. Work Habits in the Family

    a. Degree of structure and routine in the home environment

    b. Preference for educational activities over other pleasurable things

A rating scale applied to information obtained during an interview with the child's mother measured each environmental process characteristic. Several focused questions were asked regarding each environmental process characteristic during the course of an interview lasting about one and one half hours. The ratings for the environmental process characteristics comprising each environmental variable were obtained and summed to yield a score for the environmental variables. These were then summed to yield a total home environmental rating for each subject.

After the interviews and ratings were completed, achievement test information was obtained for the children from the schools. Correlations were made between the environmental ratings and scholastic achievement as measured by the Metropolitan Achievement Tests. The correlation between the total environmental rating and overall academic achievement was +.80. In contrast, the correlation between the total academic achievement score and the average level of parents' education was +.27, indicating that the home environment total score was measuring something more than parents' education. Correlations between the total environmental rating and subscores of the achievement test ranged from +.37 for arithmetic computation to +.71 for language, suggesting that the home influences were greatest in the language area and least in the area of arithmetic computation. A four-year follow-up study of the same students showed that the environmental information, obtained at grade 5, correlated +.75 with academic achievement on the Iowa Tests of Educational Development four years later at grade 9. In short, a measure of the home environment in the fifth grade was a highly accurate predictor of academic achievement four years later. A number of replications of this study have served to confirm these results.

Some examples of how the environmental process variables work seems to be in order. One environmental process characteristic that was considered to be important was the use of periodical literature, libraries, and other facilities. A set of questions was asked to obtain the needed information for this process characteristic. The initial question was whether or not the child had a library card. In all cases, parents indicated that their child had a library card. The investigators, of course, knew this, because it was school policy to take each third-grade class to the library and, if a child did not have a library card, to obtain one at that time. The follow-up question, however, was the critical one. It asked *when* the child had obtained his or her library card. It was here that the answers diverged. In some cases, the parents reported that their children had obtained the library card when the class visited the local library in grade 3. However, in other cases, parents reported that their children had obtained library cards as early as age five or as soon as they were able to write their names. It was this parent-initiated behavior that distinguished the higher-achieving students from the lower-achieving ones.

Another environmental process characteristic that was considered important was the preparation and planning for the attainment of educational goals. Parents were asked how much education they wished their children to receive. In virtually all cases, parents indicated that they would like their children to go to college. The follow-up question asked how they planned to finance their children's college education. In a number of cases, parents had given no thought to how a college education would be financed. In other cases, parents had started a savings account to pay for a college education. In the most extreme case, a mother indicated that the financing of a college education had already been completed. When asked how this had been accomplished, the mother reported that her husband had been struck by a car about six months previous and received a hefty settlement from the driver's insurance company. The bulk of the money had been put into a trust fund in a local bank to fully finance the children's college education when they graduated high school. What is notable about this story is that the family was quite poor. They didn't even have a telephone and the house was furnished in second-hand furniture. There were few books in the home other than a stack of books borrowed from the local library. However, the parents had established a trust fund for their children's college education that could not be touched until they were of college age.

A final example is the environmental process characteristic, opportunities for thinking and imagination in daily activities. A series of questions was asked about intellectual activities carried on in the home. The answers ranged from hardly anything to daily instructional efforts. In one example of the latter case, a mother reported that the child and his father, a PBX installer for the local telephone company, would sit at the Formica kitchen table every evening after dinner and work out arithmetic problems in pencil on the kitchen table while the mother washed the dishes. When she finished, she would then take a rag and wipe the kitchen table clean. Usually, the father and child would spend about twenty to thirty minutes each evening after dinner solving various problems together.

The above examples attempt to show both the kinds of variables in the family environment that not only support but also promote academic achievement, as well as how that information was obtained. The focused interviews that were conducted were delicate undertakings since they sought to obtain the needed information to derive the environmental ratings in a manner that was nonthreatening to parents. In many cases, leading questions to which the answers were already known and that were loaded with social desirability were asked to simply open up an area for discussion. The follow-up questions actually provided the information required to obtain the needed ratings.

While the results of the studies of environmental influences on achievement have yielded strong results, they need to be interpreted with caution. The studies were naturalistic ones. That is, they investigated the relationships between environmental variables and academic achievement as they naturally existed. There were no interventions to alter the environments in any way. This is both the strength and the limitation of the studies. The strength inheres from the fact that the environments had developed over a period of time and were not influenced by the data collection. The limitation of these studies lies in the fact that there is, at present, no basis for using the results from the studies in a prescriptive way without further research. In fact, one suspects that any attempt to introduce these variables into a particular home setting in a wooden or mechanical way is not likely to have a strong effect on academic achievement. It would simply be unnatural and hence not likely to be efficacious. Here, one can turn to research in child-rearing practices that has studied the relationship between the degree of stringency or leniency in child rearing. Usually, such studies show little or no relationship between the particular level of stringency or leniency in child rearing and measures of child development. In contrast, it is the degree of consistency in child rearing that seems to be related to levels of development. Parents who adopt a particular level of stringency or leniency in their child rearing and stick with it seem to have children who achieve high levels of development. In contrast, inconsistency in child rearing appears to cause confusion and result in lower levels of development. The same is likely to hold for the environments parents create in support of academic achievement. Parents can certainly benefit from knowing the kinds of things that they can do to enhance their child's academic achievement. However, it is another matter to consistently do the things that are needed to support the child's academic achievement. As one mother noted, "The weekly trips to the library do pay off." Infrequent trips to the library, however, are not likely to have much of an effect. It is with these cautions that one must approach the findings of the studies of environmental influences on academic achievement. In summing up, it seems wise to go back to Binet, the developer of the first mental test of intelligence, and see what he has to say on the matter. In 1909, Binet wrote (as quoted in Hunt 1961),

> Some recent philosophers appear to have given their moral support to the deplorable verdict that the intelligence of an individual is a fixed quantity. . . . We must protest and act against this brutal pessimism. . . . A child's mind is like a field for which an expert gardener has advised a change in the method of cultivating, with the result that in place of desert land, we now have a harvest. It is in this particular sense, the one which is significant, that we say that the intelligence of children may be increased. One increases that which constitutes the intelligence of a school child, namely, the capacity to learn, to improve with instruction.

One can paraphrase Binet and apply his words to academic achievement. The role of the home environment in increasing academic achievement is clear, and there is ample evidence to support it. The challenge at this time seems to lie in how we can make use of this information.

REFERENCES

Anastasi, A. 1958. Heredity, environment and the question "How?" *Psychological Review* 65:197–208.

Binet, A. 1909. *Les idées modernes sur les enfants*. Paris: Ernest Flamaion.

Bloom, B. 1964. *Stability and change in human characteristics*. New York: John Wiley.

Dave, R. H. 1963. The identification and measurement of environmental process variables that are related to academic achievement. PhD diss., University of Chicago.

Gould, S. J. 1981. *The mismeasure of man*. New York: Norton.

Herrnstein, R. J., and C. J. Murray. 1994. *The bell curve: Intelligence and class structure in American life*. New York: Free Press.

Hunt, J. M. 1961. *Intelligence and experience*. New York: Ronald Press.

Jensen, A. 1969. How much can we boost IQ and scholastic achievement? *Harvard Educational Review* 39:1–123.

Wolf, R. M. 1966. The measurement of environments. In *Testing problems in perspective*, edited by A. Anastasi. Washington, DC: American Council on Education.

———. 1995. The measurement of environments: A follow-up study. *Journal of Negro Education* 64 (3): 354–59.

7

The Impact of Extracurricular Activities on Standardized Test Scores

Howard T. Everson and Roger Millsap

There is little debate that public high schools in the United States need improvement. Student achievement suffers in many high schools, and innovation and change are required to address the challenge of improving learning across the curriculum, particularly when it comes to the achievement gap between minority and majority students. The contributors to this volume offer a variety of alternative approaches, all under the heading of supplementary education programs. But do these programs and interventions actually lead to increases in student achievement? What is the quality of the evidence in support of these programs and activities? Indeed, if these activities are to be expanded, as some have argued elsewhere in this book, then rigorous scientific evidence will have to be developed and made available to policymakers, parents, students, and other stakeholders.

Marsh and Kleitman (2002), writing in the *Harvard Educational Review*, present a persuasive case for the efficacy of extracurricular activities. They conclude, for example, "Whereas most school activities exacerbate the already substantial gap in academic outcomes between socioeconomically advantaged and disadvantaged students, ESAs (extracurricular school activities) appear to actually reduce this inequality gap. Although the ESA benefits generalize widely, the benefits tend to be larger, certainly not smaller, for more disadvantaged students" (508). Others (Camp 1990; Gerber 1996; Holland and Andre 1987; Holloway 2000; Marsh 1992) have reached similar conclusions. Despite these efforts, however, policymakers may be constrained in the current environment because many of these studies may not meet the standard of rigorous scientific evidence promulgated by the U.S. Department of Education.

Recently, the U.S. Department of Education's Institute of Education Sciences released a set of guidelines intended to help educators identify educational interventions that are backed by strong evidence of effectiveness (U.S. Department of Education 2003). Comparison group studies using closely matched groups are cited, albeit somewhat tentatively, by the Institute of Education Sciences as providing reliable scientific evidence of effectiveness. The research reported in this chapter, which used a matched comparison group design, provides strong preliminary evidence that extracurricular activities—a not-so-uncommon form of supplementary educational intervention—contribute to student performance on important, high-stakes tests such as the SAT. We reached this conclusion by analyzing the SAT verbal and mathematics scores of more than 480,000 high school students matched on a number of socioeconomic and academic characteristics.

EXTRACURRICULAR ACTIVITIES

High school kids call them 3:05ers. There are many of them in our nation's high schools. These are the kids who fly out the door and away from school as soon as their last class ends at 3 o'clock in the afternoon. No after-school or supplemental programs for them. Even if offered, no clubs, no band practices, no athletic teams, or other extracurricular programs keep them past the last bell. Many have questioned just how strongly these students are engaged with school. But more and more, there is a large and growing number of high school students who enjoy staying after school. These students participate in any number of extracurricular activities (ECA), including music, art and drama clubs, intercollegiate and intramural athletics, and other academic and vocational clubs. These activities are voluntary and students do not receive grades or academic credit for them (Holloway 2000).

The purpose of the study was to examine the effects of participation in a range of extracurricular activities in high school on students' SAT scores, while controlling for the effects of other important factors such as socioeconomic background, high school achievement, gender, and ethnicity. In this study, we extend previous research in this area and attempt to address policymakers' skepticism about the effects of extracurricular activities on academic achievement. We have organized the chapter to: (1) provide detail on our sample of college-bound students; (2) explain our model-based analytic approach; (3) describe briefly the data and the model-fitting framework commonly referred to as structural equation modeling and; (4) present the results of our analysis. We conclude with a discussion of the implications of our research for the validity of supplementary education in narrowing the achievement gap.

Table 7.1. SAT Verbal and Mathematics Scores by Gender and Race/Ethnicity

	Whites	*Asians*	*Blacks*	*Hispanics*
Males				
SAT-M	551	577	444	495
SAT-V	537	533	443	484
Females				
SAT-M	515	543	427	462
SAT-V	534	531	448	478

METHOD

The analyses we present in this chapter examined the relationships among and influences of socioeconomic background, academic achievement, and extracurricular activity levels on high school students' verbal and mathematics SAT scores. We looked at these relationships across eight subgroups of students, based on ethnic group membership and gender. The explanatory models we developed were tested against the SAT verbal and mathematics scores of students in all eight subgroups.

Our Sample

Our sample comes from a subset of college-bound seniors who took the SAT during their junior or senior year of high school, and who graduated from high school in 1995. This cohort of students had mean SAT verbal and mathematics scores of 504 and 506, respectively. They represent about 41 percent of all the high school seniors in the United States in 1995. Girls make up about 54 percent of this group, and the cohort is largely white (69 percent), with 11 percent black, 8 percent Asian American, 4 percent Mexican American, 4 percent other Latinos, 1 percent Native American, and 3 percent who marked "other" when noting their race or ethnicity. Since our analyses focus on subgroup differences in SAT scores, table 7.1 displays the mean SAT verbal and mathematics scores disaggregated by race/ethnicity and gender for this cohort of college-bound students.

Table 7.2. Number of Students Responding to the Survey by Gender and Ethnicity

	Males	*Females*	*Total*
Whites	170,270	212,412	382,682
Blacks	18,411	27,644	46,055
Asian American	12,333	13,732	26,065
Hispanics	13,026	16,666	29,692
Total	214,040	270,454	484,494

Table 7.3.   High School Achievement Variables

HSAVG - High School Grade Point Average
CRANK - High School Class Rank
ARTGR - GPA in Art and Music Courses
SOCGR - GPA in Social Science and History
ENGR - GPA in English Courses
LANGR - GPA in Foreign Language Courses
MATHGR - GPA in Mathematics Courses
SCIGR - GPA in Natural Science Courses

The magnitude of group differences in SAT scores is clear. Males outperform females in mathematics, and white and Asian American students, in general, score higher on both the verbal and mathematics SAT tests than black and Hispanic students.

Data Source

When students register with the College Board to sit for the SAT, they complete a lengthy questionnaire, answering forty-three questions about their high school courses, participation in a range of extracurricular activities, academic achievement levels (i.e., grades), parental education, family income, and their race or ethnicity (see www.collegeboard.org for a copy of the Student Descriptive Questionnaire). Responses to these questions formed much of the data for this study. Table 7.2 shows the number of students enrolled in public high schools, disaggregated by race/ethnicity and gender, who responded to all the relevant questions in the College Board survey, thus comprising our sample. This subset of more than 480,000 students provided the data used in the subsequent analyses.

The College Board questionnaire, for example, asked students to indicate the total number of years they took high school courses in specific subject areas, and to report their grade point average (GPA) on a scale of A to F for each academic subject. The data elements we used to model academic achievement are presented in table 7.3.

Similarly, students indicated their participation in a range of extracurricular activities. Table 7.4 provides the complete list of variables we used to

Table 7.4.   Extracurricular Activities Variables

ACTCNT - Number of Extracurricular Activities (pursued for at least 3 years)
APCNT - Number of AP Exams Intended
HNRCNT - Number of Honors Classes Taken
ENGCNT - Number of Literature Experiences
COMPCNT - Number of Computer Experiences
ARTCNT - Number of Art, Music, and Theater Experiences

Table 7.5.   Family Socioeconomic Background Variables

FATHED - Father's Education Level
MOTHED - Mother's Education Level
FAMINC - Combined Parental Income

model participation in academic and nonacademic extracurricular activities while in high school. Students in our sample also reported their best estimates of annual family income in increments of $10,000, with reporting categories ranging from a low of $10,000 to a maximum of $100,000 or more per year. In addition, they reported the highest level of education attained by both parents. These three variables were used to model students' socioeconomic backgrounds. See table 7.5.

In addition to these self-report measures, each student's SAT verbal and mathematics scores (reported on a scale from 200 to 800) were used as the outcome measures in our analyses.

A Model-Based Approach

Our approach relied on structural equation modeling (SEM). The use of SEMs in educational and psychological research has steadily grown since the late 1970s. This approach is particularly well suited for our study because of the large number, nineteen in all, of observed variables in our model, and our interest in linking participation in a variety of extracurricular activities with performance on the SAT.

SEM analyses include three broad stages: specifying the model that relate the variables to each other, estimating the parameters of the model, and estimating how well the model fits the empirical data; that is, how well the theoretical model replicates the empirical correlations between and among the variables included in the model. Specifying the model requires us to translate the theory we wish to test, in this case the relationship between ECAs and SAT scores, into a particular structural model that can be derived and tested given the empirical data on hand. Thus, the resulting models should be testable or they can be refuted by the data. During the parameter estimation stage, we used the College Board data to obtain estimates of the model parameters—the coefficients calibrating the relationships among the variables—that are optimal according to any one of several statistical estimation methods. To evaluate the fit of our model, we used the derived parameter estimates to examine whether the hypothesized model can reproduce the covariation found in the empirical data.

Model specification in SEM begins with a theory about the relationships among the variables under study. For convenience, a distinction is commonly

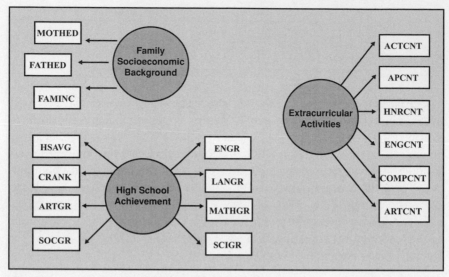

Figure 7.1.   Measurement Model of Latent Variables

made between the measurement and structural portions of the model. The measurement model describes the relations between the measured variables and the latent variables (the underlying factor that accounts for the relationships among the observed measures) hypothesized to underlie these measured variables. The nineteen measured variables in this study were believed to be represented well by three latent variables (i.e., socioeconomic background, high school achievement, and extracurricular activities), and two observed variables (i.e., the SAT verbal and mathematics test scores). This hypothetical measurement model of the three latent variables is depicted in figure 7.1.

The boxes represent measured variables from the questionnaire completed by all the students taking the SAT, and the circles represent the common factors or latent variables we hypothesized were underlying seventeen of the measured variables. The arrows linking the latent and measured variables indicate those measured variables that are hypothesized as measures of each latent variable. In our model, each measured variable is linked to a single latent variable.

The structural portion of the model specifies the directional relations among the latent variables or among the measured variables if no latent variables are included. The choice of which latent variables are linked directly or indirectly by paths is based on theory. The hypothesized structural portion of our model is depicted in figure 7.2.

Our first consideration when defining the structural model was the choice of which latent variables are exogenous and considered causally prior to the other

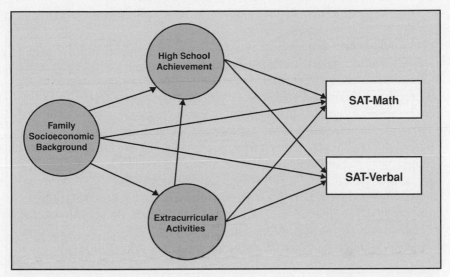

Figure 7.2. Structural Model of Relationship Among Measures of Family Background, High School Achievement, and Extracurricular Activities on SAT Verbal and Math Scores

latent variables. Our model asserts that performance on the SAT is dependent upon high school achievement and participation in extracurricular activities, which, in turn, are dependent on socioeconomic background. We also hypothesized that socioeconomic background influences directly SAT scores as well (Everson, Millsap, and Diones 1995; Everson and Michna 2004).

RESULTS

As noted earlier, the SEM approach centers on two steps: validating the measurement model and fitting the structural model. We divided our sample of N = 484,494 into eight groups based on the factorial combination of gender with the four ethnic classifications: Asian American, African American, Hispanic, and white. In this initial stage, a nested series of structural equation models were fit to the data, permitting tests of ethnic and gender invariance of the structural and measurement models. Mean structures were used to allow for tests for group differences in mean SAT performance after adjusting for the influences of the other factors. The use of means permitted tests for group differences in mean SAT performance after adjustment for modeled influences—socioeconomic background, achievement, and extracurricular activities—on the SAT scores. We proceeded by fitting a series of measurement and structural models, starting with the most general—least constrained—model and moving on to more specific models that assume invariant relationships that may or may not hold across all the subgroups of students.

Our initial model, model 1, fit a five-factor model to the nineteen measured variables within each of the eight student groups. This is the most general model, and in some ways the least interesting, though it does suggest that the underlying factors do account for the relationships among the observed variables. Table 7.6 presents the fit information for model 1, and for all of the other subsequent models we fit to these data. Three fit statistics are given for each model: the chi-square fit statistic and degrees of freedom, the root mean square error of approximation (RMSEA) (Steigler and Lind 1980), and the comparative fit index (CFI) (McDonald and Marsh 1990).

The "null" model in table 7.6 is the independence model needed for the calculation of the various fit indices, but is of little intrinsic interest. Model 1 provides a good fit, as indicated by the RMSEA and CFI indices. Again, these fit indices support the claim that five factors are sufficient to represent the nineteen measured variables in all groups.

Model 2 constrains model 1 by requiring that each measured variable load on one and only one underlying factor—constraining the cross-loading of an observed variable to more than one underlying factor. In model 2, however, two of the five factors are presumed to have nonzero loadings only for the SAT variables, with one factor representing SAT-V and the other SAT-M. This model, in short, specifies that the observed SAT verbal and mathematics scores represent the latent factors of verbal reasoning and mathematical reasoning. Table 7.6 gives the fit statistics for model 2. The overall fit is acceptable, as indicated by the RMSEA and CFI indices. Fur-

Table 7.6. Fit Statistics for Competing Structural Models

Model	Chi-square	df	RMSEA	CFI
Null	3862416	1368	—	—
(1) Meas. Model, Unconstrained loadings	87831	704	.045	.98
(2) Meas. Model, Congeneric	286713	1152	.064	.93
(3) Meas. Model, Invariant loadings	307133	1250	.062	.92
(4) Structural Model, Invariant loadings & paths	309145	1306	.062	.92
(5) Structural Model, Invariant loadings & paths	374822	1334	.068	.90
(6) Structural Model, Invariant loadings, paths partial invar. on intercepts	34637	1326	.065	.91

ther analyses suggest that the slight loss of fit in model 2 relative to model 1 results primarily from the sharp distinction between the extracurricular activities and high school achievement factors. We suspect, for example, that some of the observed variables in these factors may have nonzero loadings on *both* factors—academic achievement and ECAs—rather than only on one of the two. The variable HNRCNT, for example, which counts the number of honors courses taken, was constrained statistically to load only on the Extracurricular Activities factor in model 2, but we expected, nevertheless, that it has nonzero loadings on both the High School Achievement and Extracurricular Activities factors. The results, obviously, suggest that while the academic achievement–extracurricular activities distinction may not be as sharp as we had believed initially, the five-factor structure is, nevertheless, a good approximation of the relationships in our data.

Model 3 further restricts model 2 by forcing the loadings to be invariant across all eight subgroups. Apart from these invariance constraints, all other parameter matrices and estimates were expected to have the same structure as in model 2. Table 7.6 shows that the constraints introduced in model 3 do not degrade the fit of the model relative to model 2, suggesting that the factor loadings (or functional weights) can be presumed to be invariant without substantial loss of fit of the model. Clearly, the fit indices of these first three models provide confidence that a five-factor measurement model with invariant factor loadings fit the data reasonably well.

The next models we fit added restrictions on the relationships among the five underlying factors, creating a structural model that we then combined with the measurement model. Again, see figures 7.1 and 7.2 as representations of these hypothetical relationships.

Model 4, then, examines the invariance restrictions on the coefficients (the strength of relationship) of the paths among and between the underlying factors. The comparison between models 3 and 4 is a test of these invariance restrictions, that is, that the purported causal relationships among the latent factors are more or less the same across all the subgroups. Table 7.7 presents the estimates of the structural intercepts for SAT-M and SAT-V in each of the eight groups resulting from model 4.

The key comparison is between group differences on the intercept estimates in table 7.7, and group differences in the corresponding SAT means in table 7.1. To illustrate, table 7.1 reveals a difference of over 100 points on SAT-M between white and African American males. Further analyses show that the differences on SAT-M are only 50 points for the same groups. This reduction in score differences represents the impact of the statistical adjustment for socioeconomic background, high school achievement, and extracurricular activities. The remaining difference of 50 points represents a group difference in SAT-M

Table 7.7.   Intercept Estimates from Model 4

	Whites	Hispanics	African Americans	Asians
Males				
SAT-M	205	200	154	231
SAT-V	240	241	198	240
Females				
SAT-M	152	155	120	177
SAT-V	218	222	187	214

performance that is unexplained after adjustment for these three explanatory factors.

For example, the SAT-M and SAT-V mean differences between Hispanic and white males is essentially eliminated by the adjustment for the explanatory factors. In contrast, the gender difference on SAT-M in table 7.1 within the white, Hispanic, and Asian groups is smaller than the SAT-V gender difference within these groups. Here the adjustment for the explanatory factors served to widen the gender difference, rather than eliminate it. The basis for this finding lies in the complex pattern of gender differences on the socioeconomic background, high school achievement, and extracurricular activities variables in table 7.1. Females score higher on the high school achievement variables and on most of the extracurricular activities variables. The results suggest that after adjusting for the females' higher scores on these academic variables, we expected to see an even larger gender difference on the SAT-M than we found in the unadjusted population of males and females. The higher academic performance of the females in the unadjusted population serves to reduce the average gender difference on SAT-M. Once this higher academic performance is attenuated via statistical adjustment, the SAT-M score difference in favor of males is increased.

Model 5 is identical to model 4 with the exception that now the structural intercepts (the latent means of the SAT-V and SAT-M scores) are constrained to be invariant across all groups. This restriction suggests that after adjusting for socioeconomic background, high school achievement, and extracurricular activities, there are no group differences in expected or mean SAT scores. If model 5 fits well, we may be able to explain the observed group differences in SAT performance in terms of group differences on the three underlying factors in our theory-based structural model. Obviously, model 5 is particularly important for this reason, and its fit must be carefully examined.

Table 7.6 shows that while there is some global loss of fit associated with the invariance restrictions on the structural intercepts noted above, the overall fit is still reasonably good. A more detailed look at the fit of model 5 suggested that it does not fit perfectly, but the important question is whether the fit is below an acceptable threshold in any of the groups. Further inspection of the SAT-V and SAT-M means within each of the eight groups revealed that the African American SAT means are substantially lower than would be predicted by model 5. The discrepancy is around one-half of a standard deviation (50 points) for both males and females, on both the SAT-M and SAT-V score scales. This discrepancy suggests that while the invariance restrictions imposed in model 5 may not reduce the fit of the model globally, the restrictions are too stringent for the African American group. The key conclusion is that after adjustment for the socioeconomic background, academic achievement, and extracurricular activities latent variables, the African American students—both males and females—continue to score lower on SAT-V and SAT-M than would be expected by model 5.

The final model, model 6, relaxes the invariance restrictions on the structural intercepts for African American males and females in model 5. The remaining six ethnic/gender groups are restricted to invariance on the structural intercepts, as in model 5. All other parameter restrictions in model 5 are retained in model 6. As shown in table 7.6, the global fit indices improve slightly with the loosening of the restrictions on the structural intercepts for the African American groups. Given this improvement, model 6 is preferred to model 5.

Parameter Estimates

The standardized path coefficient estimates are based on model 6. The standardization uses a common metric across the eight groups, permitting the creation of a single set of standardized estimates. As revealed by these estimates, which are presented as the path coefficients in figure 7.3, the direct impact of extracurricular activities on SAT-V and SAT-M is larger than that of academic achievement levels.

Further, a unit change, a standard deviation difference, in the extracurricular activities latent variable produces a 45-point increase in SAT mathematics scores, and a 53-point change in SAT verbal scores. In contrast, a unit change in socioeconomic status (roughly equivalent to a $20,000 increment in family income, for example) only results in a 16-point increase in SAT verbal and mathematics scores. The direct impact of students' socioeconomic background variable is relatively small, but has indirect relations to SAT scores in the path model also. The squared multiple correlations for SAT-V ($R^2 = .49$) and SAT-M ($R^2 = .57$), an index of the explanatory power of the structural model, suggest that the structural model provides a reasonably good fit to the SAT score data. Though the squared multiple correlations are

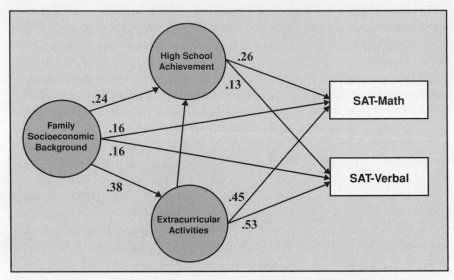

Figure 7.3.   Path Model of Effects of Family Background, High School Achievement, and Extracurricular Activites on SAT Verbal and Math Scores.

somewhat lower for African Americans, the structural model in figure 7.3, in general, accounts for about half of the variance in the SAT scores.

CONCLUSION

The application of structural modeling techniques to these data from the College Board's SAT was revealing, and supports several important conclusions. First, the measurement model holds across all eight subgroups of college-bound students. Second, the structural model is useful and informative for representing the relationships among and between the socioeconomic and academic factors and SAT scores, irrespective of race and gender. Third, with the exception of the African Americans, subgroup differences on the SAT-M and SAT-V are explained by group differences on the socioeconomic background factor, the academic achievement factor, and the extracurricular activities factor. The somewhat poorer fit of the model for African American students suggests that the model may have to be expanded to include variables and indicators of the quality of the high schools that students attend. Given the historical patterns of racial segregation in housing and educational opportunities in the United States, it would be surprising indeed if one generic model would fit this particular group of American students.

The results of this study, we contend, are methodologically stronger than most concerning the influences of extracurricular activities on high-stakes tests (see Marsh and Kleitman [2002] for a more detailed discussion of the rigor of research on this topic). Like other investigators (Camp 1990; Gerber 1996; Holloway 2000; Marsh and Kleitman 2002), our study provides compelling evidence from the SAT, a national high-stakes test, that participation in extracurricular activities provides all students—including students from disadvantaged backgrounds, minorities, and those with otherwise less-than-distinguished academic achievements in high school—a measurable and meaningful gain in their college admission test scores. The important reasoning abilities measured by tests like the SAT, evidently, are indeed developed both in and out of the classroom. To paraphrase Marsh and Kleitman (2002), participation in extracurricular activities in high school appears to be one of the few interventions that benefit low-status, disadvantaged students—those less well served by traditional educational programs—as much or more than their more advantaged peers.

Although we cannot conclude definitively from our research whether the relationship between participation in extracurricular activities and the observed increases in SAT scores is causal, the reliance on strong measurement models and large, closely matched subgroups of students certainly suggests that we may be detecting a meaningful effect in these data. Further research is needed to address the limitations inherent in this study—self-selection effects, motivation, and the qualitative differences of schools, among them. Nevertheless, given the growing body of evidence suggesting the beneficial effects associated with participating in extracurricular activities at both the elementary and secondary education levels, we remain optimistic.

REFERENCES

Camp, W. 1990. Participation in student activities and achievement: A covariance structural analysis. *Journal of Educational Research* 83:272–78.

Everson, H. T., and G. Michna. 2004. Is the SAT a wealth test? The influence of family income, ethnicity and high school achievement on SAT scores. Paper presented at a colloquium sponsored by the Institute for Urban and Minority Education, January, Teachers College, Columbia University, New York.

Everson, H. T., R. E. Millsap, and R. Diones. 1995. Exploring group differences in SAT performance using structural equation modeling with latent means. Paper presented at the annual meeting of the American Educational Research Association, April, San Francisco, CA.

Gerber, S. 1996. Extracurricular activities and academic achievement. *Journal of Research and Development in Education* 30(1): 42–50.

Holland, A., and T. Andre. 1987. Participation in extracurricular activities in secondary school: What is known, what needs to be known? *Review of Educational Research* 57: 437–66.

Holloway, J. H. 1999/2000. Extracurricular activities: The path to academic success. *Educational Leadership* (December/January). Arlington, VA: Association for Supervision and Curriculum Development.

Marsh, H. 1992. Extracurricular activities: Beneficial extension of the traditional curriculum or subversion of academic goals? *Journal of Educational Psychology* 84(4): 553–62.

Marsh, H. W., and S. Kleitman. 2002. Extracurricular school activities: The good, the bad, and the nonlinear. *Harvard Educational Review* 72(4): 464–514.

McDonald, R. P., and H. W. Marsh. 1990. Choosing a multivariate model: Noncentrality and goodness of fit. *Psychological Bulletin* 107:247–55.

Steigler, J. H., and A. Lind. 1980. Statistically based tests for the number of common factors. Paper presented at the annual meeting of the Psychometric Society, Iowa City, IA.

U.S. Department of Education. 2003. *Identifying and implementing educational practices supported by rigorous research: A user friendly guide*. Washington, DC: Institute for Education Sciences.

8

Supplementary Education, the Negotiation of Sociocultural Marginality, and the Uses of Reflexivity

Aundra Saa Meroe

Educational research across the disciplines of anthropology, psychology, and sociology has identified a constellation of attitudes, experiences, and practices relevant to patterns in the distribution of educationally relevant capital resources and scholastic achievement among ethnic minority and lower-SES (socioeconomic status) students. Such studies demonstrate that, in the course of negotiating the burdens and nuances of social stratification, these students' careers of social belonging, identity and worldview construction, and cultural consumption may be strongly correlated with either academic disidentification or engagement. While it is nearly inconceivable for any student to thrive in the midst of the insufficient school-based resources found in many of the public institutions serving ethnic minority and poor communities (e.g., curricular materials, course offerings, student-teacher ratios, teacher preparedness, academic peer networks, etc.), when the necessary elements are made accessible through interactive modes of support and tutelage, ethnic minority students can come to embrace academic achievement as a viable means for being in the world—even as the long-term struggles for social justice continue.

A number of social theorists have offered insights well suited for the dilemmas faced by students who may be at risk for academic disengagement and whose perceptions of sociocultural affiliation and political-economic resources are pivotal to the realization of their life chances. In particular, the commentaries of W. E. B. Du Bois and Georg Simmel provide characterizations of and challenges to conventional wisdom regarding social status and making one's place in the social landscape as an "outsider."

125

OUTSIDER CONSCIOUNESS: DU BOIS AND SIMMEL

In "Double-Consciousness and the Veil" (the first chapter of *The Souls of Black Folk* (1903), Du Bois addresses the quandary of reconciling the right to self-development and self-determination in the face of "doors of Opportunity closed roughly":

> This, then, is the end of his striving: to be a co-worker in the kingdom of culture, to escape both death and isolation, to husband and use his best powers and his latent genius. These powers of body and mind have in the past been strangely wasted, dispersed or forgotten. . . . Here in America, the few days since Emancipation, the black man's turning hither and thither in hesitant and doubtful striving has often made his very strength to lose effectiveness, to seem like absence of power, like weakness, and yet it is not weakness—it is the contradiction of double aims. (Du Bois 1989/1903, 2)

The intellectual, psychological, and spiritual burdens posed by the "warring ideals in one dark body" are taken up by Georg Simmel as the dance between alienation from and intimacy with others within modern social life. Furthermore, as multiple ethnic and SES groups interact, members of oppressed and marginalized communities, whom Simmel refers to as "the stranger[s]," will experience another sort of double consciousness whereby one takes a critical distance not only from everyday interactions but also from the dominant values within a particular society: "The stranger will thus not be considered here in the usual sense of the term, as a wanderer who comes today and goes tomorrow, but rather as the man who comes today and stays tomorrow. . . . This freedom, which permits the stranger to experience and treat even his close relationships as though from a bird's eye view, contains many dangerous possibilities" (Georg Simmel 1971/1908, 149).

Almost a century later, Du Bois's and Simmel's characterizations of the dilemmas and advantages of sociocultural marginality—albeit rhetorically cast in terms of "the ethnic man"—still resonate with the existential stances of people thrown into societies that may be hostile (or at best complacent) with regard to egalitarian integration. For Du Bois, the endeavors of the darker-hued "other" are diminished by the seeming contradictions between allegiance to one's (marginalized) ethnic experiences and the norms and institutions of those ethnic groups best represented by the hegemonic U.S. culture. For Simmel, the "strangeness" of the Jew within the context of European anti-Semitism lends an advantageous, and potentially subversive, perspective from the societal borderlands.[1]

The postures evoked by Du Boisian "double consciousness" and Simmel's "stranger" allow for an understanding of certain dimensions of the struggle for psychic/material well-being on the part of many members of ethnic minority groups. Educational institutions, often contentious spheres of civil societal discourse and practice (Gramsci 1971), are cultural spaces within which "the contradiction of double aims" and marginality emerge repeatedly as people vie for access to social goods and power. Regardless of—or precisely because of—the resounding consensus that "knowledge" and intellectual development are human/social goods, educational institutions are typically sites of considerable competition, exclusion, regimentation, stratification, and surveillance. As such, one's place within academic settings can bear a strong relation to understanding and making one's place in larger society. When Oliver Cox reminds us that "undoubtedly the most persistent menace to the peace and good order of the classes was the rise of popular education" (1948, 340), he is referring to the potential of educational exposure to translate into higher aspirations for life chances on the part of the poor and subjugated. Cox's observation is a more provocative view of John Dewey's famous identification of the "deeper" democratic ideal in education as "the extension in space of the number of individuals who participate in an interest so that each has to refer his own action to that of others, and to consider the action of others to give point and direction to his own, is equivalent to the breaking down of those barriers of class, race, and national territory" (1916, 101). Nevertheless, we know that, to date, such projections for the liberatory role of education and the promise of democratic practice have been only partially realized in limited sectors of U.S. society. In turn, the prognosis of this social project is found in the education of our youngest citizens.

Du Bois's observations may be used to posit that part of what appears as a weakness among some ethnic minority and lower-SES students may be attributable to the conflicts between ethnocultural belonging and alienated achievement[2] within various fields of power. Alternatively, one potential tactic for transcending these conflicts can be gleaned from Simmel's description of the negotiative savvy of strangerhood. That is, one can recognize the extent of one's social marginality within larger society while nevertheless pursuing any availed access to empowerment and influence. To stand a degree apart from the dominant and implicit norms of a society does not always give rise to isolation and meaninglessness. The stranger can discern what is necessary and what is superfluous to physical and psychological survival. And, as Simmel indicates, this stance of informed rupture from the taken-for-granted presents "dangerous possibilities" to the status quo.[3]

CULTURAL-STRUCTURAL NEGOTIATION AND RESOURCE ORCHESTRATION

The larger conditions of socioeconomic stratification, subordination, and injustice lie within conventional practices and resource distribution but are inscribed in neither stone nor genetic code. In tandem with economic, political, health, cultural, and social capital (among others), the human capital resources born of academic/intellectual development are arguably among the most central "assets," and in many cases, those most subject to our influence and intention (see, for example, Becker 1994; Friedman 1962; Wilson 1999). Our considerations of these sociocultural phenomena, situated within inequitable conditions of educational inputs across urban, suburban, and rural communities in the United States, demand multifaceted interventions that attend to individual and interpersonal practices as well as structural constraints and shortcomings.

My colleagues Gordon and Bridglall's theoretical and programmatic prescriptions for supplementary education (see chapters 2, 3, 9, and 16 in this volume) are directly concerned with the amelioration of capital resource deprivation, multicultural negotiation, academic/intellectual development, and the fostering of individual and community resilience. Taking some distance from academic and lay discourses on reform within traditional educational institutions, Gordon points to resources beyond the confines of the school that nevertheless influence academic performance. In accord with Bourdieu (1986) and Coleman (1990) among others, Gordon "demystifies" the disparities in academic achievement among ethnic groups by citing the strong contributions of background resources (e.g., material, social, psychological, ideational, etc.).

Moving beyond the mere identification of such resources, Gordon promotes an agenda that aims to (1) increase resource availability, and (2) neutralize the contradiction of Du Bois's specified double aims by taking a step outside of (hegemonic) educational institutions' monopolization of the values and modes of intellectual development. For Gordon, then, supplementary education is a domain whereby underserved ethnic minority communities may ethically, instrumentally, and politically claim academic achievement as a means for sociopolitical and economic empowerment. At the same time, Gordon's support of supplementary education echoes Simmel's observation that one need not be fully assimilated into the heart of dominant cultural forms for survival.

Having begun with a few of the views of Du Bois and Simmel regarding social marginality and Cox and Dewey's hopes for the democratic potential of education, this chapter will continue to sketch the promise of supplementary education by forging a rapprochement between the social science literature on academic inequities and ethnic minority underachievement, on the one hand, and relevant social theoretical perspectives on the interdependence among power, social status, and education as existential, cultural, and political endeavors on the other. Within this framework, Gordon's agenda for supplementary education is argued to speak to the issue of power in its myriad manifestations as it represents a practical engagement and reflexive disposition in relation to institutionalized education.

INEQUITABLE ACCESS AND SUPPORT

Educational inequity with regard to the poor and ethnic minorities in the United States has long been both colloquially acknowledged and academically documented (Berliner and Biddle 1995; Coleman and Hoffer 1987; Darling-Hammond 1998; Kozol 1991; Miller 1995; Weinberg 1977). People of color and many persons in lower-SES groups have endured a lengthy history of overt exclusion from high-quality educational inputs and resources as well as overexposure to more insidious modes of discouragement and underpreparation within educational institutions (Darling-Hammond 1998; Kozol 1991; Oakes 1985). Central indicators found in an array of standardized measures, grade point averages, and rates of secondary and postsecondary graduation demonstrate that, in general, many students of color are in special need of additional supports and interventions (see Berliner and Biddle 1995; Miller 1995; Steinberg 1996).

Data on the educational opportunities and achievement patterns of non-Asian American ethnic minorities predictably mirror the data for students of lower-SES groups, as these subpopulations largely overlap. In terms of the quality of schooling received, levels of educational attainment, and the quality of achievement, we have ample evidence that many children of color suffer from inadequate "opportunities to learn." In particular, compared to high-achieving Asian American and European American students, African American, Caribbean American, and Latin American students are underexposed to effective teaching staff, hospitable and supportive school environments (with regard to administration, teaching, and counseling staff and student peers), and they enjoy limited access to challenging curricula, instructional aids, and supplementary educational experiences and exercises (Darling-Hammond 1998; Oakes 1985). Students from low-SES and/or ethnic minority groups are more likely to be tracked into lower-skilled and remedial classes and to attend schools with less-experienced teachers, larger student populations and class sizes, greater ratios of students to teachers, and student populations that are predominantly poor (Cordero-Guzman 1997; Darity 1997; Darling-Hammond 1998; Hanushek 1989; McQuillan 1997; Miller 1995; Oakes 1985).

Statistics on the quality of academic achievement and educational attainment mirror the inequities with regard to opportunities to learn. The students most likely to drop out of high school are overrepresented among the lowest SES groups and African American and Hispanic American communities (Darling-Hammond 1998; Jordan, Lara, and McPartland 1996; Nakanishi and Nishida 1995; Rumberger and Larson 1998; Secada et al. 1998; Trueba 1989; Valencia 1991). At the levels of higher education, most Asian/Pacific Islander American groups are more likely to attend four-year colleges, followed by European Americans, African Americans, Hispanic Americans, and American Indians (Darling-Hammond 1998; Miller 1995; Nakanishi and Nishida 1995).

Data on the quality of achievement via standardized measures demonstrate that the general socioeconomic characteristics of students' neighborhoods, peer groups, and school populations have strong and positive relationships with individual achievement (Caldas and Bankston 1997). Mathematics and reading proficiency scores decrease commensurate with declines in reported levels of parental educational attainment and income. Additionally, among most nationwide and interethnic comparisons of mathematics and language/reading scores, Asian/Pacific Islander Americans tend to be represented at the high end of the distribution followed by European American, African American, Hispanic American, and Native American students (Cordero-Guzman 1997; Darling-Hammond 1998; Hao and Bonstead-Bruns 1998; Miller 1995; Nakanishi and Nishida 1995; National Center for Education Statistics 1996; Steinberg 1996; Valencia 1991).

Since the 1970s, steady and significant progress has been made by ethnic minorities in the United States (see Berliner and Biddle 1995; Darling-Hammond 1998; Miller 1995) as the achievement levels and rates of high school graduation and postsecondary matriculation have increased among African Americans, Hispanic Americans, and Native Americans. Nevertheless, these achievement levels are insufficient in light of present labor market demands and increasing competition for material and symbolic capital resources. While there are a number of intergenerational/historical and present-day factors for these achievement disparities, our intention is to explore strategies for learning from the structural, cultural, and interpersonal challenges of the past and present while forging new agendas for future gains.

SOCIOECONOMIC CONSIDERATIONS

There are many reflections of socioeconomic landscapes and cultural maneuvers in ethnic minority underachievement, particularly dialogues between discrimination and disidentification. The interpenetrating legacies of class inequality and racist and sexist discrimination are reflected in particular material, cultural, and psychological barriers to academic achievement among ethnic minority and lower-SES communities in the United States. Disparities within the distribution of a variety of human capital resources (i.e., financial, political, social, etc.) undergird a sociopolitical topography of conditions, dispositions, and practices that frustrate academic attainment and foster academic disidentification among many of our students. This is especially troubling in light of the political climate fostered during the tenure of the "New Right" leadership of Reagan and the Bush dynasty, the centrist policies of the Clinton administration, and cultural trends that appear to slip between the earlier modernist "age of anxiety" and a postmodern vulnerability to ambivalence and disjuncture (Kumar 1995).

The Socioeconomic Playing Field

The implications of these trends in the reproduction and distribution of educationally derived cultural capital are also intensified by their contextualization within the market forces of the past thirty years. The multinational exportation of industry and manufacturing jobs in a globalized economy demands that members of lower-SES groups compete for jobs in the information and service sectors alongside members of the middle classes who are comparatively better situated in terms of educational opportunity and social networks (Brown 1995; Wilson 1987). The lower-skilled jobs within these labor sectors tend not only to be less lucrative in terms of salary and benefits but also are more vulnerable to downsizing and part-time contracting in the tides of economic recession and unemployment patterns (Brown 1995; McLaren and Farahmandpur 2000; Wilson 1987, 1991). Furthermore, in spite of hopeful pronouncements that the laborers of the twenty-first century will increasingly be characterized by greater levels of skill and expertise, corporate contestants within the globalized marketplace can still make profitable use of relatively unskilled labor by choosing from among those new industrial countries that offer the lowest standards of worker protection (Brown and Lauder 1996).

In tandem with state and federal legislation that continues to dismantle the social welfare policies and services initiated to diminish (or at least ameliorate) longtime social inequalities, a "meritocratic" ethos of individualism and free-market competition has flourished (Brown 1995).[4] In our era of moderate integration, communities of color have witnessed the disintegration of supportive intragroup institutions and social networks across SES levels as more privileged members have migrated out of ethnic enclaves. Meanwhile, the restricted prospects for gainful employment, the intensified localization of extreme poverty in the central cities of the Northeast and the Midwest, and the breakdown of socially mediated "labor-force attachment" (Wilson 1987, 1991) have strained the apparent logic of "effort optimism" (Ogbu 1994) and educational attainment as a gateway to wider career options (e.g., Wilson 1987, 1991).

Subcultural Maneuvers and Conventions

As Wilson (1991) and Ogbu (1994) argue, these larger structural trends may be linked to developments in the subcultures of the students with whom we are most concerned. However, we should clearly distinguish the particular assumptions of Wilson's and Ogbu's respective positions. Wilson is likely to cite new extremes of poverty, social dislocation, and the out-migration of the middle class as causal factors in the *recent* phenomena of African American students' underachievement. On the other hand, Ogbu insists that *throughout* the history of school desegregation and compensatory education, African American students—across SES groups—have academically underperformed in comparison to many Asian American and European American students (also see Miller 1995; Steinberg 1996).

For Ogbu, the central issues involve the policies and everyday practices of racial stratification in education and "community forces"—that is, the perceptions and responses of African Americans to racist oppression. These community forces manifest in three forms: (1) an instrumental adaptation that reveals severe doubts concerning the rewards of educational attainment (even as the folk rhetoric extols the importance of education); (2) a symbolic adaptation that equates academic achievement with assimilation and the dissolution of cultural identity; and (3) a relational adaptation that engenders mistrust of school officials (of any ethnicity) and perceives a causal relationship between academic/professional achievement and community abandonment.

Cornel West (1993) suggests that the diffusion of sociopolitical solidarity (especially among the poor, "people of color," and African Americans in particular), in the face of the continuing onslaughts of economic hardship and racism, occurs alongside the development of an ethos of "nihilism" whereby cultural/historical and community standards of conduct and collective values are abandoned or equivocated. The nihilism evidenced especially within present-day youth subcultures has a curiously antidemocratic Nietzschean bent as it coincides with a pursuit of individualistic heroics. That is, in the course of further assimilation into mainstream American culture (and particularly its undercurrents of anti-intellectualism and tepid class consciousness), there is a widespread devaluing of "straight" academic and career pursuits in favor of the fairly "impossible dreams" of notoriety in the athletic or entertainment industries.

In general terms, the tendency for apathy among students is related to a number of factors, many of which occur outside the school environment. Robert Steinberg's (1996) research demonstrates that high-achieving students are more likely to have parents who, from early in the child's development, use an authoritarian style, demonstrate consistent interest in their child's schooling activities, emphasize the importance of hard work, and hold high expectations for their child's school performance. Similarly, comparisons between high- and low-achieving students predictably report that successful students spend more time doing homework and other intellectually stimulating activities as opposed to watching television, taking on time-consuming after-school employment, and spending unstructured time with academically disengaged peers (Steinberg 1996). In another vein, Bloom (1985) argues that the development of exceptionally talented young people depends upon the strong support and encouragement of parents and the child's ongoing participation in extracurricular programs and practices that enhance the mastery of necessary skills.

There are ethnic differences in terms of cultural, familial, and peer group orientations to educational achievement that may partially explain discrepancies in education attainment (Coleman 1988; Fordham and Ogbu 1986; Fuligni 1997; Hao and Bonstead-Bruns 1998; Rumberger and Larson 1998; Sun 1998). For example, in comparison to other immigrant and native-born groups, Asian/ Pacific Islander immigrant parents and children have higher expectations for academic achievement (e.g., higher grades and levels of educational attainment) (Fuligni 1997; Hao and Bonstead-Bruns 1998; Keith et al. 1998). Such parents are more likely to contribute a greater percentage of their financial resources to educational aids and savings for future college education, to believe that future economic rewards follow high achievement, to attribute academic success to effort (rather than innate ability), and therefore to expect their children to spend more time on schoolwork (Chen and Lan 1998; Hao and Bonstead-Bruns 1998; Schneider and Lee 1990; Sun 1998). In accord with parental dictates, these students are more likely to belong to peer groups who value academic achievement, report more engagement in classroom exercises, participate in cooperative learning strategies, attribute academic success to expended effort, and as a result, spend roughly twice as much time as other students on school assignments (Caplan, Choy, and Whitmore 1991; Fuligni 1997; Steinberg 1996; Steinberg, Dornbusch, and Brown 1992; Sun 1998).

Mexican immigrant families may report more ambivalent stances regarding the prospects of long-term settlement in the United States, lower expectations for their children's education, and lower levels of parent-child interactions in terms of school-related matters (Hao and Bonstead-Bruns 1998; Steinberg 1996). The literature on African American peer cultures reports a widespread tendency to devalue academic achievement in a pattern resembling Willis's (1977) findings in his research on working-class British boys' antagonism to school mores and championing of manual labor. For subaltern young people, especially boys and young men (Graham, Taylor, and Hudley

1998; Osborne 1997), the identity politics of resistance often prescribe a construction of academic achievement as "white" (i.e., the loss of ethnic identity), antithetical to "keeping it real," and irrelevant to future career goals (Fordham and Ogbu 1986; E. T. Gordon, chapter 5; Mickelson 1990; Ogbu 1994). Similarly, African American students—and again, particularly boys and young men—are more at risk of "disidentifying" with school achievement in response to negative stereotypes regarding the intellectual prowess of people of African descent. In a somewhat unconscious move *not* to provide further evidence for such stereotypes, students may not invest as much effort in schoolwork (Osborne 1995, 1997; Steele 1997; Steele & Aronson, 1995).

On the other hand, studies by Steinberg (1996) find that African American and Hispanic American students largely support the belief that a successful academic record is related to a successful adult career. However, in comparison to Asian American and European American students, African American and Hispanic American students are more likely to assume that a poor academic record will *not* significantly influence their later job options. As Steinberg puts it, "It is undue optimism, not excessive pessimism, that may be holding Black and Hispanic students back in school" (1996, 91). At the same time, Steinberg (1996) argues that the tendency to disengage with school is not restricted solely to adolescents of color. The rationales that students develop in their devaluation of academic work may vary according to their subcultural or ethnic group membership, but as a larger phenomenon, underachievement and academic disidentification appear to be rather mainstream American trends—conventions in which ethnic minority students especially cannot afford to participate.[5]

Qualitative studies of high-achieving African American students have developed more detailed analyses of the developmental processes and interactions of ethnic, gender, and class identities. These researchers find that high-achieving African American students are more likely to find strategies for managing the disdain of "disidentified" peers and negotiating ethnic identities that incorporate ethnic pride, high values for academic success, and a keen awareness of racism (and sexism, in the case of females). Their efforts are facilitated by parental support, a family history of positive racial socialization, and supportive peer relations among other African American high achievers (Datnow and Cooper 1997; Hemmings 1998; Sanders 1997).

SOCIOCULTURAL CAPITULATION

There is always the danger that the examination and critiques (explicit or implicit) of particular subcultural values (e.g., "culture of poverty" theories found in Lewis 1966; Moynihan 1965) may be read as "victim blaming" (Lareau 1987; Ogbu 1994; West 1993; Wilson 1991) or "deficit models." Indeed, it is counterproductive to blame students of color for their academic underachievement and disidentification; nevertheless, we might acknowledge that students' rejections of prosocial academic values may be a naïve enactment of resistance against status quo conventions and values that, in effect, contribute to the reproduction of social stratification and the concentration of resources among middle- and upper-SES groups.[6] (See the description of Fulani's All Stars Talent Show Network program in chapter 10 of this volume.) The writings of Antonio Gramsci (1971) and Pierre Bourdieu (Bourdieu and Passeron 1977) are relevant to these issues of ethnic minority underachievement, cultural/identity politics, and access to various forms of resource acquisition and exchange. With specific attention to the institution of schooling, the critical theories of Gramsci and Bourdieu offer frameworks for tracing the relevance of everyday practices in education to the tensions that exist between one's complicity with and resistance against the re/production of social inequities.

Gramscian Thought and the "Informal Education" Movement

Sentenced to life imprisonment under the rule of Mussolini, a major concern of Gramsci, socialist leader and intellectual, had to do with making sense of how the oppressed working-class groups of early twentieth-century Italy came to choose fascism over the seemingly liberatory ideals of communism and socialism. Borrowing some of Marx and Engel's (e.g., *The German Ideology*, 1970) theoretical premises (but ultimately eschewing the premise of economic determinism), Gramsci developed the construct of "hegemony" that emphasized the role of worldviews ("ideology"), "commonsense" assumptions, and other cultural forms in either the maintenance or potential subversion of socioeconomic stratification. In his view, extreme deprivation and violent repression (i.e., "domination") were not the only or even the most effective means of reproducing patterns of socioeconomic power. A more important consideration was the extent to which dominated social groups might (explicitly or implicitly) consent to status quo conditions of injustice by adopting views that justify the unequal distribution of power. Corresponding to his definitions of domination as violent control and hegemony as ideological consent, Gramsci identifies two means of undermining discourses and structures of domination: (1) a war of maneuver and (2) a war of position. While the first option involves violent attacks against a centralized state (fairly obsolete under advanced capitalism), the second alternative involves sustained participation within spheres of civil society (e.g., family and ethnic group traditions, popular culture, media, educational and religious institutions, etc.).

Gramsci argued that intellectual development was central to development of discourses and effective "war of position" efforts that oppose the taken-for-granted notions of how society is and should be (i.e., "a counter-hegemony"). Gramsci, like many contemporary scholars, noted that the life experiences and perspectives of many young students are often radically different and even incompatible with the pedagogic principles and curricula of mainstream educational institutions (1971; see also E. T. Gordon's discussion of the range of cultural styles among African American young men, chapter 5). Nevertheless, Gramsci believed that it was important for students to be actively engaged in the school experience in order to become "a person capable of thinking, studying, and ruling" (1971, 40).

The ethos underlying his views on intellectual development has been a central catalyst for the "informal education" movement in the United Kingdom (Burke 1999). Building upon his proposals to link intellectual pursuits with everyday praxis and thereby developing a critical awareness of self and society, these "informal educators" have shared a commitment to encouraging a variety of intellectual practices within their communities since the mid-1970s. Informal educators are commonly staff members of community centers and church organizations and are trained in the provision of a number of social services. For example, children and adults may attend community centers to build upon literacy and mathematics skills (or even incorporate a math lesson in the weekly trip to the local market). Members of multicultural communities may gather together in completing a mural or a community newsletter. "Specialist informal educators" facilitate discussions and seminars about such topics as social justice and the democratic process, employment opportunities, family relations, healthy lifestyle choices, or money management. With special attention given to the needs of young people, educators set up "study circles" and "homework clubs," help students to understand mainstream school cultures and expectations, provide individual counseling, or encourage students to participate in political forums and forge cross-cultural alliances. Informal educators also act as mediators between parents and school staff and help both parties to respond to the particular needs of students (Jeffs and Smith 1999).

Bourdieu on the Reproduction of Capital

Bearing some resonance with Gramscian thought, much of Bourdieu's critical social theory—which includes a penetrating critique of academic institutions and practices (Bourdieu and Passeron 1977)—is concerned with explaining how everyday activities, belief systems, and conditions sustain and reproduce various forms of sociopolitical oppression. Through the notion of *habitus*, Bourdieu proposes an explanatory construct of the extent to which dominated persons maintain the conventions and structures of domination. Broadly speaking, Bourdieu argues that socioeconomic and political conditions shape our taken-for-granted perspectives, motives, goals, habits, interpersonal relations, and cultural practices, which, in turn, sustain the social and material reality of such conditions. In contrast to the seemingly neutral term of "socialization," Bourdieu's use of *habitus* heightens the implications of socialized behavior and perspectives by implying that even the food we consume, the clothing we wear, or the employment we seek is delimited by our understandings of what is typically possible according to our social status: "The dispositions durably inculcated by the possibilities and impossibilities, freedoms and necessities, opportunities and prohibitions inscribed in the objective conditions generate dispositions" whereby "the most improbable practices are therefore excluded, as unthinkable, by a kind of immediate submission to order that inclines agents to make a virtue of necessity, that is, to refuse what is anyway denied and to will the inevitable" (1990, 57).

In earlier years, Bourdieu and Passeron (1977) applied the term *reproduction* to explain discrepancies in academic achievement among students from different socioeconomic classes. Here, they point to the role of dispositions in guiding students' engagement with school:

> The disposition to make use of the School and the predispositions to succeed in it depend, as we have seen, on the objective chances of using it and succeeding in it that are attached to the different social classes, these dispositions and predispositions in turn constituting one of the most important factors in the perpetuation of the relationship between the educational system and the structure of class relations. Even the negative dispositions and predispositions leading to self-elimination, such as, for example, self-depreciation, devalorization of the school and its sanctions or resigned expectation of failure or exclusion may be understood as unconscious anticipation of the sanctions the School has in store for the dominated classes. (1977, 204–5)

Bourdieu and Passeron's (1977) analysis of the role of educational institutions and their cultural practices in the reproduction of social stratification is most useful as an incisive critique and "demystification" of extant circumstances as opposed to a deterministic model of prediction (Giroux 1983; Lareau 1987). In Bourdieu's (1990) own terminology, hegemonic institutions and practices are "structuring structures" that, in turn, depend upon corresponding dispositions among social actors. For instance, the empirical research of Lareau (1987) and Wells and Serna (1996), drawing upon much of Bourdieu's theoretical premises, provides examples of how it is that socially elite parents exhibit strategies and expectations that ensure that educational institutions work in their children's interests. These practices are successful largely because their modes of enacting school-family relationships mirror the expectations of school staff. While teachers and administrators bristle at harsh criticism and scrutiny, they do expect that parents will monitor their children's schoolwork, demand high academic achievement from their children, locate and provide supplements for their children's academic or personal weaknesses, and sustain partnerships with teaching staff.

While social elites have more resources to draw upon in fostering their children's development (e.g., disposable income, prestige, high levels of parents' educational attainment, etc.), they also employ practices that are not necessarily available solely to the middle and upper classes. For example, the ethnographic data of Lareau (1987) and Wells and Serna (1996) reveal that higher-status parents do not depend upon their children to inform them about the social climate and educational exercises of the school. These parents often investigate who the leading pupils are in their children's classes as well as their own children's particular rankings and tend to know many of the other parents in their children's schools. They are likely to research the educational and performance histories of their children's teachers and are aware of how to contact counselors and special education staff. Consequently, the acquisition of this information supports their ability to promote and protect their children's interests.

High-status parents appear to be less likely to make sharp distinctions in the division of labor with regard to the education of their children. That is, they are less likely to unilaterally assume that teachers provide the education while the parents provide food and shelter. Lareau also observed that these parents expected their children to spend leisure time in structured activities as opposed to peer-directed "free play"; while most parents regardless of SES expressed the desire that their children succeed in compulsory schooling, social elites are more likely to expect their children to attend college. In other words, "getting an education" went far beyond a high school/GED diploma.

Even though these dispositions are supported by the social experiences of the elite classes, it is conceivable that less-privileged parents can benefit from similar activities melded with a sociopolitical sophistication for thwarting patterns of social exclusion and supporting the needs of their often underserved children. The inclination for parents to over-entrust the education of their children to schools and for students to adopt attitudes of academic nonchalance is especially perilous for ethnic minority and lower-SES students, as competition for employment within a postindustrial labor market, increasingly oriented toward information and service industries, is increasingly tied to heightened requirements for academic credentials (see Brown 1995). Further, Brown (1995) argues that the request for higher levels of training and credentialization is paralleled by a tendency to make distinctions according to "charismatic" skills based upon implicit sociocultural codes and personality dispositions (also see Bourdieu's discussion of "distinction" and "taste" [1986]). In this light, parents should not only encourage academic achievement but also should impart to their children a nuanced understanding of and facility with the everyday techniques and micropolitics of "the presentation of self" within a social climate predisposed to racist, sexist, and classist stereotyping and stigmatization (Goffman 1959, 1963; also see Fulani's comments on "identity play," chapter 10).

Taking on Culture, "Knowledge," and Power

For Gramsci, the development of a counter-hegemony or cultural politics depends upon our ability to reflect upon what passes for common sense. In Bourdieu's (1990) theories of *habitus* and reproduction, a crisis in the course of everyday events can lead to critical reflection and reevaluation. Still, while Gramsci and Bourdieu warn against the dangers of passive consent, there is another dimension of reflexivity that allows us to engage with hegemonic discourse and customs without wholesale internalization. This bears relevance to the potential conflict between traditional curricula and pedagogies and the life worlds of ethnic minority children—especially in cases in which students reject the content of their schooling as alien and undesirable.

Reflexivity refers to a sense of self-awareness that goes beyond typical ascriptions of social identity, everyday practices, and ways of understanding the social world. To a certain extent, reflexivity entails that we interrogate the habitual until we no longer take our beliefs and activities for granted. Nonetheless, reflexivity does not assume that we abandon our long-held values or customs; rather, we should reflect upon the importance of these beliefs relative to other worldviews and practices that we might choose to reject upon inspection.

Sociologist Alvin Gouldner advocates a practice of intellectual reflexivity that can be applied to our considerations of how ethnic minority students and others might interface with the paradigms and values inculcated in mainstream educational institutions and simultaneously declaw the threat of losing one's ethnocultural and/or ethical integrity. Warning against the inclination to see knowledge as information—that is, as a body of "objective" facts

outside of human influence—Gouldner instead suggests that we approach
knowledge as *awareness*. This involves a will to understand the social world
within the context of our actions, desires, experiences, and values. Reflexivity, then, prescribes a heightened sensitivity to the extent to which all knowledge exists in a lived dialogue with our social experiences and positions.
Gouldner argues:

> The crux of the matter is that information is rarely neutral in its implications for
> men's purposes, hopes or values. Information tends to be experienced—even if
> not expressly defined—as either "friendly" or "hostile," as consonant or disso-
> nant with man's purposes. It is the relation of information to a man's purposes,
> not what it is "in itself," that makes information hostile or friendly. News of the
> stability of a government is hostile information to a revolutionary but friendly
> to a conservative. An openness to and a capacity to use hostile information is
> awareness. . . . This is inevitably linked, at some vital point, with an ability to
> know and to control the self in the face of threat. (1970, 494)

At the same time, this recognition of the interdependence between knowledge and social life and a willingness to be on intimate terms with a range of
understandings and perspectives ultimately contributes to our ability to com-
prehend and challenge what Foucault (1980) calls the effects of
"power/knowledge" in which "each society has its regime of truth, its 'general politics' of truth: that is, the types of discourse which it accepts and
makes function as true . . . the status of those who are charged with saying
what counts as true" (1980, 131).

Applying these perspectives on the everyday politics involved in the acquisition, employment, and production of knowledge[7] to the underachievement of ethnic minority and lower-SES students presents us with the following considerations. First, having undermined the assumption that knowledge
exchange is a neutral and disinterested social process, we then might construe
the political logic of maintaining inequitable access to intellective capital between ethnic and SES groups in the United States. Second, given that these
structural impediments to the fair distribution of educational inputs are accompanied by pervasive, "naturalizing" accounts for ethnic minority underachievement in popular discourse (e.g., genetic inferiority, cultures of
poverty, the inherent Asian or European affinity for academic achievement,
the litmus tests for "blackness," etc.), we can more effectively explain how
young people may come to divest academic excellence from their horizons of
everyday life. Finally, as academic disidentification in the twenty-first century precipitates economic, intellectual, political, and social disenfranchisement, one central task entails the disruption of these cycles of reproduction.
Supplementary education represents one such mode of resistance.

THE DEVELOPMENT OF STUDENT AND COMMUNITY RESILIENCE

Gordon's theoretical framework and practical proposal for supplementary education rests upon a triad of assertions about the relationship between historically marginalized ethnic groups and traditional educational institutions. First, after more than a century of constant struggle for educational equity, Gordon suggests that we continue to advocate for and implement quality educational inputs as we simultaneously acknowledge that the school alone cannot (and perhaps will not) adequately provide for the needs of our children. Second, concerned adults and students must develop facility with negotiating the resources and demands of the schools as well as with identifying alternative means for augmenting intellectual development outside the school setting. More specifically, the needs of traditionally underrepresented students require adequate access to basic resources and complementary supports made available to comparably privileged students. Third, the agenda of supplementary education involves the development of an individual, interpersonal, and communal (and benevolent) will to socioeconomic and political power in concert with intellectual development and multicultural appreciation and exchange.

Therefore, supplementary education encourages auxiliary practice in two areas by (1) enhancing students' ability to compete in mainstream academic disciplines, and (2) elaborating the family's and community's esteem for and facility with academic achievement in the context of their own cultural values. Ultimately, the practice of supplementary education is a complex set of strategies for strengthening the resilience of communities struggling against cultural, economic, and political disenfranchisement. Supplementary education targets four issues central to countering the educational underdevelopment of many minority children and young adults: (1) the importance of an adequate base of human resource capital; (2) the importance of a sense of the cultural and political relevance of academic/intellectual experience and practice; (3) the role of mentors and guides in the pursuit of intellectual and personal development; and (4) the development and elaboration of extra-school orientations, supports, and activities typically available to more privileged social classes in the United States. (For detailed discussions, see chapters 2, 3, 5, 9, and 10; also see Greeno 2002.)

THE DEVELOPMENT OF RESILIENCE

Within the discipline of psychology, the construct of resilience refers to personal characteristics, interpersonal processes, environmental conditions, and individual and socially mediated repertoires and skills that facilitate positive adaptation and development in spite of individual disabilities, ongoing stressors, and traumatic life events. Thus, those features that would lead us to identify a person or social environment as resilient typically would be antithetical to the indicators of "at-risk" status (Cicchetti and Lynch 1995; Garmezy 1976; Hetherington 1989; Masten, Best, and Garmezy 1990; Pines 1979; Pynoos, Steinberg, and Wraith 1995; Rutter 1985).

Gordon's (Arroyo and Gordon 1998; Gordon and Song 1994) particular use of the construct of resiliency stretches beyond traditional psychological models of these phenomena to suggest an intentional praxis embodied within an attitude of ethical, political, and social resistance. In this model, sociopolitical conditions of relative deprivation (in terms of multiple forms of capital resources) are central factors in the vulnerability of ethnic minority and poor children. Another dimension that distinguishes this model of resilience from typically individualistic models is its emphasis on interpersonal relationships in the nurturance of perspectives and dispositions that protect against apathy, helplessness, and social alienation.

Gordon and Song's (1994) and Arroyo and Gordon's (1998) analyses of data collected from high-achieving African Americans suggest that the "defiance of negative prediction" (i.e., achieving in spite of significant barriers) is founded upon a confluence of factors ranging from individuals' constructions of reality to the availability of a number of material and social conditions. For example, common features among respondents' reported histories of developmental experiences consistently indicate the presence of interpersonal and material resource supports for learning and achievement. Relevant interpersonal support includes parallel or hierarchical networking and meaningful relationships with significant others who fulfill the role of mentors or models for high achievement.

"Individual" characteristics that seem to predict resilience include (a) the persistent pursuit of socially acceptable goals and an ongoing positive evaluation of such goals; (b) autonomy and self-directedness; (c) an existential orientation favoring an internal locus of control and subjective attributions that neutralize or transform objectively limiting circumstances into irrelevancies or challenges; (d) an understanding of the historical precedents and present conditions related to various forms of socioeconomic and political oppression; and (e) belief systems that ground these individual efforts within the grace of divine providence or the embrace of community. Integrating this notion of resilience with his proposals for supplementary education, Gordon suggests interventions that transform children's experiences of academic and personal development and involve parents, siblings, peers, and other community members in the development of personal and collective dispositions and practices. Supplementary education efforts are concerned with identifying and elaborating upon individual and interpersonal characteristics, processes, and structural contexts. It enhances resiliency in various social institutions (e.g., academic institutions and the workplace), family, peer-group, and community life and helps socioeconomic and political enfranchisement.

The development of resilience and resistance entails more than a reactive disavowal of norms and habits that reinforce the disengagement and underdevelopment of students of color. In proactive terms, supplementary education aims to prepare more people to join the students, families, and community members who already are *pursuing the unexpected* with regard to high academic and personal development and communal interdependence and solidarity. As demonstrated by the variety of perspectives found in this volume, supplementary education for the enhancement of ethnic minority achievement can take innumerable forms. Even so, the successful realization of these efforts depends upon our ability to reveal and attempt to dismantle the impact of structural inequities as well as the tacit assumptions and habits that contribute to inefficacy within the educational sphere.

Still, the will to academic and intellectual achievement must not be relegated to the acquisition of credentials solely as a means for gainful employment or social mobility. Intellectual and personal development reaps benefits that go far beyond individualist and free-market profiteering. The ability to avoid co-optation into exploitative social structures by taking critical distance from status quo values and developing savvy for negotiating the rules of engagement with central institutions of capital resource distribution can be critical to effecting structural transformation (e.g., landmark Supreme Court rulings with regard to ethnic and gender discrimination). A holistic incorporation of academic achievement and intellective development within the everyday practices of home and community life can endow students with the facilities to maneuver within—*and beyond*—the necessary mythologies and conventions of American meritocracy.

REFERENCES

Arroyo, C., and E. W. Gordon. 1998. Risk and protective processes among minority children: A meta-analytic review. In *Developmental perspectives on risk and psychopathology*, edited by S. Luthar, J. Burack, D. Cicchetti, and J. Weisz. New York: Cambridge University Press.

Becker, G. 1994. *Human capital: A theoretical and empirical analysis with special reference to education*. Chicago: University of Chicago Press.

Berliner, D., and B. Biddle. 1995. *The manufactured crisis: Myths, fraud, and the attack on America's public schools*. New York: Addison-Wesley.

Bloom, B. S., ed. 1985. *Developing talent in young people*. New York: Ballantine.

Bourdieu, P. 1986. The forms of capital. In *Handbook of theory and research for the sociology of education*, edited by J. Richardson, 241–58. Westport, CT: Greenwood.

———. 1990. *The logic of practice*. Stanford: Stanford University Press.

Bourdieu, P., and J. C. Passeron. 1977. *Reproduction in education, society and culture*. London: Sage.

Brown, P. 1995. Cultural capital and social exclusion: Some observations on recent trends in education, employment and the labour market. *Work, Employment and Society* 9(1): 29–51.

Brown, P., and H. Lauder. 1996. Education, globalization and economic development. *Journal of Education Policy* 11(1): 1–25.

Burke, A. 1999. *Communications and development: A practical guide*. London: Department for International Development.

Caldas, S., and C. Bankston. 1997. Effect of school population socioeconomic status on individual academic achievement. *Journal of Educational Research* 90(5): 269–77.

Caplan, N., M. H. Choy, and J. K. Whitmore. 1991. *Children of the boat people: A study of educational success*. Ann Arbor: University of Michigan Press.

Chen, H., and W. Lan. 1998. Adolescents' perceptions of their parents' academic expectations: Comparison of American, Chinese-American, and Chinese high school students. *Adolescence* 33(130): 385–90.

Cicchetti, D., and M. Lynch. 1995. Failures in the expectable environment and their impact on individual development: The case of child maltreatment. In *Developmental psychopathology: Vol. 2. Risk, disorder, and adaption*, edited by D. Cicchetti and D. Cohen, 32–71. New York: Wiley.

Coleman, J. 1988. Social capital in the creation of human capital. *American Journal of Sociology* 94 (supp.): S95–S120.

———. 1990. *Foundations of social theory*. Cambridge, MA: Belknap Press.

Coleman, J., and T. Hoffer. 1987. *Public and private high schools: The impact of communities*. New York: Basic.

Cordero-Guzman, H. 1997. Why do some children score higher than others? An empirical study of the role of the family, school, and community level resources on racial/ethnic differences in standardized test scores (AFQT). Paper presented at the National Economic Association.

Cox, O. C. 1948. *Caste, class and race*. New York: Modern Reader.

Darity, W. 1997. Programmed retardation and the theory of noncompeting groups. Unpublished monograph.

Darling-Hammond, L. 1998. Unequal opportunity: Race and education. *Brookings Review* 16(2): 28–32.

Datnow, A., and R. Cooper. 1997. Peer networks of African American students in independent schools: Affirming academic success and racial identity. *Journal of Negro Education* 66(1): 56–72.

Derrida, J. 1978. Force and signification. In *Writing and Difference*. Chicago: University of Chicago.

Dewey, J. 1916. *Democracy and education: An introduction to the philosophy of education*. New York: Macmillan.

Du Bois, W. E. B. 1989/1903. *The souls of black folk*. New York: Bantam.

Fordham, S., and J. Ogbu. 1986. Black students' school success: Coping with the burden of acting white. *Urban Review* 18:176–206.

Foucault, M. 1980. *Power/knowledge: Selected interviews and other writings, 1972–1977*. New York: Pantheon.

Friedman, M. 1962. *Capitalism and freedom*. Chicago: University of Chicago Press.

Fuligni, A. 1997. The academic achievement of adolescents from immigrant families: The roles of family background, attitudes, and behavior. *Child Development* 68(2): 351–63.

Gadamer, H. G. 1975. *Truth and method*. London: Sheed and Ward

Garmezy, N. 1976. The experimental study of children vulnerable to psychopathology. In *Child personality and psychopathology: Current topics*. Vol. 2, edited by A. Davids, 171–216. New York: Wiley.

Giroux, H. 1983. *Theory and resistance in education: A pedagogy for the opposition*. New York: Bergin and Harvey.

Goffman, E. 1959. *The presentation of self in everyday life*. New York: Anchor.

———. 1963. *Stigma: Notes on the management of spoiled identity*. Englewood, NJ: Prentice-Hall.

Gordon, E. W. 1985. Social science knowledge production and the Afro-American experience. *Journal of Negro Education* 54:117–33.

———. 1986. *Foundations for academic excellence*. Brooklyn, NY: NYC Chancellor's Commission on Minimum Standards, New York City Board of Education.

———. 1995. Toward an equitable system of educational assessment. *Journal of Negro Education* 64(3): 360–72.

Gordon, E. W., F. Miller, and D. Rollock. 1990. Coping with communicentric bias in knowledge production in the social sciences. *Educational Researcher* 19(3): 14–19.

Gordon, E. W., and L. D. Song. 1994. Variations in the experience of resilience. In *Educational resilience in inner-city America: Challenges and prospects*, edited by M. C. Wang and E. W. Gordon. Hillsdale, NJ: Lawrence Erlbaum.

Gouldner, A. W. 1970. *The Coming Crisis of Western Sociology*. New York: Basic Books.

Graham, S., A. Taylor, and C. Hudley. 1998. Exploring achievement values among ethnic minority early adolescents. *Journal of Educational Psychology* 90(4): 606–20.

Gramsci, A. 1971. *Selections from prison notebooks*. New York: International Publishers.

Greeno, J. 2002. *Students with competence, authority and accountability: Affording intellective identities in classrooms*. Monograph Series. New York: College Board.

Gouldner, A. 1970. *The coming crisis of Western sociology*. New York: Basic Books.

Hanushek, E. 1989. The impact of differential expenditures on school performance. *Educational Researcher* 18:48.

Hao, L., and M. Bonstead-Bruns. 1998. Parent-child differences in educational expectations and the academic achievement of immigrant and native students. *Sociology of Education* 71:175–98.

Hemmings, A. 1998. The self-transformation of African American achievers. *Youth and Society* 29(3): 330–68.

Hetherington, E. M. 1989. Coping with family transitions: Winners, losers and survivors. *Child Development* 60:1–14.

Jeffs, T., and M. K. Smith. 1999. *Informal education. Conversation, democracy and learning*. Ticknall: Education Now Books.

Jordan, W., J. Lara, and J. McPartland. 1996. Exploring the causes of early dropout among race-ethnic and gender groups. *Youth and Society* 28(1): 62–92.

Kao, G., and M. Tienda. 1995. Optimism and achievement: The educational performance of immigrant youth. *Social Science Quarterly* 76:1–19.

Keith, T., P. Keith, K. Quirk, J. Sperduto, J. Santillo, and S. Killings. 1998. Longitudunal effects of parent involvement on high school grades: Similarities and differences across gender and ethnic groups. *Journal of School Psychology* 36(3): 335–63.

Kozol, J. 1991. *Savage inequalities*. New York: HarperCollins.

Kumar, K. 1995. *From post-industrial to post-modern society*. Oxford: Blackwell.

Lareau, A. 1987. Social class differences in family-school relationships: The importance of cultural capital. *Sociology of Education* 60(2): 73–85.

Lewis, O. 1966. *La vida: A Puerto Rican family in the culture of poverty—San Juan and New York*. New York: Random House.

Masten, A. S., K. M. Best, and N. Garmezy. 1990. Resilience and development: Contributions from the study of children who overcome adversity. *Development and Psychopathology* 2: 425–44.

McLaren, P., and R. Farahmandpur. 2000. Reconsidering Marx in post-Marxist times: A requiem for postmodernism? *Educational Researcher* 29(3): 25–33.

McQuillian, P. J. 1997. Humanizing the comprehensive high school: A proposal for reform. *Educational Administration Quarterly* 33 (supp.): 644–83.

Mickelson, R. 1990. The attitude-achievement paradox among black adolescents. *Sociology of Education* 63:44–61.

Miller, L. S. 1995. *An American imperative: Accelerating minority educational advancement*. New Haven, CT: Yale University Press.

Moynihan, D. P. 1965. *The Negro family: The case for national action*. Washington, DC: U.S. Department of Labor.

Nakanishi, D., and T. Nishida, eds. 1995. *The Asian American educational experience*. New York: Routledge.

National Center for Education Statistics. 1996. *NAEP 1994 reading report card for the nation and the states*. Washington DC: U.S. Department of Education.

Oakes, J. 1985. *Keeping track: How schools structure inequality*. New Haven, CT: Yale University Press.

Ogbu, J. U. 1994. Racial stratification and education in the United States: Why inequality persists. *Teachers College Record* 96:264–98.

Osborne, J. 1995. Academics, self-esteem, and race: A look at the underlying assumptions of the disidentification hypothesis. *Personality and Social Psychology Bulletin* 108:330–33.

———. 1997. Race and academic disidentification. *Journal of Educational Psychology* 89(4): 728–35.

Pines, G. J. 1979. Humanizing education through counseling: The research findings. *Humanist Educator* 18(2): 51–63.

Pynoos, R. S., A. M. Steinberg, and R. Wraith. 1995. A developmental model of childhood traumatic stress. In *Developmental psychopathology, Vol. 2: Risk, disorder, and adaptation*, edited by D. Cicchetti and D. J. Cohen, 72–95. New York: John Wiley and Sons.

Rumberger, R., and K. Larson. 1998. Toward explaining differences in educational achievement among Mexican American language-minority students. *Sociology of Education* 71:69–93.

Rutter, M. 1985. Resilience in the face of adversity: protective factors and resistance to psychiatric disorders. *British Journal of Psychiatry* 147:589–611.

Sanders, M. 1997. Overcoming obstacles: Academic achievement as a response to racism and discrimination. *Journal of Negro Education* 66(1): 83–93.

Schneider, B., and Y. Lee. 1990. A model for academic success: The school and home environment of East Asian students. *Anthropology and Education Quarterly* 21:358–77.

Secada, W., R. Chavez-Chavez, E. Garcia, C. Munoz, J. Oakes, I. Santiago-Santiago, and R. Slavin. 1998. *No more excuses: The final report of the Hispanic Dropout Project.* Washington, DC: Hispanic Dropout Project.

Simmel, G. 1971/1908. *On individuality and social forms: Selected writings.* Chicago: University of Chicago Press.

Steele, C. 1997. A threat in the air: How stereotypes shape intellectual identity and performance. *American Psychologist* 52:613–29.

Steele, C., and J. Aronson. 1995. Stereotype threat and the intellectual test performance of African Americans. *Journal of Personality and Social Psychology* 69:797–811.

Steinberg, L. 1996. *Beyond the classroom. Why school reform has failed and what parents need to do.* New York: Simon and Schuster.

Steinberg, L., S. Dornbusch, and B. Brown. 1992. Ethic differences in adolescent achievement: An ecological perspective. *American Psychologist* 47:728.

Sternberg, R., ed. 1994. *The encyclopedia of human intelligence.* New York: Macmillan.

Sun, Y. 1998. The academic success of East-Asian American students: An investment model. *Social Science Research* 27:432–56.

Trueba, H. 1989. *Raising silent voices: Educating the linguistic minorities for the 21st century.* New York: HarperCollins.

Valencia, R., ed. 1991. *Chicano school failure and success.* New York: Falmer Press.

Weinberg, M. 1977. *A chance to learn: A history of race and education in the United States.* New York: Cambridge University Press.

Wells, A., and I. Serna. 1996. The politics of culture: Understanding local political resistance to detracking in racially mixed schools. *Harvard Educational Review* 66:93–118.

West, C. 1993. *Race matters.* Boston: Beacon Press.

Willis, P. 1977. *Learning to labour.* London: Saxon House.

Wilson, W. J. 1978. *The declining significance of race.* Chicago: University of Chicago Press.

———. 1987. *The truly disadvantaged: The inner city, the underclass and public policy.* Chicago: University of Chicago Press.

———. 1991. Studying inner-city social dislocations: The challenge of public agenda research. *American Sociological Review* 56:1–14.

———. 1999. *The bridge over the racial divide: Rising inequality and coalition politics.* Berkeley: University of California Press.

NOTES

1. Simmel consistently refers to the freedom of the stranger as "objectivity." I think we can recast this idea—without undermining Simmel's central argument—as something more akin to a poststructualist reading of Nietzschean "perspectivism" (see Derrida 1978), Gadamer's (1975) hermeneutic (and Heideggerian) theory of understanding as a "fusion of horizons" or "the dialogue that we are," and E. W. Gordon's (1985) "multi-perspectivity."

2. The use of this term is a weak transposition of Marx's 1844 concept of "alienated labor" and Feuerbach's notions of religious alienation. By alienated achievement, I am referring to academic accomplishment that exists solely within the confines of institutional

strictures and bears little to no relevance to a person's sense of intentionality and larger social belonging.

3. For example, in light of Gramsci's (1971) notion of hegemony, we can characterize educational institutions and other popular cultural institutions as components of civil society, instrumental in the "manufacture of consent" wherein hegemonic values and practices can either be accepted as common sense or contested within forums of "cultural politics."

4. Additionally, the gradual abandonment of national policies of social welfare and the advent of free-market devolution and competition have given rise to the federal and state constriction of social services, thereby contributing to the diminishing pool of available civil service jobs that have contributed to the attainment of "new" middle-class status for many people of color (Wilson 1987, 1991).

5 For example, research on second- and third-generation Asian/Pacific Islander students find that their levels of academic achievement tend to fall relative to that of newer generations. In fact, a common intervention among Asian/Pacific Islander immigrant parents may be to discourage association between their children and native Americans, given the latter's relatively weaker commitment to academic achievement (Fuligni 1997; Hao and Bonstead-Bruns 1998; Sun 1998).

6. As Paul Willis (1977) begins his classic study, *Learning to Labour*: "The difficult thing to explain about how middle class kids get middle class jobs is why others let them. The difficult thing to explain about how working class kids get working class jobs is why they let themselves" (1). Willis is not placing sole responsibility upon the shoulders of working-class youth; rather, he is pointing out the extent to which these people do not demand and aggressively compete for greater access to socioeconomic resources.

7. Also see Gordon, Miller, and Rollock's (1990) discussion of communicentric bias in social science knowledge production.

II

VARIETIES OF SUPPLEMENTATION PROGRAMS

9

A Taxonomy of Supplementary Education Programs

Beatrice L. Bridglall, Alan Green, and Brenda Mejia

In the preceding chapters, we have established a conceptual framework for the idea of supplementary education. We operationalize this concept in chapters 2, 3, and 16 by (1) delineating common aspects and issues of after-school programs, youth development, and other forms of supplementary education; and (2) providing several taxonomies by which the components of supplementary education programs and their exemplars may be classified. It is here that we face a dilemma of sorts. Depending upon the choice one makes from the several ways of trying to describe and understand supplementary education programs, the components of these programs can be classified in different ways. For example, the Carnegie Council on Adolescent Development (CCAD) (1992) used categories based on the nature of the organizations that sponsor the activities. We find it useful to classify these programs in relation to their purpose—that is, whether the purpose is explicit or implicit. Seppanen, deVries, and Seligson (1993) used other approaches, including a classification system that assessed availability, capacity, and utilization rates, and another that focused on income characteristics of children served, enrollment levels, use of program space, program size, child-staff ratio, staffing, staff wages and benefits, and the role of parents. Their study, called the National Study of Before- and After-School Programs (Seppanen, deVries, Seligson 1993) provided the first nationwide picture of the prevalence, structure, and features of formal programs. The authors also assessed the organizational characteristics of after-school service providers and observed that services and activities to children and families are shaped by a number of structural program features, including legal status and sponsorship, interagency cooperation, operating schedules, fees charged to parents, licensing, accreditation, and program evaluation.

The Directory of American Youth Organizations (Erickson 1998) categorizes programs by their content focus (i.e., academic clubs and honor societies; agriculture and livestock; civic education and political; science, math and technology; social welfare and community development; and youth lodges). For the purposes of our analysis, we find it useful to generate a taxonomy based on (1) the explicit versus implicit purposes of the services—that is, are the services deliberately intended to be supplemental to education or incidentally so; (2) the basis of program content, including academic instruction, remediation, socialization, recreational, religious instruction, and cultural enrichment; and (3) the nature of the organization that sponsors the service (national, local, independent, private religious, private secular, commercial, or public agency). Although we believe that our taxonomy is more appropriately descriptive and inclusive of developments in the emerging field of supplementary education, we recognize that it is not a perfect classification system. The overlaps and duplications are obvious, but they may be necessary in order that we capture the varied and dynamic status of this field.

In *The Idea of Supplementary Education*, Gordon and Bridglall (2002) used the terms *explicit* and *implicit* to categorize the services deliberately intended to be supplementary to educational programs or incidentally so. Other sources use terms such as formal and informal or deliberate and incidental as categories. It may be that the lack of a common standard for the categorization of supplementary education programs is a reflection of the lack of standard program components for this emerging field. Clearly, whether the supplementary education programs in these variously named categories are part of youth development, the after-school movement, or other explicit and implicit forms of supplementary education, the field has not agreed on nor achieved formal institutional structure. The dilemma then concerns the choice of a conceptual system by which expressions of supplementary education can be categorized.

Informed thus by conceptions reflected in this work, we have generated three categories of supplementary education interventions that comprise our taxonomy and provide examples of each—explicit vs. implicit nature of the interventions, the focus of program content, and the nature of the sponsoring organizations. Although the types and kinds of examples we cite are by no means exhaustive, they do serve as illustrations of our taxonomy.

EXPLICIT VERSUS IMPLICIT PURPOSES

Some of the explicit types of supplementary education programs and activities focus on academic development, tutorials, advocacy, remediation, SAT prepa-

Table 9.1.   Categories of Supplementary Education Interventions

Explicit
  Academic tutoring
  Advocacy
  Expeditionary learning
  Guidance services
  Remediation
  Saturday academy
  SAT preparation
  Sociocultural interventions
  Spelling bees
  Study skills
  Subject matter clubs
  Weekend and summer academies

Implicit
  Decision making
  Family talk
  Indigenous and hegemonic acculturalization
  Nutrition
  Parental employment
  Parental modeling
  Reading
  Travel

ration, Saturday academies, specialized services, and sociocultural child- and youth-centered social groups. Those interventions that are implicit include parenting, nutrition, family talk, parental employment, decision making, reading, socialization and acculturation, social networks, travel, and environmental supports (Mercer 1973; Wolf 1966). These categories of interventions are further impacted by the ethos of students' homes and communities, cultural and socioeconomic demographics, the economic and cultural infrastructure students and families may or may not have access to, incidental and informal experiences, formal and explicit exposure to high-performance learning communities, and the aspirations, expectations, and access to available resources.

Examples of Explicit Interventions

Academic Tutoring

Briefly described in chapter 3, small-group or one-to-one tutoring relationships increase learning outcomes by enabling the interpretation of necessary learning cues and fostering appropriate student participation necessary to make the learning process effective. Another advantage is that the direct contact between tutee and tutor decreases the likelihood of miscommunication due to cultural, cognitive, emotional, or stylistic learning differences that are common to group instruction (Gaustad 1992). Tutoring is often the first method employed by parents and teachers to address specific academic needs. It can also be effective with all students, be they at risk or high achieving. In general, tutoring is an effective approach for strengthening specific skills, correcting specific problems in academic subjects, and reinforcing socialization, study skills, and study habits. Tutoring is an established, effective method for enhancing learning and another example of an explicit intervention. Although cost constraints may prevent it from being used as often as needed, tutoring is highly recommended as an in- or out-of-school effort at reducing school failure (Slavin, Karweit, and Wasik 1991). Usually conducted on a one-to-one or small-group basis, supplemental programs use peers, volunteers, paraprofessionals, and professional teachers as tutors. This method is widely used because it is thought to produce better results than large-group instruction (Gaustad 1992; Gyanani and Pahuja 1995).

Advocacy

Research has consistently shown that parental participation in education is closely related to high student achievement (Taylor 1994; College Board 1999). Parents of high achievers advocate for their children in various ways. They become involved in committees that govern their child's school, join the local parent-teacher association, and influence the choice of their children's teachers, for instance. Organizations such as the National Coalition for Parent Involvement in Education (NCPIE) are also available to parents. Founded in 1980, NCPIE is a coalition of education, advocacy, and community organizations that advocate for parental involvement and strong relationships between home, school, and community. Member organizations meet monthly to share successful program projects, training, and information about family involvement. NCPIE's work is guided by objectives that privilege partnerships and effective communication between teachers and parents, active parent participation in school and home activities, and training for parents.

Expeditionary Learning

The concepts of experiential education and expeditionary travel have long influenced some savvy parents and educators to incorporate these activities in their children's education. In addition to engaging in these types of learning activities with their children, some public and private schools take students on outdoor expeditions as a regular part of the curriculum. Anecdotal evidence indicates that students often regard their field-based learning experiences as a favorite part of school. And among those students who tend to have the greatest discipline problems in the classroom, expeditionary/experiential learning activities are enjoyed and valued. Both parents and teachers seem to know that expeditionary learning programs can be a motivating factor for all students because of the sense of responsibility the programs encourage. Included among the guiding principles and philosophies of the programs are the connections between the classroom and the surrounding communities and the world beyond. Expeditionary learning programs are also characterized by student action rather than student inaction (i.e., passive receiving of processed information). Parents, teachers, and schools pursue these programs for a number of reasons, including developing life skills, career exploration, establishing connections with the community, and the application of academic skills. Additionally, expeditionary learning programs not only challenge students to cooperate and depend on each other but also emphasize strategic problem solving, logical/rational actions, and social reinforcements.

Guidance Services

According to Maddy-Bernstein and Cunanan (1995), exemplary guidance services must include thoughtful and comprehensive guidance and counseling program plans (supported by collaborative efforts with parents, businesses, and professional organizations), organizational commitment, and leadership. Exemplary career guidance programs, for example, support the following activities: self-knowledge and self-awareness (conscious examination of personal values, interests, and goals); educational and occupational exploration (presentation and integration of information and experience); and decision making and career planning (understanding the interrelations between the self and the world and developing skills to make realistic choices and rational decisions) (National Occupational Information Coordinating Committee 1989, 9).

Similarly, guidance programs address the needs of diverse student populations in addition to ensuring the delivery of essential support services (e.g., tutoring, academic advising, assessment). In exemplary programs, students undergo intensive career exploration and planning consisting of:

- A career advisement system with every faculty and staff member advising a group of students during the whole of their secondary program.
- A wide range of career materials and assessment instruments.
- Organized guidance courses and programs in the secondary and postsecondary levels.
- Individual planning and group career counseling.

- Guidance in individualized career plans and career-planning portfolios.
- Workshops on self-awareness, assertiveness, problem solving, conflict resolution, communication skills, careers, parenting, and managing relationships.
- Organized and interactive job fairs and career nights.

Another significant facet common to these programs is their availability to diverse groups of students. This diversity includes not only racial/ethnic differentials but also those that are religious, socioeconomic, and cultural in nature. Additionally, the diversity extends to students enrolled in vocational-technical programs as well as students in all other programs, those at risk of failing or dropping out of school, and displaced homemakers/single parents/single pregnant teens.

Another criterion emphasizes the importance of forging strong partnerships with parents, businesses, teachers, and community organizations. The emphasis on strong school and family partnerships is key to program success in secondary schools. Parents who are involved in various facets of the children's lives participate in career planning, educational planning, advisory committees, financial aid workshops, parent-teacher conferences, and guidance and counseling sessions. Exemplary guidance programs are also successful in getting the support of area businesses, industries, and/or community organizations.

Faculty and staff should also be partners in career development programs that include career information in the curriculum and career development activities. Some schools have teachers serve as career advisors to a group of students. In ongoing assessment meetings, teachers collaborate with school counselors and parents to identify and meet the special needs of students. Additionally, vocational and academic teachers work together with counselors during student orientation, career advisory meetings, curriculum development, career assessment, information exchange meetings, and other counseling activities. And both faculty and staff refer students to counseling staff for individual counseling.

The third criterion concerns organizational commitment and leadership, which are further defined as strong administrative leadership and support, financial backing, ongoing program evaluation, qualified personnel, organized professional development activities, and follow-up of program graduates and noncompleters.

Remediation

Like tutoring, the remediation of academic material occurs in the classroom as well as in enrichment activities outside of school. Remediation often involves some form of tutoring, but also includes providing the opportunity for extra work on different subjects and assistance with homework (MacIver 1991). Generally, this method involves slowing down the curriculum pace for students who are not performing up to academic standards. The remediation approach assumes students are not doing well in school because they cannot keep up with large-group instruction (Levin and Hopfenberg 1991). Although research findings indicate that acceleration, not remediation, is more successful in increasing academic outcomes for underachieving students, remediation is found to be widespread (Lynch and Mills 1993).

Saturday Academy

A foreign language, such as Spanish, can be taught in Saturday academies. These Saturday academies typically engage students for an hour to more than three or four hours. In a language immersion program, for example, students can be taught skills for developing language acquisition. They may also have the opportunity engage in hands-on activities such as cooking, playing a specific culture's instruments, or learning how to make arts and crafts. Another program that operates Saturday academies is the Gifted Child Society, which conducts programs for gifted children and their parents. These programs are comprised of the following components: after-school enrichment, testing services, parent seminars, and teacher training. The society's Saturday Workshop, for example, consists of about sixty one-hour Saturday-morning courses offered in ten-session semesters. The fall session operates from October to December and the spring session operates from March to May. The Saturday classes are designed to challenge the special learning needs and styles of gifted children. Curriculum and teaching strategies stimulate the development of higher levels of thinking, creativity, problem finding, problem solving, and leadership. An interdisciplinary approach is used and, where practical, courses are future oriented and globally based.

Scholastic Aptitude Test (SAT) Preparation

Academically sophisticated parents of college-bound students actively provide access to and encourage their children to participate in college-preparatory curriculum. Technology has further facilitated this process for parents, students, and teachers because of the number of preparatory courses now offered online. The College Board's website, for example, offers students the following services: a free diagnostic mini-SAT that analyzes students' strengths and weaknesses; SAT Practice, which focuses students' review of specific question types;

and an option called SAT PrepPack, which is a set of practice questions and analysis. The set includes approximately twenty to thirty sample questions by type—that is, analogies, sentence completions, critical reading, math multiple choice, quantitative comparisons, student-produced responses, a full explanation for each question, hints for answering questions when the student gets stuck, and feedback on the students' performance. The College Board's website (www.collegeboard.org) also provides simple directions for students to download their material or use it online.

Sociocultural Interventions

Sociocultural interventions include diverse cultural celebrations (such as the cotillion, for example) that some communities use as rites of passage for adolescents. The preparation for the cotillion represents the educational expression of the practice. Among certain ethnic groups, sociocultural interventions are used as vehicles in delivering religious and cultural instruction. While the main focus of these efforts may not be that of enhancing academic performance in the regular school, there appear to be indirect benefits for students engaged in additional learning opportunities (Ravid 1988; Schneider and Lee 1990). Sizer (1973) makes reference to schools and cultural institutions that are more fun and sensitive to cultural differences but nonetheless supportive of academic work. In Gordon's review of Sizer's *Places of Learning and Places of Joy*, he indicates that Sizer "identifies three purposes of education": to equip the learner with (1) "individual power" or the "intellectual and physical faculties for personal and corporate ends"; (2) "a personal style, assurance, and self-control that allow him [or her] to act in both socially acceptable and personally meaningful ways"; and (3) "joy, the fruit of aesthetic discipline, of faith and of commitment" (Gordon 1973). Theodore Sizer suggests that we separate these overlapping purposes and that we assign primary responsibility for the development of power, or skill in the use of intellectual and physical faculties, to neighborhood schools. "Let us have academies," he argues, "primarily devoted to power. And let us have different kinds of activity (Collegia) through which society may provide . . . for agency and joy. Let us have, in sum, two kinds of schools with children expected to attend both, often concurrently" (Sizer 1973). Sizer argues persuasively in support of his separation of functions. He reminds us that schools have failed to meet this dual expectation, and he suggests that while academies (neighborhood based) would likely be ethnically and economically homogeneous, Collegia could be placed—as well as managed—so as to provide for heterogeneity.

Spelling Bees

The Scripps Howard National Spelling Bee organization, together with 240 sponsors in the United States, Europe, Guam, Mexico, Puerto Rico, the U.S. Virgin Islands, the Bahamas, and American Samoa, coordinates national spelling bee finals, enrolls sponsors, and produces word lists and study materials annually. Each sponsor organizes a spelling bee program in its community, and the champion of the sponsor's final spelling bee advances to the national finals.

For example, the *Record* in Hackensack, New Jersey, is the local sponsor for the North Jersey Spelling Bee in Bergen County. Students adhere to the following qualification structure: Competition begins at the classroom level; classroom winners participate in one of three semifinal bees; and winners from the three semifinal bees advance to the North Jersey Spelling Bee. The North Jersey Spelling Bee does not have any special instructions for students attending homeschools or those attending private, parochial, or public schools. Information regarding Spelling Bee study materials is presented in a mailing sent out by the *Record* and the *Herald News*, as well as in newspaper advertisements. Scripps Howard's purpose is to assist students in improving their spelling, increasing their vocabulary, learning new concepts, and developing correct English usage that will serve them for life.

Study Skills

Study skills improvement programs focus on assisting students with the mechanics of how to study and learn effectively. The development of strategic learning approaches—summarization skills used for close reading of academic texts, rehearsal, elaboration, organization, critical thinking, planning, monitoring, self-regulation, time and study environment, effort, peer help, and help-seeking behavior have been demonstrated as effective in improving learning ability (Hidi and Anderson 1986; Payne 1992).

Subject Matter Clubs

Subject matter clubs represent traditional extracurricular activities. Houston High School (Germantown, Tennessee), for example, has a number of specific clubs targeted to students with a particular interest. The mission of their computer club, for instance, is to expose students to new software and trends in computer science. The only requirements are that students must be in grades 10 and up, and must have taken or be taking a personal computing or a programming class. The membership cost is $5.00, and members meet once a month during club schedule. Or, for example, the Houston High School Concert Choir represents the school and Shelby County as ambassadors of goodwill in TV presentations, civic organizations, churches, school concerts, conventions, and as a demonstration group at educational workshops. Students are required to have a strong ability and interest in singing and performing. They practice during class five days a week and after school as needed. Members are auditioned in the spring for participation the following year. The cost of $120.00 covers a uniform and participation in the Houston Choir Booster Club.

Or perhaps a student is interested in the German Club, which seeks to promote the study of the German language, to encourage an appreciation of German culture, and to provide a circle of friends for those studying the German language. Their activities include celebrating German holidays, such as Oktoberfest and Karneval; eating German foods at meetings, parties, and restaurants; listening to guest speakers; attending foreign language contests; creating a network of friends and peer tutors to assist in the acquisition of the language; and traveling to German-speaking countries during the summer break. Students are required to be enrolled in a German class, pay annual club dues of $7, attend meetings on a regular basis, conduct themselves appropriately at club meetings, and participate in club activities. The German Club meets once a month.

In addition to the traditional subject matter clubs referenced above, a growing number have sprouted online and via e-mail. These online programs include those sponsored by universities and private companies. The Institute for the Academic Advancement of Youth (IAAY) at Johns Hopkins University and the Education Program for Gifted Youth (EPGY) at Stanford University, for example, cosponsor the Center for Distance Education, which offers Math Tutorials, a K–8 mathematics sequence divided into five fundamental content areas. This program requires students to complete offline homework in addition to computer-guided lessons. Students must also maintain contact with their tutors via e-mail and telephone. This strategy provides a forum in which students can discuss mathematics. Students are expected to regularly send e-mail reports to their tutors, at least once a week. These reports are used by the tutor to assess progress and to isolate any difficulties that the student may be having. Tutors are subject-area specialists trained to provide instructional and technical assistance and ensure that students get feedback on their work.

Swarthmore College has an online project called Elementary Problem of the Week and Visiting Math Mentors. This program, which has just completed its second year, posts weekly nonroutine math problems to challenge third- to sixth-grade students and to encourage them to verbalize their solutions. Students have the option to participate as part of a classroom activity, weekly school assignment, or through independent interest. Participating students submit their solutions, which are reviewed by a Visiting Math Mentor. Students who correctly answer the challenge are recognized on the program's website, and the most creative solutions are highlighted. Visiting Math Mentors volunteer for one or more weeks by replying to the solutions submitted by elementary students for a given problem. As problem-solving mentors, volunteers improve their ability to develop assessment criteria and increase their own problem-solving skills while helping elementary students discover the joys of solving challenging problems. Mentors may include classes of elementary school students, high school students, preservice teachers, teachers, college professors, and anyone else interested in problem solving and a willingness to share it with others.

Weekend and Summer Academies

In addition to after-school activities, a number of effective weekend and summer programs exist. Oklahoma State University, for example, has a program called Summer Academies for High School Students at OSU. This initiative is associated with the Mathematics Department at OSU and includes the Oklahoma Principals' Science Scholars (OPSS) program, which is a four-week residential summer academy for talented junior high school students. This program is part of a larger program dedicated to enhancing science and mathematics skills and awareness among Oklahoma minority students. Each summer since 1992, through funding from the Oklahoma State Regents for Higher Education, forty bright young scholars from across Oklahoma have studied aquatic and plant biology, data collection and analysis, ecology, mathematical problem solving, computers, and graphing calculators.

OSU's Futures in Science and Mathematics program is a two-week academy for ninth- and tenth-grade students. In the 1999–2000 academic year, they recruited thirty-one students, of whom fifteen conducted research in mathematics while the others conducted research in environmental chemistry. Besides their research classes, these students took classes in mathematical problem solving, the use of the TI-82 graphics calculator, and meteorology. Each student was given a project to complete and report on when he or she returned to campus for a one-day meeting in the fall.

OSU also conducted a four-week residential enrichment program for Native American eighth- and ninth-grade students in June 1994. Thirty-two Native American students from across the United States had exposure to laboratory projects in chemistry, field studies in biological sciences, mathematical problem solving, and data analysis. This project was funded by NASA, through the American Indian Science, Technology and Engineering Consortium

Examples of Implicit Interventions

Decision Making

Teaching and socializing young people to make decisions on their own is another implicit form of supplementary education. By allowing them to make independent decisions, young people learn to take responsibility for their own actions and become independent productive adults.

Family Talk

The phenomenon of implicit supplementary education occurs in a variety of informal ways in a child's home. Activities considered routine—such as talking to and with children and including them in conversations at the dinner table, for example—seem to enable youngsters to cope with the demands of academic settings and support the intellective and social development of children (Gordon 1999).

Indigenous and Hegemonic Acculturalization

Sophisticated parents seek to balance exposure to the traditional culture of the academy and their own unique family culture (Purves 1991). Their purposes are dual in that they pursue both ends simultaneously with the belief that exposure to their own culture and traditions and to the hegemonic European culture will allow children to function well in the personal and academic worlds they are straddling and the professional world in which they will eventually participate. These parents also understand that actively engaging their children in art, music, literature, and related activities tends to promote cultural communication and identification, socialization, and the acculturation of their children. These two goals demonstrate not only what is seen, heard, and read but also *the manner* in which it is seen, heard, read, and understood. In other words, parents seek to affect their children's beliefs and attitudes by raising or shifting their consciousness or manifestations of these values. Although this discussion on indigenous and hegemonic cultures is by no means exhaustive, it reinforces the idea that sustained cultural activities provide children conceptual, descriptive, and experimental frames of reference (Gordon and Song 1994).

Nutrition

Most parents, educators, and communities know the importance of good nutrition, exercise, and disease prevention and seek to help young people improve their eating habits. In addition to raising awareness about obesity, eating disorders, dental caries, anemia, and bulimia, parental and community concerns for adequate nutrition has some support in particular programs, including the 4-H Expanded Food and Nutrition Education Program (EFNEP) at Michigan State University (MSU). Through the EFNEP, trained instructors and volunteers from MSU utilize research-based materials and relevant educational programs to teach low-income school-age children (between the ages of five and nineteen) basic nutrition, food selection and preparation, food safety and sanitation practices, and the importance of physical activity. The 4-H program for youth is an extension of EFNEP, a program that helps low-income families obtain the knowledge and skills needed to improve their diets and health. EFNEP also teaches families how to effectively use money allocated for food to improve their nutrition. The 4-H EFNEP services are delivered in various settings such as local schools, churches, soup kitchens, and Boys and Girls Clubs. The EFNEP is funded by the U.S. Department of Agriculture and receives local and private support. The program is currently implemented in ten counties throughout Michigan and can be found in all fifty states.

Parental Employment

Some organizations initiated by parents focus on increasing parental involvement in schools, train and empower parents, influence the parent-child relationship, and provide parental employment. The Parent Project in Boston strives to positively influence impoverished minority parents who are ostracized from their schools because of poverty, minority status, drugs, or violence. This parent employment initiative focuses both on increasing parents' involvement in their children's education and on improving their economic stability and growth. Parent Project's employment program, Culture Basket Employment Program, hires and trains welfare recipients, homeless parents, and high school dropouts to help create multicultural baskets. The project not only provides jobs but also trains parents in bookkeeping, sales, and management.

Parental Modeling of Activities

Much of what children and adolescents know about life they learn from watching adult role models: teachers, parents, coaches, and clergy members

(Berryman and Breighner 1994). Educated parents often access the literature and programs that professional organizations, schools, and places of worship provide. In terms of the literature parents can use to model and teach their children values necessary for learning and living, a booklet developed by early education teachers at the Ferguson-Florissant School District (1993) in Ferguson, Missouri—*Lifelong Values*—is helpful. The introduction identifies six lifelong values, discusses the important role played by parents in teaching these values, and offers a checklist of positive ways parents can interact with their children. The subsequent sections focus on each of the lifelong values, defining the skills involved, and identifying ways to encourage the child to develop those skills. The six lifelong values are:

1. confidence, which can be encouraged by giving children jobs that are appropriate to their age and ability and providing them with the tools to complete the job successfully;
2. responsibility, which can be encouraged by empowering children to do things for themselves and letting them experience the natural consequences of their behavior;
3. perseverance, which can be encouraged by extending the time spent on a task and praising the child's ability to complete a job;
4. cooperation, which can be encouraged within the family and outside the home;
5. problem solving, which can be encouraged through age-appropriate activities and materials and giving children time to think and act on their ideas; and
6. respect, which can be encouraged by parents showing respect to the child, to others, and for property.

The Pacific Northwest Cooperative Extension Service (a collaboration between Idaho University, Oregon State University, and Washington State University) also issued a seventeen-page booklet titled *Child Guidance Techniques* (Pacific Northwest Extension 1991), which discusses the role parents can play in helping their children mature, make decisions, and adjust to the challenges of the world around them. It suggests that parents and other caregivers of children keep in mind the following ideas when interacting with children: (1) focus on "do's" instead of "don'ts"; (2) build feelings of confidence; (3) try to change behavior by changing surroundings or situations; (4) provide choices for children; (5) work with children, not against them; (6) set limits for children; (7) listen to yourself and your child; (8) set a good example; and (9) show love to your children.

Reading

Parents who deliberately read with and to their children, and subsequently engage in conversations with them, understand the role and purpose of these activities in enabling children's language skills to grow. For example, reading books to preschool children helps them to grasp how stories progress. Children can easily learn familiar phrases and repeat them, thus pretending to read. "Pretend reading" gives a child a sense of power and courage to keep trying. The storyteller voices of parents help children hear the sounds of words and how they are put together to form meaning. (See chapter 3 for an elaboration of this point.)

Travel

In addition to traveling with their families, travel opportunities for young people not only promote different perspectives but also encourage understanding and awareness of other cultures. The more explicit cultural awareness programs, including study abroad and exchange programs, can facilitate friendships, emphasize multicultural competence, and expose young people to international career possibilities and the versatility of learning new languages. Clearly, although we have placed travel under our implicit category, it also overlaps with the explicit category and includes programs such as the Academy and Cultural Exchange in Moreno Valley, California, and the Institute for American Universities, which assist students in understanding and experiencing different cultures and encourages them to take active roles in their education trajectories through exchange and study-abroad opportunities.

The Academy and Cultural Exchange (ACE), founded in 1988, is a nonprofit study-abroad program that offers students opportunities to discover new ways of relating to the world through living with host families from Brazil, China, Colombia, Japan, Germany, Mexico, Peru, Yugoslavia, England, Thailand, Spain, Argentina, Venezuela, Albania, and the United States. ACE's exchange program offers foreign high school students the opportunity to stay in the United States for an academic year, semester, or a few weeks with an American family while American high school students have opportunities to study during the academic year and or over the summer in a foreign country. The requirements for high school students ages fifteen to eighteen include participation in a screening, access to medical insurance, and spending money. The students' living arrangements are coordinated by ACE and host families. ACE selects students who are emotionally mature and requires a mandatory orientation for selected students to prepare them for the cross-cultural experience. Additionally, students are paired with a counselor who provides support, answers questions, addresses potential concerns, and monitors the students' progress.

The Institute for American Universities (IAU) is a nonprofit educational institution founded in 1957 for U.S. college and university students to study abroad in Europe. As one of the oldest study-abroad education programs, IAU immerses students in a cross-cultural environment that inspires intellectual development, reflection, and personal growth. Students can study in the south of France for a semester, during the summer, or for an entire year in English or in French. Courses offered in the program include beginning to advanced French, literature, international affairs, culture art, archeology, art history, and studio art.

Applicants for the program are required to complete a general application form, submit a recommendation from a language teacher, and a nonrefundable application fee of $45. Participants must have completed one full academic year of college and have a 2.5–3.0 cumulative GPA to apply. Program costs include tuition, housing, two meals per day, orientation, textbooks, health and repatriation insurance, excursions, and scheduled cultural activities. In addition, participants are responsible for their round-trip airfare and personal expenses. Tuition grants ranging from $300 to $1,000 are awarded to students on the basis of academic achievement and/or financial need.

THE FOCUS OF PROGRAM CONTENT IN SUPPLEMENTARY EDUCATION INTERVENTIONS

Overall, after-school programs are freer than schools to use innovative curricula and activities to promote children's learning because they can be flexible in tailoring children's time to their needs, have a better student/staff ratio, and benefit from multiage groupings. In general, most programs strive to foster the psychosocial development of youth by developing their sense of self-worth, interpersonal social skills, and appreciation of cultural diversity. They reinforce school-day learning by integrating personalized educational supports into each child's schedule, such as tutoring and assistance with homework, and provide educational enrichment activities. Some also provide recreational activities to develop physical skills and constructively channel energy. A few provide age-appropriate job readiness training and information about careers and career training (*Latchkey Guidelines* 1987; Marx 1989; Brooks and Herman 1991; *What Young Adolescents Want* 1992; Carnegie Council 1994; Morton-Young 1995).

The optimal purpose of after-school programs is being reconsidered in light of the ongoing effort to institute standards for student subject mastery. Both the federal government and private foundations are now suggesting that

Table 9.2.   Categories of Program Content Interventions

Academic Instruction	*Remediation*	*Socialization*	*Recreation*	*Religious Instruction*
Chinatown Cultural Center	Tutorial	Meyerhoff Scholars Program	Little League	Jewish Yeshiva
Japanese Juku		The Posse Foundation		
Junior Achievement				
Koreatown				
Puente High School Program				
Science and math programs				

students use the after-school hours for additional educational activities, both enrichment and remedial. They assert that linking the school day to after-school activities by providing extra learning time in an environment supervised by educators can significantly increase academic achievement, and can particularly benefit urban students since many attend schools whose effectiveness is compromised by a host of factors.

The directors and staff of existing after-school programs frequently are not teachers, however, and their goals have been to provide a well-rounded afternoon of activities, not an extension of the school day. Additionally, there is little history of meshing school curricula with after-school program activities, so program staff may resist pressures to redirect their efforts to serve an academic agenda. We suggest that concerned individuals with different perspectives, interests, and experiences collaborate for the purpose of determining the kinds of after-school activities that best meet the needs of children and youth. Program content can emphasize academic instruction, recreation, and socialization, for example.

Examples of Academic Instruction Interventions

There are currently many educational programs that provide young people with an academically demanding curriculum, experiences, and activities. Junior Achievement, for example, prepares students to develop critical thinking skills useful for the business world. The goal of Puente (California) is to make a difference in the lives of minority students by enabling students to achieve high levels of academic excellence.

Chinatown

The Chinatown Cultural Center in Monterey Park, California, offers routine Chinese language classes, cultural activities, voluntary work, and employment referral. In the Chinese community surrounding the center, there is a visible presence of the middle-class ethos at different levels of leadership—that is, property owners, business owners, church leaders, customers, and workers. Both adults and children have opportunities to interact with these middle-class role models on a regular basis.

The Chinese ethnic economy also constitutes an important part of community-based social organization. For example, since this ethnic economy is owned, staffed, and patronized indigenously, it creates opportunities for contact and network building, which further reinforces mechanisms of social support and control. Second, it nurtures investments in infrastructure and education and compensates for the lack of public funds and public facilities by providing access and resources to children and their families. Third, immigrant children and their parents acknowledge the importance of education, especially college education. However, the means and strategies of helping children achieve educational goals vary significantly from one neighborhood to another. This variation may be explained in part by the level of middle-class involvement in ethnic social structures, which in turn provides information to parents about resources for their children. This focus on supplementary education can also be seen in Koreatown, Los Angeles. (See chapter 13 for a detailed examination of the supplementary education activities available in Koreatown, Los Angeles.)

East Harlem Tutorial Program (EHTP)

Initially started in the small apartment of founder Helen Webber, the EHTP is a forty-year-old nonprofit organization that provides young people ages six to nineteen with individual training in reading, writing, math, science, art, computers, and SAT preparation. EHTP resulted both from a high demand for tutoring and parents who wanted to secure educational support for their children. Today, this New York–based organization has evolved into a comprehensive program with trained staff and volunteer tutors who assess each student, develop individual plans with goals and objectives, and provide one-to-one after-school tutoring and family support programs.

Japanese Juku

In Japan, the "Juku" or after-school program preparing Japanese students for high school and university entrance examinations is regarded as the backbone of the Japanese education system. Juku programs are considered effective in that they enable high-achieving students to continue their study of advanced materials while low-achieving students work toward improving their formal educational experiences. About 60 percent of public school students and 90 percent of private school students make use of the Juku in Japan. Interestingly, the instruction is more work and time intensive when compared to regular schools. In other words, after twelve years of schooling, based on the American model, Japanese students have averaged four years more schooling than their counterparts in the United States, accounting in part for differences in test scores noted between U.S. and Japanese students (Dolly 1992).

Japanese parents (in Japan) support a six-day school week and seem committed to spending the money and time necessary to have their children enroll in extra classes to secure a competitive advantage on the tests that determine which high schools, colleges, and/or universities their children may attend. Juku's small class sizes offer students opportunities for special attention. It has been suggested that the use of this supplementary schooling system has become an important part of the Japanese student's education experience, partially because of the inflexibility of the large formal school system and its inability to meet the needs of various student populations (Harnisch 1994). According to Dolly's report (1992), Juku plays a major role in ensuring the success of Japanese students on tests administered within the country and on international comparisons made on the basis of achievement test scores.

Junior Achievement

Junior Achievement (JA) began as a collection of small after-school business clubs for students in Springfield, Massachusetts. Founded in 1919 by Horace Moses, Theodore Vail, and Sen. Murray Crane of Massachusetts, JA started as a business entrepreneurship program that taught students how to conduct business by obtaining supplies and talent, building their own products, advertising, and selling. JA has become an organization that reaches approximately four million students in grades K–12 per year. JA's national office in Colorado Springs supports 156 area offices to deliver twenty-four programs to youth nationwide. The International JA affiliate reaches another hundred countries with offices around the world.

Junior Achievement offers programs for elementary, middle, and high school students. Their elementary school programs are linked with various district, state, and educational standards. Specifically, through seven different themes (including individuals, family, community, city, region, nation, and the world), students learn basic concepts of business, economics, and the relevance of education in the workplace. Middle school programs (including JA BASE, the Economics of Staying in School, JA Enterprise in Action, JA Go Figure!, Exploring Math in Business, the International Marketplace, JA Job Shadow, Personal Economics, and JA Finance Park) build on lessons in their elementary school program and helps students to make informed decisions about the process of their educational and professional future. The eight programs in the middle school program complement standard social studies curricula and emphasize the requisite communication skills for succeeding in the business world. JA's high school programs (including JA BASE, JA Company Program, JA Economics, GLOBE, JA Go Figure!, JA Job Shadow, JA Personal Finance, JA TITAN, JA TITAN School Edition, and JA Success Skills) enable students to make informed decisions about their future and promote essential business skills. With its range of diverse programs, this curriculum emphasizes concepts varying from micro- and macroeconomics to free enterprise. In addition to its standard curriculum, Junior Achievement also offers special programs, scholarships, and online programs. In February 2000, JA launched the JA TITAN, a real-time business simulation designed to enable high school students to prepare for the economic challenges of the twenty-first century.

Existing evaluation studies of JA's K–12 programs have suggested that JA's outcomes on student achievement have been reliable and significant. Students appeared to demonstrate understanding of economics and business knowledge, especially if they are involved in the grade-appropriate curricula. JA receives funding from individuals and corporate contributors.

Koreatown

Bhattacharyya (see chapter 13) found that supplementary education in Koreatown occurs as a parallel school system that coexists with regular school during the school year and provides extracurricular and academic activities during regular school off-seasons. Supplementary education programs range from early childhood care to those that provide preparation for standardized tests used for college entrance. The Korean Youth Center, for example, offers various language classes, crime/gang prevention, tutoring, tutoring referrals, and family consulting. Bhattacharyya also found that Koreatown has a wide range of youth-oriented schools (eight Korean language schools, close to thirty hagwans, and thirty music, dance, and karate studios). Additionally, professional development of proprietors and personnel of supplementary education programs are available. Korean families rely extensively on supplementary education services, and there appears to be a growing supplementary education economy in the Los Angeles area.

Puente High School Program

The Puente High School Program enables Hispanic students to bridge the transition from high school to college. Founded in 1981 by Felix Gavaliz and Patricia McGrath, the goal of Puente (Spanish for *bridge*) is to increase the number of educationally underserved students who stay in school, enroll in college, earn college degrees, and return to the community as leaders and mentors to future generations.

Puente high school students work with a Puente counselor (who has received special training in the curriculum), who introduces them to college and career opportunities and facilitates the college admissions process. Beginning in the ninth and tenth grades, students in Puente obtain a rigorous two-year English class sequence with an academic focus on Mexican American and Hispanic literature and experiences. In eleventh and twelfth grades, students receive intensive college preparatory classes. Additionally, participants meet with either an academically successful student or an adult mentor and participate in field trips to college campuses and professional workplaces. Puente also emphasizes the significance of parent involvement. For example, parents are actively involved in the program through parent workshops, mentor events, and meetings with the Puente counselor. Parents are also required to sign a statement agreeing to provide support to the students in a variety of ways if accepted into the Puente program.

Staff development is important and is emphasized in the year-round training of their teachers, counselors, and mentors, who receive exposure to innovative and effective methodologies. A 1998 final evaluation report of three Puente sites conducted by the Carnegie Corporation of New York found that Puente students were more likely to take the PSAT in ninth or tenth grade and the ACT or SAT in the eleventh and twelfth grades. College enrollment for Puente participants was higher than for non-Puente students and Puente students were admitted to four-year colleges at almost twice the rate of non-Puente students (43 percent vs. 24 percent).

In a different study by the National Center for Education Statistics, results indicated that the percentage of underrepresented high school Puente students who enrolled in the University of California (UC) or California State University (CSU) the semester following graduation was 29 percent in 1999 compared to 9 percent of non-Puente students and 32 percent in 2000 versus 10 percent for non-Puente participants. Currently, Puente serves 8,000 students directly in forty-five community colleges and thirty-one high schools throughout California. Puente is sponsored by the California Community College and the University of California, in addition to individuals and organizations that donate their time and resources.

Science and Math Programs

Our review of science and math programs suggests that there are quite a few math and science programs that encourage students of color and females in particular. Operation SMART, a program established by Girls Inc. in 1985, encourages girls to persist in math and science by introducing them to careers in science, math, and technology and emphasizing hands-on experiences. This program is based on research, developed in consultation with the experts in the field, and rigorously evaluated. Another program of note is the Women's Action Alliance, a national organization working through community-based organizations, which has an ongoing commitment to gender equity in education. The Women's Action Alliance attempts to provide resources that work to increase girls' interest in math and science. Its most recent project is a three-tiered mentor project entitled "Buddies Exploring Science Together (BEST)." Included in this group is the Solving Problems for Access to Careers in Engineering and Science (SPACES) at the University of California, Berkeley. SPACES has developed activities for students that are intended to provide career awareness and certain mathematical skills considered critical to problem solving.

Recreation Programs

Little League

Little League Baseball is a nonprofit organization whose mission is promoting, developing, supervising, and voluntarily assisting in all lawful ways the interest of those who participate in Little League Baseball. Through guidance and leadership, the Little League program assists youth in developing the qualities of citizenship, discipline, teamwork, and physical well-being. The league focuses on the importance of the virtues of character, courage, and loyalty and is designed to develop contributing and participating citizens rather than athletes.

Socialization Programs

Meyerhoff Scholars Program

The Meyerhoff Scholars Program (MSP) at the University of Maryland in Baltimore County is exceptional given its emphasis on the achievement of excellence in addition to the nurturing and encouragement to help students achieve a high level of excellence. In 1988, Dr. Freeman Hrabowski III created a scholarship program that not only recruits but also finances thirty to fifty students a year who show promise in math or science. The MSP, named for the

Baltimore couple who first financed it, attracts black high school students sought by the best colleges but also seeks out those with promise who are less obviously headed for success. The MSP's conceptualization and implementation of the following goals enables them to create a critical mass of minority high achievers who become role models and mentors for younger students. These goals include: (1) increasing the number of underrepresented students who could successfully complete a course of study in the sciences, engineering, mathematics, and other technical fields in which they were historically underrepresented; (2) academically and socially preparing these students to pursue PhDs and/or MD/PhDs in these fields; (3) reducing the overprediction phenomenon between underrepresented and majority students at the right end of the achievement distribution; and (4) increasing the number of minority professionals in these fields and in the university professorate (thus creating much-needed role models for minority students of later generations).

The Posse Foundation

Another academic socialization program of note is the Posse program (see chapter 10 for a more detailed description of this program), which began operations in 1989 and was designed to address three issues that continue to trouble higher education. The first issue concerns the fact that recruitment and selection strategies designed to identify diverse populations of students for admission to selective institutions of higher education are somewhat limited. Such institutions seem to draw from a rather narrow pool of highly desirable students. Many capable and very promising students are overlooked or not even considered because they are not identified as belonging to that narrowly drawn pool. The Posse Foundation program challenges the narrowness of the criteria for membership in that pool of candidates for admission to college by identifying students who present leadership talent, high status among their peers and communities, and demonstrated ambition and desire to succeed, in addition to academic competence as reflected in GPA and college admissions test scores. The program presents these students to participating institutions and advocates for their admission to college as a group.

The second issue concerns the college retention and completion rates of students drawn from culturally and socially diverse backgrounds. For example, while rates of retention through graduation are rising for African American students, these rates remain considerably lower than the rates for total student populations at U.S. colleges. And although the retention rates for black students at our most selective institutions are much better than the average for the nation, African American students lag behind the mean rates for other students at these institutions.

The third issue concerns the underrepresentation in many of our colleges of the population diversity that is present in the nation. This underrepresentation is, no doubt, associated with the social and cultural homogeneity typically found in the more selective institutions of higher learning.

The Posse Foundation program tackles both the retention and the integration issues through the recruitment, selection, preparation, and support of multicultural teams of students (posses), and places these posses at participating institutions. At each college, the posse functions as a support group for the academic and personal development of its members, as a model of cultural diversity in student life, and as an agent for social change toward democratic integration on its campus. The varieties of support provided for their combined academic work and social action are designed to address issues two and three.

Socialization and Acculturation

Although this implicit intervention overlaps with those that are specifically explicit, it is especially captured in the practices of the Joseph Forgione Development School for Youth (DSY) in New York City. The DSY is a twelve-week career education program sponsored by the All Stars Project Inc. Founded and directed in 1997 by developmental psychologist Lenora Fulani and her colleague Pam Lewis, DSY is a developmental program that promotes leadership among inner-city youth between the ages of sixteen and twenty-one. Program participants are recruited from New York and New Jersey public schools after submitting written essays on leadership. The program accepts young people who aspire to be leaders. Training workshops are conducted by volunteer "program associates" who are corporate professionals (bankers, lawyers, consultants) trained to teach young people interpersonal skills, public speaking, resume writing, interviewing skills, and professional conduct, including how to dress professionally. Through these various mechanisms, young people are socialized to develop professionally, personally, and socially. They learn they can perform both as who they are and as who they are becoming. For instance, young people learn about the attitudes and skills required for success in a professional workplace and are given opportunities to visit corporate sites (such as the New York Stock Exchange) and meet with senior executives. The goal of the program is to encourage dialogue between the participants and the professionals about their daily routines and career paths. In the trainings, participants learn to behave like marketers, financial analysts, CEOs, and product developers, for example.

At the completion of the twelve weeks, participants graduate from DSY and are placed in a paid internship in corporations such as Merrill Lynch,

Morgan Stanley Dean Witter, Ernst and Young, and many more. In their internships, these young people learn what it takes to be a lawyer, an accountant, a stockbroker, or a financial manager by socializing and acclimating to the corporate culture. DSY operates with funds from friends, volunteers, and corporate donations.

THE NATURE OF SPONSORING ORGANIZATIONS

The Carnegie Council on Adolescent Development report *A Matter of Time: Risk and Opportunity in the Nonschool Hours* (1992) categorizes youth development programs under sponsoring organizations—that is, national youth organizations, independent (grassroots) organizations, religious organizations, public organizations, and private organizations. Specifically, national youth organizations include ASPIRA, Big Brothers/Big Sisters of America, Boys and Girls Clubs of America, Child Welfare League of America, National Coalition of Hispanic Health and Human Services Organization (COSSMHO), Girls Inc., National Networks of Runaway and Youth Services, National Urban League, Salvation Army, and WAVE, Inc.

Of the seventeen thousand youth development organizations now in operation in the United States, some of the several thousand that are independent are affiliated with national youth organizations such as the YWCA of the USA or Boys and Girls Clubs of America. Religious youth organizations include those with a combination of small groups of same-age peers organized and led by dedicated adult leaders; formal instruction (such as classes to prepare youth for full membership in church or synagogue); worship services, often planned and conducted by youth themselves; special events (such as camps and retreats); youth leadership councils; community service projects; and community centers (such as the networks of Jewish Community Centers). In addition, many congregations sponsor Boy Scout, Girl Scout, or Camp Fire programs, and may add their denominational component to the basic program of these organizations. Private community groups include adult service clubs, sports organizations, senior citizens groups, and museums. Public sector organizations include public libraries and parks and recreation departments.

In addition to the categories of implicit, explicit, and content-specific interventions discussed above, our third category suggests that youth-serving agencies and organizations such as churches, libraries, parks and recreation departments, private organizations, sports organizations, senior citizens groups, and national youth development programs provide various types of supplementary education that can impact the development of the children and youth they reach. According to *A Matter of Time*, 66 percent of all youth are

Table 9.3. Organizations That Sponsor Supplementary Education Services

National Organizations	Independent Organizations	Religious Organizations	Private Organizations	Public Organizations
ASPIRA	Center for Youth Development and Policy Research (CYDPR) of Academy for Educational Development	Jewish Yeshiva	Edison Schools	Libraries, Parks, and Recreation Departments
Big Brothers/Big Sisters of America	Challengers Boys and Girls Club (of Metro Los Angeles)	Project SPIRIT of the Congress of National Black Churches	Huntington Learning Center	Totally Cool, Totally Art (TX)
Families and Schools Together (FAST) of the Alliance for Children and Families (nonprofit)	El Centro de la Raza		Kaplan	Young Adult Library Services Association (YALSA)
Junior Achievement (JA)	Sponsor-A-Scholar (SAS), Philadelphia Futures		Out-of-School-Time Evaluation Database (Harvard's Family Research Project)	
National Alliance for Hispanic Health (formerly COSSMHO) (nonprofit)	The After-School Corporation (TASC)		Sylvan Learning Center	
National Youth Sports Program (NYSP) (nonprofit)	Young Citizens		The Center for Research on the Context of Teaching (CRC), Stanford University	

The American Indian Science & Engineering Society (AISES)

The Foster Grandparent Program of the Senior Corps

The Junior Leagues International (nonprofit)

The Juvenile Mentoring Program (JUMP) of the U.S. Department of Justice

The Partnership for After School Education (PASE) (nonprofit)

Youth Alive!

The 21st Century Community Learning Center Program of the U.S. Department of Education

Youth Development Inc.

The National Institute on Out-of-School Time (NIOST) at Wellesley College

Princeton Review

involved in activities, ranking youth organizations second only to public schools in the number of young people they reach each year. Youth organizations and programs provide adolescents with social and academic support; mentoring; life-skills training; positive and constructive alternatives to substance abuse, violence, and irresponsible sexual activity; and enriching opportunities to positively contribute to their communities and to society. Many youth programs are successfully facilitating the route to postsecondary education by providing opportunities to youth who drop out of school, and reducing illegal behavior. Additionally, youth programs and organizations offer a safe and beneficial environment in the out-of-school hours when neither parents nor schools are available to provide supervision.

The following are some examples of organizations providing supplementary education services and programs for youth. These organizations and programs vary in scope and size. For example, some programs such as ASPIRA Association are national, while others like the Sponsor-A-Scholar program are offered through independent organizations not associated with a national structure. Still others, such as Project SPIRIT, are based in churches; others, such as the Sylvan Learning Centers, are private. We provide two examples each of organizations sponsoring both single and multifaceted youth services.

National Organizations

Approximately four hundred national organizations serve only young people or offer significant services to them (Erickson 1998). These include the ASPIRA Association and the American Indian Science and Engineering Society (AISES), which are described below.

ASPIRA Association

Created by Antonia Pantoja with the assistance of educators and professionals to address the high dropout rate and low educational attainment of Puerto Rican youths, ASPIRA Association has been dedicated to advancing the education and leadership development of Puerto Rican and other Hispanic youth. Since its inception in New York City in 1961, the mission of ASPIRA has been to empower the Hispanic community by developing and nurturing the leadership, intellectual, and cultural potential of its youth. This nonprofit organization achieves its mission by believing that Hispanics have the collective potential to propel the community forward. ASPIRA (which means *to aspire*) believes that Hispanic youth or "aspirantes" are "leaders waiting to emerge."

Hispanic youth participate in ASPIRA's programs through ASPIRA Clubs where they learn the process of "awareness, analysis, and action." Programs offer leadership training to youth, enabling them to develop academic skills, experience cultural enrichment activities, attend career conferences, provide service to their communities, and testify before political and educational committees on issues important to Hispanic youth. Additionally, youth are provided with career and college counseling, financial aid and scholarship assistance, and continuous opportunities to implement community action projects. Parent involvement is also an important component in ASPIRA's programs.

ASPIRA has three different educational and careers programs. The National Health Careers Program, for instance, is designed to improve access to quality health care in the Hispanic community. The program recruits high school and college students and prepares them to enter health professions such as medicine, dentistry, pharmacy, public health, optometry, and clinical psychology. The Math and Science Academy (MAS) and CASA MAS programs enhance math and science skills of middle school students with hands-on activities, mentors, field trips, and academic support. This initiative operates both as an after-school enrichment program and as part of an alternative school curriculum. The CASA MAS website offers math and science education resources for students, parents, teachers, and administrators. Lastly, the Youth Entrepreneurship Venture, a partnership between ASPIRA and Youth Venture, provides youth with the opportunity to develop and utilize entrepreneurial skills to impact their communities and their own lives.

The national headquarters in Washington, D.C., provides information and assistance to a network of five thousand community-based organizations, school districts, local and national policymakers, and corporate representatives. The national office also supports local offices in the Hispanic communities of major cities in Florida, Illinois, New Jersey, New York, Connecticut, Pennsylvania, and Puerto Rico. Currently, ASPIRA serves nearly twenty-five thousand students each year in over four hundred schools.

American Indian Science and Engineering Society

The American Indian Science and Engineering Society (AISES) is a national nonprofit organization with a mission of increasing the number of American Indian scientists and engineers in the country, and developing technologically informed leaders within the Native American community. Created in 1977 by American Indian scientists to address problems of high secondary dropout rates and low college enrollment, retention, and graduation rates of American Indian students, in addition to the underrepresentation of American Indians in the science and engineering fields, AISES's primary goal is to function as a vehicle for the advancement of American Indians as they become self-reliant and self-directed members of society. AISES's secondary purpose is to educate other Americans about the Native American heritage.

AISES provides financial (yearly scholarships range from $1,000 to $5,000), academic, and cultural support to American Indians and Alaskan Natives from middle school through graduate school. Through AISES's educational programs, American Indians and Native Alaskans have opportunities to pursue studies in the fields of science, engineering, and technology. AISES's programs are in collaboration with the K–12 Affiliated Schools Program, which provides schools, tribal groups, and other educational organizations with a newsletter and information on AISES activities and deadlines for the annual science fair, summer programs, teacher workshops, and scholarships. Additionally, AISES also develops culturally appropriate curricula and publications and offers several scholarships for Native American undergraduate and graduate students. Preference is given to those students pursuing studies in science, engineering, math, health, business, natural resources/energy resource management, and secondary education.

AISES also has a Summer Work Experience Program in which Native American/Alaskan Native college students have access to a ten-week paid internship in federal agencies where they also learn about careers within the federal government. AISES's College Chapters program encourages students to develop a network of colleagues, practice leadership skills, attend regional and national leadership conferences, and join tutoring groups. To accomplish its goals, AISES builds partnerships with tribes, schools, other nonprofit organizations, corporations, foundations, and government agencies and is supported mainly by grants from both public and private funding agencies, membership dues, and marketing activities.

Independent Organizations

The CCAD study (1992) reports that only 25 percent of all independent youth organizations function on yearly budgets of more than $25,000, suggesting that the majority are small and operated by volunteers. We illustrate this category with the following two examples of nonprofit organizations: the Philadelphia Futures' Sponsor-A-Scholar in Philadelphia, and the After School Corporation in New York.

Sponsor-A-Scholar

Sponsor-A-Scholar (SAS) was created in 1989 by Philadelphia Futures, a nonprofit organization based in Philadelphia and an affiliate of the Greater Philadelphia Urban Affairs Coalition. The goal of SAS is to reduce the educational and economic gaps between low-income students and their more advantaged peers by providing scholarship funds, mentoring, academic supports, and preparation for college. SAS links at-risk youth with mentors who provide one-on-one mentoring for five years, beginning in the ninth grade and extending through the freshman college year. School staff nominates eligible participants who must be economically disadvantaged, achieving at average to below-average levels (Bs and Cs), and exhibit motivation and desire to attend college. Mentors and students meet monthly and maintain frequent telephone contact between meetings. Mentors also review students' academic progress, assist with financial aid and college applications, and maintain contact with SAS staff. SAS services are delivered to students mostly at their schools on individual or group basis. Participants attend academic enrichment activities including summer travel, campus programs, cultural events, and career exploration workshops. SAS students must also participate in college preparatory activities, including SAT workshops, campus visits, and financial aid seminars. Students who complete the program requirements and are matriculated in college are offered a $6,000 award for college-related expenses.

The Institute for Research on Higher Education evaluated SAS's effectiveness in a 1996 study. The results suggested that program participants had higher grade point averages, were three times more likely to attend college the first year after high school, and participated in more college preparatory activities than non-SAS participants. The SAS program is currently assisting about 250 high school students and more than 200 students in college. Currently, twelve communities have adopted the SAS model with information and technical assistance provided by Philadelphia Futures. Other communities throughout the country are also beginning to implement the SAS model (e.g., Milwaukee, Wisconsin, and Houston, Texas). SAS's financial sponsors include individuals, businesses, private organizations, public agencies, religious, and higher education institutions.

The After-School Corporation (TASC)

TASC is a nonprofit organization with a focus on making quality after-school programs universally available and publicly funded in New York City, New York State, and across the nation. In collaboration with the New York City Department of Education and other local school districts, TASC funds programs that are housed in public schools and operated by community-based organizations, including universities and other nonprofits. The After-School Corporation began in 1998 with a $125 million challenge grant from philanthropist George Soros's Open Society Institute (OSI). TASC is matching those funds on a three-to-one basis. According to TASC's website, TASC-supported sites serve more than 50,000 children throughout New York City and thirty-two counties in New York State. TASC has collaborated with more than 130 organizations to operate these programs. These collaborators range from neighborhood groups such as Alianza Dominicana in Washington Heights to the affiliates of large national organizations such as the YMCA in Rochester. The programs TASC supports operate from 3:00 p.m. to 6:00 p.m. each day schools are open. TASC programs are accessible to children in kindergarten through twelfth grade at a cost of approximately $1,500 per child per year. According to Policy Associates, approximately 30 percent of the children at a school enroll in the after-school program—usually two hundred to three hundred students per school. TASC's programs include the following:

- Programming that includes literacy, art, technological skills development, and homework help;
- A ratio of one adult to ten students;
- Parent participation; and
- A full-time, year-round site coordinator who is selected by the collaborating organization and the principal of the school where the coordinator is housed.

Religious Organizations

The CCAD study (1992) found that one out of every three organizations listed in the Directory of American Youth Organizations is affiliated with a church (Erickson 1998). Some organizations are associated with a particular denomination or branch of their faith, while others are autonomous or nondenominational. We illustrate this group of religious organizations sponsoring youth services through Project SPIRIT and Jewish Yeshivas.

Project SPIRIT

Project SPIRIT (Strength, Perseverance, Imagination, Responsibility, Integrity, and Talent) was launched by the Congress of National Black Churches (CNBC) in 1986. CNBC, however, has worked for twenty-three years to strengthen the black church's ministry by serving as an organizational umbrella for the eight major African American religious denominations. The program's mission is to provide constructive after-school activities to youth from low-SES backgrounds, to increase the number of caring adults in these young people's lives, to strengthen academic achievement, and to teach life skills.

Project SPIRIT enrolls young people from ages six to twelve who are unresponsive to the conventional school setting, receiving low grades, and experiencing discipline problems. After school each day, professionals and other volunteers provide tutoring in reading, writing, and mathematics and assist participants with their homework. Other activities focus on teaching life skills and improving youth self-concept through games, skits, songs, and role-playing and developing pride in the African American culture. During the weekend, parents are provided with educational programs that emphasize child and adolescent development, parent-child communication, discipline, and financial management. Additionally, pastors of participating churches are trained through the Pastoral Counseling Training to become more effective in the care, education, and guidance of African American youth. Since its first demonstration project (funded by the Carnegie Corporation of New York and the Lilly Endowment) in 1986, Project SPIRIT has provided services to more than two thousand youth and their parents in Atlanta, Oakland, Indianapolis, Kokomo, Savannah, and Washington, D.C.

Jewish Yeshiva

Some Jewish American groups use supplementary education experiences to provide cultural and historical traditions for their children. These supplemental activities run parallel to the mainstream school (Tribble 1992). Quite apart from the cultural exposure, these environments provide additional opportunities for the children to engage in intellectually stimulating activities. In the Jewish tradition, adolescent development is associated with religious training that is most often delivered through supplemental classes. An intricate part of this training is the exposure to historical facts and religious as well as other scholarly texts that develop literacy and critical thinking skills, which complement students' academic pursuits. Fejgin (1995) argues that focusing on verbal analytical skills has a positive influence on the academic outcomes of these students

Private Organizations

Many private organizations and companies also provide supplementary education services. For example, companies such as Sylvan Learning Center and Huntington Learning Center provide individualized diagnostic as well as tutoring and test preparation services.

Sylvan Learning Center

Founded in 1979, Sylvan Learning Center (SLC) was started to provide individualized instructional services to students of all ages and skill levels.

SLCs begin their work with students by analyzing and targeting the causes of academic frustrations and attempt to instill confidence and independence. The center provides instruction in reading, writing, math, test preparation, and study skills. Through the three main program components (personalized programs, individual attention, and mastery of learning), students at Sylvan work on achieving specific academic goals. Based on the findings from a comprehensive skills assessment, Sylvan develops personalized curriculums that seek to address and possibly eliminate underlying issues. Students enrolled in Sylvan programs are in groups of three students to one teacher, and experience personal interaction, attention, and immediate positive reinforcement from certified teachers.

In the personalized test prep course, students learn how to manage difficult verbal questions, deconstruct difficult reading passages, and convert complicated algebra problems into manageable arithmetic. They are also taught which geometry facts and figures appear most frequently on the PSAT, SAT, or ACT, what questions to ignore, and when to make an educated guess. Through homework exercises, students practice and reinforce their skills for improving their scores. Three full-length practice exams help students and their instructors assess student progress and provide critical feedback. Today, there are almost nine hundred Sylvan Learning Centers in North America and Asia (Hong Kong and Guam).

Huntington Learning Center

Huntington Learning Center was started by educators Eileen and Raymond Huntington, who were also parents. Since 1977, the goal of the Huntington Learning Center has been to help students excel academically by providing supplementary instruction in reading, mathematics, study skills, phonics, spelling, vocabulary, writing, algebra, and geometry. The Huntington program begins with an extensive individualized diagnostic evaluation to identify students' problem areas. Students thus receive individualized instruction based on the test results. At Huntington, students are taught how to reduce frustration by strengthening their basic skills, enhancing self-confidence, and restoring their motivation to succeed. Students are taught in small groups with one teacher to three students. Teachers adjust their pace to the individual child's needs and use materials appropriate for the student's level. The program begins at a basic level and assignments gradually increase in difficulty as new skills are mastered. Huntington also offers an in-school program for the SAT conducted by teachers who are trained, employed, and managed by Huntington. SAT courses are offered during the school year using a small-class model with a student-teacher ratio of 10:1. Huntington provides all instructional materials for both students and staff, and conducts seminars for parents on topics such as "SAT: A Parent's Survival Guide," getting into college, and topics parents may find relevant.

Public Organizations

Libraries and parks and recreation departments not only provide safe places for youth during unsupervised hours but also offer a range of athletic, social, and supplementary academic opportunities for youth. The Young Adult Library Services Association (YALSA) of the American Library Association and the Totally Cool, Totally Art (TCTA) program in Austin, Texas, are examples of supplementary education programs offered through libraries and parks and recreation departments.

Young Adult Library Services Association

The Young Adult Library Services Association (YALSA) (one of the oldest and largest library associations in the world), was founded in 1957 to advocate, endorse, and strengthen library services to young people ages twelve to eighteen in schools and public and institutional libraries. YALSA, a division of the American Library Association, is a member-driven organization based in Chicago. The association provides its members with a diverse program of continuing education, publications, awards, grants, and youth advocacy. The association advocates the young adult's right to free and equal access to materials and services, and assists librarians in enabling such access. Young adults are also encouraged to become actively involved in the library decision-making process. YALSA's goals include assisting librarians in the development, implementation, and evaluation of programs and services that address the social, educational, psychological, and recreational needs of youth.

To address the problem of poor literacy among adolescents, YALSA created "Teen Reading Week," a national literacy initiative aimed at youth, parents, librarians, educators, and booksellers. Teen Reading aspires to decrease the reading achievement gaps by advocating time for recreational reading, allowing teens to select their own reading materials, and encouraging them to acquire the habit of reading regularly. YALSA involves and actively engages young people through book discussion groups, book review message boards, book reviews linked to the library's web page, surveys evaluating reading interest, and conversations with youth about their reading interests. YALSA's website provides lists of "Best Books for Young Adults" and "Reluctant Readers" in topics raging from fiction, nonfiction, poetry, and biographies. In addition to providing book collections that are responsive to youth interests, YALSA also provides a website called Teen Hoopla (www.ala.org/teenhoopla), where youth can obtain homework help, share favorite books, and learn about sports, entertainment, and teen life issues. Currently, YALSA's three thousand members include public librarians serving young adults, library school instructors, school librarians, and youth advocates.

Totally Cool, Totally Art

Totally Cool, Totally Art (TCTA) is a nationally recognized art program for students in grades 7–12. This after-school program, offered in recreation centers, provides young people with visual art classes that include drawing, sculpting plaster, video directing, and computer graphics. The program goals include offering young people a safe place, novel experiences, a sense of belonging, participants' respect and trust for others, and encouragement of teamwork and communication skills through arts education.

This popular program operates in sixteen different recreation centers during six separate four-week sessions. Each session meets twice a week for three hours after school in groups of twenty teens or fewer. Sessions begin at 5:00 p.m. with a one-hour tutoring program or other activities planned by a teen leader, followed by a class taught by an up-and-coming artist with the assistance of a teen coordinator from the host center. The teen leaders can volunteer for as many sessions as they wish. From 1996 through the year 2000, the program reached 1,059 youth.

This program's impact has been evaluated by the Texas A&M University staff, who have illustrated that participants improved in their ability to collaborate in a group, were aware of the community resources available during non-school hours, and were less skeptical that adults were sincerely concerned about them. TCTA is coordinated by the Austin Parks and Recreation Department's Dougherty Arts School and Community Recreation Centers, with monetary contributions from the Austin City Council's Social Fabric Initiative.

CONCLUSION

As evidenced in the referenced taxonomy, a variety of supplemental or enrichment programs outside of the school's regular class time are available for at-risk, underachieving, moderately achieving, high-achieving, and gifted and talented students. Tutoring, for example, can be effective in overcoming barriers to learning often encountered in large-group instruction, if tutors and tutees are compatible (Gaustad 1992). Allowing moderate- to high-achieving students to serve as tutors can reap benefits for tutor and tutee. Although remediation is a popular method used in supplemental programs, an accelerated curriculum has been suggested to be more effective for both high-achieving and underachieving groups (Levin and Hopfenberg 1991; Lynch and Mills 1993). However, remediation can be useful in conjunction with other enrichment activities such as social and academic skill development.

In order to produce large numbers of high-achieving students of color necessary to address the economic and social equity issues facing the United States, long-term substantive supplemental activities must be developed and implemented. Preventive models targeted toward primary school children are thought by some to constitute the most efficient proactive methods for accelerating minority achievement. Given the current state of academic achievement, supplemental models should be developed that augment the entire schooling process from prekindergarten through high school. Supplemental programs for younger children should be geared toward preparing students to develop positive attitudes and long-term commitments to learning and intellectual achievement. As children get older, supplemental activities should focus on developing sophisticated oral, written, and quantitative analytic skills. Upon entry to middle school, peer group influences on attitudes, beliefs, and behaviors replace parental and family influences. It is at this time that academic peer groups should be the focus of structured supplemental activities. During the high school years, supplemental support should be geared toward correcting gaps in student preparation and preparing the student for postsecondary education and advanced intellectual activities. Finally, the array of documented activities in the taxonomy, while clearly not exhaustive, is an effort to address these concerns and hopes for students in general and students of color in particular.

REFERENCES

Berryman, J. C., and K. W. Breighner. 1994. *Modeling healthy behavior: Actions and attitudes in schools*. Santa Cruz, CA: ETR Associates.

Bhattacharyya, M. 1998. Korean supplementary education in Los Angeles: An urban community's resource for families. Paper prepared for the National Invitational Conference on Supplementary Education, Temple University, Center for Research in Human Development and Education and the National Task Force in Minority High Achievement of the College Board, October, Washington, DC.

Brooks, P. E., and J. L. Herman. 1991. *LA's BEST: An after school education and enrichment program. Evaluation report*. Los Angeles: University of California, Los Angeles, Center for the Study of Evaluation.

Carnegie Council on Adolescent Development. 1989. *Turning points: Preparing American youth for the twenty-first century. The report of the Task Force on the Education of Young Adults*. New York: Carnegie Corporation of New York.

———. 1992. *A matter of time: Risk and opportunity in the nonschool hours. Report of the Task Force on Youth Development and Community Programs.* New York: Carnegie Corporation of New York.

———. 1994. *Consultation on afterschool programs.* New York: Carnegie Corporation of New York.

College Board. 1999. *Reaching the top: A report of the National Task Force on Minority High Achievement.* New York: The College Entrance Examination Board.

Dolly, J. P. 1992. "Juku" and the performance of Japanese students: An American perspective. Paper presented at the annual meeting of the Japan–United States Teacher Education Consortium, June, Tokyo, Japan.

Erickson, J. B. 1998. *1998–1999 Directory of American youth organizations: A guide to 500 clubs, groups, troops, teams, societies, lodges and more for young people.* Rev. ed. Minneapolis, MN: Free Spirit Publishing.

Fejgin, N. 1995. Factors contributing to the academic excellence of American Jewish and Asian students. *Sociology of Education* 68:18–30.

Ferguson-Florissant School District. 1993. *Lifelong values.* Ferguson, MO: Author.

Gaustad, J. 1992. Tutoring for at-risk students. *OSSC Bulletin* 36(3). Eugene: Oregon School Study Council, University of Oregon.

Gordon, E. W. 1973. A new kind of joy. Review of Theodore Sizer's *Places for learning, places for joy. Learning Today* 6(3): 102.

———. 1999. *Education and justice: A view from the back of the bus.* New York: Teachers College Press.

Gordon, E. W., and B. Bridglall. 2002. *The idea of supplementary education.* Pedagogical Inquiry and Praxis, no. 3. New York: Teachers College, Columbia University.

Gordon, E. W., and L. D. Song. 1994. Variations in the experience of resilience. In *Educational resilience in inner-city America: Challenges and prospects*, edited by M. C. Wang and E. W. Gordon, 27–43. Hillsdale, NJ: Lawrence Erlbaum.

Gyanani, T. C., and P. Pahuja. 1995. Effects of peer tutoring on abilities and achievement. *Contemporary Educational Psychology* 20:469–75.

Harnisch, D. 1994. Supplemental education in Japan: Juku schooling and its implications. *Journal of Curriculum Studies* 26:323–34.

Hidi, S., and V. Anderson. 1986. Producing written summaries: Task demands, cognitive operations, and implications for instruction. *Review of Educational Research* 86:473–93.

Latchkey guidelines: Urban model (Cleveland City School District). After school child care program for latchkey children. 1987. Columbus: Ohio State Department of Education, Division of Educational Services.

Levin, H. M., and W. S. Hopfenberg. 1991. Don't Remediate: Accelerate! *Principal* 40:11–13.

Lynch, S. J., and C. J. Mills. 1993. Identifying and preparing disadvantaged and minority youth for high-level academic achievement. *Contemporary Educational Psychology* 18:66–76.

MacIver, D. J. 1991. *Helping students who fall behind: Remedial activities in the middle grades.* Washington, DC: Office of Educational Research and Improvement. Report no. PS 020 189.

Maddy-Bernstein, C., and E. S. Cunanan. 1995. *Exemplary career guidance programs: What should they look like?* Berkeley: National Center for Research in Vocational Education, University of California, Berkeley. MDS-855.

Marx, F. 1989. *After-school programs for low-income young adolescents: Overview and program profiles.* Working Paper no. 194. Wellesley, MA: Wellesley College, Center for Research on Women.

Mercer, J. 1973. *Labeling the mentally retarded: Clinical and social system perspectives on mental retardation.* Berkeley: University of California Press.

Morton-Young, T. 1995. *After-school and parent education programs for at-risk youth and their families: A guide to organizing and operating a community-based center for basic educational skills reinforcement, homework assistance, cultural enrichment, and a parent involvement focus.* Springfield, IL: Charles C. Thomas.

National Occupational Information Coordinating Committee. 1989. *National Career Development Guidelines. K–Adult Handbook.* Washington, DC: Author.

Pacific Northwest Extension. 1991. *Child guidance techniques.* University of Idaho; Oregon State University; Washington State University.

Payne, O. L. 1992. The effects of learning strategies on a group of Black secondary students' verbal and mathematics SAT scores. Paper presented at the annual meeting of the American Educational Research Association, San Francisco, April 20–24.

Purves, A. 1991. *The ideology of canons and cultural concerns in the literature curriculum.* Albany, NY: National Research Center on Literature Teaching and Learning.

Ravid, R. 1988. *The relationship between Jewish early childhood education and family Jewish practices.* Chicago: Phase II Metropolitan Chicago Board of Jewish Education. No. PS 018 225.

Schneider, B., and Y. Lee. 1990. A model for academic success: The school and home environment of East Asian students. *Anthropology and Education Quarterly* 21:358–77.

Seppanen, P., D. deVries, and M. Seligson. 1993. *National study of before- and after-school programs.* Washington, DC: U.S. Department of Education, Office of Policy and Planning.

Sizer, T. 1973. *Places for learning, places for joy: Speculations on American school reform.* Cambridge, MA: Harvard University Press.

Slavin, R. E., N. L. Karweit, and B. A. Wasik. 1991. *Preventing early school failure: What works?* Baltimore, MD: Johns Hopkins University, Center for Research on Effective Schooling for Disadvantaged Students. Report no. 26.

Taylor, R. D. 1994. Risk and resilience: Contextual influences on the development of African-American adolescents. In *Educational resilience in inner-city America: Challenges and prospects*, edited by M. C. Wang and E. W. Gordon. Hillsdale, NJ: Lawrence Erlbaum.

Tribble, I. 1992. *Making their mark: Educating African American children.* Silver Spring, MD: Beckham

What young adolescents want and need from out-of-school programs: A focus group report. 1992. Commissioned by the Carnegie Council on Adolescent Development. Washington, DC: S. W. Morris.

Wolf, R. M. 1966. The measurement of environments. In *Testing problems in perspective*, edited by A. Anastasi. Washington, DC: American Council on Education.

10

Varieties of Supplementary Education Interventions

Beatrice L. Bridglall

Among the issues we are concerned with and have elaborated upon are those of participation in and access to supplementary education interventions, funding, the incongruence of young people's needs and the program activities provided, and a paucity of evaluations demonstrating program effectiveness (see chapters 2 and 3). In this chapter, we examine how various supplementary education programs manage to address these concerns. We also situate these issues in the context of some common principles: parent and community participation, knowledgeable professional staff, high standards and expectations, the perspective that young people are resources to be cultivated, and the quality of implementation efforts (James and Jurich 1999).

The supplementary education interventions selected indicate the range of particular programs that have emerged to address the academic and social needs of students in general and students of color in particular. Descriptions of the following programs were adapted from papers presented at the 1998 National Invitational Conference on Supplementary Education, Temple University, Center for Research in Human Development and Education, and the National Task Force in Minority High Achievement of the College Board, Washington, D.C. (which represented an early effort at focusing attention on the value of supplementary education):

- *The National Urban League*: A community-building approach to educational improvement
- *All Stars Talent Show Network*: A project grounded in theatrical performance and traditional socialization mechanisms used in the corporate world
- The *Posse* program: Recruitment and retention of students of color for selective colleges and universities

- *A Better Chance*: Preparing students of color for college
- Supplementary education from a corporate perspective

A COMMUNITY-BUILDING APPROACH TO EDUCATIONAL IMPROVEMENT: THE NATIONAL URBAN LEAGUE

by Velma Cobb

In 1997 the National Urban League (NUL) brought together the leadership of national faith-based, professional, social, and civic African American organizations to consider ways of improving the educational achievement of youth of color. More than twenty national organizations signed on to what is now the Campaign for African American Achievement, forming a coalition with the power and influence needed to transform the education of African American children. The National Urban League is increasingly devoted to the process of systems change related to improving the development and achievement of African American children. The organization identified such indicators as improved academic standing, increased participation in constructive after-school activities, reductions in unhealthy or risky behaviors, and fewer contacts with juvenile justice systems as evidence of positive youth outcomes. Two NUL projects, the Youth Development Mobilization Initiative (YDMI) and the Academic Achievement Mobilization Initiative (AAMI), are operating at seven Urban League affiliates. These projects have become the foundation for the Campaign for African American Achievement, which is a community mobilization and advocacy initiative aimed at the collective achievement and social development of African American and other children of color. The NUL uses the strategy of advocacy and mobilization as mechanisms for community engagement and change-developing solutions. The campaign is based on the theory of a community working together under a shared set of visions and goals to promote the development of young people through systems change rather than superficial changes in local programming.

The campaign, as implemented by NUL's YDMI and AAMI, is aimed at creating systemic change in two areas. The first is comprised of youth, families, and the African American community, where the goal is to directly "spread the gospel that achievement matters." The second consists of the public policy sector of influence in the lives of children and youth: educators, administrators, policymakers, and other service providers. The focus here is on promoting and sustaining quality schools and supplementary education structures and supports for all children. Parent, family, and community engagement is the vehicle that links these two areas. Given the varying capacities of its many affiliates, NUL adopted a model that allows entry into the process of community change on three levels. Each level includes a range of activities that promote the ideals of the campaign and represent a progression of involvement that enables affiliates to focus their work.

At the organizational level, affiliates develop, strengthen, and sustain programmatic and organizational structures that promote academic achievement and subsequently replicate these structures in programs that affect children and their families. At the community advocacy and mobilization level, the programmatic and organizational structures and supports become part of a community-wide focus to create a common understanding and commitment to academic achievement. At the community change level, the community establishes a plan of action based on a common vision and set of goals that translate into a series of interim outcomes that eventually lead to improved academic achievement for youth in that community.

In order to brand the campaign as a movement and to create a synergy among the campaign partner organizations, NUL created three core elements for youth, families, and their communities: The NUL/CNBC (Council of National Black Churches) National Achievers Society seeks to encourage, recognize, and reinforce achievement among African American and other youth of color. Adapted from the McKnight Achievers Society (the brainchild of Dr. Israel Tribble), the society has inducted more than five thousand young people to date, and grandfathered in ten thousand former McKnight Achievers. The designation of September as Achievement Month also seeks to increase awareness of the importance of achievement. During September, Urban League affiliates and their campaign and community partners sponsor a series of activities that highlight achievement in their communities. Preachers use their bully pulpit to focus attention on achievement, and on the third Saturday of the month communities hold celebrations for young people "doing the right thing" in their lives, family, and community. Communities hold block parties, parades, rallies, and so forth for young people and their families, showing support for the many positive ways young people have influenced their community.

NUL has worked with the Newspaper Publishers Association on a media campaign to continue spreading the message of academic achievement. Additionally, their print ads in black newspapers speak to achievement in approximately sixty Urban League communities. This campaign has also included radio spots, billboards, and other mechanisms for publicizing the campaign's goals. To implement the second component of the campaign — creation of consumer demand for quality education and better schools — Urban League affiliates, along with their campaign and community partners, engage the community in a conversation about quality education and achievement through the forums, symposia, and leadership summits. The intent is to identify issues and barriers to achievement and positive youth outcomes, and subsequently develop solutions based on the community's expertise and resources. Through data collection and ongoing assessment, the community is able to track what currently exists for children and compare it with their vision of positive youth indicators.

The goal of NUL's Youth Development Mobilization Initiative and Academic Achievement Mobilization Initiative was to produce positive developmental outcomes for youth in a community. Though it was understood that full realization of these outcomes would not occur at the seven sites during the demonstration period, the early and interim outcomes would serve as benchmarks for ongoing progress. Building affiliate capacity, repositioning their agencies, and aligning community capacity were early outcomes seen across these sites. At all sites, affiliate CEOs and executive-level management took the lead and began to view youth and family services as the main avenue for serving their constituents. They began to develop local expertise and a presence in the supplementary education field, explored new approaches and models for improving their programs and services for children and families, and redefined their leadership roles and responsibilities by developing a knowledge base, creating a presence in the community on the issue of achievement, and establishing new measures of success.

Agency leaders became well versed in "best practices," youth development research, and policy trends. To establish a presence in the field of supplementary education, they began to share this information with the community through meetings and other forums. They took advantage of board memberships, organizational affiliations, and personal relationships to begin conversations on the issues and to develop common language and ground around supplementary education and family services. The agency leaders also redefined measures of success from those used by their individual organizations (numbers of programs, numbers of youth and families served, operating funds, etc.) to indicators of communication and collaboration with colleagues in other agencies and the quality of all youth services in the community. To reposition their affiliates as leaders in providing supplementary education services, the leaders developed a vision for affiliates, aligned organizational roles and responsibilities, and maximized resources to support their vision. They created a unified vision for the affiliate by revising their organizational mission statements, shifting focus from a programmatic approach to community-wide systems change and a common understanding of the new vision among affiliate board members and staff.

SUPPLEMENTARY EDUCATION GROUNDED IN
ACTIVITY AND PERFORMANCE: THE ALL STARS PROJECT

by Lenora Fulani

The All Stars Talent Show Network (ASTSN) has reached up to thirty thousand primarily African American youth in New York City annually for the past fifteen years and has involved them in producing and performing in neighborhood talent shows. While the ASTSN is open to every young person who wishes to participate, the leadership has focused their efforts in the areas with the highest levels of poverty and crime and the fewest resources for young people: Bedford Stuyvesant, East New York, and Brownsville in Brooklyn; the South Bronx; Central and East Harlem; Jamaica; and Far Rockaway, Queens. The ASTSN is recognized as one of New York City's most effective antiviolence programs for inner-city youth. Over the last five years, crime has dropped significantly in areas where the All Stars has had a highly visible presence; and while it is hard to establish a causal relationship, there is strong anecdotal evidence among youth participants, their families, and community leaders that the All Stars has made a difference.

The leadership of ASTSN also directs the Development School for Youth (DSY). DSY, a twelve-week after-school leadership training program for high school-age students, has operated since 1997. In this program, students visit professional job sites, such as the New York Stock Exchange, a national public relations firm, a major international investment bank, and a Seventh Avenue apparel showroom. They also produce a professional resume and participate in a mock job interview conducted by corporate professionals, many of whom have given significant financial support to the program's sponsoring nonprofit organization. Program graduates are all placed in paid summer internships in business and political offices. The target populations are diverse—African American, Caribbean, Asian, white, good students, and poor students, from the best and worst schools.

The All Stars Talent Show Network and the Development School for Youth are cultural, performance-oriented environments where students can perform in different ways from their normal behavior. They allow young people to engage in "identity play/performing" as they create new and more sophisticated performances. Performance is a central activity of both programs. In the ASTSN, young people get on stage to perform music, dance, raps, and skits. Additionally, the supports necessary to produce the talent shows are deliberately organized as a performance, including stage managing, audience building, running sound systems, and handling security. In a similar way, the Development School uses an explicitly cultural approach. The program is organized as a leadership "play" with twelve weekly "acts"; a focus on weekly workshop assignments enables students to fully participate.

The ASTSN does not specifically instruct young people to stop violence, nor does it teach young people about the impact of violence. Rather, it supports young people as they perform who they imagine themselves to be. For example, abusive behavior is all too frequently part and parcel of the "hip and cool" role in poor communities. In a confrontation between two angry young men, for example, neither one may know what else to do except hurt each other. Or a fourteen-year-old girl may assume that she has to "hold on to her man" at any cost—doing drugs with him, becoming pregnant, beating up a rival. In these situations, those involved are not likely to know that they can pursue different courses of action or contemplate differing perspectives.

Participating in the All Stars requires that students perform as creators and givers. In doing so, they discover that they can become more than what or who they are. In building their own cultural organization in which they regularly challenge assumptions about who they are and how they should behave in the world, African American youth are able to actively participate in expanding areas. For the past seven years, the youth of the All Stars have produced the annual Phyllis Hyman Phat Friend Awards through which they honor adults in government, education, entertainment, sports, and other fields whose work supports the development of young people. In 1999, they coproduced a play, *Crown Heights*, which brought black and Jewish youth together to create something new—and positive—out of the tragic history of the events that took place in Brooklyn in 1991.

Activities in the Development School for Youth are begun from the moment program staff invite young people to apply. On their recruiting trips to high schools, they speak explicitly about the cultural-performance approach of the program and open it up to dialogue. We tell them that their grades are not a criterion (something unusual in leadership training programs). Rather the criterion is their willingness to work together to create performances of professional job and career seeking, including their willingness to challenge their own assumptions about who they are, how they got to be that way, and how it was they operated within the parameters they did.

Each week they create and rehearse new performances of professionalism as they meet with lawyers, business people, and politicians in their offices. They make eye contact, shake hands, and say, "My name is _____. It's a pleasure to meet you." This scene might be seen as a potential clash of identity for the mostly poor, socially undeveloped young people who participate. However, what is significant about these professional performances is not that these young people now "have" a new identity, but that they have the capacity to create and project new identities and, given the opportunity and support, they do.

RECRUITMENT AND RETENTION IN COLLEGE:
THE POSSE PROGRAM

by Deborah Bial

The Posse Program is an initiative to enhance student achievement. It differs from other programs with the same goal by identifying students often missed by selective institutions' standard admissions measures and by employing a strategy that combines the efforts of other programs while shifting the focus away from quantitative assessments and race-based preferences. The Posse Program began in 1989 as a response to the many talented urban public school students who were leaving New York City for college and returning six months later as dropouts. At that time, *posse* was a popular word in the youth culture. It meant a group of friends who look out for one another, who "back each other up." One particular student who left college stated that if he had had his posse with him, he never would have dropped out. This simple idea, of sending a posse, or a team, of students to college together became the premise for the program as it exists today.

On average, Posse scholars score between 800 and 1100 on their SATs. Their success defies the traditional predictors. Posse scholars are urban public school students who come from diverse cultural and ethnic backgrounds. Posses include African American, Dominican, Puerto Rican, Jewish, Chinese, Filipino, Pakistani, Italian American, Burmese, and Iranian young people. Posse scholars represent a diversity of political and social views and come from varied socioeconomic backgrounds.

Program Components

The Dynamic Assessment Process (DAP) component of Posse is an alternative recruitment strategy designed to identify and recruit outstanding youth leaders from public city high schools. It emphasizes alternative predictors of success (alternative as opposed to traditional SAT and grade point average measures) with the intent of finding talented students who might be missed through traditional admissions processes. It offers these students, who might not normally be considered at elite institutions, the opportunity to enroll.

DAP begins with the premise that teachers, principals, guidance counselors, and community-based leaders can, with ease, identify a few students whom they feel could succeed at the finest college if only given the chance. The Posse Foundation, therefore, builds a network of schools and community-based organizations that can refer these students each September at the beginning of the senior year in high school. DAP then employs a four-month, three-step strategy to further assess the potential of these students. Techniques used include large interviews where candidates participate in workshops that allow trained Posse staff to assess them for leadership, motivation, communication skills, inter- and intragroup skills, and public presence skills.

Ultimately, after additional screening, university officials and Posse staff together select ten students to be in that year's posse. The colleges and universities that partner with Posse to admit Posse scholars are those that are looking for ways to increase diversity on their campus. The university partner commits to granting full-tuition scholarships to ten Posse scholars each year. The scholarships are unique in that they are neither minority nor need-based scholarships. They are granted based on a definition of merit that includes leadership, outstanding ambition, and drive to succeed. Thus, Posse scholars are honored for their potential and acknowledged by the university campus.

Another component, the thirty-four-week Posse Training Program, is a weekly series of two-hour workshops that take place during the senior year in high school and the summer before college. Posse scholars are trained in four areas—academic skill building, team building, leadership development, and becoming an active catalyst for change on a university campus—thus enabling them to make full use of their leadership talents both inside and outside the classroom.

While the workshops cover academic skill building, they do not teach students math or English. Rather they are intended to prepare students to think critically about their education and to access resources once on campus. The leadership development workshops focus on preparing students to pursue their goals and to become involved in their campus communities and include training for trainers and event planning. The team-building workshops focus on training Posse scholars to support each other, give Posse scholars an understanding of the developmental stages of a group, and teach conflict resolution skills. Finally, Posse scholars are provided with public speaking, cross-cultural communication, and negotiation skills so they can have impact on the college campus. In essence, they are charged with a mission of helping to improve the climate of diversity on their college campuses. This effort can take the form of promoting dialogue in a dormitory or becoming the student government president.

The On-Campus Program, the third component of Posse, is the maintenance program designed to support Posse scholars once they have matriculated at the partner universities. It is a response to the fact that many students drop out of college not because of their inability to handle the required academic workload but as a result of the isolation. Posse scholars often adopt an almost celebrity kind of status and many students from the larger student body have asked if they could join the Posse Program. Despite this status, Posse scholars are not necessarily seen together. Their impact as a group is achieved on an individual basis in the dormitories, in the social clubs, in the classroom. Bob Innes, chair of Vanderbilt's Human and Organizational Development department and faculty member, says, "on the simplest level, Posse kids talk in class. They are trained to promote dialogue instead of having an axe to grind."

Posse scholars meet weekly as a team on campus and also every other week with a graduate student mentor who has gone through the Posse training with them. These meetings provide academic and emotional support and help students overcome many of the freshman-year hurdles. In addition, Posse staff visit each Posse campus twice a semester to meet with administration and faculty liaisons to both ensure the continuity of the program and to plan events with Posse scholars that can involve the larger campus communities. One way Posse scholars involve the larger campus community is to host an annual Posse-Plus retreat. These retreats focus on an issue identified by Posse scholars as critical to the campus and are intended to promote serious dialogue. Posse scholars invite other students, faculty, and administrators to participate in a three-day weekend retreat off campus. Past PossePlus retreats have focused on student-faculty relationships, racism, gender and sexuality, and class issues.

Program Results

Over 90 percent of Posse scholars are persisting; they have become part of the pipeline to impressive positions in the workforce. On campus, they have started and joined numerous clubs, founded fraternity chapters, run for and won government offices, started a gospel choir, and written for newspapers. Equally important, Posse scholars' postgraduation career choices reflect a main goal of the program, which is to graduate powerful students from diverse backgrounds who can take on leadership positions in the workforce. In the year the program was evaluated, one twenty-five-year-old female Posse scholar has already finished her clinical psychology doctoral degree at Duke University. Another had just graduated from the law school at Vanderbilt University. One male graduate worked for Paramount Pictures. And another female graduate worked as a research assistant at the New York Psychiatric Institute and had plans for attending medical school in Israel.

PREPARATION FOR COLLEGE: A BETTER CHANCE

by Judith Griffin

As the oldest and only national academic talent search agency for students of color in the country, A Better Chance (ABC) has been examining effective practices in encouraging academic success, especially for students of color, for over thirty-six years. The organization's goal is to significantly increase the number of well-educated minority people who can assume positions of leadership in American society through academic and social integration of most of the selective, predominately white, independent schools in this country.

A Better Chance was founded in 1963 at Dartmouth College, which wanted to recruit higher numbers of African American students. Meanwhile, a separate but similar program, the Independent Schools Talent Search (ISTS), was developed by some of the nation's elite boys' boarding schools. ISTS and Project ABC eventually merged. Subsequently, new schools were added to the membership, and girls were actively recruited. The unique Public Schools Program (PSP) was developed, through which affluent suburban communities took on the task of annually raising the funds to provide a town residence, supervised by live-in resident directors, for six to twelve ABC students while they attend the local high school.

Assessment

A Better Chance assessment process features the distribution of twenty thousand applications, primarily through a national resource network some 4,000 strong, including 850 "feeder" middle and junior high schools. The application requires each prospective student to write an essay and complete short-answer questions; their parents must contribute a statement. The process also consists of the collection of transcripts, recommendations, and standardized test scores, and feedback from an interview.

The second part of the process is more art than science. While it is intuitive and humanitarian, it is critical to the results ABC has achieved. Each application file is read by several staff members, who consequently assign a rating based on the prospective student's academic and social strengths. The staff then meets almost daily over a period of several months to discuss each applicant and to select two or more schools to which each will be referred. This work of carefully matching student to school is the heart of A Better Chance's success. Ultimately, some 330 to 370 applicants are selected for the two hundred member schools.

Program Philosophy

A Better Chance's painstaking attention to the strengths and needs of each applicant can best be described in terms of its four longstanding commitments:

The Commitment to Believe: At A Better Chance, the first commitment is to believe that there is treasure where others believe there is none. The resource network and staff return year after year to inner cities, seeking promising students and believing in their ability to identify them.

The Commitment to Expand Organizational Thinking: Over the years, ABC has learned that reliance on traditional ways of measuring gifts and talents has meant that many children are overlooked. So a second commitment was developed: to expand the staff and network's thinking about how to identify talented minority children. Traditionally, performance on intelligence and achievement tests as well as teacher recommendations determines who is placed in gifted programs. But A Better Chance knows that, historically, many of the children in its target population may not exhibit their gifts through high test scores or other methods customarily utilized to assess potential. So ABC has learned to use other measures: (1) the ability to think logically; (2) the ability to use stored knowledge to solve problems; (3) the ability to reason by analogy; and (4) the ability to extend or extrapolate knowledge to new situations.

ABC looks for children who have a strong sense of pride and self-worth, who are individual thinkers, who will take risks, and who believe in self-determination. Staff especially seeks those with the courage to endure the anxiety, suspense, and disappointment inherent in experimenting with new situations, and still persevere. ABC, however, has not completely omitted testing from the assessment process. Applicants must take the Secondary School Admission Test (SSAT) and the results are used as part of the analysis. And when students do well, we emphasize their results. But ABC never allows test scores to become the most reliable gauge of potential or uses them to exclude a child from consideration. Were this to be done, many high-potential students would remain unidentified.

The Commitment to Avoid Blaming the Children: ABC does not blame the children for their failure to find the talented among them. According to ABC's president, Judith Griffin, it would easy to blame them, for their worlds are frequently filled with disorganized families, hunger, violence, poor schooling, and homelessness.

The Commitment to Work Unceasingly to Transmit Self-Confidence and Hope: ABC believes that, however successful they are at fulfilling the first three commitments, their efforts may well be lost unless they fulfill the fourth: to instill confidence and hope through all of their interactions with children. If during their early years at their new school students are disappointed with their grades, ABC staff remind them of others who have had similar challenges and have overcome them. Knowing that most attrition takes place after the first, most difficult year, ABC program staff invite all first-year students to reflect on and write about the challenges they have overcome, and encourage participation by awarding a $500 prize. If a child is not accepted at a member school, they talk about reapplication, if at all possible, or other options to pursue. At ABC's local Interview Days, where far more children appear than can possibly be placed, staff efforts are geared toward "uncovering gifts" not "selecting out." And often they receive letters from students thanking them for believing in them when they didn't believe in themselves.

Results to Date

During the 1998–1999 school year, 1,218 students (known as A Better Chance Scholars) were enrolled in two hundred member schools nationwide. Since 1964, 9,092 students have graduated from the program. Of this number 7,296 (70.77 percent) are African American; 1,728 (16.76 percent) are Hispanic. The remaining 12.5 percent is divided among American Indian, Asian, and "other" children of color typically underrepresented in ABC's member school population. Ninety percent of the scholars of the appropriate age were either enrolled in college or had completed a college degree.

The demographic description of the student body might have suggested a far less positive outcome. Fully one-third of A Better Chance students come from families receiving public assistance or living at or below the federal poverty line. Most are eligible for significant amounts of financial assistance from the schools accepting them. Most reside in neighborhoods known for high crime rates and beleaguered public schools with overcrowded and underequipped classrooms, low rates of graduation, and even lower rates of college attendance. Recently, the data suggests that roughly 65 percent of students are raised by single mothers.

In fairness, some less positive aspects of the ABC experience have also been reported. Some ABC scholars have described feeling isolated at school, finding it hard to "fit in" when they go home, losing interest in the lives of former friends and, perhaps most painful of all, dismissively accused of "acting white" (Fordham and Ogbu 1986). Others suggest that A Better Chance's single-minded focus on finding and placing more students left too few resources for student support activities during the school year. And while others attribute these sentiments to adolescent angst, ABC scholars indicate that despite the transition difficulties they faced, their increasing maturity has fostered a renewed appreciation of the ABC opportunity and the positive effect it has had on their lives and their families.

SUPPLEMENTARY EDUCATION FROM A CORPORATE PERSPECTIVE

by Irving Hamer

One of the issues in education worthy of reflection includes relating the increasing requirement of intellectual capacity to the commercial growth in the supplementary education field. Supplementary education—defined as formal and informal educational services delivered outside the regular classroom (Gordon 1999)—is not a new phenomenon. The affluent have purchased its treasures for a long time. This advantage may partially explain the academic achievement gap between white and Asian American students and their African American, Hispanic American, and Native American counterparts. And having worked on both sides of the blurring public and private divide, I believe that education is a business. My assertion is not meant to reduce education's place in the social sciences or the humanities but rather to suggest that education, including supplementary education, long an area of liberal and progressive traditions, has become a frontier of commerce.

On some levels, the commerce of supplementary education is not secret or subtle. While there are a number of nonprofit organizations delivering supplementary education, they are often subsidized by business interests or their foundations. And increasingly, a growing number of these supplementary education organizations charge fees for access and participation. These nonprofit organizations have quietly joined the for-profit providers of supplementary education in privatizing supplementary education. The significant dynamic of this phenomenon is that people of color are not in important decision-making positions in either the nonprofit or the for-profit supplementary education fields.

The revenue produced from a growing number of supplementary education products and services is in the millions. Likewise, the number of personnel employed by supplementary education organizations is also on the rise. While it is difficult to report accurate figures (given the lack of data in this area), an estimated $511 million worth of educational software is purchased annually for home use. Sylvan Learning Centers, as a result of a public offering in the late 1990s, is probably a $200 million organization. In addition to these supplementary products and services developed for profit, there are books, films, test preparation services, and testing services (such as the Education Testing Service, an approximately $300 million nonprofit organization that recently developed a for-profit subsidiary).

One of the noteworthy trends in supplementary education is the growth of children's museums. According to the Association of Youth Museums, attendance at children's museums has doubled. (In 1998, for example, 22 million visitors were expected, up from 9.3 million in 1996. There are 156 children's museums in the country, 62 of which have been created since 1991.) Most of the museums have youth and adult programs that are perceived as alternative education sources. For example, they provide literacy programs, hands-on science activities, multicultural education, theater programs, historical explorations, and lessons in technology, nutrition, and math. These museums are nonprofit organizations where parents pay for access. Although they are available to low-income and middle-income families of color, participation is miniscule despite some outreach effort.

The supplementary education landscape is huge, varied, and lucrative. In some instances, access is simple. Conversely, supplementary education can be difficult to know about, pay for, and understand. Some for-profit (and nonprofit) providers almost always suggest connections to students' regular schooling, but often the supplementary educational experiences have no overt relationship to children's school-based education, although they may be quality experiences.

What is new in supplementary education? In 1999, basic information on nonprofit community-based supplementary education organizations was scant and fragmented. This is beginning to change as Gordon's (1999) concept of supplementary education takes hold and the field begins to document and evaluate the various interventions detailed in our taxonomy chapter (see chapter 9). Second is its growth. Third, the possibility that supplementary education can assist in closing the academic achievement gap between majority and minority students is new. Fourth, perhaps the recognition of the role supplementary education has played in middle- and upper-income communities is new. And finally, conferencing about supplementary education, and publishing a book about it, may foreshadow rigorous study and research.

Of particular note is the large amount of private funds (with almost no government regulation, certification, or accreditation requirements) associated with supplementary education. Education, it seems, has become everybody's business. And the perception that education is a type of elixir has spurred consumers to pay for access, in part because schooling alone has not, cannot, and will not provide children with all they need to succeed (Comer 1997). Until recently, supplementary education was not considered in debates about the academic achievement gap. For years achievement gaps have been explained by noting family income but not by considering what family income purchases for children. It is clear that compensatory education (Gordon and Wilkerson 1966) efforts, including Head Start and Title I, are attempts to "supplement and not supplant" local educational initiatives, but most public efforts do not rival what the supplementary education industry makes available to those discerning and networked families that can purchase services.

Additionally, the private nature of supplementary education may enable it to function in the shadows of public scrutiny. Conventional wisdom suggests that an entity operating in the private sector according to the rules and demands of the market is better than a comparable service or product in the public sector, even if the cost is significantly higher. Yet, as providers of supplementary educational interventions, for-profit programs do benefit from public dollars in direct and indirect ways. For instance, it is partly parental anxiety about the shortcomings of public schools and the desire to prepare their children for higher education and/or meaningful employment that fuel supplementary education.

The nonprofit domain of private supplementary education further complicates understanding. Although services are often free for qualified children, operating costs are supported by philanthropic, corporate, and, increasingly, public dollars. These arrangements force issues such as universal access to supplementary services, sustainability of the service, and quality control from program to program. The entire area of supplementary education demands careful and rigorous research. Deepening the field's understanding is critical because supplementary education providers are working in both nonprofit and for-profit organizations. And properly configured, supplementary education may serve a societal need to increase high academic achievement among some ethnic minority students. Supplementary education is a frontier, particularly in low-income communities. It appears to be a new terrain for scholarly inquiry and—for underrepresented students—it may even be a solution.

ANALYSIS OF COMMUNITY-BASED ORGANIZATIONS

One of the characteristics the National Urban League, the All Stars Talent Network, Posse, and A Better Chance share in common is their engagement with the community in various ways. Indeed, according to program personnel, these interventions not only produce positive differences in young people's lives but are also evidence that communities—in the shape of the organizations and activities they support—can help young people rise above the negative predictors. While funders and program administrators may perceive the effects of programs according to formal criteria—including use and capacity, for example—young people are less constrained about how they judge a program's effectiveness. Vandell and Shumow (1999), Quinn (1999), and the Carnegie Council on Adolescent Development (1992) suggest that youth judge a program's effectiveness according to whether they are good places to spend their time, whether these organizations engage young people in challenging and supportive ways, whether they provide a safe haven from often-dangerous streets, and whether they offer opportunities to spend free time in ways that contribute significantly to their learning and their social development.

From young people's perspective, the referenced programs are not "typical" of other organized opportunities that may also be available in their communities—which they may gauge as uninteresting, inappropriate, or otherwise off-putting. In these community-based organizations, young people are not "typical" American youth (traditionally defined in terms of the schools they attend, the communities they live in, and their family socioeconomic status). Rather, they are considered isolated, hard to reach, and designated high risk. Almost without exception, the urban youth come from families struggling with low, often uneven, employment and social disruption.

Our review of program descriptions and existing evaluations of All Stars and A Better Chance, for instance, indicate that some of the achievements and successes of active young people engaged in community organizations are impressive. We are reminded of how important these organizations are in playing critical roles in filling gaps left by families and schools that are underresourced and lack capacity to provide supports to young people. Other encouraging aspects are the opportunities provided to young people to engage in positive activities, to cultivate close and caring relationships, and to find value in themselves in the face of personal disruption, poor schools, and neighborhoods generally lacking of supports. They offer a means for reaching youth and can have considerable impact on the skills, attitudes, and experiences young people need to take their places as confident, contributing adults.

Young people's achievements range from formal and informal to social and academic, and matter in varying degrees. With regard to A Better Chance (ABC), academic success—in terms of participation in rigorous courses, good grades, and high school graduation—plays a major role in a young person's ability to continue to postsecondary education. In addition to a measure of academic success, young people need a sense of personal worth, a positive assessment of the future, and the knowledge of how to plan for it. These skills include attitudes of persistence, reflection, responsibility, and reliability. Self-confidence and a sense of efficacy (Bandura 1986) are crucial if young people are to succeed both academically and socially. One of the marks of ABC, Posse, All Stars, the National Urban League, and the supplementary education programs in Koreatown (see chapter 13) is their focus on developing these life skills in addition to strengthening more traditional academic outcomes.

The literature suggests that young people in effective community organizations perceive their local schools as lacking and/or inadequate as learning institutions and as places where they feel safe and valued (CCAD 1992). Compared to most American youth, students of color are more likely to experience violence in their schools, to encounter drugs, to have something stolen from them, and to feel personally threatened at school. Yet compared to American youth generally, young people who participate in the community organizations tend to achieve at higher levels and hold higher expectations for their academic careers (Hrabowski, Maton, Greif, and Greene 2002).

Further, young people who participate in high-quality supplementary education programs seem to be more optimistic about their futures and appear to have increased their knowledge and confidence to plan and reach for success. As opposed to the disparaging estimations many youth from difficult environments have of themselves, young people engaged in community supplementary education organizations appear to hold markedly different views of themselves.

Community-based organizations with an emphasis on learning are similar in some critical ways. The core elements of an effective organization appear to correspond closely with the core elements of an effective learning environment. As different as they may seem on the surface, the supplementary education activities or interventions are similar with respect to their mission, goals, and youth-, knowledge-, and assessment-centered approaches.

We define *youth centered* as responsiveness to diverse talents, skills, and interests; developing youth strengths; providing a selection of appropriate materials; providing personal attention; and encouraging youth leadership. *Knowledge centered* means having a clear focus, quality content and instruction, embedded curriculum, diverse teachers—including volunteers, senior citizens, peers, coaches, directors, consultants, organizers, and peer tutors. *Assessment centered* includes integrating continuing feedback and recognition and regular periods of planning, practice, and performance.

Common Principles

As indicated at the beginning of the chapter, the interventions we feature also share the following principles: parent and community participation, knowledgeable professional staff, high standards and expectations, the perspective that young people are resources to be cultivated, and the continuing attempts to ensure the quality of implementation efforts.

1. *Parent and community participation*: Over the years, scholars (Lopate, Flaxman, Bynum, and Gordon 1970; Epstein 1995) have increasingly emphasized the significance of adults who are concerned about young peoples' lives and their resulting need for supplementary education programs to provide mechanisms enabling parents and communities to actively participate in nurturing and developing their young people in academic and social domains. For instance, parent and community participation was an important factor in Project Rockland (NY) Youth Supplemental Education (RYSE)'s success (see chapter 12). The theoretical conceptualization and implementation of RYSE's success appear to have gone beyond traditional measures of parent and community in-

volvement (i.e., the occasional parent meeting or note sent home to indicate "participation") to include home visits, involvement in specific school activities, adult education classes, brokering of community services for family members, and ongoing communication between program staff and families. With regards to community, Lopate, Flaxman, Bynum, and Gordon (1970), Epstein (1995), and Heath and McLaughlin (1993) emphasize the importance of the community in deliberate and continuing efforts to serve young people. As the founder of Project RYSE, Gordon actively brokered community collaboration and was equally sensitive to adapting his activities to the community needs. In the case of RYSE, this tacit understanding of the potency of communities in addition to the engagement of community members in decision making contributed significantly to the program's success.

2. *Knowledgeable professional staff*: Effective supplementary education initiatives connect young people with adults who care about them, serve as role models, advise, mentor, chide, sympathize, encourage, and praise. The simplicity of this reality should in no way detract from its great importance. Adults who take time with young people, who advocate and broker on their behalf, who guide them, who connect them to the broader institutions of society, and who have the training and professional skills to help them develop and grow are central to effective youth policies and programs. A young person's continued access to caring, knowledgeable adults is crucial in gaining his or her trust and commitment. This professional staff can be mentors, teachers, case workers, counselors, program directors, community members, or trained volunteers who are concerned about young people, devote substantial time and attention to young people, and effectively demonstrate that they are "in for the long haul."

   With regards to the Posse program, caring, supportive adults contribute to effective outcomes. Similarly, the low turnover rate of professional staff and volunteers in All Stars Talent Network permits young people to build stable relationships with staff who simultaneously take an active interest in the welfare of young people by encouraging and following up. While it is important for programs to have sympathetic adult staff and volunteers, it is also crucial that these adults are knowledgeable about working effectively and providing age-appropriate activities that follow sound supplementary education principles.

3. *High standards and expectations*: It is critical that parents, communities, and professional staff in supplementary education programs guide young people's behavior, challenge them, and insist on personal responsibility and accountability. Epstein (1995) suggests that young

people will not only rise to the expectations of adults they trust but also tend to achieve more positive outcomes in program settings with these characteristics (Maton, Hrabowski, and Schmitt 2000; Hrabowski, Maton, and Greif 1998; Hrabowski, Maton, Greif, and Greene 2002). In A Better Chance, for example, middle school African American and Hispanic students are selected to attend prestigious high schools with high expectations, a demanding curriculum, and a strong support system. These successful programs do not dilute their standards to accommodate students considered to be "at risk"; rather, they maintain high standards and provide support so that these students can achieve those standards. The ABC model stands in sharp contrast to the unfortunate practice some urban and suburban schools engage in—namely, enrolling low-income students of color in less academically demanding courses under the assumption that they would fail otherwise and might drop out of school. ABC demonstrates that low-income students of color, including limited-English-speaking students, can achieve academically at high levels when challenged. One of the implicit objectives of ABC is to increase the number of economically disadvantaged students pursuing postsecondary education, and increase enrollment for students of color in college preparatory courses, including advanced math and science courses. This exemplary program also suggests that high expectations and standards result in academic achievements and postsecondary attendance that are equal to or better than that of young people in traditional academic education.

4. *The perspective that young people are resources to be cultivated*: Many effective programs have moved away from focusing on eliminating youth deficits and toward supporting youth assets. Service learning and community service programs in particular give youth opportunities to show themselves, their parents, and their communities that they are able to contribute to society in positive ways. Youth not only receive services but also provide them. In this way, they change from participants into partners, from being cared for into key resources for their communities. This change in approach helps build youth resiliency and protective factors in powerful ways. The regard for young people as resources is one of the defining characteristics of the All Stars Program.

5. *Implementation quality*: While it may be obvious that programs work better when they are implemented well, some of the particular factors contributing to effective implementation include ample start-up time; unambiguous goals; adequate, timely, and sustained resources; effective leadership; relevant professional development; and use of data to improve performance. We suggest that programs would increase their ef-

fectiveness in providing relevant services if they can follow-up with participants who may either go on to postsecondary education or self-select into the labor market.

Clearly, in both common and unique ways, the referenced examples of supplementary education programs featured in this chapter seem to enable underrepresented students from some ethnic minority groups to achieve academically and to develop social and cultural competencies. While some of these programs have not been evaluated on formal levels, they do attempt to address some of the more prevailing issues, including participation, access, and the incongruence of activities and children's and youth's actual interests. The program developers also seem to be in the midst of creating and/or increasing their capacities for program monitoring. Most regard this strategy as enabling them to be responsive to changing community demographics and dynamics. Conversations with some of these program personnel suggest that they perceive themselves as a collective system of supports for children and families and are committed to their roles in a larger framework of supports for young people of color.

REFERENCES

Bandura, A. 1986. *Social foundations of thought and action: A social cognitive theory*. Englewood Cliffs, NJ: Prentice-Hall.

Carnegie Council on Adolescent Development. 1992. *A matter of time: Risk and opportunity in the nonschool hours*. Report of the Task Force on Youth Development and Community Programs. New York: Carnegie Corporation of New York.

Comer, J. 1997. *Waiting for a miracle: Why our schools can't solve our problems—and how we can*. New York: Dutton.

Epstein, J. 1995. School/family/community partnerships: Caring for the children we share. *Phi Delta Kappan* 76:701–12.

Fordham, S., and J. Ogbu. 1986. Black students' school success: Coping with the burden of acting white. *Urban Review* 18:176–206.

Gordon, E. W. 1999. *Education and justice: A view from the back of the bus*. New York: Teachers College Press.

Gordon, E. W., and D. A. Wilkerson. 1966. *Compensatory education for the disadvantaged*. ERIC Document Reproduction Service no. ED 011 274.

Heath, S. B., and M. W. McLaughlin, eds. 1993. *Identity and inner city youth: Beyond ethnicity and gender*. New York: Teachers College Press.

Hrabowski, F. A. III, K. I. Maton, and G. L. Greif. 1998. *Beating the odds: Raising academically successful African-American males*. New York: Oxford University Press.

Hrabowski, F. A. III, K. I. Maton, G. L. Greif, and M. L. Greene. 2002. *Overcoming the odds: Parenting successful African-American females*. New York: Oxford University Press.

James, D. W., and S. Jurich, eds. 1999. *More things that do make a difference for youth: A compendium of evaluations of youth programs and practices.* Vol. 2. Washington, DC: American Youth Policy Forum.

Lopate, C. E., E. Flaxman, E. Bynum, and E. W. Gordon. 1970. Some effects of parent and community participation on public education. *Review of Educational Research* (February). ED 027 359.

Maton, K., F. A. Hrabowski III, and C. Schmitt. 2000. African American college students excelling in the sciences: College and postcollege outcomes in the Meyerhoff Scholars Program. *Journal of Research in Science Teaching* 37(7): 629–54.

Quinn, J. 1999. Where need meets opportunity: Youth development programs for early teens. *Future of Children* 9(2): 96–116.

Vandell, D., and L. Shumow. 1999. After-school childcare programs. *The Future of Children* 9(2): 64–80.

11

Families as Contractual Partners in Education

Hank M. Levin and Clive R. Belfield

The educational achievements of the young depend on both family and school, but are much more dependent on the former than on the latter. While educational policy has established an extensive set of legal and contractual obligations for schools, the only contractual obligation for families is to meet compulsory education requirements. The establishment of "performance expectations" or "contracts" between families and society may be an effective way to enhance educational outcomes. This chapter investigates the need for, feasibility of, and possible content of such "performance expectations" by suggesting the construction of metaphorical contracts for families to provide for the education of their children. We begin by documenting the overwhelming ties between socioeconomic status (SES) and student educational results. We then look at the research literature on what families do that improves educational results for their children—that is, what is it that SES reflects? Next, we consider what a comprehensive family contract that embodied these behaviors would look like. Finally, we add greater specificity to such a family contract by asking: (a) What can families do on their own if properly informed, even low-income families? (b) What can families do with training and support? (c) What gaps in the contract must be filled by other service providers? Answers to these questions are important for education reforms that seek to capitalize on parental efforts and energies within the context of privatization.

In recent decades, privatization of elementary and secondary education has become an increasingly common topic. Usually, privatization is meant to refer to enrollment in private or independent schools, as opposed to public schools, or as contrasted with mechanisms that would subsidize private education such as educational vouchers and tuition tax credits (Levin 2000,

2001b; Belfield 2001). However, at its core, the purest form of privatization in education begins with family effort. Studies of educational achievement or educational attainments consistently find that differences in family circumstances have a large influence on educational outcomes, typically greater than the impacts of differences among schools. For this reason, education is already heavily "privatized."

More than 90 percent of a child's waking hours from birth to the age of eighteen are spent outside of school in an environment that is heavily conditioned, both directly and indirectly, by families (Sosniak 2001). Data on early childhood demonstrate the extent to which school readiness varies significantly and substantially across children of different races, socioeconomic groups, and genders; before children reach school age, their family environments has had a powerful effect on their educational future (Coley 2002). The most elemental form of educational privatization is found in the high level of control that families have over the activities that directly and indirectly determine educational outcomes (Belfield and Levin 2001).[1] Yet the thrust of formal educational policy is devoted overwhelmingly to school improvement, ostensibly to raise student achievement and to improve educational equity. While many schools also attempt to incorporate various means of parental involvement, such involvement is limited largely to the margins of the educational process rather than viewed as a critical component of that process (Epstein 2001; Jordan, Orozco, and Averett 2002).

In this chapter, we suggest a way of viewing families as contractual partners in education, that is, having contractual obligations on behalf of their children. To a large degree, this notion of a "contract" is metaphorical because a democratic society permits families to rear their children in diverse ways with wide latitude among practices. Nonetheless, one can still view the family as an educator and raise the question of what type of contractual obligations could maximize the educational success of its offspring. One of the earliest efforts in this direction is *Families as Educators* (Leichter 1975). Our attempt here is to do more than to propose specific programs; it is to identify in a comprehensive manner the links between family behaviors and educational outcomes, and to codify these links into a metaphorical contract that might be implemented by families in conjunction with a variety of social institutions.

FAMILIES, SCHOOLS, AND EDUCATIONAL ATTAINMENTS

Prior to the 1960s, it was assumed that differences in school resources and other characteristics of the school environment were the dominant causes of differences in educational outcomes such as achievement scores and years of schooling attained (Coons, Clune, and Sugarman 1970).[2] The Coleman Report (Coleman et al. 1966), a study requested by the U.S. Congress under the 1964 Civil Rights Act, represented a massive effort to determine the impact of both families and schools on educational achievement (Bowles and Levin 1968). It concluded that differences in family background characteristics were overwhelmingly more important than school characteristics in explaining differences in student achievement. Although the Coleman study was criticized, in part for using a statistical technique that overstated the impact of families on achievement, its overall finding has been replicated in virtually all of the studies done in ensuing decades.[3]

Although some policymakers and advocacy groups argue that the family is the key to educational improvement (Steinberg 1996; Hoxby 2001) and others argue that it is the school (Edmonds 1979; Mortimore 1998), the conflict between the two positions lacks merit. Both families and schools are important in educational development. From an economist's perspective, they are joint inputs into the production function for education,[4] and they are partially interdependent rather than separable in their effects. School inputs and family inputs may interact in ways such that students from some backgrounds may benefit more from specific resources and school policies than do other students. For example, reductions in class size seem to have a larger impact on minority students and those from lower-SES backgrounds than on Anglo students or those from middle-class backgrounds (Krueger 1999, 497; Molnar et al. 1999). This pattern of different effects for different races and social classes has been found in several studies (Grissmer, Flanagan, Kawata, and Williamson 2000; Levin 1970, 24). As another example, when students enter schools with stronger preparation and higher expectations, teachers are able to provide more demanding challenges than when students are less prepared.

Preoccupation with Schools

While the importance of families in determining educational outcomes is highly recognized in the literature, it is less emphasized in educational policy. The main focus of educational policy has been on institutional reform of teaching practices and curriculum, or on changes in the organization of the educational system.[5] Much of this reform has emphasized privatization and more parental choice. Privatization includes the promotion of private school provision and greater opportunities for private funding of education. Public choice examples include magnet schools, open enrollment among schools within districts and states, and most recently, charter schools.[6] Charter schools are relatively autonomous public schools that are exempted from most rules and regulations in exchange for their pursuit of an approved mission or charter. Many are operated under contract by private and for-profit educational management organizations, although some are run by nascent community groups that include local parents. In 2002 there were more than 2,400 charter schools with about 580,000 students in thirty-seven states and the District of Columbia, a rapid expansion considering that the first charter schools were only established in 1992.[7]

Market approaches to privatization and increased choice include the provision of publicly funded educational vouchers that can be applied to the cost of private education, as well as tuition tax credits that create tax subsidies for families and businesses for paying tuition at private schools. The use of educational vouchers, however, is still rare and small-scale. For instance, although in 2002 educational voucher plans had been operating in Milwaukee for eleven years and in Cleveland for about seven years, annual enrollments were fewer than twenty thousand students.[8] Florida has a voucher statute for students in public schools that have been designated as "failing" for two consecutive years. Except for a single year when students in two schools were eligible for vouchers, no schools have met the failing criteria since. Education vouchers have also been challenged as unconstitutional: In 2002, the Cleveland program was under scrutiny by the U.S. Supreme Court, with plaintiffs arguing successfully in the lower courts that the plan violates the First Amendment's separation of church and state, as almost all the vouchers are being used in religious schools.[9] Although the Supreme Court ruled in favor of the program in June 2002, it is unlikely to expand significantly.[10]

Almost all of these efforts at policy reform recognize that families are important in determining educational results of offspring. Indeed, advocates argue that school choice will energize parents to improve family practices in the education of their students, while also creating incentives for schools to improve their performance in order to maintain and attract clientele (Hoxby 2001, 104–18). School reform projects also make at least some attempt to expand parental involvement in the education of students, particularly in the school but also at home. Yet most of the focus of in-school reforms is on changes in pedagogy, curriculum, and governance. While "no topic about school improvement has created more rhetoric than 'parent involvement'" (Epstein 2001, 3), this "rhetoric" substantially exceeds the actual magnitude of effective interventions. Indeed, the substance of parental involvement has been marginal relative to the possibilities for families to improve the education of their children. School policy for improving educational outcomes has been far more obsessed with pressuring schools to change than inducing change in families.

A recent strand of school policy reform is the preoccupation with raising academic standards and closing gaps among social groups. This reform is motivated by the concern about mediocre performance on achievement tests and unequal outcomes by race and SES. The "standards movement," which is found in almost all of the states, emphasizes improving achievement test results as a condition of graduation and promotion, as well as reducing test score inequalities between minority and Anglo students (Heubert and Hauser 1999). But a school-based approach, without more focus on families, may have disappointing results because test score gains from educational reforms that are limited to schools are modest. In addition, such gains show only a limited relation to productivity or earnings (Levin 2001a). For example, dramatic reductions in class size from about twenty-five to fifteen students per class in the famous Tennessee Class Size experiment resulted in an increase in student achievement of about .25 standard deviations (Finn and Achilles 1999). Minority students improved by about .30 standard deviations and white students by about .20 standard deviations (Krueger 1999, 530).[11] Only about one-tenth of the black–white achievement gap was reduced by this very costly reform (Hedges and Nowell 1998).[12] Among reforms that have been shown to succeed in improving educational achievement, impacts are relatively small, and little of the achievement gap has been closed (Levin 2002).[13]

Besides emphasizing standards, market advocates have pushed for greater competition among schools for students in order to provide an incentive to raise school effectiveness. But summaries of studies measuring the effects of school competition have found that impacts on achievement are extremely modest, in the range of .1 of a standard deviation (Belfield and Levin 2001).[14] To give some idea of how small these effects are when translated into a practical application, this amounts to a ten-point increase on the SAT verbal or mathematical test for college admissions, a test that has a mean of about 500 and a range from 200 to 800.[15] An improvement of .1 of a standard deviation is likely to be associated with less than a 1 percent increase in earnings.[16]

In summary, strategies to improve education generally focus on change within the schools, with some involvement from families being bolted on. However, because much educational success is based upon family actions, circumstances, and behaviors that are either unrelated to schooling or that take place in the preschool period, these efforts are likely to have only marginal effects. Both families and schools are central to obtaining strong educational results, and the imbalance of educational policy in the direction of school reform is detrimental to improving the quality and distribution of educational outcomes.

Seeking Balance between Families and Schools

One measure of the present imbalance created by policy emphasis on schools rather than on families is to compare the formal strictures placed on schools with those placed on families to produce educational results. The schools that our children attend are subject to a sheaf of laws, rules, regulations, directives, guidelines, and policies that are far too extensive for enumeration. Although providing less than 10 percent of the funding for elementary and secondary schools, the federal government sets numerous complicated rules and procedures that affect the operations of all schools. Federal laws and regulatory provisions have proliferated, especially for such functions as education for handicapped students, economically disadvantaged students, bilingual students, and gender equity, racial stratification, and vocational education. The recent No Child Left Behind Act of 2001,[17] which took effect in January 2002, constitutes over one thousand pages in itself. In addition, there will likely be thousands of pages of supplemental regulations set out by the U.S. Department of Education for implementing the law.

Overall, government involvement in schooling is vast and complex. Federal courts have been active in setting standards for the operation of schools under the U.S. Constitution. State laws are even more multitudinous than the federal ones and are administered by activist state departments of education setting their own regulations and policies and monitoring school districts. Federal and state laws are further augmented by the actions of local school boards. Furthermore, state courts have become deeply involved in interpreting state laws and constitutions.

It is probably not even possible to document fully all of the laws, regulations, and policies that frame the operations of schools. One can view these mechanisms as an overlapping set of contracts that function as "binding agreements among the parties."[18] Many of these agreements are enforceable via government sanctions. Government agencies can withhold funds and official recognition of schools, can close and reshape institutions, or can change personnel.

In addition, there are less-formal agreements that might be more temporary in nature, such as agreements with students and their families, that constitute informal contracts on school activities or expectations (Powell et al. 1985; Bishop 1996). Such informal contracts are subject to change with changes in clientele and can be enforced by sanctions available to families through political channels or exit (Hirschman 1970, 21–29).[19]

These enforceable contracts have two main features. First, public schools, other than those embedded in educational voucher arrangements or public choice, are largely answerable to federal, state, and local authorities rather than to parents or students. Moreover, there is little or no bargaining over contractual provisions because the schools are agencies of state government and are expected to fulfill those responsibilities mandated by federal and state authorities. Hence, contracts are imposed, not negotiated. Second, the contracts are procedural rather than outcome based. Schools are required to follow procedures set out by Congress, courts, legislatures, and administrative branches rather than to produce specific educational outcomes. Only recently have schools been sanctioned for failing to produce specific educational results, either in terms of reconstitution of schools by external authorities or by allowing students in failing schools to seek other alternatives such as those under the Florida voucher plan.

If families have a powerful influence on the educational results for their children, both separately and in concert with schools, however, one might expect to find formal obligations set out for them as well. In fact, the formal requirement for family participation in education as embodied in law is so trivial that it is in stark contrast to the overwhelming accretion of formal demands and procedures set on schools. Basically, there is a single requirement: A child must meet compulsory attendance requirements; he or she must be in attendance at a recognized school during regular school hours or must meet other participation requirements as set out for homeschooling. Of course, families are not the property of the state, whereas schools are state agencies. But, if better educational results, and particularly more nearly equal outcomes in education are to be achieved, it is obvious that schools cannot do it alone.[20] Rather, changes in family behavior will be necessary as well, particularly among those families at the bottom of the SES ladder whose children are most challenged in terms of educational outcomes.

Accountability across Public Services—A Comparison

The educational policy trends outlined above are mirrored in other public services, where similar questions are being raised regarding optimal forms of governance (Diller 2000). Specifically, the development of site-based management, devolved decision making, and organizational change (for example, into charter schools and contract schools) have their counterpart in reforms to the welfare system. In that system, "ground-level agency personnel" have been given substantially more discretion since 1996, along with "performance-based evaluation systems" and redefined "institutional culture" serving to mitigate any corresponding loss of accountability at higher levels of government (Diller 2000, 1121). Thus, the education and welfare systems are tending toward hollowing out, with any side effects being addressed through stricter (or more directly specified) accountability mechanisms. But whereas in the educational system parents can serve as one check on the loss of higher-level accountability, no such check exists to protect recipients of benefits in the welfare system. The concern for welfare recipients who face external constraints can be compared to the concern for parents with underdeveloped parenting skills. With recent reforms, these groups are inevitably facing greater self-responsibility. Yet, in part, these reforms are motivated by a belief that the individuals are themselves integral to raising their own welfare levels.

The parallel between welfare and education sectors can be extended. Education systems should not only be efficient but also equitable. Welfare reform also reflects such a trade-off: "Regardless of whether one agrees with the goals and philosophy of welfare reform, the lack of accountability and potential for unfairness in the new administrative regime are causes for concern. One can favor the new emphasis on work in many [Temporary Assistance for Needy Families] programs and still value fair process and public participation in administrative decision-making" (Diller 2000, 1128).

Interestingly, the solution in education of parental choice—where it has been successful—has largely been supported as a way of making the system more fair, not less fair (for example, the parental choice programs targeted at low-income families). The specters perpetually on the horizon are parental choice programs that are expanded to upper-income families with potentially greater inequities (Levin 1998, 379–82). Last, we also recognize the tension arising from a system with "agency personnel as motivators, guides, and overseers of recipients, constantly promoting the message of self-sufficiency" (Diller 2000, 1129). In education, we could stylize school professionals as "motivators, guides, and overseers" of what learning takes place in the home (Diller 2000, 1129). Such stylization emerges because of the facts regarding the overwhelming importance of home activities to the educational outcomes of children.

A more general discussion of a private role in public governance has been offered recently by Jody Freeman (2000).[21] Freeman begins by asserting that private participation in governance is neither "marginal nor restricted to the implementation of rules and regulations" and that "the relationship between public and private actors in administrative law cannot properly be understood in zero-sum terms, as if augmenting one necessarily depletes the other" (Freeman 2000, 547). This assertion parallels our argument that parental influence over educational outcomes is not marginal, and—for higher-SES families certainly—cannot be limited to following rules. Indeed, we characterize the relationship between parents and schools as strongly interdependent. Hence, as "public and private actors negotiate over policymaking, implementation, and enforcement" (Freeman 2000, 548), Freeman rejects the notion of a hierarchy of governance and control. This rejection comports with our skepticism regarding solutions that bolt on parental engagement to existing school practices (as recent policy initiatives have tended to do), and it echoes our proposal for stronger "contracts"—or at least stronger dialogue—between parents and schools.

The richer notion of accountability that Freeman articulates also comports with our claims for future betterment of public and private education. Freeman writes,

Accountability is more plural and contextual than traditional administrative law theory allows. In light of public/private interdependence, I propose that we think in terms of "aggregate" accountability: a mix of formal and informal mechanisms. . . . Taken together, these mechanisms can allay our concerns about the particular risks posed by arrangements of public and private actors, while capitalizing on their capacities. (Freeman 2000, 549)

For education services, the analogous concern might be to weigh the risks to the welfare of the children against the benefits from effective parenting. The greater need for dialogue, as opposed to efficiency mandates or legal challenges, extends across public services. Freeman refers to the traditional focus of administrative law as "heavily court centered" (Freeman 2000, 556) with a "quest for legitimacy . . . understood as the pursuit of public acceptance of administrative authority" (Freeman 2000, 557). In other words, the conventional "solutions" to governance problems appear to be government agencies maintaining their autonomy but simply being better honed to their purpose. The equivalent "solutions" in education reform are the search for the efficient school and the elimination of wasteful bureaucratic agencies (Hanushek 1998, 11). Neither solution has yet yielded much fruit, nor—insofar as they neglect the role of the family—do they appear promising for the future.

Instead, public agencies and private individuals are interdependent in the production of education outcomes for children, with private individuals performing "key functions that are not traditionally considered the responsibility of the state and that are not easily reduced to contractual obligations. . . . [T]he delivery of a service involves discretionary decisions that are difficult either to prevent through delineated delegation or to police with formal oversight mechanisms" (Freeman 2000, 597). In the case of parenting, we suggest these discretionary decisions are intimately bound up in the family's lifestyle.

Freeman also offers an explanation for the public/private demarcation that may be pertinent for education provision. Simply put, even when governance structures include private actors, they do so warily, fearing regulatory capture by these private actors. A similar aversion may exist in schooling, where teachers cultivate their professional status, and where parents are reluctant to negotiate with professionals regarding the education of their children. We further concur with Freeman that new contractual relationships (metaphorical or otherwise) need not lead to a diminution in the engagement of the state (Freeman 2000, 568). Indeed, it may be the private actors themselves who resist greater dialogue with government, fearing greater regulatory oversight or doubting government's expertise and their own parenting skills. Yet, the imperative in education—as in many other government activities—is for "structuring and capitalizing upon desirable private contributions to governance," that is, for making families contractual partners (Freeman 2000, 575).[22]

Finally, we perceive the same tensions between the public and private spheres as Freeman does. On the one hand, much is made of the "hallowed" autonomy of the private family in their children's upbringing without governmental intervention. On the other hand, the importance of the family in the education process is clearly acknowledged in research evidence. We concur with Freeman's proposal for further scrutiny of policies that draw on the unavoidable interdependence of family and government (Freeman 2000, 638). At issue is how to frame policy to exploit this interdependence—in the terms used here, how to develop the metaphorical family contract.

DEVELOPING A METAPHORICAL FAMILY CONTRACT

Presumably there is a knowledge base on what schools need to do to educate children effectively, and this is translated into financial support, resources, and procedures, much of which are embodied in laws, rules, and regulations. This knowledge base is always expanding on the basis of experience and research, although it is hardly unequivocal. Debates over the choice of practices and over how they should be implemented are common in education, in part because of different theories of sound educational policy and practice. John Chubb and Terry Moe suggest that schools based upon democratic decisions must necessarily adopt a hodgepodge of goals and practices that are largely unworkable because they must necessarily be a compromise among many different and conflicting views (Chubb and Moe 1990, 215–26).[23] In fact, however, decisions are made and practices are adopted that are viewed as effective strategies for achieving given goals.

Paradoxically, the knowledge base on which family practices have educational consequences is less equivocal than the knowledge base for schools, but it has been less employed to impact educational policy. Here we provide an overview of what makes families effective in terms of the education of their students. Although indicators of SES, such as parental education, income, occupation, race, language, and family structure (number of parents and siblings) have been used to explain achievement, these are only markers or indicators of social class, not the family practices that account for such differences. Therefore, we must contemplate what a metaphorical "contract" that sets out the required contributions of families to the education of their children would contain.

We call this a metaphorical contract because there are no ready mechanisms to enforce it. Furthermore, much of such a contract might require resources that go beyond the capacity of some families, particularly low-SES families. More broadly, we might conceive of this contract as a "social contract," including more agents than the direct family (Rousseau 1973/1762). It is, however, useful to translate the indicators of family SES that account for such substantial portions of educational success into actual behaviors. If high-SES families are following successful educational practices in the home and in relation to the school, it is important to know what those practices are. Conceptually, these activities can be placed into a metaphorical contract of good practices for all families, and we can seek ways of helping families meet the condition of the contract. Enforcement and monitoring are problematic, but evidence of the likelihood of success for their children might be an important motivation for families.

It should be noted that this is a distinctively different approach from that found in the literature emphasizing either school-induced parent participation or more out-of-school experiences. This school-based literature is important in improving the educational success of children at the margin by trying to get low-SES families more involved in the schooling of their students and by providing additional school-based special programs (Epstein 2001; Hoxby 2001, 118–23),[24] These programs are useful, and reflect a genuine effort to improve educational outcomes. But such approaches tend to be scattershot rather than systematic. They are not embedded in a more comprehensive picture of what is needed. Moreover, such approaches often require additional funding rather than emphasizing the reallocation of activities toward a specific goal. In contrast, a metaphorical contract would attempt to encapsulate comprehensively the various practices that parents would need to pursue in order to ensure a high chance of educational success for their students. As we suggest later in the chapter, an overall solution to incorporating families more fully into the education of their children will require some social investment, but this is of necessity required for executing every aspect of the contract.

What follows is not an exhaustive catalog of parental behaviors that can be linked to educational success, but a representative set that might be used to construct an initial metaphorical contract. Normally, any attempt to review the impacts of families on the educational achievement of their children is limited to measures of SES.[25] In contrast, we are asking what SES measures represent in terms of actual family practices that positively affect student achievement.

High-SES Families and Education of Children

Strong ties between SES and student educational outcomes have been affirmed in numerous studies. SES appears as an important predictor of children's cognitive development, school readiness, school achievement, and school completion, as well as other measures of child and adolescent well-being (Duncan and Brooks-Gunn 1997; Stipek and Ryan 1997; Rothstein 2000, 11–14). Three specific pathways have been identified through which the influence of SES is most clear. These pathways are summarized in tables 11.1 through 11.3, in which the impact of being in a low-SES family is described.

Table 11.1.   Home Environment Pathways between SES and Student Achievement

Home Environment Variables	*Impact on Children of Being in a Low-SES Family*
Learning environment	Lower likelihood of a "school-like" home (Epstein 2001; Bradley 1995).
Language and literacy	Weaker language interaction with parents (less talking; fewer object labels; shorter, noncontingent conservations; more controlling speech) (Lareau 2000). Weaker literacy engagement (value placed on literacy; press for achievement; availability and instrumental use of reading materials; reading with children; and opportunities for verbal interaction) (Hess and Holloway 1984).
Parent-child interactions	Conflicting interactions with parents; more controlling, restrictive, and disapproving parents (Liaw and Brooks-Gunn 1994).
Daily routine	Less likely to follow a daily routine (Rebello-Britto, Fuligni, and Brooks-Gunn 2002; Newacheck, Stoddard, and McManus 1993).
Health and nutrition	Poorer health; less health care (for example, immunization delay; more conditions limiting school activity) (Brooks-Gunn and Duncan 1997, 55).
Parents' mental health	Have parents with greater risk of depression (Adler, Boyce, Chesney, Folkman, and Syme 1993).
Choice of neighborhood	Residence in more socially disorganized neighborhoods, with fewer child development resources and greater exposure to violence (Leventhal and Brooks-Gunn 2000; Sampson, Raudenbush, and Earls 1997). Higher school mobility from residence mobility (U.S. General Accounting Office 1994).

The first pathway is "home environment." Evidence clearly indicates that the home environment of higher-SES families is more conducive to educational advancement (see table 11.1). The strongest effects are through parent-child interactions, such as the creation of "school-like" homes, stronger language and literacy relations, and less conflict within the home. In addition, higher-SES families have better health and nutrition and follow a more structured daily routine at home. In terms of the local environment, higher-SES families reside in more socially organized neighborhoods, and they are less likely to move residence such that their children must change schools. This pathway is the most important, and yet the one most neglected in current policies and school practices.

The second pathway is "use of out-of-school time." Higher-SES families tend to use out-of-school time (including summertime) in a more educative way: They are more likely to use preschool and day-care centers for their children, and they spend more time on reading (see table 11.2). These differences are evident in the widening of educational performance over the summer period; lower-SES students have been found to fall further behind during the summer months (Alexander, Entwisle, and Olson 2001). Such differences are also evident in the variation in school readiness across children of various SES backgrounds (Coley 2002). Much of this variation is attributable to SES differences. For example, whereas 85 percent of kindergartners in the highest SES quintile can recognize letters of the alphabet, only 39 percent of kindergartners in the lowest SES quintile can do so. Moreover, when differences in SES are controlled for, nearly all differences across races disappear. Racial differences in school preparedness appear to be substantially explained through their correlation to SES differences. This

Table 11.2.   Out-of-School Pathways between SES and Student Achievement

Out-of-School Variables	*Impact on Children of Being in a Low-SES Family*
Child care	Lower-quality child care (Gallinsky et al. 1994). Choice of child care based on cost and location, rather than quality (Peyton, Jacobs, O'Brien, and Roy 2001). Care by relatives rather than center care or nannies (Ehrle, Adams, and Tout 2001).
Preschool	Less likely to attend preschool (U.S. General Accounting Office 1994).
After-school and summertime activities	Spend more time in informal play, outside play, or television watching (Lareau 2000; Posner and Vandell 1999). Spend less time on sports and reading (McHale, Crouter, and Tucker 2001).

evidence offers some justification for our basing a parental partnership on what high-SES families do for their children.

The third pathway is "parental involvement." High-SES parents are typically more involved in their children's schooling (see table 11.3). They are more likely to have exercised a direct preference for a particular type of school and are more likely to be involved in school-based activities. In addition, higher-SES parents are more likely to monitor the performance of their children's schooling more intensively and more effectively. Finally, higher-SES parents are more likely to assist their children in their homework. It is this pathway that has received the most attention in terms of policy reform (and has been promoted by school choice advocates). Yet it is a relatively weak pathway to educational advancement; the majority of children's time is spent in home environments. Plausibly, and indeed as is established in table 11.1, the home environment pathway is the strongest.

Collectively, these three pathways suggest a substantial educational advantage for children of higher-SES parents.[26] Therefore, these pathways allow us to identify specific practices and behaviors that parents can employ to improve educational outcomes that can then be introduced into the metaphorical contract. In fact, it is possible to be more precise, identifying actual tasks that parents may engage in. For example, in relation to effective parental in-

Table 11.3.   Parental Involvement with Schooling Pathways between SES and Student Achievement

Parental Involvement with Schooling	Impact on Children of Being in a Low-SES Family
Choice of school	Less likely to have chosen a private school (Woodhouse 1999; Hoxby 2001). Less likely to have had home location chosen in conjunction with schooling decision (Woodhouse 1999; Hoxby 2001). Less likely to have taken advantage of public choice programs (Witte 2000).
Communication with school and requests made	Less involved in school-based practices (Epstein 1986).
School involvement	Less involved in evaluation of school provision (less monitoring of child's schooling; less intervention in children's program; less critical of teachers; fewer supplementary materials to reinforce classroom experience) (Lareau 1989).
Homework help	Less homework help in terms of valuing, monitoring, assisting, not interfering and doing (Scott-Jones 1995).

volvement with homework, Kathleen Hoover-Dempsey identifies how high-SES parents interact with the student's school or teacher about homework; provide general oversight of the homework process; respond to the student's homework performance; engage in homework processes and tasks with the student; and engage in metastrategies to create a fit between the task and student skill levels (Hoover-Dempsey et al. 2001). Each of these tasks may enhance educational performance. Nonetheless, the information in tables 11.1 through 11.3 is intended to illustrate what might be included in a parent-school contract. We want to point out that some of these behaviors are only possible with higher family income. Others may require a substitution of a more effective set of behaviors for ones that are less effective.

Of course, some schools have established contracts with parents. These, however, are very brief and tend to focus on highly specific and functional contractual terms, such as the time the student should arrive at school, the number of hours the student should spend in school, student comportment, and parent volunteer requirements.[27] They are certainly highly incomplete specifications of behaviors that parents might exhibit to maximize the educational performance of their children. Parental contracts can be enforced if the school has the power to select its students, as in many public schools of choice, charter schools, and independent schools. However, we are unaware of any enforceable contracts that reflect the activities listed in tables 11.1 through 11.3.

Implementing the Contract

Of course, just taking what we know about the potential of the family for contributing to educational success and encapsulating that into a contract does not change very much. The real challenge is to alter family-school practices by implementing the provisions of the contract. This seems daunting because of the inability of the state to monitor and enforce family behavior, particularly given the subtleties of behavioral impacts on child development. Yet the license provided by a metaphorical contract permits us to conceptualize the purposes that such a contract might serve, even in the absence of strict enforcement.

Incentives

Families have a motivating self-interest in attempting to comport with the terms of a proposed contract. Most families have a deep interest in the success of their children both in school and in life, and if families can thus be convinced that actions that they might take will improve their children's chances, they will be motivated to undertake them within their abilities and resources. This incentive is a powerful one. It is important to note, however, that there are constraints upon families in fulfilling such contracts.

Information on practices to improve the educational prospects of children is not common or widespread in a form that spells out specific actions that families can take. It is costly to obtain such information. Moreover, families are "socialized" by their experiences and circumstances to behave in certain ways and not in others. These differences are particularly poignant in Shirley Brice Heath's work on *Ways with Words* (1983), in which she compares parental language interactions with children among families of different SES and racial backgrounds.[28] They are also found in the important work of Melvyn Kohn, in which families are shown to prepare their children for occupational success by transmitting the values and behaviors of their own occupations (Kohn 1969). Thus, a working-class adult will often emphasize conformity, obedience, following rules, and reluctance to challenge authority or seek alternatives. Children of professional parents are taught to challenge authority, negotiate, and consider options. Each is preparing offspring for success as the parents understand its requirements from their own occupational experiences, but the consequence is transmission of class status from generation to generation. We can call this a knowledge constraint, but it may also entail a capacity constraint. These differences in child language and orientation also result in different expectations and treatments of children in school, an example of the interaction between parental and school effects (Carnoy and Levin 1985, 110–43).

By capacity constraint, we mean that some families, even if informed of practices that will improve educational outcomes for their children, may not have the capacity to act on that knowledge. Clearly, transmitted language styles are not just determined by knowledge acquisition by parents about which approaches are more effective at socializing children for school experiences. Language is deeply embedded in culture and personality and does not simply shift when parents are informed that another style will be more advantageous for children's success.[29] In other cases, families do not have the income to provide their children with expanded opportunities such as enriched child care, effective preschools, health care, nutrition, and housing. Nevertheless, there is scope for parents to be made more aware of effective practices in these domains; such knowledge is a necessary condition for change.

It is also worth noting that schools with pressures to improve student achievement—particularly among minorities and low-income students—also have incentives to mobilize family resources on behalf of better school performance. Likewise, the larger society that will benefit from the better civic behavior, economic performance, and political decisions of those whose education has improved will also have incentives to mobilize family resources for better school performance (Haveman and Wolfe 1984).

Implementation Strategies

A metaphorical contract for parents could be divided into three parts, each dedicated to a different type of strategy: (1) information, (2) assistance, and (3) externally provided activities.[30]

Information

A metaphorical contract for parents to enhance the education of their children would be a repository of information, much of it presently unfamiliar to families, on what types of activities are effective. Simply knowing what is exemplary serves an important function as parents make decisions about their offspring. Many of the activities are feasible for almost any family: setting aside reading time for children, rewarding good school performance, discussing school experiences, reviewing a child's schoolwork, meeting with teachers for progress reports, taking children to the library on a regular basis, guiding television viewing, and so on. We believe that there are many activities that parents would be willing to undertake both at home and in conjunction with schools if they knew that these activities would have a positive effect on their child's education.

Assisted Activities

The metaphorical contract would contain other responsibilities that parents cannot do alone because of a lack of resources or other capacity constraints. For example, students may need help on homework that parents are unable to provide. In this case, school- or community-provided homework assistance or tutoring will be necessary, even though it will be up to parents to monitor their children's needs and to make appropriate arrangements. Other areas that may require assistance are training in parenting skills, orienting children toward college and learning the academic requirements, visiting colleges, and using community services such as those provided by public agencies and nonprofit providers, as well as religious organizations. All of these represent an intermediate range of activities in which parents can take responsibility if they have assistance.

External Support

These are activities in which parents may require substantial assistance to be able to fulfill the contract. At one extreme are basic necessities for human and educational development, such as decent housing in safe neighborhoods, health care, employment opportunities, and adequate income to provide amenities.[31] In addition, they may include quality preschooling, summer schools, tutoring centers, after-school programs, the provision of summer jobs for students, and test preparation courses, including those for college entrance examinations. External support may entail longer school years and school days for children to accommodate educational enrichment.[32] Both assisted and externally supported activities will likely entail a variety of providers including schools, other governmental organizations, philanthropic groups, community organizations, and faith-based organizations.

STEPS FOR THE FUTURE

The next step in moving in the direction of a family contract would be to conduct a fully comprehensive survey of the knowledge base linking family activities to the educational success of offspring. We have attempted only a sampling of that knowledge base, but a much fuller survey and synthesis is called for. This comprehensive knowledge base would then be transformed into a metaphorical contract that would set out categories and specific types of activities that families would commit themselves to on behalf of their children. The contract would be accompanied by the "reward" of predicted educational progress associated with these types of activities.

Activities would be divided according to those whose performance would require one of the three proposed intervention strategies: information, assistance, and external provision. Each of the three strategic areas would require design and implementation of programs that would be effective in assisting parents to honor substantial parts of the contract. Social policy would balance efforts to provide support for families to fulfill their obligations with efforts to provide similar support for schools to fulfill theirs. School activities and parent involvement programs could also be refined to support parent partnership contracts. Increasingly, economists are suggesting that reforms to support families' educational activities will provide a considerably larger improvement in the education of at-risk populations than direct investments in schools (Rothstein 2000, 29–31; Hoxby 2001, 118–23).

Clearly, this exploration of metaphorical contracts for families has raised as many questions as it has suggested directions to pursue. In addition to further details on the knowledge base and how it might suggest different implementation strategies, there are at least two larger issues for using the contract. First, as we construct the metaphorical contract and its different parts, it is not clear who, beyond families, are the potential parties to the agreement. Obviously, schools become a potential partner when the child reaches school age, but probably not during the preschool years. Schools have incentives to provide assistance to families in exchange for better student performance on which schools are judged. The larger impact of educational attainments on labor force productivity, citizenship, and social participation means that society and its governmental and nongovernmental organizations also have a stake in the contract.[33] However, how these particular groups will participate in the contract and how this will be coordinated is certainly not clear.

Second, there is the question of whether there are any grounds for enforcement of any part of the contract. Enforcement requires both monitoring and sanctions. Monitoring of family behavior—particularly the more subtle components—is not likely to be appropriate or feasible; sanctions for most family behaviors are also unlikely to be available. Thus, we suspect that there must be greater reliance upon incentives, not only the rewards of better child performance but incentives for such results as good grades, student achievement, attendance, and school completion. For example, income supplements can be made conditional on these types of outcomes.[34] These types of questions need to be more fully addressed in order to make significant progress on metaphorical contracts for family education partnerships.

REFERENCES

Adler, N. E., W. T. Boyce, M. A. Chesney, S. Folkman, and S. L. Syme. 1993. Socioeconomic inequalities in health: No easy solution. *Journal of the American Medical Association* 269(24): 3140–45.

Alexander, K. L., D. R. Entwisle, and L. S. Olson. 2001. Schools, achievement, and inequality: A seasonal perspective. *Educational Evaluation and Policy Analysis* 23(2): 171–91.

Belfield, C. R. 2001. *Tuition tax credits: What do we know so far?* Occasional Paper no. 33. New York: Teachers College, National Center for the Study of Privatization in Education. ERIC Document Reproduction Service no. ED 463 568.

Belfield, C. R., and H. M. Levin. 2001. *The effects of competition on educational outcomes: A review of U.S. evidence.* New York: National Center for the Study of Privatization in Education, Teachers College. ERIC Document Reproduction Service no. ED 463 564.

Bernstein, B. 1971. *Class, codes and control.* London; Boston: Routledge.

Bishop, J. H. 1996. Incentives to study and the organization of secondary instruction. In *Assessing educational practices: The contribution of economics*, edited by W. E. Becker and W. J. Baumol. Cambridge, MA: MIT Press.

Block, J. H., S. T. Everson, and T. G. Guskey. 1995. *School improvement programs: A handbook for educational leaders.* New York: Scholastic.

Bourdieu, P., and J. Passeron. 1977. *Reproduction in education, society and culture.* London: Sage Publications.

Bowles, S., and H. M. Levin. 1968. The determinants of scholastic achievement—An appraisal of some recent evidence. *Journal of Human Resources* 3(1): 3–24.

Bradley, R. H. 1995. Home environment and parenting. In *Handbook of parenting*, edited by M. Bornstein, 235. Mahwah, NJ: Lawrence Erlbaum.

Brooks-Gunn, J., and G. J. Duncan. 1997. The effects of poverty on children. *Future of Children* 7(2): 55–71.

Carnoy, M., and H. Levin. 1985. *Schooling and work in the democratic state.* Stanford, CA: Stanford University Press.

Chubb, J. E., and T. Moe. 1990. *Politics, markets, and America's schools.* Washington, D.C.: Brookings Institute

Clune, W. H., and J. F. Witte, eds. 1990. *Choice and control in American education.* Vol. 2: *The practice of choice, decentralization and school restructuring.* Philadelphia: Falmer Press.

Coleman, J. S., E. Q. Campbell, C. J. Hobson, J. McPartland, A. M. Mood, F. D. Weinfeld, and L. R. York. 1966. *Equality of educational opportunity.* Washington, DC: U.S. Government Printing Office.

Coley, R. J. 2002. *An uneven start: Indicators of inequality in school readiness.* Policy Information Report. Princeton, NJ: Educational Testing Service.

Committee for Economic Development. 2002. *Preschool for all: Investing in a productive and just society.* New York: Author.

Coons, J., W. Clune, and S. Sugarman. 1970. *Private wealth and public education.* Cambridge, MA: Harvard University Press.

Dearing, E., K. McCartney, and B. A. Taylor. 2001. Change in family income-to-needs matters more for children with less. *Child Development* 72:1779–93.

Diller, M. 2000. The revolution in welfare administration: Rules, discretion, and entrepreneurial government. *New York University Law Review* 75(5): 1121–220.

Duncan, G., and J. Brooks-Gunn, eds. 1997. *Consequences of growing up poor.* New York: Russell Sage Foundation.

Edmonds, R. 1979. Effective schools for the urban poor. *Educational Leadership* 37(1): 15–18, 20–24.

Ehrle, J., G. Adams, and K. Tout. 2001. *Who's caring for our youngest children? Child care patterns of infants and toddlers.* Occasional Paper no. 42. Washington, DC: Urban Institute. ERIC Document Reproduction Service no. ED 448 908.

Epstein, J. 1986. Parents' reactions to teacher practices of parent involvement. *Elementary School Journal* 86(3): 277–94.

———. 2001. *School, family, and community partnerships: Preparing educators and improving schools.* Boulder, CO: Westview Press.

Finn, C. E., B. V. Manno, and G. Vanourek. 2000. *Charter schools in action: Renewing public education.* Princeton, NJ: Princeton University Press.

Finn, J. D., and C. M. Achilles. 1999. Tennessee's class size study: Findings, implications, misconceptions. *Educational Evaluation and Policy Analysis* 21(2): 97–109.

Freeman, J. 2000. The private role in public governance. *New York University Law Review* 75(3): 543–675.

Friedman, M. 1962. *Capitalism and freedom.* Chicago: University of Chicago Press.

Fuller, B., ed. 2000. *Inside charter schools: The paradox of radical decentralization.* Cambridge, MA: Harvard University Press.

Gallinsky, E., et al. 1994. The study of children in family child care and relative care—Key findings and policy recommendations. *Young Children* 50(1): 58–61.

Gordon, E., and B. L. Bridglall. 2002. *After school and other forms of supplementary education*. Presentation at the After-School Programs and Supplementary Education Conference, May, New York.

Grissmer, D. W., A. Flanagan, J. Kawata, and S. Williamson. 2000. *Improving student achievement: What state NAEP test scores tell us*. Washington, DC: RAND.

Grissmer, D. W., S. N. Kirby, M. Berends, and S. Williamson. 1994. *Student achievement and the changing American family*. Washington, DC: RAND.

Gutman, A. 1987. *Democratic education*. Princeton, NJ: Princeton University Press.

Hanushek, E. A. 1998. Conclusions and controversies about the effectiveness of schools. *Federal Reserve Bank of New York Economic Policy Review* 4:1–22.

Haveman, R. H., and B. L. Wolfe. 1984. Schooling and economic well-being: The role of nonmarket effects. *Journal of Human Resources* 19(3): 377–407.

Heath, S. B. 1983. *Ways with words: Language, life, and work in communities and classrooms*. New York: Cambridge University Press.

Hedges, L. V., and A. Nowell. 1998. Black–white test score convergence since 1965. In *The black–white test score gap*, edited by C. Jencks and M. Phillips, 149, 154. Washington, DC: Brookings Institution Press.

Henig, J. R., and S. D. Sugarman. 1999. The nature and extent of school choice. In *School choice and social controversy: Politics, policy, and law*, edited by S. D. Sugarman and F. R. Kemerer, 13–35. Washington, DC: Brookings Institution Press.

Hess, R. D., and S. D. Holloway. 1984. Family and school as educational institutions. In *Review of Child Development Research*. Vol. 7, edited by R. D. Parke, 179. Chicago: University of Chicago Press.

Heubert, P., and R. M. Hauser. 1999. *High stakes: Testing for tracking, promotion, and graduation*. Washington, DC: National Academy of Sciences, Committee on Appropriate Test Use.

Hirschman, A. O. 1970. *Exit, voice, and loyalty: Responses to decline in firms, organizations, and states*. Cambridge, MA: Harvard University Press.

Hoover-Dempsey, K. V., A. C. Battiato, J. M. T. Walker, R. P. Reed, J. M. Dejong, and K. P. Jones. 2001. Parental involvement in homework. *Educational Psychologist* 36(3): 195–209.

Hoxby, C. M. 2001. If families matter most, where do schools come in? In *A primer on America's schools*, edited by T. M. Moe, 89–126. Stanford, CA: Hoover Institution Press.

Jordan, C., E. Orozco, and A. Averett. 2002. *Emerging issues in school, family, and community connections: Annual synthesis*. Austin, TX: Southwest Educational Development Laboratory.

Kagan, S. L., and B. Weissbourd, eds. 1994. *Putting families first: America's family support movement and the challenge of change*. San Francisco, CA: Jossey-Bass.

Kohn, M. L. 1969. *Class and conformity: A study in values*. Homewood, IL: Dorsey.

Krueger, A. B. 1999. Experimental estimates of education production functions. *Quarterly Journal of Economics* 114(2): 497–532.

Lareau, A. 1989. *Home advantage: Social class and parental intervention in elementary education*. Philadelphia, PA: Falmer Press.

———. 2000. *Contours of childhood: Social class differences in children's daily lives*. Berkeley: University of California, Berkeley Center for Working Families.

Lawson, H. A. 2002. Meeting the needs of low performing urban schools. A policy and practice brief. Unpublished manuscript. Available online at www.albany.edu/~hlawson/urban-schools.pdf. ERIC Document Reproduction Service no. ED 466 507.

Leichter, H. 1975. *The family as educator.* New York: Teachers College Press.

Leventhal, T. L., and J. Brooks-Gunn. 2000. The neighborhoods they live in: The effects of neighborhood residence upon child and adolescent outcomes. *Psychological Bulletin* 126(2): 309–37.

Levin, H. M. 1970. A cost-effectiveness analysis of teacher selection. *Journal of Human Resources* 5(1): 24–33.

———. 1998. Educational vouchers: Effectiveness, choice, and costs. *Journal of Policy Analysis and Management* 17(3): 373–92.

———. 2000. The public-private nexus in education. In *Public-private policy partnerships*, edited by P. V. Rosenau, 129–33. Cambridge, MA: MIT Press.

———. 2001a. High-stakes testing and economic productivity. In *Raising standards or raising barriers? Inequality and high-stakes testing in public education*, edited by G. Orfield and M. L. Kornhaber, 39–50. New York: Century Foundation Press.

———, ed. 2001b. *Privatizing education: Can the marketplace deliver choice, efficiency, equity, and social cohesion?* Boulder, CO: Westview Press.

———. 2002. Issues in designing cost-effectiveness comparisons of whole-school reforms. In *Cost-effectiveness analysis in education: Methods, findings, and potential*, edited by H. M. Levin and P. McEwan. Yearbook of the American Educational Finance Association.

Liaw, F., and J. Brooks-Gunn. 1994. Cumulative familial risks and low birth weight children's cognitive and behavioral development. *Journal of Clinical Child Psychology* 23:360–72.

Ludwig, J., H. F. Ladd, and G. J. Duncan. 2001. The effects of urban poverty on educational outcomes: Evidence from a randomized experiment. In *Brookings-Wharton Papers on Urban Affairs*. Vol. 2, edited by W. G. Gale and J. Pack. Washington, DC: Brookings Institution Press.

McHale, S. M., A. C. Crouter, and C. J. Tucker. 2001. Free-time activities in middle childhood: Links with adjustment in early adolescence. *Child Development* 72(6): 1764–78.

Molnar, A., P. Smith, J. Zahorik, A. Palmer, A. Halbach, and K. Ehrle. 1999. Evaluating the SAGE program: A pilot program in targeted pupil-teacher reduction in Wisconsin. *Educational Evaluation and Policy Analysis* 21(2): 165–78.

Morse, J. R. 2002. Competing visions of the child, the family, and the school. In *Education in the twenty-first century*, edited by E. P. Lamar, 148–49. Stanford, CA: Hoover Institution Press.

Mortimore, P. 1998. The vital hours: Reflecting on research on schools and their effects. In *International handbook of educational change*, edited by A. Hargreaves, A. Lieberman, M. Fullan, and D. Hopkins, 85, 92–94. New York: Kluwer Academic.

Murnane, R., J. Willett, Y. Duhaldeborde, and J. Tyler. 2000. How important are the cognitive skills of teenagers in predicting subsequent earnings? *Journal of Policy Analysis and Management* 19:547–68.

Nathan, J. 1996. *Charter schools: Creating hope and opportunity for American education.* San Francisco, CA: Jossey-Bass.

Newacheck, P. W., J. J. Stoddard, and M. McManus. 1993. Ethnocultural variations in the prevalence and impact of childhood chronic conditions. *Pediatrics* 91:1031–39.

David and Lucile Packard Foundation. 2002. Children and welfare reform. *Future of Children* 12(1): theme issue.

Peyton, V., A. Jacobs, M. O'Brien, and C. Roy. 2001. Reasons for choosing child care: Associations with family factors, quality, and satisfaction. *Early Childhood Research Quarterly* 16(2): 191–208.

Posner, J. K., and D. L. Vandell. 1999. After-school activities and the development of low-income urban children: A longitudinal study. *Developmental Psychology* 35(3): 868–79.

Powell, A.G., et al. 1985. The shopping mall high school: Winners and losers in the educational marketplace. *NASSP Bulletin* 69(483): 40–51.

Rebello-Britto, P., A. Fuligni, and J. Brooks-Gunn. 2002. Reading, rhymes, and routines: American parents and their young children. In *The health and social conditions of young children and their families*, edited by N. Halfron, M. Schuster, and K. McLearn. New York: Cambridge University Press.

Reisner, E. R., R. N. White, J. Birmingham, and M. Welsh. 2001. *Building quality and supporting expansion of after-school projects: Evaluation results from the TASC after-school program's second year*. Washington, DC: Policy Studies Associates.

Rothstein, R. 2000. "Finance fungibility: Investigating relative impacts of investments in schools and non-school educational institutions to improve student achievement." In *Improving educational achievement: A volume exploring the role of investments in schools and other supports and services for families and communities*. Washington, DC: Center on Education Policy.

Rousseau, J. 1973/1762. *The social contract and discourses*. Trans. G. D. H. Cole. New York: Dutton.

Sampson, R. J., S. W. Raudenbush, and F. Earls. 1997. Neighborhood and violent crime: A multilevel study of collective efficacy. *Science* 277:918–24.

Schauble, L., and R. Glaser, eds. 1996. *Innovations in learning: New environments for education*. Mahwah, NJ: Lawrence Erlbaum.

Scott-Jones, D. 1995. Parent-Child Interaction and School Achievement. In *The family-school connection: Theory, research, and practice*, edited by B. A. Ryan et al. Vol. 2 of Issues in Children's and Families' Lives. Thousand Oaks, CA: Sage.

Shaul, M. S. 2001. *School vouchers: Publicly funded programs in Cleveland and Milwaukee*. Washington, DC: U.S. General Accounting Office. GAO-01-914.

Sosniak, L. 2001. The 9% challenge: Education in school and society. *Teachers College Record*. Available online at www.tcrecord.org/Content.asp?ContentID=10756.

Steinberg, L. 1996. *Beyond the classroom: Why school reform has failed and what parents need to do*. New York: Simon and Schuster.

Stipek, D. J., and R. H. Ryan. 1997. Economically disadvantaged preschoolers: Ready to learn but further to go. *Developmental Psychology* 33(4): 711–23.

Taylor, D., and Y. M. Goodman. 1998. *Family literacy: Young children learning to read and write*. Portsmouth, NH: Heinemann.

Tolman, J., K. Pittman, N. Yohalem, J. Thomases, and M. Trammel. 2002. Moving an out-of-school agenda: Lessons and challenges across cities. Takoma Park, MD: Forum for Youth Investment.

U.S. General Accounting Office. 1994. *Elementary school children: Many change schools frequently, harming their education*. Washington, DC: Author. GAO/HEHS-94-95. ERIC Document Reproduction Service no. ED 369 526.

Weiss, A. D. G., and R. J. Offenberg. 2002, April. Enhancing urban children's early success in school: The power of full-day kindergarten. Paper presented at the annual meeting of the American Educational Research Association, April, New Orleans, LA.

Wenglinsky, H. 2002. How schools matter: The link between teacher classroom practices and student academic performance. *Education Policy Analysis Archives* 10(12). Retrieved November 15, 2003 from http://epaa.asu.edu/epaa/v10n12/.

Witte, J. F. 2000. *The market approach to education: An analysis of America's first voucher program.* Princeton, NJ: Princeton University Press.

Woodhouse, S. 1999. Parental strategies for increasing child well-being: The case of elementary school choice. Working Paper. Berkeley: University of California, Sloan Center for Working Parents.

World Bank. 2001. Brazil: *An assessment of the bolsa escola programs.* Report no. 20208-BR. Washington, DC: Author. Available online at http://lnweb18.worldbank.org/External/lac/lac.nsf/4c794feb793085a5852567d6006ad764/ed5eeaaed4101b9385256a53007492a4/$FILE/Bolsa%2OEscola.pdf.

NOTES

The authors greatly appreciate the research assistance of Elizabeth Rigby.

1. Although families may also expand their control over education through school choice mechanisms, there is little evidence at this time of a powerful effect on educational outcomes from such expansion.

2. It should be noted that fiscal support of schools was extraordinarily disparate among states, school districts, and schools during those years.

3. The methods for measuring the relative home and school influences are the source of some controversy. For example, at one extreme, Harvard University Professor Caroline Hoxby evaluated the statistical determinants of achievement among a sample of more than sixteen thousand twelfth-grade students in 1992. Hoxby found that family variables accounted for more than 93 percent of the variance in mathematics scores, with less than 3 percent being explained by school input variables and the remaining 4 percent associated with neighborhood variables. See Caroline M. Hoxby, *If Families Matter Most, Where Do Schools Come In?* (Hoxby 2001, 96–98). Depending upon which subject is tested, she found that family variables accounted for from 34 to 105 times as much variation as the school input variables (97). Hoxby also did a parallel analysis for thirty-three-year-olds in attempting to explain their educational attainments in terms of years of schooling and found a similar result—an overwhelming influence of family background (98–99). One criticism of Hoxby's method is that she used measures of family characteristics for each individual student, but only cruder school averages for the school inputs. Therefore, the measures of school inputs are insensitive to the variance in student experiences reflected by differences among specific teachers and among classroom groups to which individual students were exposed. In a very recent study, using a method that accounts for some of these within-school differences, Harold Wenglinsky (2002) found that teaching variables might have a weight equivalent to socioeconomic variables.

4. An excellent study that tries to explain improvements in educational achievement of the population over time by both demographic and educational changes is *Stu-*

dent Achievement and the Changing American Family (Grissmer, Kirby, Berends, and Williamson 1994).

5. A large range of school reforms is found in *School Improvement Programs* (Block, Everson, and Guskey 1995). See also *Innovations in Learning* (Schauble and Glaser 1996). A comprehensive survey of interventions for urban schools is given by H. A. Lawson. See Hal A. Lawson, *Meeting the Needs of Low Performing Urban Schools: A Policy and Practice Brief*, 60–62, table 2 (2002).

6. The best overall source on traditional public choice options is *Choice and Control in American Education* (Clune and Witte 1990). The more recent charter school movement is discussed in *Inside Charter Schools* (Fuller 2000) and in the picture provided by *Charter Schools in Action* (Finn, Manno, and Vanourek 2000). Its origins are found in Joe Nathan, *Charter Schools: Creating Hope and Opportunity for American Education* (1996).

7. See News Alert, Center for Education Reform, "CER Releases National Charter School Directory 2001–2002: Nearly 2,500 Schools Open in Just 10 Years" (January 7, 2002), available online at www.edreform.com/press/2002/ncsd0102.htm. The Center for Education Reform in Washington, D.C., collects comprehensive information on charter schools.

8. For a summary of the Cleveland and Milwaukee voucher programs, see U.S. General Accounting Office, *School Vouchers: Publicly Funded Programs in Cleveland and Milwaukee*, GAO-01-914 (Shaul 2001). The Milwaukee voucher program is described and analyzed in detail in John F. Witte, *The Market Approach to Education* (2000, 29–51, 83–156).

9. See *Simmons-Harris v. Zelman*, 234 F.3d 945 (6th Cir. 2000), rev'd, 122 S. Ct. 2460 (2002).

10. See *Zelman*, 122 S. Ct. 2460.

11. Krueger reports an average effect size of .22 from being in a smaller size class (Krueger 1999, 530). This effect size varies between .19 and .30 according to grade level (Krueger 1999, 514). It also varies according to ethnicity. Krueger's Table X shows that the effect size for blacks is approximately 50 percent higher than for whites (Krueger 1999, 524 and table X). Approximately, therefore, the effect size for minorities is .30, and for whites it is around .20.

12. The black–white achievement gap is about one standard deviation.

13. Even these "successful results" overstate the case because they do not account for highly mobile students. That is, they evaluate achievement gains for students who have been in the school reform continuously over one year or more. The most disadvantaged students are highly mobile, moving frequently among schools.

14. See Belfield and Levin 2001, note 4, at p. 35.

15. The most competitive colleges and universities require SAT scores in the 700 range; the second tier of competitive institutions requires scores in the 600 range. For state institutions and less selective private colleges, it is the 500 range. An improvement of 10 points is unlikely to increase a student's eligibility for a more selective institution. For a review of SAT scores of enrollees, see Best Colleges, www.usnews.com/usnews/edu/college/rankings/rankindex.htm (accessed June 30, 2002).

16. These calculations are based upon the findings of Richard J. Murnane et al. (Murnane, Willett, Duhaldeborde, and Tyler 2000, 447). Their estimate would be about 1.5 percent, but this is overstated by their technique, for reasons elaborated on in Levin 2001a, 43–44.

17. Pub. L. No. 107-1.10, 115 Star. 1425 (2002).

18. The concept of contracts is a well-established area of law. We are using the concept of contract in a less formal way to encompass the agreed-upon functions that are required of agencies in fulfillment of their obligations to another entity. Of course, these contracts are so complex that only a small portion of them are effectively operable at any one time, given that the overwhelming numbers and complexities of the provisions make them impossible to monitor fully. School personnel are familiar with those provisions that are presently salient or that are indeed monitored, but others are ignored or are found to cover such limited circumstances that they are rarely identified. Monitoring of contracts is costly, so it is not surprising that only a small portion of the provisions are enforced in this manner.

19. Hoxby (2001, 104–10) estimates that almost 70 percent of parents can make intentional choices of schools. Henig and Sugarman (1999) estimate the figure at about 60 percent.

20. Other writers have sought to reassess the balance between schools and families: Roback Morse argues that many existing government programs crowd out family behaviors rather than supplement them—so universal preschool programs or school breakfast programs are held to weaken or undermine relationships within the family rather than to aid them (2002).

21. It should be noted that, in her discussion of public services and benefits, Freeman does not refer to education provision.

22. In addition, Freeman recognizes the tension that private individuals may face in contracting with the government; her suggestion is to allow for the possibility of "independent third parties to set standards, monitor compliance, and supplement enforcement," along with "professional norms," "internalized rules," and "informal sanctions" (Freeman 2000, 666). These suggestions go beyond our argument here. At this stage, we are seeking to identify what families can achieve. Nevertheless, such suggestions may be appropriate for education provision.

23. John Chubb and Terry Moe advocate a market approach in which scholarships or vouchers are given to families to use at any school in a marketplace of choices that meet some minimal government requirements (1990, 221–29). The initial voucher plan was set out in Milton Friedman (1962, 85–98).

24. A recent work in favor of considerable out-of-school investments to assist families educationally is Richard Rothstein, "Finance Fungibility: Investigating Relative Impacts of Investments in Schools and Non-School Educational Institutions to Improve Student Achievement" (2000).

25. For example, Grissmer et al. (1994, 39–48), uses family structure, family size, education of parents, age of mother at child's birth, family income, maternal employment, and race to measure the effects of family background on student achievement.

26. We also note that these pathways refer to specific *educational* advantages that parents pass to their children, and we have not addressed more general economic, social, and behavioral advantages that may accrue.

27. The parent/guardian "Achievement Agreement" at Bronx Preparatory Charter School lists eight commitments, of which only one refers to a parental role outside the school. This commitment expects the parents to read at night, attend parent/teacher conferences, make themselves available to staff, read all papers sent home, schedule student absence during the afternoons; purchase necessary materials, and allow the child to contact the teachers about attendance and homework. Similarly, the pledge by parents at North Star Academy Charter School of Newark has ten items, of which only one refers to the type of activities identified in tables 11.1 through 11.3: "I will check our child's homework

each night and provide quiet time and space for the work to be completed." A third example, Hyde School, makes no reference to family behaviors beyond attendance at a school retreat. At the Accelerated School, Los Angeles, the agreement expects the parent to provide home academic support (for example, ensuring the child is ready to learn), provide school support, and participate in at least three hours of school-based activity. Other countries have developed policies on home-school agreements. In England, the School Standards and Framework Act of 1998 expects each school to adopt an agreement relating to the standard of education, the ethos of the school, regular and punctual attendance, discipline and behavior, homework, and the information schools and parents should give to each other. Again, the actual content of the agreement is loosely specified. Similarly, school handbooks specify rules that apply within the school.

28. See also *Family Literacy* (Taylor and Goodman 1998).

29. The classic work on this topic is *Reproduction in Education, Society and Culture* (Bourdieu and Passeron 1977). Also, see generally the linguistic foundations in Basil Bernstein (1971).

30. As we note, much of the contract will require direct support for families in the form that will encourage greater educational effectiveness of family behavior. This will not only entail school-based strategies but major commitments to families as well. For examples of general programs of family support, see generally Kagan and Weissbourd (1994).

31. For concrete evidence on the effects of housing on student achievement, see generally Ludwig, Ladd, and Duncan (2001). The impact of increased family income for poor families on educational achievement is found in Dearing, McCartney, and Taylor (2001).

32. External support may be given in numerous ways, some of which are already being undertaken or developed. See generally Reisner, White, Birmingham, and Welsh (2001); Tolman, Pittman, Yohalem, Thomases, and Trammel (2002); Gordon and Bridglall (2002); Weiss and Offenberg (2002). Furthermore, much of this external support may be incorporated into existing welfare systems for children (for a full description and investigation of these systems, see the collected volume of *The Future of Children* (David and Lucile Packard Foundation 2002). Incorporating the contractual obligations into existing programs would be cost effective.

33. A forward-looking proposal by business interests for universal preschools to raise educational results (and improve the future labor force) is Committee for Economic Development, *Preschool for All: Investing in a Productive and Just Society* (2002). The citizenship and social participation rationales are found in Amy Gutman, *Democratic Education* (1987).

34. In Mexico, Brazil, and other countries, income supplements to poor families for student educational attainments have been shown to be effective. See World Bank (2001).

12

Parents as Advocates for Education

Patti Smith

In acknowledging the essential need to supplement public education, it may be helpful for parents who are not accustomed to providing such activities for their children to acquire the tacit knowledge and written information of school practices and policies in order to effectively support their children's academic and social maturation. The development of this understanding, appropriate supplements to the education of their children can be identified and implemented. Even so, the development of supplementary education activities and experiences for families who do not have access to high levels of human resource capital require treatments that address conditions born of social and economic disenfranchisement.

For parents of low economic status who have not experienced positive intellectual activities outside of school, it is important to demonstrate that such experiences are critical for their children's academic success. Those parents who have not been exposed to a variety of supplementary educational experiences during their childhood years may not have the background knowledge or experience with which to judge the value of these activities. Historically, these parents have been led to believe that their children are academically inferior when the case may be that their children suffer from inadequate exposure to intellectually stimulating experiences. Given these circumstances, parents of color are more likely to feel disenfranchised in relation to the school system (Menacker, Hurwitz, and Weldon 1988).

A disproportionate number of families of color have infrequent encounters with peers and adults whose sophistication is relevant to the pursuit of academic excellence and personal development. It is important that any programmatic efforts to remedy this situation facilitate close associations between such families and individuals who can impart repertoires for sustaining academic and social development. It is also helpful if at least some of these individuals are persons with whom these families feel a sense of commonality. Parents of color and their children often discover that there are too few members of school leadership with whom they can identify ethnically—a condition that exacerbates the absence of trustworthy and sophisticated role models in their children's immediate environment.

THE PARENTS FOR ROCKLAND YOUTH SUPPLEMENTAL EDUCATION (RYSE) PROGRAM

In an effort to address some of the issues raised by my colleagues in this book, Parents RYSE was initiated in two suburban communities north of New York City. These communities were chosen for three reasons: (1) the school districts in these communities had experienced a growth in their minority student populations; (2) these communities of color were experiencing problems with reversing the trends of their children's academic underachievement; and (3) there existed two community-based organizations in the districts that were also eager to support parent and student programs to enhance academic, political, and social involvement in school affairs and community empowerment. In addition to RYSE's primary intentions of increasing parental involvement in the academic lives of their children, cooperative efforts with community-based organizations were key aspects of the Parents RYSE program (Gordon and Smith 1999). The RYSE founders were convinced that it was critical to locate the program and activities in sites that were considered "safe havens" by communities of color.

The twofold program goals included, first, providing families with the human resource capital that is typically available to families from more-advantaged homes, and second, making explicit the connections between education, cultural integrity, and political empowerment. These goals were achieved by providing parent education that was focused on facilitating a better understanding of the school's curriculum and educational services, the responsibilities of parents as teachers of their children outside of school, and the development of highly effective parenting skills. Supplementary education services were also provided for the children of these families. These direct services to students were designed to enhance the impact of school-based academic practices and to model effective out-of-school intellectual experiences. Ultimately, this package of parent and student services would increase parents' sophistication in understanding the scope and breadth of experiences in which their children should participate (Gordon and Smith 1999).

RYSE targeted students who were at risk of underachieving. That is, RYSE sought out a broadly defined group of middle school–aged children whose academic performances could improve if their families were more actively involved in the schooling process. Although the RYSE staff worked directly with middle school staff in these districts to identify potential participants, this criterion ("at risk of underachieving") was not easily understood by school faculty or parents initially. RYSE staff met with guidance counselors and teachers to explain the objectives of the program and to solicit assistance with the identification of potential students and their families. Typically, the schools' staffs were more likely to refer special education students, students with behavioral problems, or students who were failing courses and were less likely to consider students who were passing but who had the capacity to achieve higher levels of academic progress. Parents of passing students were concerned when they and their children were recommended for the program. They construed this referral as a reflection of their children's purported failure. Fortunately, trusted leaders in the community assisted the RYSE staff in convincing parents that participation in the program was not synonymous with academic failure. In this vein, focus group meetings were held at the community-based organizations to explain the goals of the program to parents. It was fruitful to discuss the historically poor relationships between schools and families of color and the impact that cultural differences and prejudices have on student achievement. Furthermore, many discussions focused on parents' own experiences of academic difficulties and their reports of recent and unpleasant encounters with school officials concerning their children. In some cases, parents had been conditioned to believe that their children could not achieve academic success. During these preliminary focus group meetings, parents helped to develop realistic and necessary strategies for addressing the challenges of underachievement and their contributions were incorporated into the program content.

RYSE'S PROGRAM CONTENT

The RYSE program for parents included formal parent workshops and informal cottage meetings (with guest speakers). RYSE offered students Saturday academies and regular tutorial sessions. Both parents and students were involved in trips to colleges and periodic cultural activities.

Parent Activities

Parent Workshops

A series of workshops were held in the evening twice a month (during which dinner and child care were provided). The workshops were divided into three specific areas: (1) "Parents as Advocates," (2) "Parents as Teachers," and (3) "Parents as Parents." Each workshop was divided into the following seven components:

1. Community Bulletin Board: Parents were asked to bring information regarding school functions, library activities, and church or cultural events to share with members of the group.
2. Ground Rules: The group developed a set of operating principles at the first meeting. These rules were reviewed and modified as necessary at each subsequent session. Participants were also encouraged to develop family ground rules and to review them periodically with members of their families.
3. Icebreakers: During each workshop, an icebreaking exercise was introduced that was consistent with the program content for the evening and facilitated a sense of familiarity among the participants.
4. Homework review: For most sessions, parents were given homework assignments that emphasized school-related information gathering and the initiation of frequent communication and effective alliances with teachers and guidance counselors.
5. Skills Development: In each workshop, a hands-on exercise was used to introduce new parenting skills and to introduce the discussion topic.
6. Discussion: In each workshop, a topic related to the preceding skills development component was introduced in order to engage parents in discussions that enabled their ease and confidence with public speaking.
7. Review and Preview: At the end of each session, facilitators guided participants through a review of the workshop and presented a preview of the upcoming workshop content.

Parents as Advocates

These workshops provided parents with pertinent information about the administrative structures, practices, and curriculum content of public schooling, what parents could do to improve schools, and what they must do outside of school to support the academic, political, and social development of students. Workshop activities engaged parents in activities that would enable them to create political and social networks in support of high student achievement in the community. For example, workshop content was designed to prepare parents to be active members of community organizations such as Parent-Teacher Associations and school boards. Additionally, parents were prepared to engage in informative and effective meetings with school personnel. Topics that were discussed at the workshops included:

- The historically poor relationships between parents of color and school institutions

- The basic skills of "parent advocacy"—that is, knowing what to do at home to support children's academic endeavors, knowing what kinds of questions to ask of teachers and school administrators, and knowing how to engage in political activity
- The expectations parents should have of schools
- The importance of visiting schools, attending school functions, and communicating with teachers and school administrators on a regular basis
- The importance of working with teachers as allies (as opposed to adversaries) in the educational process.

Through role-playing, handouts, and skills-building practices, parents developed the ability to work effectively in the schools on behalf of their own children and in support of other parents.

Parents as Teachers

Given my experience that academically successful students are involved in extracurricular activities that support their scholastic abilities, these workshops provided parents with examples of activities that parents could initiate with their children (with a particular emphasis on access to affordable activities). Parents were led to identify their personal, academic, and social skills and talents—as well as their limitations—in providing such resources to their children. Parents developed the ability to identify the specific needs of children that could be addressed through supplementary resources such as mentors, tutors, after-school programs, and family excursions. Specific workshop topics and activities included:

- Visits to libraries and cultural centers
- Visits to colleges and exposure to college life
- Finding tutors and positive role models
- Recognizing learning styles and finding appropriate mentors

Parents as Parents

Several workshops addressed critical issues concerning parenting. Parents were reminded that the atmosphere created in the home and the attitudes demonstrated about learning have powerful influences on children's academic expectations and values. RYSE facilitators stressed the importance of providing loving support and, simultaneously, expecting children to uphold the standards established in the home. By providing children with structure, appropriate discipline, and praise, parents create an environment for learning and self-esteem. There are many aspects of the home that can be structured in support of academic development. Parents were informed about the value that children give to having their parents show interest in their schoolwork and maintain trusting relationships that, nevertheless, provide age-appropriate guidance and limits.

Children can be very sensitive to parents' fatigue from managing the demands and stressors of the workplace and the household. RYSE emphasizes that parents need to make time for their children and to remember how difficult it is to be a child—especially a child of color—in our society. Parenting is important not only as a source of nurturing and security but also as a source of acculturation. What is emphasized in the home with regard to academic success will have a profound impact on how a child functions in the larger society. These workshops featured the following topics:

- Developing good parent-child communication
- Creating a nurturing environment for study and encouraging homework completion
- Parents as intellectual and social role models
- The importance of consistent discipline and praise

Cottage Meetings

The RYSE program was developed according to the goal of empowering parents. This meant that RYSE staff listened for opportunities to support ideas that were generated by the participants. One such example of a parent-generated activity was the informal cottage meeting. These meetings arose as a result of parents' increased understanding of the importance of creating social networks. Parents wanted an opportunity to discuss problems and concerns with members of the community (more sophisticated others) who would be sensitive to their specific needs. These informal meetings were held in homes or at a community center. Parents generated topics of interest and the RYSE staff arranged for guest speakers with expertise in particular fields (Gordon and Smith 1999).

For example, one evening, a middle school principal of color spoke to parents about her expectations of parents and of teachers in her school. She was able to provide an administrative perspective on issues concerning student behavior and academic expectations. Another evening, in response to parents' concerns regarding child abuse, an activist who advocates for parents with children with behavioral difficulties spoke about the legal issues surrounding corporal punishment and child abuse. These meetings, conceived by the parents, proved to be an important addition to the RYSE program. These meetings increased parents' social capital as they became friends and partners in the educational endeavors of each other's families.

Family Activities

In an effort to address the need for parents and students to develop cultural integrity and pride, as well as to model examples of appropriate family activities, cultural excursions, dinners, and trips were provided by RYSE. These experiences included visits to traditionally black colleges and to cultural centers that provided historic information that demonstrated the richness of black culture in this country. Another example of a family activity was a "Pot Luck with Professionals" dinner, held to expose families to professionals in various fields. These professionals of color shared their struggles and their routes to academic and career success. Recurrent themes in their stories included consistent help and support from parents, mentors, and tutors who provided support, and extracurricular activities that generally provided sources of financial support during college attendance. These various family experiences demonstrated to parents the importance of providing mentors and tutors, encouraging student participation in extracurricular activities, and exposing students to historical and cultural activities.

Student Activities

The Saturday Academy provided supplementary educational experiences for students. The activities were structured as models of activities that more affluent families provide for their children and were fashioned to demonstrate the quality and breadth of out-of-school experiences that are necessary for academic success. The Saturday Academy was designed to provide assistance to the children, to model activities and behaviors that parents could implement in their homes, and to enable parents to identify characteristics of quality and content in supplementary educational programs for future acquisition.

The Saturday Academy operated during the pilot year of the program for three hours each session. The program was divided into several six-week sessions, each focusing on a specific area of intellectual development. For instance, the content areas included storytelling and literature through the visual arts and music, literacy skills, game strategies (e.g., chess), and team building with Outward Bound staff. The program was structured to include working in a content area for an hour, working on school assignments for one hour, and in the final hour, lunch was served, followed by community service activities. Parents were encouraged to participate in the weekly activities, and college interns were available during these sessions to assist students.

During the second year of the program, the Saturday activities were scaled down to include library tutorials with college-aged mentors. The change occurred because we observed that parents were likely to enroll in the program to enable their children to participate in the Saturday Academy; however, parents' participation was not especially strong. Although it was important for students to engage in the Saturday activities, these programs were initiated to provide parents with hands-on experience; they were not designed for students whose parents were not participating regularly in the program. In order to maintain the program's primary function of empowering parents, it was necessary to focus more acutely on the parent and family activities.

LESSONS LEARNED: STRENGTHS AND PROBLEMS IN PROGRAM IMPLEMENTATION

The greatest strength of the program was the ability to provide comprehensive and resource-rich programming for underserved communities. The exposure to sophisticated others from similar ethnic backgrounds served as a strong motivating factor for participants. Several parents enrolled in college and technical programs as a result of the program. Parents also experienced the potency of creating social and political networks to support them in dealing with the academic enrichment of their children. Many families developed lasting personal relationships as a result of the program.

Another strength of the program was reflected in RYSE's cooperative efforts with community-based organizations. Given that parents of color have traditionally had difficult relationships with schools and that they do not necessarily trust institutional leadership to share their concerns, it was our intention to develop the program in connection with organizations that traditionally provided support to the minority community. For this reason, the RYSE program was developed by and facilitated in organizations other than schools. With this priority in mind, it was important to develop strong links to establishments and individuals that actively support the development of minority students. On the other hand, RYSE's ability to capture the imagination and support of fraternities and sororities was not as successful as anticipated. Nonetheless, strong links to these organizations are necessary for future efforts to identify mentors and tutors and for assistance with appropriating financial resources.

We learned that our challenges were not dissimilar to those of other parent involvement projects. Transportation and child care often are difficult for families to negotiate, and any program's provision of these services can be time-consuming and expensive. Many parents in the minority community work at least two jobs and often have inconsistent schedules at work; such demands make regular participation in supplementary programs impossible. Some parents have not developed good organizational skills and have difficulty organizing their time to enable them to meet regular commitments. Although the development of personal and organizational skills was addressed in the program, it takes time to change long-term patterns that individuals have developed over time. Our window of opportunity may have been too short to impact a portion of the population we were targeting.

ALTERNATIVE STRATEGIES FOR DEVELOPING PARENT SUPPORT

RYSE's founders are committed to the further identification of alternative strategies for developing parent programs that support student academic and social development. The following issues were key factors in the consideration of alternative strategies: (a) the quality of the content of the program, (b) access to and availability of human resources, especially high-quality facilitators, (c) client recruitment and participation, and (d) the knowledge that there are limited financial resources available for such programs.

Organizations often identify the need to provide parent education to their constituents, but do not have the financial or human resource capital to develop and deliver quality programs. Prepackaging the content would provide an alternative strategy that addressed both content and financial concerns. The financial burden on organizations to generate content would be alleviated. Relieving this burden is significant, given that it is often a factor that preempts the development of parent education programs—especially those specifically addressing the needs of communities of color.

To address program participation and recruitment concerns, delivery strategies would need to be developed that provided a wide range of access to the program at various times and in multiple settings. To address considerations of program facilitation, delivery methods should include opportunities for potential facilitators to view effective program leadership techniques. The facilitators of the original RYSE program were trusted professionals in the community who could provide frank, sometimes tough, feedback to parents. Finding such facilitators could be difficult in alternative programs. Modeling their techniques would be an important component of any effective alternative strategy.

RYSE to the Challenge

It was determined that the most effective way to address identified concerns was to create a video series that documented key program content of the Parents' RYSE program. This would address our concern that appropriate alternative program strategies be developed with quality research-based content. It would also address our concern that the leadership style of the original facilitators could be modeled by potential facilitators when implementing the program.

The creation of such a documentary series would provide on-demand viewing options for clients. The video could be used by a small group of families in a cottage-meeting environment, could be aired on local television stations viewed by our target population, or could be viewed by individuals in their homes. Furthermore, a video documentary series could be used by churches, libraries, schools, and other parent organizations.

The *RYSE to the Challenge* video series was directly developed from the research-based, comprehensive, and interactive content of the original RYSE program. The series was divided into three 25-minute segments: "Parents as Advocates," "Parents as Teachers," and "Parents as Parents." Each video provides a conceptual framework for the specific topics, provides interviews of parents, students, teachers, and community leaders addressing the topic, and provides snapshots of the Parents' RYSE program in action. A manual for facilitators was developed to accompany the video that explains the video content and provides directions for implementing various components of the original program.

Given the need to inform parents of the significant role that supplementary education plays in the academic and social development of their children, this documentary—the first of its kind—is an inexpensive, easily accessible resource. Through the voices of educationally sophisticated persons of color, parents and students learn the rationale for the importance of parent involvement in supplementary educational experiences and additional, practical hands-on activities for future implementation are clearly explained.

The video series will be disseminated to various community-based organizations and other national organizations interested in providing parent education programs that address the specific academic, social, and political concerns of communities of color. Local and regional workshops will be held to train facilitators to implement the program. Additional material that outlines the workshop series is available as an appendix to the manual that accompanies the video collection.[1]

Future Replications

In subsequent years, we hope to refine the models and specifications for each of the components and seek to involve local community organizations in the sponsorship of elements of this program. In addition, as the model programs are perfected and documented, effort will be directed at promoting the sponsorship of high-performance learning communities nationwide through such community organizations as:

American Indian Movement
ASPIRA chapters
Jack and Jill Clubs and the Links
Local organizing committees of the Million Man March
Local chapters of Greek letter organizations
NAACP chapters
National Congress of American Indians
100 Black Women's Clubs
100 Black Men's Clubs.
Urban League chapters

REFERENCES

Gordon, E. W., and P. Smith. 1999. *The facilitator's manual for* RYSE to the Challenge: *Parents supporting student academic development.* New York: College Board.
Menacker, J., E. Hurwitz, and W. Weldon. 1988. Parent-teacher cooperation in schools serving urban poor. *Clearing House* 62(3): 108–12.

NOTE

1. For more information about the video series or to inquire about upcoming training sessions, please contact the RYSE Program, care of Gordon and Gordon Associates in Human Development, 3 Cooper Morris Drive, Pomona, NY 10970, or call 845.354.5809.

13

Community Support for Supplementary Education

Maitrayee Bhattacharyya

Although many types of ethnic education initiatives exist,[1] the published description and evaluation of ethnic supplementary education programs specifically in the scholarly literature is limited. This chapter describes only one of these many ethnic efforts, namely Korean supplementary education. Specifically represented are schools and after-school programs that the author observed, organized by people of Korean origin to serve Korean families in the section of Los Angeles called Koreatown. Since the study of Korean supplementary education in the United States is a relatively new area of inquiry, the main purpose of this chapter is descriptive. This chapter describes and interprets what was reported to the author and observed by the author on visits to various schools. What was learned is related to the existing literature on the influence of parents and families on academic development and on the effects of after-school programs on academic development. This chapter also explores limited aspects of the interplay between parents, children, and the larger systems or the multiple sociocultural contexts of which they are a part and among which they must negotiate. Conceivably, there are positive effects of Korean supplementary education on academic achievement. However, determining the effects of Korean supplementary education will require further systematic investigation.

ACADEMIC ACHIEVEMENT AND ITS CORRELATES

The literature on academic achievement has explained achievement through a variety of competing hypotheses. The greatest tension has been between those who argue that achievement is a fact of nature, or innate qualities, versus those who argue that achievement is a result of nurture, or environmental circumstances. In recent years, scholars have debated the relative contribution of IQ versus socioeconomic status and have debated the contributions of societal structural factors including discrimination, preselection, access to opportunities, and economic changes; of family cultural factors including cultural repertoires and dispositions, habits, beliefs, and expectations, and language abilities; and of family socioeconomic resources including parents' education, wealth, employment, and income.

While the relative importance and causal relationships of different factors remain in dispute, it appears that many of these factors are at work together. It is safe to say that academic development is a result of numerous and complex influences. Among these, scholars recurrently find that a number of familial characteristics exert positive influence across families. Greater parental educational experience, high parental expectations and aspirations, higher per-child parental financial resources, early monitoring and supervision of children's activities, interactive activities like help with homework and reading to children, low family disruption stress, good health and nutrition, quality schooling, and structured after-school environments facilitate academic achievement.

In the context of this scholarly interest in determining the correlates of academic achievement, scholars have been concerned with explaining the differences in achievement patterns of different ethnic groups. Currently, students of Asian descent in the United States have the reputation for outperforming European Americans, whose test scores represent the standard on traditional measures of performance. Results of various studies and data reviewed by Miller (1995) indicate that Asian students on average outperformed or performed equally as well as European Americans on standardized tests and GPAs. Asian Americans also maintained high levels of school enrollments comparatively based on 1980 and 1990 census data (Barringer, Gardner, and Levin 1993). Korean Americans are among those Asian American groups who maintain high levels of school enrollment through college, which is one of the more universal measures of school engagement (Barringer, Gardner, and Levin 1993).

In order to explain Asian achievement patterns, scholars have examined a number of the aforementioned correlates of achievement in various degrees of detail. Scholars have explored the reasons behind the academic achievement of Asian groups habitually in the aggregate, and usually this includes Koreans. The explanations for high academic achievement have ranged from demographic and structural accounts to cultural accounts. From a demographic view of human and cultural capital distribution, scholars routinely hypothesize that the children of educated families will become educated as well, and have found evidence supporting this relationship. The relationship between economic and educational backgrounds of parents also has been found across and within groups to exert a powerful influence on children's academic performance, and Korean children are unlikely to be an exception.

Since parents' education and experienced payoffs on education may facilitate children's academic engagement, in the Korean case, parents' backgrounds probably enhance Korean children's average educational achievement levels. A high percentage of early post-1965 Korean immigrants came from middle-class professional backgrounds (Kim et al. 1981), and Korean householder college completion rates exceed those of whites, blacks, and Hispanics (Barringer, Gardner, and Levin 1993, 188). Also, Korean immigrant cohorts post-1965 are college educated compared to native-born Americans, even though the percentage of high school and college graduates decreased significantly in the 1975–1980 cohort compared to those who immigrated between 1965 and 1974 (Barringer, Gardner, and Levin 1993). As such, it is reasonable to assume that at least some Korean youths' parents represent a "preselection of well-educated" immigrants who experienced "real payoffs on education" (Hirschman and Wong 1986). In addition, there are some other factors to consider regarding Asian American student environments; these reportedly often also include intact homes, time spent on homework, relatively high educational expectations, and lessons and activities outside regular school (Peng and Wright 1994).

An informal experiment shows how some of these factors might interact. Parents' education levels can be converted to occupation and income statistics, which can translate into purchasing power and extended support and information networks (Barringer, Gardner, and Levin 1993). Certainly this impacts parents' abilities to provide adequate food and health care. Also, parents' education, through the purchasing power it enables from employment, can affect the educational resources available to children. For example, some evidence suggests that college students are more likely to have been enrolled in preschool than those who are not in college (Barringer, Gardner, and Levin 1993). Parents' education also enables parents to assist children in the navigation of school systems and educational experiences and serve as educational mentors. In fact, some have found mother's education and mother's expectation play as strong a role—if not stronger—in academic development as preschool attendance (Baker and Entwisle 1987; Wadsworth 1986). Parents' education can indicate familiarity with educational institutions. If "preexistence of institutional instruction" is not part of the family background, it may be more difficult for children to engage in the institutional structure of learning (Kruger and Tomasello 1996).

Along these lines, some scholars theorize that inequality occurs as the product of cultural resources and social interaction (Lamont and Lareau 1988), and some posit that there is more chance of a cultural gap or mismatch between low-SES families and school institutions than for high-SES families (De Graaf 1988). Power differentials and displays may also impede student achievement. Since teachers act as active gatekeepers who reward general skills, habits, styles, and appearances through course grades (Farkas, Grobe, Sheehan, and Yuan 1990), derogatory attitudes and behaviors toward cultural diversity and unexamined assumptions about ethnic groups can contribute to the higher- or lower-status maintenance of various groups. Thus, a lack of institutional savvy or parental familiarity with institutional instruction may be exacerbated by teachers' attitudes and behaviors on the microlevel and lead to or reproduce inequality on the macrolevel. Further, scholars hypothesize that educational success is due to perceptions of education as a means for mobility (Caplan, Marcella, and Whitmore 1992; Sue and Okazaki 1990; Steinberg 1989). In turn, children may learn that the rewards differ for different groups, and that even with similar background characteristics there are very real differences in the rates of return for different ethnic groups (Tienda and Lii 1987).

It must be acknowledged that socioeconomics plays a role in explaining aggregate differences in achievement at the group level, but differences that persist after individuals are matched on socioeconomic status must be explained (Mercy and Steelman 1982; Alwin and Thornton 1984). In addition to arguments that stress the importance of economic resources and educational resources, some assert that ethnic cultural resources and diversity in a co-ethnic community can facilitate adaptation and incorporation in the United States (Portes and Zhou 1993).

Bicultural or multicultural adaptations, compared to monocultural adaptations, may help maximize resources and mediate against poverty. With an "Asian" culture in mind, scholars have posited that high Asian achievement may stem from a Confucian ethic and a family orientation (see Barringer, Gardner, and Levin, quoting Liu, 1993, 134). In other words, Asians are thought to have "a desire for education . . . because East Asian societies made education a prerequisite, at least ideally, for high status positions" coupled with "obedience to elders and respect for status" and "strong family support" or stability (Barringer, Gardner, and Levin 1993, 164 and 144). As Kim (1998) notes, the traditional Asian American family is described as patrilineal, patrilocal, collectivist, and cohesive, and also one that controls children through shame and guilt, according to Uba (1994) (see also Barringer, Gardner, and Levin 1993, 134). A related argument, one that is not uniquely Asian, is that immigrants, more generally, have higher expectations. Immigrant parents may immigrate for the express purpose of enhancing children's educational opportunities (Chao 1996; Suarez-Orozco 1989). It is believed that children may work to succeed because a child's achievement reflects on family reputation, and failure to meet family expectations may result in a psychological cost (Kim 1998).

Several studies support the idea of a family mechanism in Asian achievement. While Sigel finds that Chinese parents are less likely to be directly involved with schools and homework help in the United States than they would have been in their country of origin (Sigel 1988), findings from a Texas survey of two-parent middle-class Asian American families published in 1985 included the finding that Asian American families have more structure and push children to study more than white families (Yao 1985). Similarly, Hedges (1988) argued that Asian parents' involvement and interest in their schools was higher than that of European Americans. Another study finds that Korean students feel more pressure from parents than Caucasian students to succeed; the caveat is that this also differentiates Korean from Caucasian students' depression levels (Aldwin and Greenberger 1987). While Kim (1998) argues that it is not clear that depression scales hold the same construct validity for Asians as for Caucasians, the possibility exists that family pressure has both positive and negative consequences for human development. Further examination of the effects of family and culture on achievement should be undertaken to understand what appears to be a complex relationship.

Kim (1998) argues for further examination of the possible influence of parent-child relationships, parenting style, and family dynamics, particularly the interplay of acculturation, parental expectation, family cohesion and obligation, and marital conflict that potentially leads to both high academic achievement and also to higher emotional distress. Although high family expectation among Asian and immigrant families may mediate some of the risks associated with low SES, the relationship is probably not a linear one. Tseng (1998) argues similarly for further examination of family obligation and its role in academic achievement among immigrant families and posits a curvilinear model of diminishing return to high family responsibility. At very high levels of demand and very low levels of financial resources, the positive academic impact of greater emphasis placed by immigrant families on education may be diminished.

Studies suggest that all of these factors concerning the family and family status contribute to Asian academic achievement patterns and that the interaction of family expectation/obligation, family socioeconomic status, and immigrant status deserves further inquiry. While these factors play a role, it is clear that the ability to succeed academically depends on the education a child receives. The ability to gain admission to college, attend, and succeed there depends largely on the educational institutions to which families have had access before that time.

A factor that may be involved in the achievement of Korean children that is not often considered in the scholarly literature is the access many of these students had to supplementary education. Higher percentages of Korean children than white children ages three to four in the 1980 census (i.e., those going to college now) attended preschool. It is not clear from census data whether these were ethnic preschools, but access to ethnic supplementary education also may be an important factor to consider. S. Kim (personal communication, March 1999) believes that more than 80 percent of Korean children in Koreatown are involved regularly in supplementary education. For many years, there has been a growing number of ethnic supplementary education programs in Koreatown, which may positively impact the college attendance and success of Korean children, even those who may not have access to high-quality urban public education and whose parents struggle to survive economically. In order to find out more about Korean after-school and day-school programs, the author went to Koreatown to conduct research on schools open during the summer.

METHODS AND COMMUNITY PROFILE

School sites were selected by using the Korean phone directory to select schools in Koreatown for site visits. Inclusion of schools of different types that served a broad age range of clientele was achieved with the assistance of a bilingual young man of Korean American origin who had lived in the Koreatown area. He served as an informant and his assistance helped in many ways since the author is not of Korean descent, cannot speak Korean, and is not from the Los Angeles area. Together, schools were contacted by phone to schedule visits; a total of nine schools and one educational bookstore in Koreatown (from a pool of nearly three hundred schools in the greater L.A. area) were visited. Two schools were family businesses, one was a family business with a religious affiliation, three programs had a church affiliation, one ran through a community center, and one ran through a private elementary school; one school was actually a school franchise headquarters.

Only one school declined the phone request of visitation; the director said he worked alone, was busy, and would not be available. He said the school was a franchise and suggested contact with their corporate headquarters for the information the author expressed interest in gathering. The author followed this suggestion. All other school officials agreed to site visits, although some visits and interviews were more extensive than others. Contact with schools was not made too far in advance to minimize the possibility that schools might artificially prepare for visits or alter their programming, but this also may have limited access to some schools as a result. In the best visits, the author observed all the classrooms and facilities; observed classes and activities; observed children; interviewed school directors, assistant directors, and/or teachers; and learned about daily and weekly schedules, staff, cost, and parental involvement.

Koreatown in Los Angeles was selected because of the suitability of Los Angeles for this project, and the access the author gained there to the community. Los Angeles and New York City are the two main areas where there are large, concentrated Korean populations making efforts to maintain Korean language and culture through networks of churches, social institutions, and language schools (Byun 1990). In Los Angeles, efforts also include Korean language mass media and bilingual education in public schools and business organizations (Kim et al. 1981). Los Angeles is particularly interesting because of the Proposition 187, 209, and 227 debates, since public bilingual education has been voted out de jure but reportedly continues de facto, and since some schools operate year-round due to the size of the school-age population.

Although Korean immigration to the U.S. mainland dates to World War II (Byun 1990), the majority of the Korean population in Los Angeles came after 1970. Through 1980, the population included a high percentage of middle-class professionals (Kim et al. 1981), but it has since diversified (Barringer, Gardner, and Levin 1993). It should be noted that a high percentage of Korean immigrants have limited English proficiency, and most Korean children in Koreatown attend public (not private) day schools during the school year. Koreatown is urban, not suburban, and is by no means uniformly middle-class even within the Korean population.

As reported in the Korean Youth and Community Center pamphlet based on 1990 U.S. Census data,

> Korean Americans constitute one of the fastest growing populations in the United States, growing 127% from a reported 354,593 in 1980 to 798,949 in 1990, and over 25% of them live in L.A. County. Approximately 80% are foreign born, and over 80% of Korean American households speak limited or no English. Approximately half of Koreatown residents are Hispanics. Korean Americans are the second largest group followed by whites and African Americans. Over 35% of Koreatown households earn less than $15,000 per year. Over 25% of the entire Koreatown population live in poverty, and approximately one third of Koreatown youth live in poverty. 90% of households do not own their housing. The unemployment rate in Koreatown is 9.6%.

DISCUSSION AND FINDINGS:
KOREATOWN SUPPLEMENTARY EDUCATION

While not an economically wealthy community according to the aforementioned statistics, Koreatown appears to house a fairly healthy urban economy built around supplementary education. Some members of the Korean population in Koreatown have drawn on whatever human, cultural, and economic capital they can to meet a demand for enlightened child care. The community has produced more than one hundred local area programs, enough programs to serve thousands of children. Supplementary education is not only economically viable in Koreatown, it appears to promote itself by increasing employment among Koreans and by ensuring that Korean wealth is circulated among Koreans, not to mention the human capital and social support it builds by fostering child development and intraethnic community ties.

Since there is still unmet need, more new supplementary schools and franchises have been emerging both in the suburb areas and in the city. There is even enough demand for supplementary schooling to sustain a school in the business of teaching how to run schools. There is also a healthy demand for tutors, and some Korean youth will tutor younger Korean children as they get older, though tutors reputedly cost more than supplementary schools.

The concern that it would not be easy to find many examples of ethnic after-school programs was quickly mitigated. The author had heard of isolated examples of supplementary school initiatives in immigrant and ethnic communities from time to time in the popular press, but concerns stemmed from the very little reference to such programs in the scholarly literature. Indeed, the author was not prepared to find so many examples of rather densely situated Korean after-school programs.

Before conducting site visits, the author had heard of Asian supplementary education existing in the Los Angeles area. Interestingly, even in Los Angeles, not everyone knew of the existence of Asian supplementary education initiatives. Since there are multiple Los Angeles–area phone directories, reliance on these could lead to oversight of ethnic programs. However, ethnic community after-school programs were rather readily located through multiple inquiries. A local professor, who had studied the Korean community and was also of Korean origin himself, said that there were reputed to be two hundred Korean ethnic supplementary schools in the Pico area of Koreatown, and he mentioned that they were all within a four-square-mile area (D. Park, personal communication, July 1998). By this time, the author also had heard several reports of the existence of ethnic community phone directories. With the generous assistance of a young Korean associate, the author gained access to the Korean community directory and examined school listings. The author also learned that in the Korean community these schools had a name; they were called *hagwans*, meaning "study place." Unlike Los Angeles phone directories at large, a look at listings for schools in the Korean community phone directory makes very manifest what some might otherwise take to be an invisible phenomenon.

The mostly private Korean after-school programs in and around Los Angeles are a visible phenomenon, immediately obvious if you drive or walk through Koreatown or pick up a local Korean phone directory and look up "schools." Driving around to visit schools, one finds advertisements in newspapers for schools and billboard advertisements or banners for schools. On a typical drive through the Wilton residential area, you see the Heidi Preschool and Art, the U.S. Academy, the Hosanna Presbyterian Church, the Wilton Place School, the Korean Youth Community Center (a.k.a. KYCC), and a teen karaoke hangout. If you are driving down Wilshire Boulevard, one of the main boulevards, you see a church advertising its preschool toddler program, the Newton SAT Center, the ECC Academy, the Saint James Infant Toddler Development Center, the Wilshire Boulevard Methodist Church Summer School, and an information center. You do not necessarily see many young people hanging out on the streets, but there are clearly many young people in the community and services geared for them.

After driving extensively around the area, contacting schools and visiting a number of schools, there are several informed conclusions that can be made about the supplementary programs in the area. Korean supplementary education in Koreatown can be described as (1) profuse, densely concentrated, and available for almost all grades; (2) supervisory, structured, and curriculum diverse; (3) multiculturally oriented; (4) functional, convenient, accessible, and relatively affordable; and (5) highly utilized, generally popular, economically viable, and currently expanding due to unmet need and industry competitiveness.

Looking through non-Korean phone directories before the Korean directory, the author had found some listings for ethnic group–based education initiatives particularly of Asian aspect. There are listings of language schools and Noonoppi- and Kumon-style mathematics preparation programs. Notwithstanding the ethnic supplementary schools elsewhere in the Los Angeles area, the Korean community directory indicated the very high concentration of Korean ethnic schools in Koreatown.

In fact, it became clear that members of the Korean community had created a near-parallel school system outside regular schools. In the Korean directory there were roughly 295 listings for Korean schools in Los Angeles. There were seventy-seven schools that advertised as formal nursery schools and kindergartens, twenty-six "family nursery and preschools," ninety-six "art" schools, and ninety-five "school institutes," mostly for older children. Multiple listings ran the spectrum from preschool through tenth grade, and there was a choice of many supplemental programs that provided child care through the eighth grade.

The institutions that the author is referring to as "schools" can be seen essentially as need-driven child-care services. Most schools offered very parent-friendly schedules and hours, pick-up to and from the school, and extended operating hours. Supervision of children was available in some locations from as long as 7 a.m. to 6:30 p.m. with breakfast, lunch, and two snacks provided, all for a fee of $335 a month. Part-time schedules and fees also existed in the $200 monthly range. Strictly after-school hours could cost even less at roughly $90. Workbooks and special music or dance lessons and field trips were billed separately. Schools operated Monday through Saturday and year-round. However, besides their fundamental child-care services, these institutions had a scholastic orientation. A director at a school mentioned simply that they serve two needs at once: day care and homework supervision.

It seemed that while locations and buildings differ among schools, all places visited had adequate, not fancy, facilities and small classes. Facilities ranged from attractive homes to church buildings to very plain, square, brick or stucco buildings with old linoleum floors and small classrooms with parking lot playgrounds. Inside, the schools usually had a piano, several computers, many books, and some light colorful decor of animals, rainforests, and award certificates. Although the interior of some schools was also quite plain with windowless classrooms not uncommon, it is clear that students were exposed in many of these schools (regardless of their level of interior decor or charm) to what scholars have called cultural capital, that is, objects and skills related to literature and fine arts. At each site, the classes were small, fewer than fifteen students per teacher. Students were busy. One might argue that while exposed to cultural capital during classes, these young children were insulated from the outdoor urban environment. A sheltered Korean atmosphere may not be integral to learning, but it may help younger children achieve a basic education.

Korean schools were serving parents with a much-needed sense of support and formed a reliable system where other adults could perform parenting roles in a way that is not culturally unfamiliar or insensitive to parents and their needs. From this author's point of view, schools were helping thicken thin resources for both immigrant and postimmigrant-generation parents. According to one working mother who is second generation and sends her two children to supplemental schools, the schools offer many benefits. Schools are conveniently located in the neighborhood near work or home, provide "home-cooked Korean meals and snacks, not poor quality American junk food, and have lots of activities." She said the buildings "aren't great," even "yucky" but the schools make up for that in other important ways, and are "efficient." For example, they are strict on timing of activities and meals, and are relatively inexpensive. She also found Korean schools more flexible than American schools since they have longer hours than American schools. According to parent testimony, it appeared that many parents believed their children learned in these environments and were generally pleased with the content. For example, parents perceived that their children learned "some Korean and good math."

Based on site visits, several features seemed common to most of the schools. The schools offered systematic and diverse program options and curricular preparation structured around certain basic elements. Simultaneously, programs ranged from preschool for ages two to five, kindergarten for ages five to six, after-school programs for all ages through eighth grade, and kindergarten through eighth-grade programs, special reading programs, ESL programs, art, music, and computer programs.

School brochures and schedules indicated availability of instruction in a wide number of areas and a variety of closely supervised activities. Schedules and curricular options named phonics, listening and reading comprehension, writing composition, journal entry, vocabulary building, computer, mathematics, SSAT, PSAT, SAT, science, study time, Bible time, art, history, English, Korean, and Spanish. Most schools demonstrated a core emphasis on English literacy and math skills, students working or learning in small-group settings, and Korean staff of different ages and both genders. Almost all faculty and staff at the schools were co-ethnic, Korean; in addition to both male and female personnel, school personnel came from immigrant, postimmigrant, monolingual, and bilingual backgrounds.

Programs were not haphazardly or incoherently scheduled. The schedules indicated participation by all in certain language and math academic activities rather than schedule conflicts between academic activities. In other words, there were required core activities from which students were not withdrawn to receive remedial instruction. This may have been possible, in part, by many schools' use of workbook-driven curricula.

While workbooks are not a highly creative teaching method, their use may help make delivery of services more uniform, even as it encourages students to learn at their own pace. All together, a typical day program offered several hours of academic activity, some physical activity, time for meals and homework, and usually a field trip on Fridays. There was regular testing of progress, particularly in math; for example, in one school there were bimonthly tests, perhaps a monthly math and spelling bee, and an award day.

Although the schools embodied "no frills" and the basics, they did appear to capitalize on "Korean" culture and demonstrate multicultural education. School features seemed to accommodate and accept U.S. tests as performance measures and yet retain Korean influences—or at least the imagery of Koreanness. Schools offered English, Spanish, and Korean. Schools might also simultaneously do the pledge of allegiance, offer Bible study, teach Korean history and world history, and teach about Korean traditions. Schools appeared to teach to math tests and focus on improving English instruction. One school had developed Korean instructional materials, such as textbooks on learning Korean. As aforementioned, many of the school personnel were of Korean descent, yet they brought to schools different backgrounds. Despite the broken or limited English of some staff, others were on hand who spoke English fluently.

Discussions with community members and school proprietors (and that is not mutually exclusive) suggest that Korean competition and supplementary education continue to act as points of reference that contribute to the high emphasis on education among transplanted Koreans in the United States. The noticeable presence of cultural imagery played a seemingly integral role in the success and existence of these schools. Images of Korean authenticity, perhaps real but also mythic elements, were intertwined with images of Asian achievement and Korean success. Asian achievement, Korean success, and ethnic authenticity were invoked as the backdrop for these programs, and as a reason for choosing these over "American" schools.

Contrasting education in Korea to the education in the United States, one school director spoke at length about the early age at which students learn in Korea, saying how early students learned double-digit multiplication and so forth in Korea. He spoke with pride of Korea's high national rank in test performance. He said that despite Korea's status as a small country, Korea was trying to develop, and that informs parents' drive and emphasis on education. He also said compared to Korea, so many colleges in America make it less competitive here; this is viewed by parents as an opportunity for their children. He said students in Korea have no free time, only study time; the goal is to get to college. Thus, in the United States, 70 to 80 percent of Korean parents send their children to after-school programs since both parents work 80 to 90 percent of the time; 50 percent in Korea get some tutoring also. He believed the achievement and performance of those in after-school programs surpassed that of others who did not attend after-school programs.

Similarly, another school director said, "In Korea all children begin school by age five, and kindergarten is for three- to five-year-olds where they learn to read and count. But here you don't have to go to school until you are six. It is drilled into children from young ages that Korean students know they must do well or else disgrace the family—not to do well would be unacceptable." The sense that educational achievement is honorable and integral to a Korean child's development and the sense that after-school programs promote educational achievement seem to permeate the after-school environment and parental thought in Koreatown. It is not merely thought that participation in after-school programs may provide an advantage, but that nonparticipation in after-school programs is a disadvantage. Through widely accessible educational beliefs and reinforcing school structures, pressure on Korean parents and children to consume educational services has been generated in Koreatown.

On the whole, persons with whom the author spoke indicated the presence of strong endorsement of supplemental education among Koreans and, not surprisingly, a feeling of connection for both parents and the youth attending these supplemental programs. Nonetheless, despite organized community efforts to maintain Korean language and culture, pressure to change comes both from outside and within the community as U.S. education and ideals and the Korean younger generations challenge elders and the traditional hierarchical family structure (Kim et al. 1981). Some members of the younger generation expressed concern over the pressure to use supplementary education that grew out of the perception that everyone else used supplementary education. Some members of the younger generation voiced an interest in seeing the supplementary educational philosophy evolve to include work on social interaction, more creative problem solving, and more questioning.

In addition, the laws in California play a role in encouraging and discouraging these schools. It seemed clear that parents patronized Korean schools because they were looking for a good value, desired flexibility, and low cost, but wanted more than day-care service. Demand is also fostered, according to one school director, because parents fear social service will take their children away if children are unsupervised; so every parent with children under age fourteen needs the service.

The demand for services extends beyond Koreatown to greater Los Angeles. Korean families who live in the suburbs have been known to send their children into the city to attend schools. There is so much Korean demand for good teachers, education, and schools that schools are proliferating in areas where there are many Koreans so that now some children from the suburbs no longer have to commute to Koreatown. There is competition among programs and a pressure, generated particularly by the younger generations, to open "better programs" and make them more prestigious and expensive. Furthermore, the school board sets requirements for day-care, after-school, and preschool programs. Some institutions are perhaps not able to meet all requirements. Indeed, rumors of official campaigns to close schools made some schools wary, particularly of outside visitors. At one school, the author was initially suspected of being an auditor, even though the author produced university identification. Due to these and other factors, changes in schools are foreseeable, and increase in costs may be likely, particularly if less expensive schools are shut down. Whether or not all foreseeable changes will be beneficial on the whole remains to be seen.

IMPLICATIONS

Korean supplementary education may play a significant role in the academic performance of Korean students. This observer would generally hypothesize a positive impact on children's academic development and on community development. Also, this impact might be observable at the group level, and may partially explain the forthcoming academic achievement patterns of Korean children in the United States as well as the current patterns, since supplementary schools have been a part of Korean education as far back as the seventies. It appears that Korean supplemental initiatives act as functional structures that create smoother transitions from home to school environment and from one grade to the next. Though designed separately, together they create a promising supplemental system that should be promoted.

Further inquiry into Korean supplementary education and other ethnic supplementary education initiatives, and determination of their potential transferability as educational technologies is strongly indicated. Individual communities may be able to integrate these strategies with their own, as well as design and adapt these strategies in ways that are nevertheless unique to their needs. Successful yet isolated programs already exist in many communities as a result of their sheer will, but densely situated programs may have greater impact still.

Of course, supplementary education has been proposed and implemented before. Programs have been developed as interventions in order to improve the life chances of those with very limited socioeconomic resources. Chapter 1, Title 1 funds reportedly reach fifty-one thousand schools, including over 75 percent of the elementary schools in the United States, to provide supplementary education services to low-achieving students in poor areas (Kober 1991). There are not only many programs, but there are reportedly many good programs for urban residents. Schwartz (1996) reports that in most urban communities there are good after-school programs, that parents can choose to provide extra learning opportunities. Just as the literature on family resources makes frequent reference to certain findings about the characteristics of families that facilitate scholastic achievement, the literature on after-school programs suggests generally that these programs have a positive influence. By some accounts, there are already many supplementary programs, and many good programs to serve ethnic groups or the poor. Why, then, highlight Korean supplementary education?

The answer simply is that one must have some reservations about the programs described in the scholarly literature and the availability of supplementary education systems. After reviewing the supplementary education efforts mentioned in the literature of both private efforts and Chapter 1, Title 1 efforts, this author finds that despite reports of the availability of programs and mostly favorable impacts, several critical observations can be made. Regarding supplementary instruction initiatives, such as peer or other tutoring to help in particular courses, these occur primarily at the college level and primarily for math and science courses. Regarding other non–Chapter 1, after-school, and supplementary efforts, many are inspired by practicums and thus lack permanence. Many take place one or two days a week or less, and even as little as a one half-hour a week, or on a pullout basis, and thus offer insufficient exposure or regularity. Many are optional for children and result in irregular attendance. Many rely on volunteers, and may thus lack continuity of mentoring. Many lack a diverse or culturally responsive curriculum. Many are run by schools, similar to Chapter 1 programs, and may replicate the shortcomings of standard school pedagogy, including teacher fatigue, lack of parental control or input, and little diverse or co-ethnic faculty. Finally, many programs target adolescents and are not maximizing risk prevention or enrichment starting at younger ages. This leaves a gap in the supplementary program system at the elementary school level, which Chapter 1 programs are left to fill. However, Chapter 1 programs are often remedial and potentially stigmatizing rather than enriching in character and have been shown to have fallen short of intended goals over the last thirty years, despite some positive impacts (Borman and D'Agostino 1995).

Urban areas in general may not have as many options for students of all ages or economic backgrounds or as complete a system of supplementary education as exists in Koreatown. In addition, many urban communities may lack programs that are community based, self-determined, or well informed by parents' investments and needs. One of the apparent quandaries of Chapter 1, Title 1 supplementary education is that supplementary education for the poor becomes compensatory education and by definition temporary. In some cases, if students improve to the desired standard, they become ineligible for further participation—but if the program does not show improvement occurring among students, then it becomes ineligible for funding. Despite Chapter 1, supplementary education for those who may need it most may be lacking and limited to compensatory education, as contrasted with programs providing continued enrichment. Finally, this also leaves a large gap in supplementary summer school choices. This break should increasingly concern scholars and educators since studies have found that loss of knowledge over the summer or during nonschool times may be particularly high for students from disadvantaged backgrounds (Morse 1992). Furthermore, the availability of summer enrichment programs seems even more limited for less-advantaged communities or students who are performing poorly academically.

We know that supplementary education can have a positive impact, particularly if designed in certain ways. Having physical activities, structure and clear limits, positive interaction with adults and peers, diversity of experience, and an understanding of what parents and children want form the criteria for successful after-school programs (Marx 1989). In addition, reaching the goal of improving preparation of students to attain high achievement in secondary school and beyond depends on beginning at the elementary school level, especially for the educationally disadvantaged (Levin 1987). Children who have more supervision (Folsom 1991) and continued and lengthy academic engagement and mentorship show the greatest positive academic results (Kennedy 1996). Seven or more years of supplementary education produce better results than one or two years, and may even be necessary to make a difference for some boys (Fuerst and Fuerst 1993).

Of course, Korean after-school programs and summer day-school programs in Koreatown do not always meet all of the recurrently mentioned criteria of successful after-school programs in the scholarly literature. However, overall they form a system that does appear to meet many of the above criteria. Other communities are nevertheless often missing systems of supplementary education or lacking in programs that meet all of these criteria. Restated, based on observation, Korean supplementary education in Koreatown may be simply described as follows. As a group of initiatives:

- They are densely situated and age diverse.
- They exhibit program diversity and curriculum diversity in a structured and developmental manner.
- They are designed to suit most working parents' schedules and budgets, and are service oriented for profit.
- They are interested in doing a good job and compete with each other. The competition gives parents choices, and it appears parents see school cost as a necessity; a free program is not perceived as a good quality program according to proprietors and parents I spoke with.
- They also display multicultural adaptivity in programming.
- Their facilities are not usually fancy or large, but their classes are, more importantly, usually small.
- Finally, their programming appears to engage students, and their teachers appear energetic and attentive.

There is a dense array of schools that have the capacity to act as a parallel school system and a community scaffolding. For Korean parents who may not be able to personally supervise children after school due to employment or other commitments, Korean after-school programs satisfy an important childcare need in dual-worker homes. For parents who may perceive potential difficulties of language, culture, and socioeconomic barriers to being involved in the mainstream education their children receive, Korean after-school programs may provide parents with a sense of familiarity, continuity, and control in fulfilling an educational need for children without extensive demands on the parents' own time. For children this may facilitate the development of a bicultural or multicultural adaptation, which has been found to enhance intellectual and cognitive development (Portes and Hao 1998).

At the very least, Korean after-school and summer day-school programs provide a quiet and safe place to study and learn in an urban environment, enrichment in the arts, math and literacy skills useful on standardized tests, regular physical activity, supervised summer activities that include and promote summer learning, and potentially an academically oriented peer group. For all these reasons, Korean supplementary education's popularity with parents would be understandable. Moreover, it is reasonable to expect that the directionality of the impact of these initiatives on Korean student academic development is on average positive.

The practice of doing for one's ethnic group by members of that ethnic group may be named a co-ethnic strategy. An inquiry into co-ethnic efforts indicates there are a number of supplementary education efforts organized around religious or ethnic affiliation besides those of Korean origin. The presence of ethnic initiatives can teach us a number of lessons. We develop structures, sometimes inadvertently, that deter self-determination or ignore parents' needs—then we ask whether groups value education if participation is low or irregular. Even if groups value education, developing academic abilities depends on what groups can do about it. Historical and economic factors have prevented some from doing something about it, and continue to threaten to do so. As a society, we have not been as tolerant or supportive of the efforts of various ethnic groups to create their own schools or embrace cultural traditions, particularly the more these initiatives are situated in public space. Remember the outcry at the use of public moneys for developing African American male academies. Another example is a case where Southeast Asians studying together as a group came into conflict with the library they used because the other patrons disliked listening to their discussions. The students argued this method of studying was a cultural tradition. Even private programs come under siege. In Los Angeles, the Korean schools have been threatened with state-enacted shutdown. Rather than create barriers to initiatives that seem ethnic or different, perhaps we should support the broader development of co-ethnic initiatives.

With some support and information about ethnic systems that are making it, other communities can have a better chance of producing systems of programs and practices that increase the resilience of children who face adverse economic conditions and unequal opportunity in regular public schooling.

Access to supplementary education programs run by co-ethnic community members appears to increase resources families can draw upon to educate children and may enhance child development in multiple ways. It seems important to increase family access to educational opportunities in any way possible when financial resources are most limited or ethnic or racial discrimination are suspected. In particular, education programs organized by ethnic groups around cultural traditions may help foster academic development and reduce susceptibility to common risk factors that may make it more difficult for a child to succeed. Contrary to some scholarly expectations, the retention of family cultural traditions and ethnic identity arguably might offer a better path than straight-line, one-way assimilation to Anglo conformity.

Although the discussion in this chapter has not focused specifically on structural discrimination as it is usually conceived, structural inequalities are a major concern. It is suggested that after-school and supplementary school programs can be scaffolding or enriching structures developed to help mediate the impact of declining or unequal opportunity structures and limited family resources.

Indeed, community development of these systems will not be easy. Even promoting the idea may be difficult. Some will argue that family cultural deficiency or innate genetic and biological predispositions, rather than structural barriers to equal and quality educational opportunities, cause academic underachievement and underdevelopment. It is important to remember that it is quite likely that many more families value education and wish to see their children succeed academically than are offered quality opportunities for academic development. The interest in differential levels of academic performance between ethnic groups and the comparison of minority groups has led unfortunately to a problematic stereotyping and essentializing about the nature and disposition of different groups with regard to their learning abilities. We must go beyond these ideas.

Interpreting the development of Korean supplementary education as evidence of Korean cultural superiority or innate abilities is problematic. An alternative interpretation is that cultural imagery of superiority is a resource that can be drawn upon by groups to develop their own service structures when they perceive that the services they otherwise receive are less than adequate. Individuals may believe their success or survival depends in part on maintaining a distinct cultural identity and may believe in their group reputation of superiority. Channeling this belief toward the development of supplementary education initiatives may have positive enabling properties. Some educational practices may have cultural origins in reputation more than in reality, but belief and sense of claim or proprietorship can be powerful tools in making and shaping reality. With a multicultural orientation, supplementary strategies can also help young people tackle standard measures of academic performance. Whether we agree with standard measures of performance or not, these cannot simply be dismissed. Mastery of these tests opens doors to further schooling.

Where will the money come from to finance community initiatives? Although start-up costs are required, the Korean supplementary education available in Koreatown suggests the possibility of a self-perpetuating system. We should expect academic development for all students, but this must be coupled with the resources that enable all students to value education and help families do something about it. Enabling folks to open ethnic-owned and -operated educational businesses calls for greater direct funding in the form of loans and grants for community development.

In the end, we cannot speak about family, culture, and attainment without highlighting the prominent role of structural blockages. Because such blockages do exist, efforts to foster academic success must be multipronged. One question is: How do you change antagonist learning structures that maintain inequality of educational opportunity? Another question is: How do you create structures and mechanisms for better integration of diverse learners and learning organizations? Yet another question is: How do you foster strategies that help individuals overcome structural blockages and unequal opportunities? These questions must be addressed simultaneously.

In other words, the value of education may depend on how attainable education, employment, and upward mobility are (regardless of the demerit or merit of the cultural argument about how much value different groups place on education). We cannot let lending institutions, discriminatory housing and employment practices, or public schools off the hook. Regarding public schools specifically, we must offer reminders that all cultures engage in learning; schools must recognize this and act aware of this. While there is a dominant culture that may believe there is only one right way to learn, that is not the case. Likewise, there is not one way to characterize an appropriate environment for learning (White 1986).

Public schools must assume greater responsibility in certain areas, but not necessarily in supplementary education areas. There is still an unmet need for public school educators to expect learning from all students, offer more individualized instruction, validate different life experiences, diversify curricula, assume responsibility for employing diverse teaching strategies and connecting with the knowledge and learning strategies each child brings, and to change negative response to individual diversity. Schools might look toward ethnic group-based schools that result at least in part from initiatives to maintain cultural traditions or at schools that have implemented more multicultural curriculums or culturally responsive pedagogy. Unfortunately, too often there remains a tendency to blame the victims of historical oppression and view ethnic cultures as pathologies, liabilities, and deficits as opposed to useful resources.

Ultimately, access to quality education must be improved. This is partly a question of schools and partly a question of supplementary schools. In order to prevent schools from becoming a place of power struggle rather than a place to learn useful skills (Sheets 1996), teachers and schools must employ diverse teaching strategies. In addition, intentional teaching of parents about the structure of instruction may help empower parents with less educational experience. Moreover, greater access to ethnic after-school programs may help bridge between family and institutional instruction, supplement substandard public education, supplement family resources, and help develop a chain of social support and mentoring.

CONCLUSION

There is marked heterogeneity in educational opportunity among so-called ethnic and racial groups. Perhaps not surprisingly, though certainly of great concern, there is also marked heterogeneity in educational attainment among groups. The variance of educational opportunity includes disparities in access not only to regular schooling but also to supplementary education programs that take place after school or during the summer. Access to such programs (in addition to access to quality regular schooling) and attainment appear correlated, and results of most studies suggest that participation in supplementary education programs positively impacts child development. However, differential access to supplementary education programs may exacerbate existing educational inequalities and uneven patterns of developed abilities and attainment.

Dissimilar access to programs may be caused at least in part by differences in family resources. The roles of the family and familial resources have long been thought to be central to learning and educational attainment, and a broad range of family resources has been cited to provide proximal and distal explanations for group discrepancies in academic success. Scholars have presented evidence of the effects of family resources such as wealth, income, and educational experience on children's upward socioeconomic mobility. Included among family resources, one resource in particular that families also have differential access to that may deserve further examination is ethnic education, that is, education organized by ethnic and cultural groups, often around cultural heritage.

This chapter described only one of many ethnic community efforts: Korean supplementary education initiatives in Koreatown, Los Angeles, California.

Supplementary education in Koreatown appears to provide a parallel school system that exists in addition to regular schooling during the school year and provides academic and extracurricular activities during regular school off-seasons. Supplementary initiatives range from early childhood care to preparation for standardized tests used for college entrance to training of supplementary school proprietors and personnel. Korean families of diverse economic backgrounds heavily use supplementary education services, and new supplementary education business growth does not seem unexpected. The Korean schools visited appear well attended and interviewees believe supplemental education and enrichment enable high performance. Furthermore, the general sentiment that Korean students are high achievers due to family and cultural factors exists.

Whether cultural or economic factors are mainly at work or not, the structure of Korean supplemental education probably enhances achievement. Of course, a thorough examination and comparison of such programs and their effects is needed, but was not possible here; that is, a larger project would require the utilization of multiple research methodologies. At the very least, serious historical and ethnographic research must be undertaken, since there is little published work of any sort on most of these efforts, and the risk of reifying cultures and propagating stereotypes is high.

The study of Korean supplementary education in the United States is a new area of inquiry, and there is little in the way of literature on this subject, although research is ongoing (Kim, personal communication, April 1999, July 1999). To the author's knowledge, there are few studies or ethnographies that appropriately evaluate the relationship of family cultural traditions and academic development, whether family cultural traditions have a sizable or unique effect, which family traditions seem to matter most, and whether the effects are universally positive. Determining the effects of Korean after-school programs will require further study; nevertheless, the sheer number of schools and their diversity offer compelling testimony to the high academic engagement of many Korean Americans and the local orientation toward academic success.

There are always difficulties promoting change. Difficult changes in public schools are necessary; however, promoting supplementary education also seems necessary. Supplementary education created by communities themselves may do as much, if not more, for communities. We need to support ethnic group supplemental programs and take down some of the hurdles that stand in their way. This may even be more realistic or efficient than changing public education in diverse areas, and may stand a higher chance of addressing the needs of diverse families and spilling over to boost local economies.

REFERENCES

Aldwin, C., and E. Greenberger. 1987. Cultural differences in the predictors of depression. *American Journal of Community Psychology* 15(6): 789–813.

Alwin, D. F., and A. Thornton. 1984. Family origins and the schooling process: Early versus late influence of parental characteristics. *American Sociological Review* 49(6): 784–802.

Baker, D. P., and D. R. Entwisle. 1987. The influence of mothers on the academic expectations of young children: A longitudinal study of how gender differences arise. *Social Forces* 65:670–94.

Barringer, H. R., R. W. Gardner, and M. J. Levin. 1993. *Asians and Pacific Islanders in the United States*. New York: Russell Sage Foundation.

Borman, G. D., and J. V. D'Agostino. 1995. *Title I and student achievement: A meta-analysis of 30 years of test results*. Paper presented at the annual meeting of the American Educational Research Association, April, San Francisco, CA.

Byun, M. S. 1990. Bilingualism and bilingual education: The case of the Korean immigrants in the United States. *International Journal of the Sociology of Language* 82:109–28.

Caplan, C., H. C. Marcella, and J. K. Whitmore. 1992. Indochinese refugee families and academic achievement. *Scientific American* 266(2): 36–42.

Chao, R. K. 1996. Chinese and European American mothers' beliefs about the role of parenting in children's school success. *Journal of Cross-Cultural Psychology* 27(4): 403–23.

De Graaf, P. M. 1988. Parents' financial and cultural resources, grades, and transition to secondary school in the federal republic of Germany. *European Sociological Review* 4(3): 209–21.

Farkas, G., R. P. Grobe, D. Sheehan, and S. Yuan. 1990. Cultural resources and school success: Gender, ethnicity, and poverty groups within an urban school district. *American Sociological Review* 55(1): 127–42.

Folsom, H. P. 1991. Before and after school child care and enrichment for school age children. Unpublished manuscript.

Fuerst, J. S., and D. Fuerst. 1993. Chicago experience with an early childhood programme: The special case of the Child Parent Center Program. *Educational Research* 35(3): 237–53.

Hedges, W. D. 1988. Comparing the United States and the Orient: Are American schools really so bad? *NAASSP Bulletin* 72:84–87.

Hirschman, C., and. M. G. Wong. 1986. The extraordinary educational attainment of Asian Americans: A search for historical evidence and explanations. *Social Forces* 65(1): 1–23.

Kennedy, J. W. 1996. Opus Dei tutors kids in Aquinas and algebra. *Policy Review* 77:12–13.

Kim, K. K., et al. 1981. *Korean language maintenance in Los Angeles*. Professional Papers K-1. Los Alamitos, CA: National Center for Bilingual Research.

Kim, S. Y. 1998. Developmental trajectory of emotional distress and academic achievement in Asian American immigrant adolescents: Role of parent-child acculturation, parenting, and family relations. Paper presented at Social Science Research Council International Migration Program Workshop.

Kober, N. 1991. *The role and impact of Chapter 1, ESEA, evaluation and assessment practices. Part I: The legal and regulatory framework for Chapter 1 Evaluation and Assessment. Part II: General findings from background research. Part III: Case studies. Part IV: Federal policy options*. Washington, DC: United States Congress, Office of Technology Assessment.

Kruger, A. C., and M. Tomasello. 1996. Cultural learning and learning culture. In *Handbook of education and human development: New models of learning, teaching and schooling*, edited by D. R. Olson and N. Torrance, 369–87. Oxford: Blackwell.

Lamont, M., and A. Lareau. 1988. Cultural capital: Allusions, gaps, and glissandos in recent theoretical developments. *Sociological Theory* 6:153–68.

Levin, H. M. 1987. *New schools for the disadvantaged*. Aurora, CO: Mid-Continent Regional Educational Lab.

Marx, F. 1989. *After school programs for low-income young adolescents: Overview and program profiles*. Working Paper no. 194. Wellesley, MA: Wellesley College, Center for Research on Women.

Mercy, J. A., and L. C. Steelman. 1982. Familial influence on the intellectual attainment of children. *American Sociological Review* 47(4): 532–42.

Miller, L. S. 1995. *An American imperative: Accelerating minority educational advancement*. New Haven, CT: Yale University Press.

Morse, S. C. 1992. The value of remembering. *Thrust for Educational Leadership* 21(6): 35–37.

Peng, S. S., and D. Wright. 1994. Explanation of academic achievement of Asian American students. *Journal of Educational Research* 87(6): 346–52.

Portes, A., and L. Hao. 1998. E pluribus unum: Bilingualism and loss of language in the second generation. *Sociology of Education* 71(4): 269–94.

Portes, A., and M. Zhou. 1993. The new second generation: Segmented assimilation and its variants among post 1965 immigrant youth. *Annals of the American Academy of Political and Social Science* 530: 74–98.

Schwartz, W. 1996. *A guide to choosing an after-school program. For parents about parents*. New York: ERIC Clearinghouse on Urban Education, Teachers College, Columbia University.

Sheets, R. H. 1996. Urban classroom conflict: Student-Teacher perception: Ethnic integrity, solidarity, and resistance. *Urban Review* 28(2): 165–83.

Sigel, I. E. 1988. Commentary: Cross-cultural studies of parental influence on children's achievement. *Human Development* 31(6): 384–90.

Steinberg, S. 1989. *The ethnic myth: Race, ethnicity, and class in America*. Boston: Beacon Press.

Suarez-Orozco, M. 1989. *Central American refugees and U.S. high schools: A psychosocial study of motivation and achievement*. Stanford, CA: Stanford University Press.

Sue, S., and S. Okazaki. 1990. Asian American educational achievements: A phenomenon in search of an explanation. *American Psychologist* 45(8): 913–20.

Tienda, M., and D. T. Lii. 1987. Minority concentration and earnings inequality: Blacks, Hispanics, and Asians compared. *American Journal of Sociology* 93(1): 141–65.

Tseng, V. 1998. Youth from immigrant families in 4-year colleges: The role of family background, attitudes, and responsibilities in academic adjustment. Paper presented at Social Science Research Council International Migration Program Workshop.

Uba, L. 1994. *Asian Americans: Personality patterns, identity, and mental health*. New York: Guilford Press.

Wadsworth, M. E. 1986. Effects of parenting style and preschool experience on children's later verbal attainment: Results of a British longitudinal study. *Early Childhood Research Quarterly* 1(3): 237–48.

White, M. I. 1986. Cultural factors in the transfer of western educational models to non-western environments. Paper presented at the annual northwest regional meeting of the Comparative and International Education Society, November, Cambridge, MA.

Yao, E. L. 1985. A comparison of family characteristics of Asian American and Anglo American high achievers. *International Journal of Comparative Sociology* 26:198–208.

NOTE

1. There are many examples to choose among that could fall into the category of ethnic education strategies. The array of such initiatives demonstrates that supplementary ethnic or cultural group–based education is not a new or isolated idea. There are examples of these efforts abroad from East to West, from Yobiko in Japan to Afro-Caribbean and Asian after-school programs in Britain. In the United States, education strategies organized by ethnic groups range from the establishment of private bilingual education by French immigrants and efforts to create African American male academies to supplementary education efforts such as Saturday or Sunday schools organized around Judaism, Catholicism, African American heritage, and even socialism. Others examples include Hebrew Teachers Colleges, mentoring or family and peer study groups commonly employed by some Mormons and Southeast Asian groups, and weekend language academies developed by various immigrant and ethnic groups. There are also after-school cultural programs and preventative programs developed by Native American tribal nations, and child-care academies in some Korean, Chinese, and Japanese communities. These are just some of the examples, but this list is by no means an exhaustive one.

III

THE IDEA OF SUPPLEMENTARY EDUCATION

14

The Institutionalization of Supplementary Education

Beatrice L. Bridglall and Edmund W. Gordon

It is clear that supplementary education is a well-established and implicitly effective instrumentality of high levels of academic achievement. Its practice is ubiquitous in the experiences of highly successful students, and seems to be widely utilized on the behalf of children by well-informed and academically sophisticated parents. However, one of the challenges for the field of supplementary education is that of using and extending existing resources and creating programs and practices that have developed quite naturally in well-resourced segments of the population into institutionalized practice for those segments of the population that experience inadequate or nonexistent cultural, economical, and motivational resources. Consistent with the perspective represented in this book, we are essentially advocating the development and application of educational and social practices in marginalized and less-affluent populations. In this context, it appears that we may need to consider institutionalization in several ways, especially since it typically takes many forms. Given our purpose of introducing and encouraging the specific use of supplementary education in African American, Hispanic American, and Native American communities, we may need to explore the utilization of at least three different approaches, including creating new institutions, utilizing relevant services in existing institutions, and, in some instances, expanding the functions of extant institutions established for other purposes to include supplementary education.

There is, however, yet another sense in which institutionalization is indicated; supplementary education may be as much a reflection of a cultural ethos as it is a set of experiences and practices. Supplementary education may be a virtual phenomenon in that it need not have a material presence, but an attitudinal, dispositional, almost spiritual presence—as in a way of life or a way of doing things. We are convinced that in some instances the effectiveness of supplementary education may be more a function of the commitment and interest of parents and other significant adults than of what actually happens to children who participate. It is not that the developmental and educative treatments provided by supplemental education are not important, but the weight of the impact may be carried by the cultural and emotional values that attach to cultural- and parental-endorsed participation. Thus, the institutionalization of supplementary education as a virtual phenomenon in marginalized and subordinated communities may require that we influence the popular culture and folkways of the people in these communities. In addition to creating, utilizing, and expanding existing institutions, we may also need to influence the belief systems, values, and consequent behaviors of parents, other significant adults, students, and their peers.

In defining prevalent issues related to the institutionalization of supplementary education, we find it is useful to examine the following manifestations of its emerging significance in contemporary society. These manifestations include:

1. Implementation of local programs that are sponsored by national organizations. The local group benefits from the institutional status, stability, national reputation, and sometimes the programs and financial resources of the national group. Examples include Girl Scouts, Camp Fire, Boy Scouts, the YMCA, and so forth. In the Scouting movement, the local sponsors of Boy Scouts and Girl Scouts follow a prescribed curriculum so that Scout activities in any part of the country are similar. YMCAs and YWCAs, on the other hand, have flexibility and tailor their programs to reflect the local context.

2. Supplementary education programs implemented by institutions established for other purposes. Again, supplementary education programs benefit from the institutional stability, reputation, and resources of the host institutions. Examples include faith-based institutions, community centers, schools, and cultural institutions. There is a strong likelihood that faith-based institutions will infuse some aspects of their denominations' values and privileges in their supplementary education programs. There is an implicit distinction that community centers give more attention to the activities rather than the purpose driving it whereas schools tend to favor the purpose, which in their case is academic. And certainly, cultural values are reflected in the exhibits museums showcase and invest in.

3. Supplementary education as a cultural/social phenomenon sponsored or mediated through existing social groups that lend the prestige of mem-

bership to the sponsored activity, making participation the thing to do. Examples include Cotillion, Jack and Jill, and Links, Inc. Links, Inc. is a national women's organization dedicated to improving the quality of life for African Americans. Founded in 1946, Links has 241 chapters throughout the United States and in Nassau, the Bahamas, and Frankfurt, Germany. Their program, Project LEAD: High Expectations, was developed as a national demonstration program in 1987 with financial support from the federal Office for Substance Abuse Prevention (OSAP). The program is designed to help African American youth refrain from using alcohol and other drugs or engaging in other high-risk behaviors. It also seeks to enhance young people's self-esteem and pride in their cultural heritage, to teach about career options, and to help youth establish high education and career aspirations (Carnegie Council on Adolescent Development 1992, 56).

4. Supplementary education as noninstitutionalized cultural practices in which institutionalization is a function of "folkways"—colloquial notions of how things are done. Stability and status of the practice is a function of the establishment of a set of social norms and expectations. Examples include family travel, reading at home, prep school, faith-based schooling, mealtime conversations, and the explication of models. In chapter 9, where we present a taxonomy of supplementary education programs and activities, these interventions would fall under an implicit or incidental category.

Clearly, these forms of supplementary education interventions may involve different approaches to institutionalization that confront us with different types and levels of problems related to policy and institutional dilemmas that may seem contradictory but in some cases are actually complementary and do represent an alternative perspective. For example, parents, educators, and youth leaders are aware of how some strict religious institutions and/or very traditional, old-fashioned grandparents have kept some young people in school and out of trouble. Currently, however, foundations and/or other public sources that partially or fully fund community youth organizations could not publicly support these venues or their practices, although they might privately approve of the church's impact on young people's lives, for instance. This dilemma, in addition to others we address in this chapter, emphasizes the quandary scholars, educators, and youth leaders often find themselves in as they acknowledge not only the needs of youngsters but also that of funding sources. Specifically, scholars, social scientists, and policymakers often quietly affirm the significance of understanding and basing youth policy on the reality of multiple pressures, competing demands, and the worldviews of low-income youth in urban, suburban, and rural contexts. These informal, quiet affirmations, however, are usually reduced in importance as more formal economic demands for "efficiency," bureaucratic instructions for organizational control and accountability, and political calls for "equity" and neutrality with respect to religion redirect attention away from the chaotic, strident, and unruly realities of low-income youth in urban, suburban, and rural areas.

Clearly, these two perspectives not only coexist uneasily but often also pose crucial and unyielding dilemmas for policymakers. Thus, policy responses to these rigorous questions—that is, the degree to which policy represents diagnosis of the problem and framework for the solution—have everything to do with whether low-income youth will respond as policymakers hope or whether youth policy initiatives ostensibly designed to serve young people and society will again disappoint.

CONTRADICTORY POLICY DILEMMAS

Apparently, some of the dilemmas for youth policy stem from traditions in the United States of pluralism, democracy, age-appropriate sexual behaviors and preparation for child rearing. These norms underpin the measures created to reassure foundation boards and taxpayers that their dollars are spent conscientiously and judiciously. While these traditions may still have relevance for certain policy issues, they hinder more than help low-income youth in general and young people of color in particular who need a policy model and policy approaches that differ in critical, elemental ways from those in place today. The following is an attempt to outline and briefly elaborate on seemingly contradictory policy dilemmas that include value-laden vs. value-neutral programs; standardized programs vs. locally constructed practices; seemingly nondiscriminatory policies vs. policies that recognize the relevancy of ethnicity, gender, and race in developing appropriate programs; the needs of the privileged vs. the needs of the disadvantaged; professionalism vs. indigenous knowledge; accountability vs. adaptability; responses to immediate and colloquial activities vs. responses to longer-term societal demands; relaxation and recreation vs. remediation and work; and professional or bureaucratic boundaries vs. comprehensive needs.

Value-Laden vs. Value-Neutral Programs

Few, if any, supplementary education organizations in existence today can be regarded as value free. Indeed, most emphasize certain values that they attempt to instill in the young people participating in their activities. Both the

Girl Scouts and the YWCA, for instance, emphasize serious commitments to gender equality. The YWCA's overarching mission is to reduce racism through their program's focus while the Girl Scouts' affirmative action position emphasizes their organizational position on equity and race. Although the Boy Scouts' organization does not explicitly focus on affirmative action, they do value achievement, patriotism, community service, and religiosity, which are unmistakable in the activities and experiences they sanction.

It may not be obvious, however, that the dilemma for policy involves publicly supporting institutions that promote a particular religious or ideological position (such as a specific religious denomination or a moral position on an aspect of private life) in addition to general support for the organizations that pursue these broad philosophical positions. Most of us are aware that constitutional law separates church from state in the United States and that public norms oppose the use of public dollars to support activities distinguished by specific ideological perspectives. We are suggesting, however, that organizations with these "missionary" characteristics are undoubtedly among the more significant resources low-income youth particularly need, especially in the oppressive contexts of depressed urban, suburban, and rural neighborhoods in which they grow up. Importantly, these groups offer a clear, coherent value system in addition to reliable, supportive, and firm environments for learning that may be lacking in either the families or the schools of youth who are often in the most difficult of circumstances. It is our impression that certain categories of youth can be reached by these groups when nothing else seems to provide them with a way to achieve a sense of control over their lives. Hence, the range and scope of supplementary education organizations available within low-income communities needs to include churches and/or religious groups that are youth centered, rigorously disciplined, and effectively demanding of responsibility. However, we are acutely aware that the particular religious or moral teaching of these organizations may provoke questions concerning their eligibility for public support.

Standardized Programs vs. Locally Constructed Practices

A part of the rationale for consistent program methodology includes the ease with which programs can be managed with respect to underlying ideas concerning equity. One of the current trends concerns policymakers, leaders, and administrators of national organizations, who worry that decentralized programming could result in organizational chaos, sparking issues of management and control. As a result, they may support opportunities and programs equally across different locations. However, according to program leaders and administrators who interact with youth, programs that are unrelated to local needs, disconnected from the local ecology, and neglectful of neighborhood cultures will inevitably fall short. For example, one national organization's approach to locating facilities resulted in a well-equipped downtown athletic center that is empty of youth while glass-strewn parks in their areas are overflowing with young African American males unwilling or unable to travel downtown.

The policy dilemma involves effectively balancing not only some of the legitimate needs of administrators and policymakers for control and direction but also local/community needs for independence and flexibility. Those supplementary education organizations sensitive to local youth needs are aware that inflexible requirements for standardized practices and strictness with consistency or program replication are only superficial efficiencies and are more likely than not to result in inefficient allocation of resources. Heath and McLaughlin (1993) cited an instance of a nationally sponsored supplementary education program that succeeded in one community where school administrators and community leaders were able to work with each other—yet achieved very little of substance in another community because the schools were abysmally weak and feelings of resentment characterized the relationship between community leaders and neighborhood schools. Clearly, in this instance, community leaders could have planned and implemented a program using other community resources, but were constrained because of national guidelines.

According to Epstein (1995), and Heath and McLaughlin (1993), the range of approaches and methods that are particularly effective for low-income youth depend on the context of the activities and experiences and the specific realities of young peoples' lives, not on static bureaucratic guidelines. There are tangible differences, however, between and among different supplementary education organizations concerning this aspect: Girl Scouts, Boy Scouts, and Camp Fire, for instance, follow a top-down model of program development but allow and reward local improvements. The YMCA, YWCA, Boys and Girls Clubs, and Girls Incorporated adhere to a different model that emphasizes local autonomy (within national guidelines, of course) in program development. The trend within most national organizations, however, is to centrally develop program models as one way of controlling the cost of program development while integrating effective ideas. Given the reality of inadequate resources for supplementary education programs targeted to low-income youth, in addition to incentives for achieving economies of scale and efficiency by shifting responsibility for program development away from communities, the challenge for national organizations is to find ways of incorporating indigenous knowledge and realities without redirecting resources away from program development and the maintenance of services and activities.

Nondiscriminatory Policies vs. Policies That Recognize Ethnicity, Gender, and Race

Despite espoused values of nondiscrimination and democracy in the United States, supplementary education programs designed to benefit low-income youth often fall short of expectations because significant differences in design and implementation related to race, gender, and culture are often disregarded. Heath and McLaughlin (1993) cited another example of how ignorance of Hispanic American culture caused a well-intended effort sponsored by the business community to fail in a target group of Latina teenage mothers. Specifically, a fund to provide up to $10,000 to any Latina teenage mother willing to return to school went largely unspent because sponsors disregarded the cultural norms that require Latinas to remain at home and raise their children. Obviously, the "benefit" determined by the program ran counter to cultural values and expectations. Similarly, the Boy Scouts' refusal to adequately adjust their programming (predicated on European American middle-class values and norms) continues to restrain urban Scouting efforts targeted to African American, Hispanic American, and Asian American low-income youth.

Another example concerns underlying issues of assimilation or accommodation that a Boys and Girls Club facility was compelled to acknowledge when they provided exactly the same locker room and shower facilities for girls and for boys. Consequently, the young women perceived that since their differing needs for privacy were not taken seriously, they questioned whether or not they were welcome to use the facility (Heath and McLaughlin 1993). Additionally, policies that are inconsiderate of cultural differences reveal other attitudes toward diversity, that is, differing ways of thinking and different worldviews that may have little to do with fairness and more to do with comfort. Indeed, the general reluctance to probe beyond the food and festivals (marking cultural awareness for most of us) to critically interpret and understand the meaning of cultural differences in speech, ideas about time, and beliefs about child rearing, for example, relegates policy to a superficial level. As a result, those of us responsible for developing, funding, implementing, and evaluating supplementary education programs for low-income ethnic minority groups often do not engage the implications of deeply rooted cultural differences, partially because we are wary of being perceived as supporting the idea of "stereotypes." So we coast over particularly sensitive, volatile issues of race, ethnicity, and gender that are continually impacted by the complexities of local demographics, youth perceptions, and economic realities.

The Needs of the Privileged vs. the Needs of the Disadvantaged

It is disturbingly apparent that the quality and level of public schools, recreation and park facilities, hospitals, and other public services in low-income areas are alarmingly dissimilar to those available in wealthy parts of town. And while city officials recognize these inequalities, they justify them in terms of relative political voice and influence. Indeed, most of us are aware that the political calculus that bestows more and better resources to the affluent not only denies equal treatment to poor neighborhoods but also deprives them of the very resources they need to develop a constructive environment for young people: clean, well-equipped, supervised recreation; good schools; responsive medical care; and other social services (Littell and Wynn 1989, 66). These wealth-based inequities are among the many ways in which low-income youth are disadvantaged by local political processes. Another has to do with the small percentage of voters in low-income areas who have a direct interest in the services available to youth—for example, those voters with children in the public schools. Consequently, when local politicians set priorities, supplementary education services for low-income youth rank low on their list of priorities compared to public services such as roads, drainage problems, and senior services. When these and other services are allocated resources, there is usually not much left when we get to youth needs. It appears that although some communities are concerned about providing supplementary education services for low-income youth, the demands from more powerful constituencies relegate programs and resources for youth to low places on the priority list.

Professionalism vs. Indigenous Knowledge

While assurances of program quality and issues of public safety are driving some of the demands for the professionalization of supplementary education programs and the credentialing of practitioners, Heath and McLaughlin (1993) suggest that the knowledge that matters most is locally contrived and sensitive to the situativity of schools, communities, and families of low-income youth (Gordon and Bridglall, 2002). Heath and McLaughlin (1993) also emphasized that many of the people leading supplementary education organizations were former schoolteachers who had found their way to these organizations to "escape" what they perceived as the callous responses of schools to the needs of low-income youth. Others included local folks who were staunch advocates of youth development programs or trained professionals with a strong commitment to place. They suggested that the expertise gained through formal education might have little to do with creating ties to the local situation, which is a necessary ingredient for effective programs. While these researchers are not suggesting that we discard programs that professionalize this emerging field of supplementary education, they do suggest that professionals in these organizations balance their career aspirations for mobility with the equally important need to create viable and genuine relationships with the community. In other words, professionally trained and well-educated service providers need to balance professionalization of the staff who implement supplementary education services without losing the skills, resources, and perspectives of the volunteer population. Those professionals who honor the local knowledge and their ties to the community and to its young people appear to have respect for the community and its people. This is especially significant to residents of low-income communities who are rarely heard because they are prevailed over by those without accurate impressions of what it is like to subsist in the community.

Accountability vs. Adaptability

According to most supplementary education service providers, the requirements of both private and public funding agencies for accountability remain one of the primary barriers to the flexible and responsible programming associated with effective program design and implementation. We should clarify that their concerns are not about evaluation per se, but rather about the categories of evidence required. Specifically, program staff are asked to identify treatments and outcomes in program development and implementation that can be easily calibrated and demonstrated, whereas, for program staff, the real dilemma is how to assess "soft" outcomes such as an improved self-concept, a wonderful sense of future prospects, a coherent system of values and beliefs, and a sense of personal and emotional safety. These outcomes characteristically elude usual and customary evaluation instruments. We would hypothesize that these outcomes make a difference to young people and have a bearing on their futures. Yet, funding agencies often require evaluations that must demonstrate substantial outcomes over very short periods of time. Those of us who are familiar with the youth development literature and/or have significant experience in this field, are aware that generating substantive change in young people whose lives have been and will, in all likelihood, continue to be overwhelmed by violence, poverty, abuse, and unpredictability will take time. Given this reality, we argue that the success of supplementary education programs needs to be evaluated with respect to what they accomplish for young people.

Immediate and Colloquial Activities vs. Longer-Term Societal Demands

It is ironic, but vulnerable young people seem to regard many well-intentioned educational programs as another source of alienation rather than as inclusionary. Programs and policies targeted at exposing low-income youth to education and support for achievement—that is, programs that (1) award scholarships to college-bound youngsters; (2) award honor roll status; or (3) bring professionals to low-performing schools as part of a career fair—may encourage some low-income youth but for many others, these programs may further erode their impression of their own value and dignity. This may be attributed to student perceptions that the expectations established are beyond them and the "options" given distinction are largely white-collar professional positions. However, these are not contradictory but rather related perspectives. In other words, if we cannot provide the conditions that will literally enable these students to survive in viable ways, how can we worry about conjoining these two goals and recruiting personnel who would recognize its duality and commit to its implementation?

Relaxation and Recreation vs. Remediation and Work

Those of us (scholars, educators, and policymakers, etc.) involved in conceptualizing, designing, implementing, evaluating, and funding supplementary education programs need to be aware of the choices that must be made with regard to focus, message, and environment. As we engage in these significant and necessary considerations, we must also be aware of the need for young people to simply relax in a supportive environment at safe remove from recurring threats, anxieties, and challenges that typify daily life in many low-income areas. Simultaneously, however, we need to balance their needs for assistance, structure, and opportunities that will enable them to acquire the basic skills and information required not only for success in school but also for the development of healthy and informed responses concerning substance and drug abuse, unsafe sexual activity, crime, or other destructive behaviors. Clearly, striking a balance between these goals and objectives stretches already inadequate resources and often goes against the guidelines from funding agencies and/or public officials.

In chapter 3, we discussed the issue of low participation rates of adolescents in supplementary education programs and some of its causes. One of the reasons hinges on some young people's perception that purely recreational program activities that are without concrete purpose or product are humiliating because the developers and practitioners of these programs fail to recognize or understand the adult roles and responsibilities that many of these young people have played since their early childhood. These activities are thus considered to be a waste of time because they do not produce anything practical. The Carnegie Council on Adolescent Development (1992) and Heath and McLaughlin (1993) suggest that programs based on activities and experiences that have traditionally served European American middle-class youth are frequently mistaken in their theories about the preferences and perspectives of the ethnic minority youth they hope to involve.

On the other hand, however, adolescents who can no longer be compelled by a parent, guardian, or youth worker to show up for counseling or a tutoring session may also rebuff programs with an exclusive focus on mediating, "fixing," or otherwise managing their behavior. Alternatively, funding agencies and policymakers are usually disappointed with programs that focus on single issues, such as academic performance, substance use, irresponsible sexual behavior, and parenting skills, partially because young people fail to attend or to respond consistently. The dilemma for policy involves finding the appropriate balance between relaxation and serious work, between "time off" or recreational activities and a conscientious effort at developing skills and attitudes necessary to effectively negotiate negative environments. Many supplementary education programs have been unsuccessful in striking this balance and have defined themselves in terms of one or the other focus, as stipulated by their institutional identity or policy mandate. As a result, most youth organizations report a reduction in young people's participation once they reach teen years and can "vote with their feet." Despite this impression, we cannot sweepingly conclude or rationalize that adolescents will not participate or are unresponsive to organized activities. Gordon and Bridglall (in press) suggest that the exceptions to this common pattern can be found in organizations whose activities and experiences are designed to demonstrate that young people, particularly those for whom supplementary education opportunities are unavailable, are resources to be developed.

These organizations provide recreational activities that not only enable young people's social and intellective competence (Gordon 2001) but also their agenda, which explicitly values and empowers young people. It is interesting that these supplementary education organizations do not identify themselves as "after" or "out of" with respect to schools; they simply exist for young people and for the projects, performances, and participation they can enable (Heath and McLaughlin 1993). One of the related dilemmas for policy involves shifting from an ideological position that privileges specific institutional (often national) identities and society's objectives (i.e., lowered rates of school dropouts, reduction in crime, and lowered rates of teen pregnancy and substance abuse) to defining and conceptualizing institutions, activities, and experiences that develop from the needs and perspectives articulated by young people. We recognize that this youth-centered stance, however, is not popular in state legislatures, foundation boardrooms, or national organizations, whose impression of the problems, the resulting solutions, and categorical ways of allocating limited resources are somewhat narrow.

Professional or Bureaucratic Boundaries vs. Comprehensive Needs

It may not be apparent to some of us, but anyone who has either worked, lived, or spent time in neglected low-income neighborhoods knows that the problems of families and youths who live there do not come in neat packages labeled "educational," "medical," "economic welfare," and so on, but in chaotic, complicated bundles that reflect differing contexts and personal conditions. Staff members in effective programs are aware of the impossibility of meeting the needs of low-income youth without crossing the boundaries of profession and agency. As we have indicated in our discussion concerning standardized programs vs. locally constructed practices and professionalism vs. local knowledge, effective programs craft their shape, substance, and progress from the needs and nature of those they serve rather than from the rigid guidelines or parameters mandated by funding agencies and their political ideology.

Essentially, we are emphasizing that the significant disconnect between the conventional requirements and limitations of funding sources and government agencies. The needs of low-income youth may partially explain the scarcity of effective programs and the prevalence of disappointing initiatives. At the core of this emerging field of supplementary education is perspective—how the problem is understood, where it is located, and the formation of possible responses that inform and influence policy, parents, educators, and students. The very small number of effective programs for low-income adolescents also mirrors a narrow perspective—that is, it is "too late" to do much with adolescents; they are a lost cause and thus an inefficient target for policy investment.

Heath and McLaughlin's (1993) fieldwork in supplementary education organizations in low-income areas suggests that there is sufficient evidence to the contrary. Indeed, some low-income adolescents with access to the diverse supplementary education services available have not only evaded early pregnancy, school failure, or death but have become productive as workers, parents, and citizens. While others may not behave as funding sources and policymakers would ideally wish them to do (some may become pregnant in their early teens, drop out of school, and go on welfare), many do maintain their relationships with youth organizations, find their way to night school, and wind up working for youth groups or assist as volunteers or aides in their children's schools. Some may have several children, scrapes with the law, and leave school, but if they emerge through the athletic program of a supplementary education organization and find their way to a vocational education program, for example, their chances of supporting themselves and their families and of participating in the larger society becomes greater.

We are aware that for such struggles to be perceived as small victories, funding sources and the diverse supplementary education programs must acknowledge that such paths—unusual from a purely academic or professional career orientation—do merit support and respect. When we think of some of the staff in supplementary education organizations whose lives have followed such directions, it is not so farfetched to imagine that they can provide realistic models of hope and dignity for young people. Gordon and Yowell (1999) suggest that when we attempt to diagnose and prescribe from the perspective of society's needs rather than from those of youth, we place the burden of change on youth and their families as opposed to the institutions that serve them. Thus, the culture of supplementary education services for low-income youth should support the necessary trust, social cohesion, and respectful relationships that will enable young people to become less cynical and defeatist, and improve their self-esteem; a lesser organizational culture might serve to perpetuate the problems that concern society.

COMMON ISSUES IN IMPLEMENTING
SUPPLEMENTARY EDUCATION PROGRAMS

As we indicate in chapter 3, no consistent standards or guidelines characterize supplementary education organizations across the country. Implicit in our discussion concerning the dilemmas for policy, wide disparities exist in program features that can be standardized, like child-adult ratios, staff education, and staff size. According to the National Study of Before- and After-School Programs, the number of children per staff ranged from a low of 4:1 to a high of 25:1 (Seppanen, deVries, and Seligson 1993). Staff education ranged from those with graduate education to those with less than high school diplomas. A few comprehensive studies demonstrate that these program features have implications for children's experiences. Rosenthal and Vandell's (1996) study documented observations of 180 third-, fourth-, and fifth-grade students in thirty different after-school programs that focused on the positive or negative quality of children's exchanges with staff, and the variety and flexibility of program activities. According to this study, staff interactions with children were negative in the programs with more children per adult and less-educated teachers. In programs with a larger range of activities and more flexible programming, children experienced more positive interactions with staff.

Staff turnover, which is less likely to be regulated, comprises another aspect of program quality. Although some after-school and youth programs are able to sustain a stable staff, many experience high rates of turnover. The National Study of Before- and After-School Programs indicates that 58 percent of the programs surveyed had undergone significant staff turnover (at least 60 percent of their staff had changed) during the previous year (Seppanen, de-Vries, and Seligson 1993). Halpern's 1992 study of eight inner-city after-school programs in Chicago found that more than 40 percent of the staff had been with the documented programs for less than one year; those staff members with longer tenures were more likely to follow up when children were absent because they knew the children better. Not surprisingly, the Child Care Staffing Study (Howes, Phillips, and Whitebook 1992) found that higher compensation is one of the key elements in reducing staff turnover.

One of the challenges of evaluating supplementary education programs is accurately gauging the consequences of program participation on outcomes, defined broadly as children's development. Available studies compare the school success and social adjustment of children who attend programs with outcomes for children who spend their afternoons in other care settings. This research challenge is further complicated by the fact that no form of after-school care exists in a vacuum but rather within a wider context of family and community, which not only affects the after-school arrangements that are accessible to certain children, but also situates their reactions to their after-school experiences (Gordon and Bridglall 2002; Epstein 1995). In addition, the individual child's own attributes (i.e., age, temperament, and gender) play a role in shaping the choice of after-school programs and arrangements for other supplementary education activities for that child.

Existing early studies of individual programs did find benefits that the researchers credited to program participation. Howes, Olenick, and Der-Kiureghian (1987) found that kindergarten children who were involved in an extended-day program at a university lab evinced better peer relationships than classmates who were not involved in the program. Sheley's (1984) study reported that compared to a matched control group, low-income children who participated in an after-school tutoring program demonstrated improved performance on a standardized math test. The researchers documenting the recent Ecological Study of After-School Care (Posner and Vandell 1994) suggested that the third-graders who participated in this study had better reading and math grades, work habits, emotional adjustment, peer relationships, and fewer antisocial behaviors than children in other forms of after-school care.

Still, not all studies have documented conclusive program effects. As opposed to the studies referenced above, Vandell and Corasaniti (1988) found the reverse to be true for those middle-class children who participated in programs. Specifically, the teachers, parents, peers, and students themselves rated the program more negatively than children in other forms of care. Some researchers (Marshall et al. 1997) did not suggest overall links between children's adjustment and program involvement. These disparate findings imply that perceptions concerning both positive and negative implications of a program are influenced by family and community variables, and the students' own dispositions and related program experience.

Throughout this chapter, we have established that supplementary education programs do not reach those who need it most. In one of its summary reports, the Carnegie Council on Adolescent Development (1995) documented that, nationally, more than seventeen thousand organizations provide community-based youth programs after school, on weekends, or during vacation periods, yet only about 29 percent of all young adolescents are reached by these programs (106). Clearly, participation in existing after-school programs is considerably lower among those most in need: youth from low-income families. The young people more likely to take advantage of fine arts experiences, activities, and music lessons, for example, are from higher socioeconomic backgrounds (Miller 1998, 24). Those supplementary education programs that do provide services to low-income children constantly struggle with structural and operational problems, including competitive, aggressive interactions between children; high turnover of children; lack of time for planning, team building, training, and orientation for staff; lack of staff training in child development, activity planning, and group process; low staff–child ratios; and lack of opportunities to work with parents and social workers (Halpern 1992). Similarly, other challenges in serving low-income or language-minority students include recruiting and retaining a dependable staff that are not only able to communicate in the native language of the students, but can assist with providing community support.

PRINCIPLES FOR POLICY

From the perspective of low-income young people, the principles that fundamentally drive effective institutions, program activities, and experiences are simple and few. The crucial components that define programs and policies for youth include motivations and goals (Gordon, personal communication, 2003). There is an emerging literature that suggests that young people evade programs defined from the perspective of societal need for "social control"—for instance, reduction of teen pregnancies, dropout rates, or involvement in substance and drug abuse or illegal activities. It may not be common knowledge that many low-income youth do not participate in programs that define them as deviant, "at risk," or in some way deficient or negative. Indeed, low-income youth, similar in this respect to youth in more privileged circumstances, want to participate in activities that perceive them and their development in positive ways. They gravitate to activities and experiences that communicate respect rather than condemnation for who they are, and hope rather than fear for what they can become. Effective programs and policies for low-income adolescents strive to avoid labels that sort youngsters into categories of more or less socially desirable behaviors or problems partially because they are aware that for their target population to participate, they must challenge the perceptions held by the general public about the value and potential of adolescents in low-income areas. Specifically, these beliefs suggest that low-income youth:

- Do not have much to offer the community;
- Are not to be trusted with responsibility;
- Do not have any interest in supplementary education services/organizations;
- Are beyond redemption;
- Are just lazy and just want to hang out or have fun; and
- Do not have the interests or the abilities required to achieve much.

Clearly, these beliefs not only limit the quality of strategies for youth but they also communicate disrespect and prevent the empowering approaches vital to the development of social and intellective competence (Gordon 2001; Gordon and Bridglall, in press). Low-income adolescents and the adults who work with them recognize the irony and waste resulting from policy decisions that maintain and bolster social control goals while undermining developmental efforts (Heath and McLaughlin 1993). Specifically, policy choices—for example, recreation initiatives scaled back to support increased park security, and job programs terminated while drug prevention programs proliferate—seek to fix and control rather than develop and support. Gordon (2001) implicitly argues that the resources spent on human development may generate a higher return than those allocated to problem management and social control, while efforts at "fixing" may have a better chance of success when situated in a nurturing, positive milieu than in a punitive framework.

Given the lack of standardization of program components and effective practices, and a consideration of the referenced policy and practical issues, we suggest that it is possible to arrive at some additional principles that are fundamental to this work. The principles that follow have been adapted from a list developed by the Carnegie Council on Adolescent Development (1992). Although these principles provide general guidelines rather than a specific blueprint for standardization of program design, they can, in combination with concrete program examples, facilitate the move from conceptual frameworks to implementation.

1. *Adapt relevant content and processes to the interests and needs of young people.* Effective programs solicit and consider the input of young people at the planning stage and offer active, meaningful roles for young people throughout implementation.

2. *Distinguish, appreciate, and respond to the diverse conditions and experiences that adolescents currently experience.* Effective programs are aware of the differences among young adolescents, especially those based on race, ethnicity, geographic location, family income, gender, sexual orientation, and first language.

3. *Collaborate individually as well as collectively to broaden their reach to underserved youth.* Effective programs work to improve access and participation of young people living in low-income areas and focus on keeping youth needs rather than organizational interests at the core of their outreach efforts.

4. *Seriously contend for young people's attention and time.* Effective programs consider their competition (everything from youth gangs to television) and discover alternate methods for producing engaging and attractive rather than passive or antisocial programs.

5. *Reinforce the quality and diversity of their staff.* Effective programs conscientiously recruit and invest in both staff and volunteer development as a normal cost of doing business and acknowledge the centrality of volunteers to their program success.

6. *Consistently engage with families, schools, and other community partners.* Effective programs support consistent working relationships with parents and other community institutions on behalf of young people.

7. *Develop the role of young people as community resources.* Effective programs counsel young people to play meaningful leadership roles within their organizations and actively ensure that youths have opportunities to contribute their talents to the larger community.

8. *Advocate vigorously for and with youth.* Effective programs regard advocacy for and with youth a part of their work and ensure that the needs and interests of children and youths are not neglected in decision-making forums.

9. *Identify and assess their intended outcomes.* Effective programs are unequivocal about the goals and results they want to achieve, and develop
uniform documentation systems and sensible evaluation measures.

10. *Create and maintain sound organizational structures, including vigor-
ous and committed board leadership.* Effective programs are typically
found in well-governed and well-managed organizations that privilege
stability of relationships for young people at this important period in
their lives.

CONCLUSION

We began this chapter with broad questions that are not easily answered.
While we have attempted to conceptualize some of the dilemmas an institutionalization agenda might consider, we are also aware that we have only begun to scratch the surface. We can agree, however, that it is a beginning, and
issues will emerge and gather importance as we struggle with what the implications are for not only low-income youth but also for ethnic minority
groups on each level in the socioeconomic scale. Ultimately, the institutionalization of effective supplementary education services and programs should
(1) support and progress beyond simple, single-identity categorizations of
race, ethnicity, and gender to impart a positive social identity, broadly conceived; (2) seek not to control or remediate youth but to develop and cultivate
their spirit and their strength to negotiate successfully the collective dilemmas
of low-income neighborhoods; and (3) respect and support knowledgeable,
independent, and innovative local leadership because (a) these professionals
and volunteers usually understand the socioeconomic milieu in which adolescents construct their senses of self and (b) because they promote ownership
and social investment in the neighborhood and its youth.

Finally, given the presence of diversity in and the explicit and implicit nature of supplementary education activities and experiences, institutions that
organize to provide different yet essential services for youth ultimately implement services that are extrinsically and intrinsically connected to the reality of youths' lives. Our discussion in this chapter, implicitly and explicitly reflected throughout the other chapters, suggests that in order for academic
persistence and performance and personal and social development to become
institutionalized, we need to enable high participation levels in some ethnic
minority populations, access for youths in low-income communities, adequate financial resources, evaluations concerning program effectiveness, coordination with other youth-supporting services, including schools, and the
congruency between actual activities and perceived needs of adolescents.

REFERENCES

Carnegie Council on Adolescent Development. 1992. *A matter of time: Risk and opportunity in the nonschool hours. Report of the Task Force on Youth Development and Community Programs.* New York: Carnegie Corporation of New York.

——. 1995. *Great transitions: Preparing adolescents for a new century.* New York: Carnegie Corporation of New York.

Epstein, J. 1995. School/family/community partnerships: Caring for the children we share. *Phi Delta Kappan* 76:701–12.

Gordon, E. W. 1999. *Education and justice: A view from the back of the bus.* New York: Teachers College Press.

——. 2001. *The affirmative development of academic ability.* Pedagogical Inquiry and Praxis, No. 2. New York: Teachers College, Columbia University.

Gordon, E. W., and B. L. Bridglall. 2002. *The idea of supplementary education.* Pedagogical Inquiry and Praxis, No. 3. New York: Teachers College, Columbia University.

——. In press. *The affirmative development of academic ability.* Boulder, CO: Rowman & Littlefield.

Gordon, E. W., and C. Yowell. 1999. Cultural dissonance as a risk factor in the development of students. In *Education and justice: A view from the back of the bus*, edited by E. W. Gordon. New York: Teachers College Press.

Halpern, R. 1992. The role of after-school programs in the lives of inner-city children: A study of the "Urban Youth Network." *Child Welfare* 71(3): 215–30.

Heath, S. B., and M. W. McLaughlin, eds. 1993. *Identity and inner city youth: Beyond ethnicity and gender.* New York: Teachers College Press.

Howes, C., M. Olenick, and T. Der-Kiureghian. 1987. After-school child care in an elementary school: Social development and continuity and complementarity of programs. *The Elementary School Journal* 88(1): 93–103.

Howes, C., D. A. Phillips, and M. Whitebook. 1992. Thresholds of quality: Implications for the social development of children in center-based child care. *Child Development* 63(2): 449–60.

Littell, J., and J. Wynn. 1989. *The availability and use of community resources for young adolescents in an inner-city and suburban community.* Chicago: University of Chicago, Chaplin Hall Center for Children.

Marshall, N. L., C. G. Coll, F. Marx, K. McCartney, N. Keifc, and J. Ruh. 1997. After-school time and children's behavioral adjustment. *Merrill-Palmer Quarterly* 43(3): 497–514.

Miller, B. 1998. Border zones: Out of school time and young adolescents. Unpublished paper. Wellesley, MA: Wellesley College, National Institute on Out-of-School Time.

Posner, J. K., and D. L. Vandell. 1994. Low-income children's after-school care: Are there beneficial effects of after-school programs? *Child Development* 65(2): 440–56.

Rosenthal, R., and D. L. Vandell. 1996. Quality of care at school-aged child care programs: Regulatable features, observed experiences, child perspectives, and parent perspectives. *Child Development* 67(5): 2434–45.

Seppanen, P., D. deVries, and M. Seligson. 1993. *National study of before- and after-school programs.* Washington DC: U.S. Department of Education, Office of Policy and Planning.

Sheley, J. F. 1984. Evaluation of the centralized, structured, after-school tutorial. *Journal of Educational Research* 77(4): 213–18.

Vandell, D. L., and M. A. Corasaniti. 1988. The relation between third graders' after-school care and social, academic, and emotional functioning. *Child Development* 59(4): 868–75.

15

Conceptual and Practical Issues in Evaluating Supplementary Education Programs

Edmund W. Gordon and Beatrice L. Bridglall

Existing studies of after-school and supplementary education programs demonstrate that children have participated in after-school programs sponsored by organizations like Boys and Girls Clubs, 4-H, YMCA, and YWCA for years. Initially focused on custodial care, these and related programs have recently evolved to emphasize academic development (see chapter 3 for a more detailed description of this shift). The growing number and reach of supplementary education programs and increased funding by the federal government, foundations, and other sources has generated calls for accountability, expectations of certain outcomes, and data that demonstrate program effectiveness. The increasing demands for empirical evidence may be a function of the relatively little systematic and comprehensive data to guide conceptual development, practical implementation, and informed policy about after-school programs and other forms of supplementary education (Caspe 2001).

Some research studies have associated after-school programs with an academic emphasis to increases in academic and social competencies in underrepresented students (Engman 1992; Henderson 1990; Mercure 1993; Posner and Vandell 1994; Schinke, Cole, and Poulin 1998). Fashola (1998) suggests that this literature is primarily focused on common aspects of after-school programs as opposed to discrete models. Other studies have related access to and participation in after-school and youth development programs with decreases in antisocial behaviors (violence and substance abuse) and increases in constructive behaviors (improved refusal and conflict resolution skills, social skills, and self-efficacy) (Beuhring, Blum, and Rinehart 2000; Pierce, Hamm, and Vandell 1999; Catalano, Berglund, Ryan, Lonczak, and Hawkins 1998; Roth, Brooks-Gunn, Murray, and Foster 1998; Pettit, Laird, Bates, and Dodge 1997; Marshall et al. 1997; Miller 1995).

A report published by the Center for Research on the Education of Students Placed at Risk identified and reviewed thirty-four after-school programs (Fashola 1998) with foci on study skills, academic content programs, tutoring in reading, and community-based programs. Fashola's review discussed "these programs in terms of their evidence of effectiveness for improving student outcomes and their evidence of replicability in other locations." His report also summarized "correlational research studies that have examined the effects of after-school programs" (v).

Fashola's results suggest that (1) research on after-school and youth development programs were preliminary, and (2) that "few studies of the effects of after-school programs on achievement or other outcomes [met] minimal standards of research design" (54). One of the more prominent research design weaknesses includes the issue of selection bias. Fashola acknowledges that since after-school programs are rarely required for all children in a school, there are usually uncontrolled factors that determine why some children attend these programs and others do not. In other words, merely controlling for grades, socioeconomic status, previous academic achievement, or other factors can result in a neglect of the overt and subtle differences in motivations between students whose parents enroll them into a range of programs. Fashola indicated that while there are different remedies for this methodological problem, they have been used infrequently. He suggested that the ideal solution is to randomly assign students (who have independently applied for a certain program) to participate in the program or to a waiting list control group. "The fact of applying and meeting other admission requirements ensures that the waiting list control group is equivalent" in significant ways to the experimental group. Of all the programs Fashola reviewed, only two used random assignment of this kind. Nevertheless, he concluded that successful programs designed to increase academic achievement provide:

- A well-defined structure and a predictable schedule;
- Alignment with the school-day curriculum;
- Well-qualified and well-trained staff; and
- Individual and/or small-group tutoring.

Fashola (1998) cautioned, however, that "these conclusions depend more on inferences [drawn] from other [bodies of] research than from well-designed studies of the after school programs themselves" (55). The different bodies of research Fashola referenced make both explicit and implicit associations between certain demographic indicators (gender, ethnicity, socioeconomic status, first language, mobility, and disability), and student's academic performance and socioemotional adjustment and outcomes (Finn, Folger, and Cox

1991; Finn, Pannozzo, and Voelkl 1995; Trueba 1983). These associations are discussed throughout this book where we document the various supplementary education programs that enable access to and participation in curricula and activities (usually to majority-group students and less so to ethnic minority groups). We also emphasize that the long-term goals of these programs include the provision of social experiences that enable students to develop into responsible and productive adults and citizens. The more immediate goals include academic achievement (indicated by students' positive attitudes toward school, improved school attendance, effective work habits, reduced dropout rates in high school, and future aspirations); and socioemotional development (indicated by satisfying friendships, self-efficacy, a good understanding of other people's feelings, and relatively little loneliness) (McGuire and Weisz 1982; Zill and Rogers 1988). The Carnegie Council on Adolescent Development's report (1992) echoed these goals and objectives when it suggested that supplementary education programs can encourage expressions of student resiliency. This is achieved by offering students a structured, predictable, developmentally appropriate, and culturally relevant environment in tandem with concerned staff members and clearly defined and enforced limits (Wang, Haertel, and Walberg 1994; Wang, Frieberg, and Waxman 1996).

Scott-Little, Hamann, and Jurs's (2002) metaevaluation of after-school evaluation methods and related findings is a more recent attempt at determining these programs' relative quality, merit, and worth. The Joint Committee for Standards for Educational Evaluation (1994) defined a metaevaluation as an evaluation of an evaluation (or evaluations). The purpose of a metaevaluation is to identify the strengths and weaknesses of the individual evaluations and their adherence to utility, feasibility, propriety, and accuracy standards. These researchers also tried to include a meta-analysis (a statistical analysis of data from several studies) in their synthesis of findings. They were not able to perform a complete meta-analysis because the after-school program evaluations they considered did not include enough data (e.g., means and standard deviations) for them to calibrate meaningful effect sizes. Thus, their metaevaluation was directed at resolving or answering research queries concerning (1) the common characteristics of widely distributed after-school evaluation studies; (2) adherence to accepted practices for research design and the evaluation standards referenced above; and (3) the possible implications of these findings for program effectiveness.

Scott-Little, Hamann, and Jurs's (2002) findings indicate that the varied types of evaluations of after-school programs are generating formative and summative data associated with process and outcomes. While a fair number of evaluations utilized external evaluators and several sources of data, few included on-site observations and most used nonstandardized measures. Additionally, most evaluations were not published in peer-reviewed journals. The researchers suggest that "given the current emphasis on scientifically based research evidence for programs, after-school programs and evaluators may need to consider the need to utilize more standardized measures and more structured peer review processes to guide evaluation designs and reports" (410).

As suggested above, little quantitative evidence exists in support of the effectiveness of supplementary education. This does not mean that supplementary education programs are not effective, but rather that this emerging field has yet to meaningfully conceptualize and empirically evaluate the assumptions that undergird a program, the processes in place and outcomes. The Mathematica Policy Research national evaluation of 21st Century Community Learning Centers Program (Dynarski et al. 2003) is one of the more recent attempts at empirically investigating the effectiveness of after-school programs.

THE MATHEMATICA POLICY RESEARCH STUDY

The Mathematica Policy Research's study, *When Schools Stay Open Late: The National Evaluation of the 21st Century Community Learning Centers Program*, was conducted for the U.S. Department of Education and focused on school-based programs that are part of the 21st Century Community Learning Centers Program (CCLC). According to the study's authors, the evaluation was designed to explore the characteristics and outcomes of mainstream CCLC programs. Their first-year findings suggest that (1) while 21st Century after-school centers modified with whom and where participating students spend some of their time after school, and (2) although CCLC enabled an increase in parental involvement, they were less effective with regard to academic performance, general feelings of safety among participants, and may have had some damaging effects on behavior. The key findings of the study include:

Limited academic impact: Grades and reading scores for participating students at the elementary school level were not higher than those for non-enrolled students. Neither did the elementary CCLC programs have any effect on whether students completed general assignments or homework to their teachers' satisfaction. This finding also held for middle school students. However, while math grades were higher for CCLC participants, the overall difference was small. The researchers conducted a subgroup analysis and found (1) significant grade point improvements for black and Hispanic middle school students, and (2) indications of less absenteeism and tardiness in contrast to nonparticipants. Middle school students were also more likely to complete assignments to their teachers' satisfaction, "although program participants were not more likely to do or complete the homework assigned. Another subgroup analysis found that students who attended programs more frequently, both at the middle school and elementary school levels, did not have higher academic outcomes compared with students [who] attended less frequently. Other analyses did not find statistically significant relationships between program characteristics, including program maturity, and academic impacts" (xii).

Adult care of participants increased but student self-care remain unaffected: The study found that CCLC programs increased the percentage of students being cared for by nonparent adults and reduced the percentage of students being cared for by older siblings and parents. CCLC programs did not reduce the proportion of students in self-care. Students in grades K–2 were determined to be in self-care if their parents indicated that they were without any type of supervision after school or if students said they were by themselves. In the control group, 53 percent of nonparticipating middle school students and 67 percent of elementary school students were cared for by a parent after school.

No improvement in safety and behavior: CCLC programs "did not increase students' feelings of safety after school. At the middle school level, participants were more likely to report that they had sold drugs 'some' or 'a lot' (although the incidence was low). Participants also were more likely to have had their property damaged" (xiii). (The researchers did not collect data on these items for elementary school students.)

Increased parental involvement: More parents of elementary school participants assisted their youngsters with homework or inquired about their classroom assignments. Parents of middle school participants increased their involvement at their child's school. Parents also volunteered at their children's schools and attended parent-teacher meetings.

Negligible Impact on Developmental Outcomes: Researchers found that programs had no impacts on developmental outcomes including "whether students felt they were better able to plan, set goals, or work with a team" (xiii). Participants at the middle school level were less likely to regard themselves as "good" or "excellent" at resolving conflicts with others.

Implementation Findings

Researchers found that CCLC grantees had largely done well in implementing their programs, obtaining support, and nurturing collaborations with teachers and principals in elementary and middle schools. Most CCLC programs provide academic enrichment activities centered mainly on homework help and recreation, based on students' needs and preferences. While only a few programs emphasized academic activities, none focused exclusively on recreational activities. Other implementation findings include:

Low levels of student participation: Despite program availability from four to five days a week, participant attendance averaged less than two days a week.

Programs staffed predominantly by school-day teachers: Regular school-day teachers made up a third of CCLC program coordinators and "three out of five program staff members" (xiii).

Limited efforts to form partnerships and plan for sustainability: CCLC programs did not form any notable working relationships with other community organizations. In most cases, centers contracted with community organizations to supply particular after-school activities as opposed to functioning as partners with shared oversight or combined operations. Sustainability planning for CCLC programs was also negligible.

Methodology

The study's evaluation design is comprised of separate elementary and middle school studies. The study of elementary group centers was a random assignment (or experimental) design that consisted of a participant group (587 students) and a nonparticipant control group (381 students). Although the study included fourteen school districts and thirty-four centers, the elementary school study findings were from seven school districts chosen in the study's first year. The researchers suggest that while the elementary school programs in the study were in urban communities, served a larger proportion of students of color than average elementary school programs, and were representative of elementary school 21st Century programs, they were not systematically sampled. The findings, consequently, could not be generalized to all elementary school programs.

Middle school centers were evaluated using a quasi-experimental design with a matched comparison group. A total of 1,782 participants were evaluated against a demographically similar nonparticipant group of 2,482 students. The researchers claim that the middle school study is also based on a nationally representative sample of after-school programs. A total of sixty-two centers in thirty-four school districts were included in the middle school study.

The evaluation included a sample of CCLCs and focused on project implementation, participant outcomes, and efforts made by grantees to sustain funding. The study of elementary school centers drew upon student, parent, and teacher surveys, and program attendance records. The study of middle school centers drew upon student, parent, and teacher surveys, school records, center and school staff surveys, and program attendance records.

Issues Related to the Study

The findings and methodology of the Mathematica study need to be viewed in the context of the criticisms made of the study. Specifically, these findings are currently debated by various supplementary education stakeholders and research scientists and are, ironically, refuted among some of the working group members who collaborated on the report. According to *Education Week* (Jacobson 2003), seven out of twelve working-group members claimed that some of the report's conclusions were not justified because the study did not reflect that middle school students in the control group started out scoring higher than participants in the treatment group. In their judgment, "the first-year analyses and any subsequent analyses are un-interpretable given these substantial baseline differences on key measures" (Jacobson 2003). Mathematica's lead researchers countered that while the treatment and control groups were different in some respects, the study did use "statistical methods specifically designed to adjust for the differences" (Jacobson 2003). The seven working-group members further asserted that the sample size in the elementary school evaluation was too small for them to have much confidence in the results.

The After-School Corporation's critique of this study compared findings from the Mathematica evaluation to those of the Policy Studies Associates report (After-School Corporation 2003). According to this critique, the Mathematica report did not clearly indicate if the nonparticipating students who comprised the comparison group were selected from the same schools as their participating counterparts. Nor does the report clearly explain how or if the evaluation controlled for student mobility or "crossing over." That is, if an elementary school student included in the comparison group began to participate midyear, was he or she removed from the comparison group and treated as a participant or was this student excluded from the analysis? This issue was also not addressed in the middle school study.

For both the elementary and middle school studies, the study suggests that the control/comparison groups were statistically different on a variety of measures, including gender, ethnicity, and household income. Additionally, information for all participants in the treatment and control groups in the elementary school centers study were not collected nor discussed. It also appears that the comparison group for the evaluation of middle school centers did not represent the study's participants. While statistical models were created to adjust for the differences among middle school center groups, the relative strengths or weaknesses of this methodology were not made clear.

With regard to participant outcomes, the researchers did not use standardized test scores in math for elementary or middle school participants. With respect to the standard test scores in reading for elementary school participants and nonparticipants, no statistically significant differences were found. Further, the researchers did not use standardized test scores in reading for middle school participants, nor did they find conclusive effects of the program with respect to classroom and peer interactions. In some instances, there were increases in negative behaviors or delinquent activities.

The debate over the Mathematica findings is indicative of an indefinite, conflicting, and confusing study. It suggests that the value of supplementary education may be obfuscated in part because the practice of evaluation research is poor. This reinforces the need for evaluations based on program and process theory and relevant research designs that inform socially relevant policy decisions. This conceptualization may be at odds with the current administration's hasty and radical overemphasis on empirical investigations as the sole conduit for decision making and funding of educational research and program implementation. The call for scientifically validated research and the use of scientifically questionable research by the current administration to influence policy decisions is not new. Administrations over the years have used studies of a dubious nature to argue against continuing socially necessary programs like Head Start and compensatory education, for example. This strategy is reflected in Deputy Secretary of Education William D. Hansen's testimony before a Senate Appropriations subcommittee to explain the Bush administrations proposal to cut funding for the 21st Century initiative by $400 million. Hansen claimed that the program grew "rapidly with little consideration of its effectiveness" (Jacobson 2003). He may be referring to the increase in funding for the CCLCs from $40 million in 1998 to $1 billion in fiscal 2002. (Approximately 7,500 schools in more than 1,400 communities participate in the CCLC program and provide an array of academic, recreational, and enrichment activities.)

Clearly, we are not disputing the need for evaluation research to better inform policy; we are suggesting, however, that the field needs to be sensitized to the tendency for such studies to be used inconsistently with their purposes.

CURRENT EMPHASIS ON EVIDENTIAL WARRANTS

On November 5, 2002, the Institute of Education Sciences (IES) was established though the Education Sciences Reform Act of 2002. (This act also terminated the Office of Educational Research and Improvement [OERI], formerly responsible for education research and statistics). The IES suggests that their focus on experimental design may be a way to reverse "decades of stagnation in American education, and spark rapid, evidence-driven progress" (www.ed.gov/about/offices/list/ies/index.html). IES claims that (1) the use of data from randomized controlled trials can provide better predictors of effective educational interventions, and (2) that their collective effort to build a knowledge base of effective interventions would increase with the use of experimental design. These assertions appear to reflect the current administration's implicit belief that the study designs commonly in use (including most comparison-group and pre–post designs) do not hold up in careful empirical investigations nor do they generate reliable conclusions.

IES's perspective promotes the idea found in the No Child Left Behind legislation of 2001 that federal funds should support interventions that are anchored in scientifically based research. According to the report *Bringing Evidence-Driven Progress to Education: A Recommended Strategy for the U.S. Department of Education*, developed under a collaborative initiative between the Coalition for Evidenced Based Policy and the Department of Education, with funding from the William T. Grant Foundation, educational interventions, such as grade retention and ability grouping, are used with little regard to the evidence. According to the report's analysis of the past thirty years of National Assessment of Educational Progress (NAEP) scores, this practice seems to have resulted in minimal academic achievement gains for elementary and secondary school students despite a 90 percent increase in real public spending per student.

"The success of federal education programs depends ultimately on the ability to evaluate which programs are working as intended and which are not. With rigorous evidence on effectiveness we can begin to focus our resources on programs that work," said Grover "Russ" Whitehurst, assistant secretary for educational research and improvement (www.ed.gov/news/pressreleases/2002/04/04242002a.html). IES asserts that its initiative draws on models from medicine and welfare policy, where rigorous evaluation seems to have been instrumental in policy and funding decisions.

While the administration's rationale for evidence-based research may be well intentioned, it does not appear to have considered the potential problems associated with randomized trials when used in connection with highly valued resources in underrepresented ethnic minority communities. This policy also ignores the possible value of different ways of knowing, and that different knowledge sources do not operate in exclusion of each other. We argue that empirical research should not be privileged over qualitative or hermeneutic ways of knowing. We believe that this dilemma can be addressed more appropriately with the selective and thoughtful integration of qualitative and hermeneutic ways of knowing to enhance the power of quantitative investigations. Proponents of this idea, elaborated by Suchman (1967), Eisner (1967), and Gordon (1995), advocate for the integration of quantitative, qualitative, and hermeneutic data in program evaluation. This integration is captured in what Gordon calls connoisseurial evaluation, in which available data of various kinds are supplemented by expert knowledge, broad experience, and extensive exposure to the kind of intervention being evaluated. Suchman (1967) proposed five categories of criteria (adapted from James 1958) by which the success or failure of an intervention may be evaluated. These categories, as further elaborated by Gordon (1995), inform the methods and procedures used in the connoisseurial evaluation and are described as follows:

1. *Effort*: Evaluations in this category have as their criterion of success the quantity and quality of activity. This represents an assessment of input, or energy expended, regardless of output. It is intended to answer the questions "What did you do?" and "How well did you do it?" Gordon (1976) has referred to this aspect of evaluation as the assessment of implementation. At this level, the investigator goes beyond what is described as intended treatment or done from the perspectives of the doers and the receivers.

2. *Performance*: Performance or effects criteria guide the measurement of the results of effort rather than the effort itself. This requires a clear statement of objectives. How much is accomplished relative to an immediate goal? Did any change occur? Was the change the one intended? This is, perhaps, the most commonly utilized category of evaluation, where we examine the intervention's impact on some person, institution, situation, condition, etc. For example, did the students learn anything? Is there a change in the behavior of teachers? Did institutional policy or practice change? Were the results consistent with the objectives of the intervention?

3. *Adequacy of Performance*: This criterion refers to the degree to which effective performance is adequate to the total amount of need. Thus, a program of intensive psychotherapy for a small group of mentally ill individuals may show highly effective results, but as a broader public health measure may prove thoroughly inadequate to meet the problem of mental illness in an entire community. Given the current level of minority student underachievement, did the intervention result in a significant reduction in the gap between the targeted group's mean achievement level and the level specified by the criterion of success? Adequacy is obviously a relative measure, depending upon societal standards and how high one's goals are. Gordon and Shipman (1979) have introduced another test of adequacy that addresses the specific needs of the targeted group. In contrast to a concern for equality of treatment in which all are ensured equal access and equal treatment, Gordon and Shipman (1979) suggest that social justice requires appropriateness and sufficiency of service to achieve a common learning or achievement criterion. This is

especially important for the differential requirements that are essential to the achievement of an agreed-upon level of competence in populations whose baseline characteristics differ. The connoisseurial approach is ideal for determining adequacy, which is too often ignored in evaluation research.

4. *Efficiency*: A positive answer to the question "Does it work?" often gives rise to a follow-up question: "Is there a better way to attain the same results?" Econometricians have introduced a concern for cost effectiveness. Is this the most economical way of achieving the results, and are the results obtained worth the cost of the intervention to the recipients, the implementers, and the sponsors?

5. *Process*: In the course of evaluating the success or failure of a program, a great deal can be learned about how and why a program works or does not work. An evaluation study may limit its data collection and analysis simply to determining whether or not a program is successful, according to the preceding four criteria, without examining how and why it succeeds or fails. An analysis of process can have both administrative and scientific significance, particularly where the evaluation indicates that a program is not working as expected. Locating the cause of failure may result in modifying the program so that it will work, instead of its being discarded as a complete failure. On the other hand, understanding why a treatment works can provide a basis for separating ritual from substance.

In addition to using both qualitative and quantitative data, connoisseurial evaluators are also free to make use of objective and subjective measures. The connoisseur's judgment is not used to supplant empirically based evaluation, but rather to supplement, amplify, and explain more traditional evaluation research.

CONCEPTUAL AND PRACTICAL ISSUES

The Practice-Theory Relationship in Evaluation

Shadish, Cook, and Leviton (1991) indicate that one of the goals of evaluation is to consider the quality and merit of educational and social programs that are intended to improve the welfare of people, organizations, and society. The nature and scope of information derived from evaluation done systematically and deliberately is also critical in formative decision making and related policy (Cronbach 1963; House 1980; Patton 1997; Stufflebeam and Shinkfield 1985; Worthen and Sanders 1973). There is somewhat of a tension, however, in the perspective that evaluation is a pragmatic or professional field rather than an academic one. We do not make this overt distinction but rather acknowledge that while academic research is pursued to advance knowledge, it is informed by evaluation research that, as a practical matter, questions and considers the applicability of basic theories to practical situations (Shadish, Cook, and Leviton 1991).

Alkin and Ellett (1985) distinguish between the uses of evaluation and academic research theories of evaluation. They assert that evaluation research theories identify the key elements guiding evaluation practice, implying that there's a standard method for conducting evaluation. "These elements include the focus and role of the evaluation, the specific evaluation questions to be studied, the evaluation design and implementation, and the use of evaluation results (Shadish, Cook, and Leviton [1991] as cited in Christie 2003). Various evaluation research theories emphasize, prioritize, and combine these elements differently.

In contrast, academic research theories provide statements and generalizations that seek to explain and predict practical phenomena (Alkin and Ellett 1985). In other words, academic research theories enable an understanding of when a particular theory is appropriate, how it functions best, and what it can be expected to accomplish and under what conditions (Cousins and Earl 1999). Christie (2003) however, indicates that "with the exception of a few focal areas in the evaluation theory literature (such as evaluation utilization), there are very few academic research theories. This limitation has resulted in an evaluation field built on, and constrained by, [evaluation research] ideas" (1–2). If this is indeed the case, then the evaluation field has not yet perceived the utility of an interdisciplinary theoretical approach to inform professional practice. For example, if we assume that behavior is a function of the interaction between the characteristics of persons and the environment in which they develop, then we would be guided by theoretical constructs that inform these interactions and possibly these behaviors.

Evaluation Standards

Despite the limitations of existing efforts to evaluate supplementary and other education programs, some progress is being made in the development of standards that can guide these endeavors. The most current version of *The Program Evaluation Standards*, developed by a committee chaired by James R. Sanders (Joint Committee on Standards for Educational Evaluations 1994), resulted from a pioneering project in 1975 that aimed to develop guidelines for conducting useful, feasible, ethical, and sound evaluations of educational programs. Since the 1970s, the field of evaluation practice has rapidly expanded beyond educational programs to include institutions, programs, or services in health, rehabilitation, emergency management, economic development, and other community- and nation-building efforts. Institutions, programs, and services in both public and private sectors now serve as objects of evaluations. Sponsors (for programs and evaluations) vary greatly, and include government, nongovernment, and private agencies/foundations that cross national boundaries.

The 1994 *Standards*, consisting of thirty standards for appraising evaluation practices in four broad domains—utility, feasibility, propriety, and accuracy—resulted from a collaborative effort among sixteen professional associations in the United States, including the American Educational Research Association, the American Psychological Association, and the American Evaluation Association. The *Standards* defines evaluation as "the systematic investigation of the worth or merit of an object" (Joint Committee 1994, 3). The *Standards* is intended to serve as

- Guides for designing and carrying out sound evaluations and stimulating the use of evaluation findings in appropriate ways;
- Resources for teaching clients/stakeholders about the purposes for evaluations and what they can expect from evaluative efforts;
- A framework for conducting metaevaluations or appraisals of the quality of evaluation practices in given projects and programs;
- Resources in proposal development for developing and evaluating new programs or projects; and
- Guiding criteria for assessments of evaluator knowledge and credibility.

The general intentions of the four broad domains in the *Standards* are as follows:

1. Utility standards (U1–U7) are intended to ensure that an evaluation will serve the information needs of intended audiences and users. These standards address the identification of relevant stakeholders; formulation of evaluation questions to address stakeholder information needs; and the usability, clarity, and timeliness of the reports for stakeholders and clients. Evaluation impact is also addressed here.
2. Feasibility standards (F1–F3) are intended to ensure that an evaluation is designed and conducted in a manner that is prudent, practical, diplomatic, and cost effective. These standards acknowledge the social and political context in which social programs and institutions reside, and stipulate that evaluations be conducted in politically viable ways.
3. Propriety standards (P1–P8) are intended to ensure that evaluations are conducted legally, ethically, and with due regard to the welfare of those

involved in the evaluation, as well as those affected by the results. These standards include properly addressing the rights of human subjects, compliance with agreements about the confidentiality of information gathered, and the appropriate release of results.

4. Accuracy standards (A1–A12) address the methodological rigor and technical adequacy of information concerning the product, program, institution, or service area that is evaluated. They are intended to ensure that quantitative and qualitative procedures employed are credible and that the information gathered, analyzed, and conveyed about various aspects of the program is technically defensible.

The *Standards* text provides the reader with an extensive array of illustrative examples of violations and repercussions of particular standards on the quality of evaluation practices and evaluator credibility. Additionally, the cases suggest a particular value orientation of the Joint Committee:

• Evaluations primarily involve "judgments of worth" of the object evaluated and are thus summative in orientation;
• Evaluations should be conducted by external rather than internal evaluators;
• Evaluator roles are distinct and separate from program participants or stakeholders at large;
• Evaluators possess formal training as methodologists; and
• Various approaches for delivering evaluation services should have a metaevaluation plan that will inform and guide all of the procedures and ensure that the quality of the investigation is aligned with the utility, feasibility, propriety, and accuracy standards advocated by the Joint Committee for Standards for Educational Evaluation (1994).

Purposes and Applications of Evaluations

Evaluation purposes can be formative (defined as an orientation toward conceptualizing, planning, modifying, or improving programs, projects, or services), summative (defined as an orientation toward judgments of worth, effectiveness, or merit), or some combination of the two. In each of the following models, the role of the evaluator (the individual or team conducting the evaluation research) and the evaluator-stakeholder relationship is somewhat differently defined. Further, differing values drive the design and conduct of research in models with differing organizing units. In some models, the program goals and objectives are the primary organizing unit. In others, the types of decisions to be made with the results serve as the primary organizer. Chatterji (2002) suggests that specific evaluation questions or issues can be investigated through the following broad categories of evaluation models (which can utilize qualitative, quantitative, or a combination of the two):

Context Evaluation

Context evaluation questions are concerned with variables in the context in which a program, project, or service area is situated, and how these affect program design or delivery. Needs assessment falls in this category.

Input Evaluation

Input evaluation questions are concerned with input variables, including how resources are allocated to implement a program, project, or service area.

Process Evaluation

Process evaluation questions are concerned with process variables such as monitoring how well a program, project, or service area is being implemented.

Outcome Evaluation

Outcome evaluation questions are concerned with determining the impact of a program, project, or service area and the extent to which the desired outcomes have been achieved with target populations.

Systematic Evaluation

Systemic evaluation questions examine the functioning of a program, project, or organizational system as a whole, focusing on all or some combination of context, input, process, and outcome variables and their interdependencies.

Lesson Learning

These are the subjective and relatively informal appraisals of a program, project, or service area based on brief site visits, generally early in the program's history.

Pseudoevaluation

Subjective judgment(s) of a program, project, or service area by advocates primarily for public relations and promotion purposes are referred to as pseudo-evaluations.

As suggested, the effectiveness of supplementary education programs can be judged through a particular form of social science. Evaluation research— sometimes called program evaluation—refers to a research purpose rather than a specific method. This purpose is to evaluate the impact of social interventions (such as innovations in parole) and educational interventions (such as new teaching methods). Various methods—surveys, experiments, focus groups, and interviews, for example—can be used in evaluation research. Evaluation research is not a new phenomenon. Whenever people have established a social program or intervention to serve a specific purpose, they have paid attention to its actual consequences even if they have not always done so in a conscious, deliberate, or sophisticated fashion. In recent years, however, the field of evaluation has become an increasingly popular and active research specialty, as reflected in textbooks, courses, and projects. Moreover, the growth of evaluation research points to a general trend in the social sciences. This is attributed in part to social scientists' increasing desire to link social activism with scholarship that may make a difference.

In conducting evaluation research, we distinguish three levels of concern. The first attempts to discover whether or not a particular intervention program is effective: Are developmental and learning processes supported following the application of a particular teaching method, curriculum, and so forth? The second level of concern is comparative: Is the particular intervention more effective than other approaches? The third level is explanatory: What is the nature of the relationship between specific interventions and particular changes in behavior? Most evaluation research is directed at the first two levels of concern. We argue that attention to the third level is critical because queries on this level can enable us to (1) establish a rational basis for action, and (2) begin to specify treatments relative to known characteristics of the target population. At this third level, the distinction between academic and evaluation research collapses. The questions posed demand a quality of design that is not only appropriate to academic research but also serves the purposes of evaluation research. Unfortunately, evaluation research of this quality has seldom been applied to supplementary education.

All of these approaches are made more complex by technical operational problems. The closer investigations of supplementary education programs approach conditions comparable to those in laboratory experiments, the more the researcher may discover what, how, and why certain educational treatments affect educational underdevelopment. Yet various obstacles preclude establishing the necessary degree of precision and control in isolating variables and discovering the effectiveness of specific treatments on targeted behaviors.

One obstacle involves difficulties in the utilization of an adequate method for selecting subjects. As Campbell and Erlebacher (1970) suggest, experimental participants are often not selected on a random basis. While the control group is selected to closely match the experimental group according to various indices, the control group is often too different from the experimental group in crucial aspects, however small the degree. Without random selection of subjects, program outcomes may reflect differences that are unrelated to the experimental treatment in question. Additionally, the matching procedures themselves may produce regression artifacts. As for analysis of covariance and partial correlation, these biases may be found in pretest scores. Campbell and Erlebacher (1970) suggest that true experiments that privilege randomization of subjects will avoid the difficulties that quasi-experimental designs have encountered. However, parental objections, coupled with political pressures, have made large-scale application of random assignment of students impossible. Controlled comparative studies of this sort are often resisted by communities that want the benefit of special treatment but will not accept arbitrary selection of subjects for experimentation.

Another difficulty in establishing comparable experimental and control groups can be attributed to the influence of what has been called the radiation effect. Even if the two groups are initially comparable, the effect of experimentation on the experimental subjects is radiated onto their families, siblings, and eventually onto the control subjects if there is any contact, direct or indirect, between these several groups. Obviously, control subjects should be selected in a manner such that they can in no way be affected by the experimental treatment. However, this condition is increasingly difficult to maintain in large-scale field studies and demonstration projects.

In addition, investigators have discovered other effects that are associated with an intervention program—effects that are not direct results of the treatment itself. Rosenthal and Jacobson (1968) reported that a teacher's expectations can have an important influence on the performance of students (the Pygmalion effect). Shepard (1962) reported a similar observation in the early stages of his work in St. Louis. Where the teacher's expectation of the child's performance is high, the child is likely to show high achievement. Where expectations are low, achievement tends to be low. Consequently, in any supplementary education program, the teachers' expectations of the subjects may influence their students' subsequent performances. The Hawthorne effect, in which the mere fact of experimentation or altered learning conditions may cause a temporary change in performance that is unrelated to the specific intervention method applied, can also influence the results. In the evaluation of supplementary education, such interferences have not been identified or controlled for; hence, meaningful consequences of various treatments cannot be determined from these studies.

Other problems with evaluation research design can confuse, distort, or limit the initial data as well as subsequent findings. Most evaluations of supplementary-education studies depend primarily on static variables and quantitative measures to the neglect of the process variables and the qualitative analysis of behavior, process, circumstances, and conditions. This dependence on quantitative measures of status raises questions concerning the validity of the measurement instruments and ignores the growing appreciation of situational and transactional factors as determinants of function. Supplementary education programs both include and influence a wide variety of independent and dependent variables that are insufficiently accounted for in the more narrowly designed evaluation research studies that have dominated the field to date. This rather static approach to assessment has led some investigators to view student characteristics that differ from some presumed norm as negative, as well as to consider any correlation between these negative characteristics and learning dysfunction as support for a deficits theory of intervention.

In practice, researchers have perceived the differences between the target populations and the standard group as deficits to be overcome rather than characteristics to be utilized and developed. Little opportunity is provided to study the dynamic processes by which success or failure may be more adequately understood (Gordon and Armour-Thomas 1991). Likewise, the relationships between stereotypical and fairly static input and output variables (often isolated in pairs) are usually investigated. Scant attention is paid to the complex dialectical relationships between patterns of dependent variables and patterns of independent variables, many of which may be idiosyncratic to individuals and situations. These inadequate attempts at the assessment and treatment of student characteristics are often accompanied by an even less adequate appraisal of program variables. In practically all of the so-called national impact studies and most of the evaluations of specific programs, little or no attention is paid to the fact that intervention treatment is uneven and control of that treatment almost nonexistent. When national impact data are pooled, we could easily have results that show no net effect, that is, the positive impact of discrete programs is canceled out by the absence of positive effect of other programs. Even more serious is the apparent disregard of our growing conviction that individual students respond differently to treatments. We may again have negative responders canceling positive responders to indicate no net effect—even though the treatment may be highly effective for specific individuals under specific circumstances—when mean changes in status are used as the indices to outcome.

Several possible explanations have surfaced to illustrate how these confusing data can be interpreted to demonstrate program ineffectiveness. The most extreme is the theory that the subjects involved are simply genetically inferior and incapable of "being raised" to "hoped-for" standards. Those who have advanced such hypotheses have been discredited for the questionable nature of their supporting "scientific evidence" and for the dubious value (to today's society) of advancing such theories when they cannot be adequately proven.

Given the range of possible interpretations of apparently discouraging data, what cannot be ignored is that most underrepresented students are failing to master the traditional learning tasks of schooling. The problem is not only tragic but also staggeringly complex. Perhaps the most meaningful response to the discouraging data presented by various evaluation reports (after allowing for many of the research problems already discussed) is a rigorous examination of the appropriateness of what is actually taking place in educational practice during and after school.

Even where extraordinary programs of supplementary education have brought about some beneficial results, they may be negated in the long run by larger social factors. Outside the classroom, underrepresented students confront a society that is hostile to their healthy development. Learning in structured situations may be irrelevant in the context of life outside of school. There is some evidence to suggest that ethnic, economic, or social integration has beneficial effects on students from disadvantaged backgrounds. While achievement levels have increased after desegregation in many schools, identification of the exact variables leading to this result have been inconclusive. Improved teacher morale, for example, may be the product of desegregation and, where enabled, has resulted in an overall increase in the quality of education throughout the system. Other evidence points to the perspective that integration on the basis of social status has beneficial effects for underrepresented students if the majority of their peers are from higher-status groups. Even these results, however, are not sufficiently conclusive to legitimize large-scale generalizations.

The dilemma is further complicated by the resurgence of cultural nationalism among ethnic minorities, a movement that affects the assumptions made about ethnic integration and education. In a society that has alternately advocated ethnic separation and ethnic amalgamation, yet has never truly accepted cultural and ethnic pluralism, African Americans, Hispanic Americans, and Native Americans are insisting that the traditional public school is guilty not only of their children's intellectual and social annihilation but also of cultural genocide. There are class and caste conflicts to which insufficient attention has been given in the organization and delivery of educational services. If cultural and ethnic identification are important components of the learning experience, to ignore or demean them is poor education, at best. Even if these factors were sufficiently taken into account in schools, we would be far from any guarantees that the society would honor such values outside the classroom. It is not at all clear that intensive, short-term, in-school treatment can counter the negative external forces working upon underrepresented students.

The schools face a difficult challenge if they are to make learning an exciting and stimulating experience, relevant and effective for all students of all cultural and social backgrounds. However, meeting these criteria would not be enough. Educators would still face the problem of matching the developmental patterns, learning styles, and temperamental traits of individual learners to the educational experiences to which they are exposed. Many researchers have concentrated on differences in level of intellectual function, a concern reflected in the tracking of students based on standardized tests of educational achievement. This tradition has emphasized quantitative measurement, classification, and prediction to the neglect of qualitative measurement, description, and prescription. These latter processes are clearly essential to the effective teaching of children who come to the schools with characteristics different from those of both their teachers and the other children to whom most teachers are accustomed.

Research data indicate wide variations in patterns of intellectual and social function across and within subpopulations. Variations in function within privileged groups may be less important because of a variety of environmental factors that support adequate development and learning; however, among disadvantaged populations—where traditional forms of environmental support may be absent—attention to differential learning patterns may be crucial to adequate development. Understanding the role of one set of behaviors as facilitators of more comprehensive behaviors is at the heart of both differential analysis of learner characteristics and differential design of learning experiences. Schooling for disadvantaged children—indeed, for all children in our schools—comes nowhere near meeting these implied criteria. Assessment technology has not seriously engaged the problem. Curriculum specialists are just beginning to face the task of "individually prescribed learning."

The problems of social disadvantage in the society at large, and the failure of schools to integrate their students' cultural differences and individual learning styles in their practices are not the only obstacles to successful supplementary education. Social disadvantage gives rise to a variety of harmful health and nutritional problems that militate against healthy development and adequate utilization of educational opportunities. It is becoming increasingly recognized that low income results in poor health care and frequent malnutrition; these disadvantages are related to high risks for the pregnant mother and fetus, and for the child after birth, in terms of mortality and/or maldevelopment. Poor health conditions may result in either a direct impairment of the nervous system or an indirect interference with the learning process, such as a low level of energy or high level of distractibility. Such health-related conditions have probably had a crucial effect on school and general social adjustment. We now know that impaired health or organic dysfunction can influence school attendance, learning efficiency, and developmental rate, as well as personality development. Clearly, adequacy of health status and adequacy of health care in our society are influenced by adequacy of income (see Gordon and Bridglall's chapter 2 for a more detailed discussion).

CONCLUSION

Despite the many problems in the design, implementation, and evaluation of programs of supplemental education, and the equivocal status of most evaluation efforts, we are nonetheless constantly called upon to make judgments and policy decisions based upon experience and the available data. To guide such decisions, the following observations may be useful.

1. The search for the best or the generic treatment is clearly a futile search. Problems of human development and learning are so complex and conditions of life so varied that the chances of finding a curriculum that is universally superior are quite modest. In several well-designed studies comparing different approaches to early childhood education, differences in curriculum orientation were found to be less important than such factors as systematic planning, clear objectives, intensity of treatment, attention to individual needs and learning patterns, opportunities for individual and small-group interaction, support in the home environment for the learning experiences provided at school, and the presence of personnel committed to the pedagogical procedures prescribed. It seemed that as these conditions were met, no matter what the content or method for personal development and content mastery were advanced. Empirical data in support of these conclusions are scarce since few studies have been designed to be particularly sensitive to this constellation of variables. Nonetheless, logical and impressionistic evidence mounts in support of the validity of these observations.

2. Although the concept of individual differences has been with us for a long time, individualization is underrepresented in interventions and related program evaluations. Confusing interpretation of evaluation data may occur because of this neglect and the countertendency to generalize too freely. In a few longitudinal studies of experimental school programs, where impacts on individuals (or on youngsters identified as having been exposed to known treatments over time) have been investigated, emerging achievement patterns are encouraging. There appear

to be insufficient studies of highly sophisticated programs of individually prescribed learning experiences to draw definitive conclusions. Yet some of the more generalized approaches to individually prescribed instruction do seem to be widening the range of achievement among students so exposed. The true matching of pace, prior knowledge, and conditions of learning to the specific characteristics of each learner is not yet a part of empirical studies. Insufficient progress in the qualitative analysis of the actual behavior of learners may be partially responsible for this situation. We contend that qualitative analysis is clearly prerequisite to any serious effort at achieving sophistication in the individualization and personalization of instruction and learning.

3. The absence of broader representation and utilization of the social sciences in the evaluation of supplementary education has contributed to the neglect of psychological, social, and political factors in these programs. Yet as important as the strictly pedagogical problems are, the politics of education delivery systems, the psychology and political economy of education, and the sociology of knowledge and learning share the stage with pedagogy in accounting for the success or failure of supplementary education. Whether we are considering the role of students in directing their own learning or the roles of parents and community in shaping school policy, the influences of involvement, participation, commitment, and values are critical. They are so critical as to render much of our evaluation and our treatment invalid if these factors are not included. We must give these factors greater consideration. In the very inadequate studies of several informal education situations (storefront academies; the adult education programs of groups like the Black Panthers, Black Muslims, Young Lords; the offerings of community-based and faith-based institutions, etc.), the blending of these factors appears to have an important role in the participants' educational development and rehabilitation. These factors include efficacy, commitment, engagement, opportunity to learn and be rewarded, politics, and privileged values (Bridglall 2004).

REFERENCES

After-School Corporation. 2003. *A comparison of Mathematica's national evaluation of the 21st Century Community Learning Centers and Policy Studies Associates' evaluation of the TASC after-school program*. New York: Author.

Alkin, M. C., and F. S. Ellett. 1985. Evaluation models: Development. In *International Encyclopaedia of Education: Research and Studies*, edited by T. Husen and T. Postlethwaite. Oxford: Pergamon Press.

Beuhring, T., R. W. Blum, and P. M. Rinehart. 2000. *Protecting teens: Beyond race, income, and family structure.* Minneapolis: Center for Adolescent Health, University of Minnesota.

Bridglall, B. L. 2004. Structural and individual characteristics that enable high academic achievement for underrepresented students of color. Unpublished PhD diss., Teachers College, Columbia University.

Campbell, D. T., and A. Erlebacher. 1970. How regression artifacts in quasi-experimental evaluations can mistakenly make compensatory education look harmful. In *Compensatory education: A national debate*, edited by J. Hellmuth. New York: Brunner/Hazel.

Carnegie Council on Adolescent Development. 1992. *A matter of time: Risk and opportunity in the nonschool hours.* Report of the Task Force on Youth Development and Community Programs. New York: Carnegie Corporation of New York.

Caspe, M. 2001. *Family–school–community partnerships: A compilation of professional standards of practice for teachers.* Cambridge, MA: Harvard Family Research Project, Harvard University.

Catalano, R. F., M. L. Berglund, J. A. M. Ryan, H. S. Lonczak, and J. D. Hawkins. 1998. *Positive youth development in the United States: Research findings on evaluations of positive youth development programs.* Washington, DC: U.S. Department of Health and Human Services.

Chatterji, M. 2002. Models and methods for examining standards-based reforms and accountability initiatives: Have the tools of inquiry answered pressing questions on improving schools? *Review of Educational Research* 72(3): 345–86.

Christie, C. A., ed. 2003. *The practice-theory relationship in evaluation: New directions for evaluation #97.* San Francisco: Jossey-Bass.

Cousins, J., and L. Earl. 1999. When the boat gets missed: Response to M. F. Smith. *American Journal of Evaluation* 20:309–18.

Cronbach, L. C. 1963. Course improvement through evaluation. *Teachers College Record* 64:672–83.

Dynarski, M., M. Moore, J. Mullens, P. Gleason, S. James-Burdumy, L. Rosenberg, W. Mansfield, S. Heaviside, D. Levy, C. Pistorino, T. Silva, and J. Deke. 2003. *When schools stay open late: The national evaluation of the 21st-Century Community Learning Centers program, first year findings.* Princeton, NJ: Mathematica Policy Research.

Eisner, E. W. 1967. *Instructional and expressive educational objectives: Their formulation and use in curriculum.* ERIC Document Reproduction Service no. ED 028 838.

Engman, R. 1992. On a roll: A successful after-school tutoring program at Patrick Henry School, Alexandria, VA. *Principal* 71:24–25.

Fashola, O. S. 1998. *Review of extended-day and after-school programs and their effectiveness.* Report no. 24. Baltimore, MD: Center for Research on the Education of Students Placed at Risk.

Finn, J. D., J. Folger, and D. Cox. 1991. Measuring participation among elementary grade students. *Educational and Psychological Measurement* 51:393–402.

Finn, J. D., G. M. Pannozzo, and K. E. Voelkl. 1995. Disruptive and inattentive-withdrawn behavior and achievement among fourth graders. *Elementary School Journal* 95:421–34.

Gordon, E. W. 1976. Group differences vs. individual development in educational design. In *Individuality in learning*, edited by S. Messick and associates. San Francisco: Jossey-Bass.

———. 1995. Toward an equitable system of educational assessment. *Journal of Negro Education* 64(3): 360–72.

Gordon, E. W., and E. Armour-Thomas. 1991. Culture and cognitive development. In *Directors of development: Influences on the development of children's thinking*, edited by L. Okagaki and R. Sternberg, 83–100. Hillsdale, NJ: Erlbaum.

Gordon, E. W., and S. Shipman. 1979. Human diversity, pedagogy, and educational equity. *American Psychologist* 34(10): 1030–36.

Henderson, D. 1990. Expanding the curriculum with after-school classes: Oak Park Valley Union Elementary School District, Tulare, California. *Thrust* 1:32–33.

House, E. R. 1980. *Evaluating with validity*. Beverly Hills, CA: Sage.

Jacobson, L. 2003. After-school report called into question. *Education Week* 22(37): 1, 15.

James, G. 1958. Research by local health departments: Problems, methods, results. *American Journal of Public Health* 48(3):353–61.

Joint Committee on Standards for Educational Evaluations. 1994. *The program evaluation standards: How to assess evaluations of educational programs*. Ed. J. Sanders. Thousand Oaks, CA: Sage.

Marshall, N. L., C. G. Coll, F. Marx, K. McCartney, N. Keife, and J. Ruh. 1997. After-school time and children's behavioral adjustment. *Merrill-Palmer Quarterly* 43(3): 497–514.

McGuire, K. D., and J. R. Weisz. 1982. Social cognition and behavior correlates of preadolescent chumships. *Child Development* 53(6): 1478–84.

Mercure, M. 1993. Project achievement: An after-school success story. *Principal* 73:48–50.

Miller, B. M. 1995. *Out-of-school time: Effects on learning in the primary grades*. Wellesley, MA: National Institute on Out-of-School Time Center for Research on Women, Wellesley College.

Patton, M. Q. 1997. *Utilization-focused evaluation*. Thousand Oaks, CA: Sage.

Pettit, G. S., R. D. Laird, J. E. Bates, and K. A. Dodge. 1997. Patterns of after-school care in middle childhood: Risk factors and developmental outcomes. *Merrill-Palmer Quarterly* 43(3): 515–38.

Pierce, K. M., J. V. Hamm, and D. L. Vandell. 1999. Experiences in after-school programs and children's adjustment in first-grade classrooms. *Child Development* 70(3): 756–67.

Posner, J. K., and D. L. Vandell. 1994. Low-income children's after-school care: Are there beneficial effects of after-school programs? *Child Development* 65:440–56.

Rosenthal, R., and L. Jacobson. 1968. *Pygmalion in the classroom: Teacher expectation and pupils' intellectual development*. New York: Holt, Rinehart and Winston.

Roth, J., J. Brooks-Gunn, L. Murray, and W. Foster. 1998. Promoting healthy adolescents: Synthesis of youth development program evaluations. *Journal of Research on Adolescence* 8(4): 423–59.

Schinke, S., K. C. Cole, and S. R. Poulin. 1998. *Evaluation of Boys' and Girls' Club of America's educational enhancement program*. Atlanta, GA: Author.

Scott-Little, C., M. S. Hamann, and S. G. Jurs. 2002. Evaluations of after-school programs: A meta-evaluation of methodologies and narrative synthesis of findings. *American Journal of Evaluation* 23(4): 371–519.

Shadish, W. R., T. D. Cook, and L. C. Leviton. 1991. *Foundations of program evaluation: Theories of practice*. Newbury Park, CA: Sage.

Shepard, S. 1962. A program to raise the standard of school achievement. In Programs for the Educationally Disadvantaged, U.S. Department of Education report of conference, May 21–23.

Stufflebeam, D. L., and A. J. Shinkfield. 1985. *Systematic evaluation*. Boston: Kluwer-Nijhoff.

Suchman, E. A. 1967. *Evaluative research*. New York: Russell Sage.

Trueba, H. T. 1983. Adjustment problems of Mexican and Mexican-American students: An anthropological study. *Learning Disability Quarterly* 6:395–404.

Wang, M. C., H. J. Freiberg, and H. J. Waxman. 1996. Case studies of inner-city schools. Paper presented at the annual meeting of the American Educational Research Association, April, New York

Wang, M. C., G. D. Haertel, and H. J. Walberg. 1994. *The effectiveness of collaborative school-linked services*. Philadelphia, PA: Temple University, National Center on Education in the Inner Cities.

Worthen, B. R., and J. R. Sanders. 1973. *Educational evaluation: Theory and practice*. Worthington, OH: Charles A. Jones.

Zill, N., and C. Rogers. 1988. Recent trends in the well-being of children in the United States and their implications for public policy. In *The changing American family and public policy*, edited by A. J. Cherline, 31–115. Washington, DC: Urban Institute Press.

The Idea of Supplementary Education

Edmund W. Gordon

I grew up in segregated St. Louis during the 1950s and early 1960s. From talking to my parents, reading, and interviewing people about St. Louis during those years, I know that racism was harsh. My personal experience there as a child, however, was almost completely devoid of any awareness of racism. For I had the benefit of a web of caring adults who must have spent twenty-four hours a day figuring out ways to protect their children from racism. Part of their job was made easy by the complete separation of the races. The schools, churches, social events, service organizations, and neighborhoods where we played and volunteered were all black. But separation from whites did not satisfy these adults; their aim was higher. They wanted their children to have exposure to the best that St. Louis had to offer without coming into contact with those who would seek to diminish us. What's amazing is that they succeeded.

When I was growing up, St. Louis (then the ninth-largest city in the United States) was known for its outdoor opera, its wonderful museum (with the steep hill behind used for sledding in the snow), its world-class zoo, its magnificent city park, and its symphony orchestra. While all of these attractions did not hold my interest equally, they were all a regular part of my life. These determined black adults would take us to enjoy these activities, literally shielded from the rest of the world. At the outdoor opera, for instance, the children sat on the inside seats and the adults sat on the perimeter, shooting stares and threatening gestures at any child who might embarrass them or us. When there was a special exhibit at the museum, we were taken as a group to explore the arts with our own private docent. And so it was; racism all around and the children of the black middle class in St. Louis oblivious to its sting and burn, playing in St. Louis as if it were ours.

When we weren't on reconnaissance missions, we were having a grand time within the community: Sunday school picnics, block parties, activities at the Phillis Wheatley Y (this, too, was all black), hay rides and apple picking in the fall, neighborhood Trick or Treat and Christmas caroling, social clubs, dances, and church, church, church.

Of course, it has taken the benefit of hindsight for me to appreciate the richness of the community that surrounded me as a child. At the time I felt constrained and watched. I have come to understand that for black people growing up in America during those and earlier years, community was the scaffolding around the mainstream of society that allowed us to move up. We were locked out, but we were not locked in. Through ingenuity and collaboration my black community created a parallel universe that took from the outer world what it needed to expand my horizons and make me feel that I could do anything. That strong, caring, resourceful, creative, demanding community shaped me, and its values and expectations continue to nurture me.

It was not until I went to college that I began to understand the racism that had surrounded me in St. Louis. Few of my classmates went to college because not all black children in St. Louis had the experience that I did. Our group of middle-class children, while large for a social group, represented a tiny minority of black children in St. Louis. Most of the black children were poor and were not protected. Segregation and racism hit them with full force. And those proud black adults I described were disrespected and beat down daily as they tried to earn livings, shop, buy homes, and generally provide for their families. In fact, every good thing that I experienced had an ugly flip side. For example, I received a great education in St. Louis's segregated public schools partly because the well-educated, well-trained teachers that I had were not allowed to do anything else. Then, I never thought about how frustrating it must have been for the journalists, scientists, actors, singers, athletes, mathematicians, and would-be senators who taught me to spend their entire professional lives in the only career available to them.

After college I became an organizer, a public interest lawyer, a community builder, a foundation executive, and a policy advocate. I've had many jobs, but only one project—to do something about racism, injustice, and inequality; to help build a society in which all people can thrive, contribute, and participate fully—socially and economically. In searching for solutions, I never forget that community matters.

—Angela Glover Blackwell (2002, 27–29)[1]

Supplementary education is about the scaffolding that caring members of our families and communities create around "the mainstream of society" that enables our children "to move up" (Blackwell, Kwoh, and Pastor 2002, 28). The essence of what we call supplementary education is as much about the ethos of caring and concern, and the acts of enablement, nurturance, and protection, as it is about the institutions, resources, and services that are stressed in this

book. The à la carte or supplemental components of education include attitudes and expectations. Included are the demands, the routine provisions, the
things that are done for fun, and even things that are forced under duress in
the effort to ensure that optimal development and effective education are
achieved. I have often said that supplementary education is what parents who
know and are able do to ensure that academic achievement and personal development are, in fact, achieved. Well-resourced families and communities
are better able to provide such supplements than are underresourced communities and families—but that does not mean that such supplements must remain unavailable to families of modest means. It certainly does not mean that
such learning opportunities are inappropriate to the needs of such children.
We are convinced that well-resourced schools, while essential, are not sufficient for the optimal education of many children. These supplementary learning experiences may be even more essential for young people from underresourced families and schools. Various expressions of these supplements
appear to be equally important, as are good schools. In my view, nothing may
be as important as the fact that parents and other concerned adults participate
in the building of the scaffolds for learning, and in the mediation of their use
by children to enable children to "move up."

Lest we become too much focused on the role of adequately resourced
families and parents in providing supplemental education, an anecdotal report
and some emerging research are useful. A young African American professional is reported to have told the story of his grandmother's participation in
his rearing. The young physician claims that his grandmother regularly supervised his doing his homework and listened to his reading. He reports that
it was not until he reached junior high school that he realized that his grandmother was illiterate. But she knew that education, effort, and self-regulation
are important, and she made certain that he learned those values and pro-
gressed in school. Recent research findings indicate that the role of this
grandmother is not atypical. Several studies report an association between the
survival of human infants and the presence in the home of the maternal grandmother. While grandmothers may be especially important (and it appears that
the presence of the maternal grandmother is of even greater significance), my
own research suggests that the crucial factor is the presence of a knowledgeable and caring adult. In my studies of black men who defied the odds against
success, consistently we find the presence of a knowledgeable and caring
adult—not necessarily well educated, but informed and caring. Even in the
absence of resource abundance, these adults found ways to build scaffolds, to
encourage, to open opportunities, and to protect.

There is controversy concerning our use of the academic standards of the
mainstream society as a reference point for academic achievement. The con-

ference in 1998, which provided some of the impetus for this book, was principally concerned with supplementary education as an instrumentality for reducing the gap in academic achievement between African American, Hispanic American, and Native American students and students who trace their recent ancestry to Asia and Europe. That conference, which was sponsored by the Education Laboratory for Student Success at Temple University and the National Task Force on Minority High Achievement of the College Board, took as its focus the relationship of a variety of rather formal education supplements to the improvement of academic achievement. This concern with the underproductivity of our schools relative to certain ethnic minority groups is by no means new. Beginning at least with the 1965 War on Poverty, our nation has seen a range of activities directed at improving the quality of academic performance in ethnic minority populations. These efforts may have foundered on the politically based concern that the academic standards toward which these efforts were directed were alien to and disrespectful of the people we were trying to help.

For several years now, I have begun to realize that it is possible that I had been handicapped in my own thinking about the problems of education for the poor and other low-status populations. It is a self-imposed handicap, born of the manner in which I have permitted aspects of my ideology to constrain the way in which I have conceptualized the problem. In one of the first articles that I published concerning the education of disadvantaged students (Gordon 1965), I wrote about the more typical characteristics of this population. It was my thinking at that time that many of the characteristics of the population were inconsistent with high levels of academic achievement or that those characteristics created special challenges for educators. Influenced by Frank Riessman's book *The Culturally Deprived Child* (1962), I argued that the children that we are concerned with are not without culture, but had cultural experiences that made them behave differently from other children with whom the schools were more effective. These characteristics were thought of as deficits that these children and their schools needed to overcome. We later came to believe that these "deficits" might more appropriately be referred to as differences. This emphasis on differences rather than deficiencies came to dominate the discussion of the problems of educating the poor. I bought into the parallel arguments that the focus on the deficiencies of the group was to blame the victims, and that a focus on differences placed the responsibility on the school. While I somehow managed to avoid romanticizing the fact of difference and many of the actual characteristics, my attention correctly turned to how those characteristics might be better utilized in the education of low-status children. This need for the adaptation of schooling to the characteristics of learners continues to be a central tenet of my approach to pedagogy. However, increasingly, it has become clear to me that while adapting to the characteristics of learners and building on students' strengths (and many of these characteristics should be viewed as potential sources of strength) is appropriate, it is not sufficient to their effective education.

In my first book-length treatment of the education of low-status persons, I introduced the term "compensatory education." The late Doxey Wilkerson and I argued that for education to be effective with students disadvantaged by economic and ethnic status, pedagogy should compensate for the deficits and disadvantages our children had suffered as well as adapt to the differences in their characteristics. We recognized the importance of culture, but viewed cultural experiences as phenomena to be celebrated and utilized in the education of our children. We avoided the deprivation construction and privileged the differentiation construction.

Reuven Feuerstein (1978) was more accurate than was Riessman (1962) in his conceptualization of the problem of cultural experience. Feuerstein used cultural deprivation to refer to students being deprived of aspects of the hegemonic culture that provided the foundations for academic learning. Feuerstein described many educated parents as being engaged with their children in the mediation of environmental encounters in ways that provided the children with many of the instrumentalities essential to academic learning. According to Feuerstein, these children were not deprived of culture, but their cultures did not emphasize those attitudes, behaviors, experiences, and values that are instrumental to academic learning. His curriculum of "instrumental enrichment" was an attempt at building the explication of the demands of academic excellence and acculturation to the habits of intellective competence into the directed learning experience. It took a while for me to see beyond the rather formalistic structure of Feuerstein's initial emphasis on the intellective tasks of Raven's Progressive Matrices. (Raven's Progressive Matrices is an untimed test of general intelligence that seeks to evaluate an individual's ability to perceive and analyze perceptual relations and make sense of complex data. It is a nonverbal test created to measure reasoning ability, relatively independently of linguistic and educational background [Raven 2000]).

Raven and his colleagues have subsequently broadened the focus of those tasks to include less abstract and more practical mental tasks. Nonetheless, I have come to recognize the importance of behavioral analysis, structured intellective demand, mediation, explication, and reinforcement in the lives of those who would become academically sophisticated. Instrumental enrichment became and continues to be a part of the armamentarium that I bring to the education of low-status populations.

I see, then, several instrumentalities of academic learning that may be essential for persons whose natural life experiences do not dispose them toward the development of academic ability. Among these are:

- the functional analysis of the academic behavior of the learner as a basis for the design of all instruction and especially remediation;
- the explication of the principal features of the stimulus material, the salient components of the process, and the critical demands of the criterion standard;
- the explication of the critical importance of situative and tacit knowledge referable to content and procedure;
- repeated, structured, and incidental exposure to on-demand performance experiences; and
- the explication of names and meanings of common features of the content to be learned and its context.

Now what is important about these instrumentalities is that they are not routinely addressed in school, perhaps because schooling was designed on the assumption that most of these learning needs are met, incidentally, in the home and community. Some years ago, Frederick Strodtbeck (1964) reported from his research on decision making in lower-class and middle-class families that there appeared to be greater parity in decision making in the middle-class families than in the lower-class families. He argued that lower-class children learned from family decision making to listen for answers, directions, and signals. The middle-class children learned to listen to the subtleties of the arguments made by the discussants, so that they could anticipate which side to team up with. Strodtbeck (1964) argued that these children became more analytic and reflective listeners, and thus were better prepared for what would be demanded of them in school. Basil Bernstein (1974) came to similar conclusions concerning language differences between working-class and upper-class children. Since the number of words used and the complexity of the vocabulary were greater in the upper-class families, the children who grew up in these more-affluent families had stronger language skills and language habits than children from working-class families. Competence in the manipulation of more complex language forms is a distinct advantage in school learning. These habits and skills are in keeping with the demands of academic learning, but they are products of the informal learnings that are incidental to the quotidian exposure to educated or otherwise intelligent persons. This is a more subtle expression of supplementary education. Strodtbeck (1964) called it the "hidden curriculum of middle-class families."

I have often made reference to my wife's and my four children who could not avoid growing up as well-educated persons. These four young people are intelligent, but they are not geniuses. Each has become well educated; two of them exceptionally well educated. But why should they not be so? They are members of the fourth generation of educated families. Some of their ancestors were being educated while most persons of African descent were still enslaved. Both of their parents have earned doctoral degrees. These children were born into a highly literate environment, where family discussion of important (and not-so-important) issues was common. This is a family where the importance of academic learning was stressed, where these children had ready access to all of the resources necessary to optimal academic and personal development, and where graduating from college was the default expectation. If children growing up in these circumstances do not become well educated, they would have to explain why they failed to do so. Discussing one such child, a friend of mine once explained that growing up in such an academic achievement-oriented family, the young woman had three choices: she could be valedictorian, she could be salutatorian, or she could leave home! I don't mean to advocate such pressure on children, but it is clear that members of high-performance learning communities sense the expectation, feel the pressure, and are often motivated to achieve at levels that are consistent with the standards of the group. Under such conditions, high performance becomes a way of life.

In this book, we have called attention to the variety of human resource development capital that is required for investment in the academic and personal development of children. The examples above reflect the cultural and human capital resources that are grounded in some black families and the communities in which they live. We cannot stress too much the importance of these resources to the developmental outcomes to which they are related — linguistic competence, habits of mind, dispositions, acquisition skills, information, identity, and purpose are examples. However, there are other essential categories of capital that are related to still other outcomes. We have called attention to the crucial importance of health and nutrition. Children can function and survive in the presence of ill health and poor nutrition, but impairments in these domains take their toll on the efficiency with which humans function and the quality of the human effort invested in learning. Poor health and nutrition impede attention, attendance, and energy deployment. Some conditions of poor health so compromise the integrity of the organism as to interfere with learning.

One of the most intriguing varieties of capital is Bourdieu's (1986) conception of "polity capital." We use the term to refer to sense of membership in and by the social order as reflected in social commitment, social concern, and participation. If I do not feel that I belong in the group, I am not likely to take the group's standards and values seriously. If the group does not consider that I belong, it is not likely to take my needs or my development seriously. Banks, McQuarter, and Hubbard (1979) make a telling point in research that suggests that when one sees inappropriate behavior in a person considered to be like or related to the observer, the cause of the behavior is attributed to the context or environment. When the same behavior is observed in one who is considered "other than me" or "unlike me," the cause of the negative behavior is attributed to the nonbelonging person. Polity is an often ignored but critically important resource for learning and survival.

Unfortunately, all children do not have easy access to this important resource. The irony is, of course, those children who are most lacking polity capital are also likely to be those most in need and hardest to reach. It is the underresourced families and those most alienated by the hegemonic culture that are least likely to utilize or to be reached by supplemental education. It is these families who seem to have the least awareness of available services. In focus group discussions with some such parents, they seemed unaware of even the need for supplements to schooling. Schools were thought to be both responsible for meeting their children's educational needs and sufficient to do so. In our experiments with the delivery of supplemental education services, two groups of parents were more likely to request service: parents of children who were very much identified with the culture and whose children were doing quite well readily reached out for additional educational services, and so did some well-informed parents of children with special needs. Special efforts were required to reach families of students who were surviving in school, and we were not very successful in reaching families that were socially and/or financially stressed. While the families of the students who were getting along in school probably need better information and education relative to the importance of supplementary education, it is our impression that the stressed group not only was in need of the information but also needed a greater sense of polity. They are the population that most agencies indicate difficulty in engaging.

My early fear that too sharp a focus on what is missing in the lives of children who have been placed at risk of educational failure by their status in the society could lead to our further blaming them for their condition was a misplaced fear. It is certainly true that an emphasis on deficits in a population can become stigmatizing, but that need not necessarily become the case. Placed in the context of situational demand, it is possible to recognize the absence of a characteristic that is necessary for participation. If the recognition is coupled with sufficient opportunity for correction, without demeaning the indigenous practice, the recognition of the deficit can be enabling. Despite the tendency to identify the intellective demands of modern technologically advanced societies with hegemonic cultures that are alien and dominating, the fact is that meaningful participation in the social order requires high levels of intellective competence. If the cultural experiences and the resulting abilities of certain segments of the population are lacking in those experiences and developed abilities, they are deficient with respect to the standard for survival. To make a "politically correct" apology or try to deny the fact that the society has not equally prepared all segments of the population is simply wrong. I am now convinced that it is dysfunctional to our efforts at the optimal academic and personal development of these persons who were initially discriminated against by exclusion, and now by refusal to recognize the functional reality.

Low levels of developed academic ability are ubiquitous in certain ethnic minority and low-income families. Our schools seem unable to adequately address the developmental needs of many of these children. Emerging evidence suggests that effective schooling is associated with the presence of certain kinds of experiences and developed abilities that are peculiar to specific kinds of life experiences. Many of these experiences tend to occur in well-resourced families and communities and are mediated through agents who function in and outside of the school. I am convinced that the optimal education of the children who are now a special target will require more than the educational reform that occurs in school—thus, this collection of essays that advocate for strengthening the many forms of supplementary education and making these resources more widely available.

We began this book with the challenge of universal access to academic excellence. We followed with a discussion of possible alternatives in the acceleration of academic achievement with special attention given to supplementary education. The balance of the book has been devoted to various manifestations of this out-of-school education phenomenon, its rationale, and its implementation. Why have we devoted this kind of attention to non-school interventions?

We have referred to Comer's *Waiting for a Miracle* (1997) in which he makes the argument that we cannot wait for schools to solve the problems of children of color and poverty. Hugh Price has published his book *Achievement Matters* (2002), in which he makes the case for our giving much more serious attention to high academic achievement. Both of these authors turn attention to how parents and other interested adults can do something about high academic achievement in minority student populations. The 2001 No Child Left Behind Education Act, influenced by the excellent work of the Children's Defense Fund and the writings of Comer, Dryfoos, Epstein, Gordon, Halpern, Heath, McLaughlin, Price, Quinn, Steinberg, and Vandell, places the U.S. government behind the idea of attention to after-school and out-of-school interventions. This act makes $1 billion available to the states for the support of such work. What is clear is that there is growing recognition of the importance of educational interventions that are supplemental to formal schooling.

We have defined *supplementary education* as the formal and informal learning and developmental enrichment opportunities provided for students outside of school and beyond the regular school day or year. Some of these activities may occur inside the school building but generally are beyond those included in the formal school curriculum. There cannot be a sharp distinction between school and nonschool activities as schools increase their participation in these informal curricular functions. In fact, the No Child Left Behind Act encouraged school systems to sponsor such activities in collaboration with nonschool-based community groups and faith-based organizations. In the wide variety of activities that may be referred to as supplementary, it is easy to focus on those that are institution based or sponsored. Several of these are described in chapters 9 and 10, but equally important, and perhaps more significant, are those varieties of activities implicit in Richard Wolf's chapter (chapter 6) on family environments and the quotation from Angela Glover Blackwell that began this chapter.

The values that are privileged by parents and the experiences that parents and communities can provide are critical to the mix of regular and supplemental educational experiences. They are so important that I am convinced that enabling and teaching parents how to support academic development, and to be advocates for their children's academic and personal development need much greater emphasis. In our current research, three related efforts are included in our program of work:

1. Strengthening the capacity of families and parents to support the academic and personal development of children;
2. Educating and supporting parents and other interested adults as advocates for the academic and personal development of students; and
3. Better enabling parents to function as competent adults who are capable of directing and supporting the optimal development of children. We argue that it takes a well-developed adult to support the optimal development of a child.

In the first of these activities, the emphasis is on encouraging and teaching parents to function as supporters of the academic and personal development of children. The second activity is more sharply focused on assisting, demonstrating, and enabling parents to interact with school people and programs and to advocate for the best interests of children. In the third set of activities, we are seeking to better enable parents to function as competent adults do—at home, at work, in their communities. We are convinced that the absence of such competence is one of the problems faced by teenaged parents. We have also observed adults trying to function as parents when their own development has been so arrested that they are incapable of providing for themselves or their children. In cases such as these, the support for the academic and personal development of children rests on very weak reeds. We repeat, the optimal development of children requires that well-developed adults mediate their developmental experiences. This may be a part of the explanation for the relationship between stable and competent families, on one hand, and student academic success on the other.

In one of our experiments, we were able to engage parents in a number of workshops where school observation, analysis of school records, school visitation, and negotiation and advocacy skills were developed and practiced. This work is described in chapter 12 under the Rockland Experiment. In the same experiment, materials and resources were made available to parents designed to be used in help with homework, to encourage college attendance, and to offer guidance in the selection of high school courses. In a related project, books, book reviews, writing assignments, and suggestions for family projects around materials read were used to encourage family literacy. In none of this work have we conjoined a direct attack upon general adult competence with parental support for academic development. However, the model for the enhancement of such adult competence has been successfully demonstrated in the Life Skills work of Adkins (1984). In the Adkins work, adults were taught self-presentation skills. Adults were placed in vocational development settings. Some participants were involved in counseling directed at improved self-understanding and psychosocial rehabilitation. In an experiment currently in design stage, the Life Skills and the parent-educator initiatives will be combined.

This concern with the quality of human capital present in parents is mirrored by a concern for the human capital necessary to initiate and staff supplementary education initiatives in low-income communities and communities of color. Although some elements of supplemental education have developed professional leadership and utilize professional staff, most of what we call supplementary education is led and staffed by ordinary parents and laypersons who volunteer. However, this field—like early childhood education, athletics, and recreation—requires professionalization of some of the people who staff the endeavor. Yet some parts of supplementary education benefit from and may always have to depend on layperson involvement. It may not be cost efficient to depend mostly on professional workers. It is possible that the involvement of parents and other especially interested adults is a part of what makes supplementary education an effective intervention. There may be aspects of the interaction between served and serving persons that cannot and should not be professionalized. On the other hand, some of the teaching and learning that occur in supplementary education should be informed by expert knowledge of how people learn. Some of the delivery mechanisms are so large and complex as to require professional direction. Some of the personal and interpersonal issues require the attention of experts in mental health, social work, social organizational theory, health and nutrition, pedagogy, and so on. Thus, there are tensions in this emerging field around the availability and the nature of the required human capital and the nature of the involvement of the diverse human resources necessary to the success of the enterprise.

CONCLUSIONS

We have introduced the idea of a system of supplemental education experiences and resources as a partial solution to the challenge of universal access to academic excellence. We argue that schooling and continued improvement of schooling is necessary but is not a sufficient condition for closing the gap in academic achievement between privileged and disadvantaged populations of students. Throughout this book, we have embraced the idea that families, communities, and students themselves will have to become actively engaged in the support of the academic and personal development of children if high levels of academic achievement are to be achieved universally. We believe, with Comer (1997), that waiting for schools alone to achieve that end is like "waiting for a miracle." We agree with Comer (1997) and Price (2002) that ordinary people in our homes, communities, and peer groups can make a difference. We do not advocate working alone, but in concert with schools and a wide variety of educative institutions. And we concur with Edmund T. Gordon's notions (see chapter 5) that concerted educational efforts must include the active participation of the learning persons—academic pursuit must map onto the political agenda of the learners.

We have pointed to a wide range of educational activities that occur in and out of school, most of which are initiated or sponsored independent of schooling. Some few years ago, I called these activities supplementary education. I sometimes think that the activities to which I refer are the core of education and that schooling is supplementary, but the relative weight of these efforts is not the issue. What is important is that education can and does occur almost everywhere. Some segments of the population, generally the more affluent

and academically sophisticated, actively and deliberately orchestrate these
varieties of educative experiences for their children, mediate their children's
educative encounters, and activate specialized resources for their children as
needed. Studies of persons who achieve academic excellence support the conclusion that these orchestrations, mediations, and activations are modal behaviors among the academically successful. In this book we have suggested
that such behaviors must become the modal pattern for African American,
Hispanic American, Native American, and a variety of low-income children
who are underrepresented among the population of high-achieving students in
the United States.

Although we are convinced that these supplemental experiences are the
way to go, we recognize that such a movement is not without its problems and
tensions. We conclude with the iteration of some of the issues.

1. Supplementary education requires adequate human and social capital.
   We argue that optimal child development requires support from adequately developed parents or parent surrogates. The supplemental education enterprise will require an adequate cadre of professional workers
   without supplanting the rich resources resident in lay personnel and parents themselves. As in communities like Koreatown, supplementary education requires the presence of a network of community- and/or faith-
   based social and cultural agencies committed to the provision of
   supplemental educational services.
2. Education that is supplemental to schooling and supportive of academic
   development is grounded in the hegemonic culture to which many of
   our targeted students and families have a subaltern relationship. (Subaltern groups adapt to some of the dominant cultural forms, develop alternatives to others, and actively resist still others.) In trying to replicate
   in lower-class and ethnic communities a model from middle-class Asian
   American and European communities, we are confronted with problems
   of cross-group adaptations. While spontaneous adaptations between
   groups occur, we do not have a lot of experience with the deliberate im-
   portation into host cultures artifacts and customs that are alien to the
   host, even though the behaviors may prove to be functional. Certainly
   the black middle class has not rushed to replicate the white middle-class
   use of supplementary education.
3. In the Koreatown example, we found that most of the services involved
   some payment from the user families. The growing presence of commercial institutions offering supplemental services highlights the fee-
   for-service nature of this work. The communities that we have targeted
   tend to be low-income families for whom the fee for service may be

prohibitive. One possible solution is to turn to tax-levied funds or to the philanthropic community in order to provide a very low-cost or free service. But we do not know if the fact of the family's investment in supplementary education is an important part of the treatment. It is possible that when a young person realizes that education and its supplements are so important to the parent that the family sacrifices to pay for them, that fact and awareness may be as important as the actual service that is purchased.

Most complex systems that achieve effectiveness and stability are characterized by redundancy—that is, systems in which all critical mechanisms have back-up or alternative components in case of failure in the primary system. We routinely see such redundancy in biological, electronic, and mechanical systems. It is possible that the educative systems of human societies also require redundancy—multi-layered mechanisms by which the developmental tasks of human learning are engaged, supported, and mastered. At best these layers should complement each other, but the critical function of each is to compensate or take over when one mechanism or another fails. Supplementary education just may be a part of that ubiquitously redundant system concerned with motivating, preparing, enabling, mediating, facilitating, consolidating, and ensuring that high levels of academic learning and personal development are achieved.

NOTES

1. From *Searching for the Uncommon Common Ground: New Dimensions on Race in America* by Angela Glover Blackwell, Stewart Kwoh, and Manuel Pastor. Copyright © 2002 by the American Assembly. Used by permission of W. W. Norton & Company, Inc.

REFERENCES

Adkins, W. R. 1984. Life skills education: A video-based counseling/learning delivery system. In *Teaching psychological skills: Models for giving psychology away*, edited by D. Larson. Monterey, CA: Brooks/Cole.

Banks, W. C., G. McQuarter, and J. Hubbard. 1979. Towards a reconceptualization of the social-cognitive bases of achievement in blacks. In *Research Directions of Black Psychologists*, edited by A. Wade Boykin, A. J. Franklin, and J. F. Yates, 381–97. New York: Russell Sage Foundation.

Bernstein, B. 1974. *Class, codes and control*. 2nd rev. ed. London: Routledge and Kegan Paul.

Blackwell, A. G., S. Kwoh, and M. Pastor. 2002. *Searching for the uncommon common ground: New dimensions on race in America*. New York: Norton.

Bourdieu, P. 1986. The forms of capital. In *Handbook of theory and research for the sociology of education*, edited by J. Richardson, 241–58. Westport, CT: Greenwood.

Comer, J. 1997. *Waiting for a miracle: Why our schools can't solve our problems—and how we can*. New York: Dutton.

Feuerstein, R. 1978. *Instrumental enrichment: Just a minute . . . Let me think!* University Park, FL: University Park Press.

Gordon, E. W. 1965. Characteristics of socially disadvantaged children. *Review of Educational Research* 35(5): 377–88.

———. 1999. *Education and justice: A view from the back of the bus*. New York: Teachers College Press.

Price, H. 2002. *Achievement matters: Getting your child the best education possible*. New York: Kensington.

Raven, J. 2000. The Raven's Progressive Matrices: Change and stability over culture and time. *Cognitive Psychology* 41:1–48.

Riessman, F. 1962. *The culturally deprived child*. New York: Harper and Row.

Strodtbeck, F. L. 1964. The hidden curriculum of the middle class home. In *Urban education and cultural deprivation*, edited by C. W. Hunnicutt. Syracuse, NY: Syracuse University Press.

Wolf, R. M. 1966. The measurement of environments. In *Testing problems in perspective*, edited by A. Anastasi, 491–503. Washington, DC: American Council in Education.

———. 1995. The measurement of environments: A follow-up study. *Journal of Negro Education* 64(3): 354–59.

Index

About the Editors and Contributors

Editors

Edmund W. Gordon is the Richard March Hoe Emeritus Professor of Psychology and Education and director of the Institute of Urban and Minority Education (IUME) at Teachers College, Columbia University. He is also the John M. Musser Professor of Psychology Emeritus at Yale University. He has authored or edited over 15 books and monographs, including *Compensatory Education: Preschool Through College*, which continues to be regarded as the classic work in its field. He is also the editor of the *American Journal of Orthopsychiatry* and the annual *Review of Research in Education*. Edmund Gordon is one of the conceptual leaders of several of the major developments in public education, viz. Head Start, compensatory education, career education, school desegregation, alternatives in educational assessment, and supplementary education. He continues to guide the Taskforce on Minority High Achievement at Teachers College and The College Board.

Beatrice L. Bridglall is currently assistant research scientist and editor at the Institute for Urban and Minority Education (IUME) at Teachers College, Columbia University, The Educational Testing Service, and The College Board. She is coauthor of *The Affirmative Development of Academic Ability* (in process) with Edmund W. Gordon and coeditor of IUME's and The College Board's *Pedagogical Inquiry and Praxis Newsletter*, which (1) emphasizes the bidirectionality of knowledge production through practice and research, and (2) distills issues associated with increasing the number of high academic achieving students who come from African American, Hispanic American, and Native American families.

Aundra Saa Meroe, a postdoctoral research scientist at The College Board and Research Associate at IUME, Teachers College, Columbia University, is currently an AERA/OERI Postdoctoral Research Fellow.

Contributors

Maitrayee Bhattacharyya is a doctoral candidate in the sociology department at Princeton University.

Clive R. Belfield is assistant director of the international and transcultural grant department of Columbia University's Teachers College.

Deborah Bial is president and founder of the POSSE Foundation, Inc.

Velma L. Cobb is vice president of education and youth development for the National Urban League.

Howard T. Everson is vice president for academic initiatives and chief research scientist for The College Board.

Lenora Fulani is a cofounder of the All Stars Project, Inc. and codirector of the Joseph A. Forgione Development School for Youth.

Edmund T. Gordon is associate professor of anthropology at the University of Texas at Austin.

Alan Green is assistant professor of counseling and human services at Johns Hopkins University.

Judith Griffin is a former president of A Better Chance.

Irving Hamer is professor of practice and education at the Teachers College, Columbia University.

Henry M. Levin is the William H Kilpatrick Professor of Economics & Education at the Teachers College, Columbia University.

Brenda Mejia is a research coordinator for the Institute for Urban and Minority Education (IUME) at the Teachers College, Columbia University.

Roger Millsap is associate professor of quantitative psychology at Arizona State University.

Patti Smith is a managing specialist for strategic development at The Education Alliance/LAB at Brown University.

Donald M. Stewart is president and CEO of Chicago Community Trust.

The late **Richard M. Wolf** was professor of psychology and education emeritus at Teachers College, Columbia University, where he served for more than thirty years. He specialized in educational evaluation and measurement.